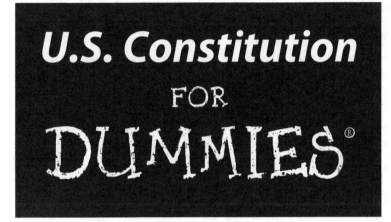

U.S. Constitution FOR DUMMIES®

by Dr. Michael Arnheim
Barrister at Law

Sometime Fellow of St. John's College, Cambridge

Foreword by Ted Cruz
Partner, Morgan, Lewis & Bockius LLP

Former Solicitor General of Texas

WILEY

Wiley Publishing, Inc.

U.S. Constitution For Dummies®

Published by
Wiley Publishing, Inc.
111 River St.
Hoboken, NJ 07030-5774
www.wiley.com

WILEY

About the Author

Dr. Michael Arnheim is an English Barrister who also sits periodically as a court-appointed mediator. In addition, he is a member of the Irish Bar and is of counsel to Brown & Welsh P.C. of Meriden, Connecticut.

Michael Arnheim's active interest in the U.S. Constitution started with a comparative paper he wrote at the age of 17, for which he was awarded a special prize in the Royal Commonwealth Society Essay competition. As a junior barrister he wrote a fortnightly column in the *Solicitors Journal,* in which he dealt with U.S. constitutional issues among others. He has also written on U.S. constitutional themes for publications such as the *New Law Journal* and *Counsel* magazine. In 1994, he was invited to edit the comparative *Common Law* volume in the prestigious *International Library of Essays in Law and Legal Theory,* published by Ashgate Dartmouth. He has also been consulted on matters involving immigration, healthcare, protectionism, states' rights, and same-sex marriage.

Dr. Arnheim is the author of numerous articles and 15 books to date, including the following titles: *Drafting Settlements of Disputes* (Tolley, 1994), *Civil Courts Practice & Procedure Handbook* (Butterworths, 1999), *A Handbook of Human Rights Law* (Kogan Page, 2004), and *Principles of the Common Law* (Duckworth, 2004).

Dr. Arnheim has been interviewed on television on a number of occasions, particularly in South Africa and Sweden. In 1985 he spent several enjoyable hours on David Brudnoy's radio talk show on WRKO in Boston, fielding calls from listeners on topical legal and political issues.

Michael Arnheim started life as a member of the "Quiz Kids" team on South African national radio. He went to university at 16, took his first degree when he was 19, received a First Class Honours degree at 20, and was awarded a master's degree (with distinction) at age 21. He then won a national scholarship to St. John's College, Cambridge, where he took his PhD and was elected a Fellow of the College.

After spending several years researching and teaching Classics and Ancient History as a Fellow of St. John's College, Cambridge, at the age of 31 he was appointed a full Professor and Head of the Department of Classics at his original university in South Africa. Returning to Britain, he was called to the English Bar by Lincoln's Inn in 1988.

When he is not trying cases or advising clients, Michael Arnheim spends his time teaching, writing, and (less often than he should) swimming.

For updates on the U.S. Constitution, comments, and reviews on the subject, go to www.michaelarnheim.com.

Dedication

To the memory of my beloved parents.

To my students over the years, who kept me on my toes.

And to the spirit of American liberty, in the light of Abraham Lincoln's challenge:

Must a government, of necessity, be too strong for the liberties of its own people, or too weak to maintain its own existence?

Acknowledgments

My classical and historical training has stood me in good stead in my practice of law, and, not least, in my study of the U.S. Constitution. Professor Theo Haarhoff taught me how difficult it sometimes is to differentiate between objective views and subjective views that mimic objectivity. Professor Hugo Jones and Professor John Crook of Cambridge University were two of the most tolerant minds that I have ever come across, but they never made the mistake of equating toleration with acceptance of all views as equally valid.

Special thanks to my editors at Wiley: Kathy Cox, Diane Steele, and Joan Friedman. My thanks also to Susan Ellis Wild for her review of the manuscript. I owe a particular debt of gratitude to Kathy Nebenhaus, Vice President and Executive Publisher at Wiley, who, beyond the call of duty, took this book under her wing and saw it through to completion.

As I don't have a cat, I can't blame it for clambering over the keyboard. The sole responsibility for any mistakes rests on me. The law as stated in the book is correct as of Washington's Birthday (Presidents' Day), February 16, 2009. For updates, go to www.michaelarnheim.com.

Publisher's Acknowledgments

We're proud of this book; please send us your comments through our Dummies online registration form located at `http://dummies.custhelp.com`. For other comments, please contact our Customer Care Department within the U.S. at 877-762-2974, outside the U.S. at 317-572-3993, or fax 317-572-4002.

Some of the people who helped bring this book to market include the following:

Acquisitions, Editorial, and Media Development

Project Editor: Joan Friedman

Acquisitions Editor: Lindsay Sandman Lefevere

Assistant Editor: Erin Calligan Mooney

Editorial Program Coordinator: Joe Niesen

Technical Editor: Susan Ellis Wild

Senior Editorial Manager: Jennifer Ehrlich

Editorial Supervisor: Carmen Krikorian

Editorial Assistant: Jennette ElNaggar

Cover Photos: © Comstock Images

Cartoons: Rich Tennant
(`www.the5thwave.com`)

Composition Services

Project Coordinator: Patrick Redmond

Layout and Graphics: Reuben W. Davis, SDJumper, Sarah Phillipart, Christin Swinford

Proofreaders: Laura Albert, Nancy L. Reinhardt

Indexer: Becky Hornyak

Publishing and Editorial for Consumer Dummies

  Diane Graves Steele, Vice President and Publisher, Consumer Dummies

  Kristin Ferguson-Wagstaffe, Product Development Director, Consumer Dummies

  Ensley Eikenburg, Associate Publisher, Travel

  Kelly Regan, Editorial Director, Travel

Publishing for Technology Dummies

  Andy Cummings, Vice President and Publisher, Dummies Technology/General User

Composition Services

  Debbie Stailey, Director of Composition Services

Contents at a Glance

Table of Contents

Part III: Balancing the Branches of Government: The President, Congress, and the Judiciary 113

Chapter 10: Looking at the Role of Commander in Chief..........115

Chapter 11: Giving Everyone a Voice: The House of Representatives and Senate 139

Part IV: The Bill of Rights: Specifying Rights through Amendments.......................... 193

Chapter 14: The First Amendment: Freedom of Religion, Speech, and Assembly.............................195

Chapter 15: The Second Amendment: Bearing Arms..............207

Foreword

· ·

"*W*e the people" are the opening words of the U.S. Constitution, and it is fitting that this book is written for "We the people." Both the Constitution itself, and this book explaining it, were meant for everybody, for all of the American people.

This book can be read on several different levels. If you just want to understand the basics of the Constitution, this book offers you an easy, enjoyable, and at times humorous way to do so. But the book also offers a much deeper insight into the Constitution and all the controversies surrounding it.

Michael Arnheim does not pull his punches. He makes no secret of his own views on the Constitution. However, the book always presents both sides of every argument fairly, so that you, the reader, can decide what take to adopt on any issue.

The U.S. Constitution is the world's oldest written constitution, and it was a revolutionary document. Written by men who just a few years earlier had won American independence from Britain, it changed the relationship altogether between people and government.

Indeed, that was the genius of the Constitution — limiting government to protect the liberty of the people. Because the Framers recognized that unchecked government can strip the people of their freedoms, they designed a constitution to prevent that from happening.

James Madison, the primary author of the Constitution, explained as follows:

> *If men were angels, no government would be necessary. If angels were to govern men, neither external nor internal controls on government would be necessary. In framing a government which is to be administered by men over men, the great difficulty lies in this: you must first enable the government to control the governed; and in the next place oblige it to control itself.*

Because men are not angels, the Constitution was designed to create an effective national government and, at the same time, prevent the government from overreaching.

At the time of this writing, our Nation is facing some of the greatest challenges in its history. One possible solution to these problems is to allow the government ever-expanding power. But it remains to be seen whether that would really be the best choice either in practical terms or in terms of the Constitution.

For good or for ill, the meaning of the Constitution has often been very much in the hands of the nine justices of the U.S. Supreme Court. This book goes in depth into the different approaches adopted by different justices over the years. Dr. Arnheim explains his own interpretations in simple, direct language, and he also explains why he favors the approach that he adopts — while at the same time setting out the opposing views.

For example, Justices William Brennan and Thurgood Marshall both believed that the death penalty always constituted "cruel and unusual punishment." Dr. Arnheim explains why he believes they were wrong — based on the text of the Constitution itself. But Dr. Arnheim goes further, arguing that Justices Brennan and Marshall were really confusing what the Constitution actually *says* with what they as judges thought it *ought* to have said. There are serious policy arguments both for and against capital punishment — but given that the constitutional text twice explicitly authorizes capital punishment, the only proper way to change that would be a constitutional amendment as laid down in Article V of the Constitution. And an amendment is unlikely to be passed, because large majorities of the American people have consistently supported capital punishment for the very worst criminals. Accordingly, a judge imposing his or her views on the issue is not only unconstitutional, it is also undemocratic.

Chief Justice Rehnquist, for whom I had the honor of clerking, was an original dissenter from the Court's opinion striking down the death penalty. And, over his three decades on the Court, he helped overturn that decision and return the Court to a more limited view of judicial authority. Indeed, the very last opinion he ever wrote was a case I was privileged to litigate for the State of Texas, *Van Orden v. Perry,* which upheld the Texas Ten Commandments monument and repudiated many years of judicial hostility to expressions of religious faith (discussed in Chapter 14).

Likewise, in 2008, the Supreme Court decided *District of Columbia v. Heller,* holding for the first time that the Second Amendment protects an individual right to keep and bear arms (discussed in depth in Chapter 15). Texas led 31 states in defense of the Second Amendment in that case, and our arguments for giving force to the plain text of the Constitution and the original understanding of the Framers prevailed by a vote of 5 to 4.

The Constitution is designed to limit government and to protect all the freedoms that you and I cherish as Americans. And this book is a clear, straightforward roadmap to understanding how it works — and a lot more.

Ted Cruz

Partner, Morgan, Lewis & Bockius LLP

Former Solicitor General of Texas

Introduction

· ·

*O*kay, so you bought this book (or you got it as a present, or you borrowed it, or you're browsing through it in a bookstore). Obviously, you have some interest in the U.S. Constitution, but maybe you're afraid the Constitution isn't really that interesting.

Well, you're in luck. Even if you don't find the Constitution itself to be the most riveting read, it's a never-ending source of debates and arguments. And we all know how interesting debates and arguments can be!

About This Book

This book explains the Constitution simply and thoroughly, including all the juicy controversy it evokes. Whether you're a student, a lawyer, or just a concerned citizen, I hope you find it to be both a good read and a great resource.

You don't have to read this book from cover to cover, and you don't have to read the chapters in order. I've written each chapter so it can be understood on its own; if it refers to topics that aren't covered in that chapter, I tell you where to find information about that topic elsewhere in the book. Using the Table of Contents or the Index, feel free to identify topics of the greatest interest to you, and dive in wherever you want. Even if you dive into the middle or end first, I promise I won't let you get lost.

I cover the entire Constitution in this book, but I don't give each article or amendment equal attention. That's because some parts are more important, more difficult to understand, more controversial, or more relevant to modern society than others. If I believe a particular part of the Constitution requires or deserves more explanation than another, I give it lots of real estate in the pages that follow. Parts that are easier to understand or less important to your 21st-century life get less space in the book.

Throughout the book, I offer not just facts but also a variety of opinions about constitutional issues that have created debate for more than 200 years. In some cases, the opinions belong to Supreme Court justices, advocates for or against specific rights, or any number of other sources. In other cases, the opinions are my own — and I alert you to that fact. I may sometimes try to persuade you of the rightness or wrongness of a certain opinion, but you're welcome to disagree — that's the fun and the privilege of becoming a more informed citizen!

Conventions Used in This Book

Whenever I quote or refer to a specific part of the Constitution, I tell you the name of that part. You'll often see this reference in the form of an *article,* a *section,* and maybe a *clause* — for example, Article I, Section 8, Clause 3. If you turn to the Appendix at the back of the book, where the text of the Constitution is provided, you can see that it's broken into seven articles, some of which are divided into sections. If a section contains more than one paragraph, I refer to each paragraph as a clause. So if you're looking for Clause 3 within Section 8 of Article I, just find the third paragraph in that section.

The amendments to the Constitution appear in the Appendix after the main body of the document (and after the list of people who signed it). It's pretty easy to locate an amendment, as long as you aren't too rusty on Roman numerals.

When you see the term *the Constitution,* it always refers to the U.S. Constitution. Each of the 50 states also has its own constitution, but if I'm referring to one of those, I include the state name (such as *the Virginia Constitution*). Similarly, when I refer to *the Supreme Court, the high court,* or just *the Court,* that means the U.S. Supreme Court. If I refer to a state supreme court, I always give the name of the state concerned (such as *the Texas Supreme Court*).

You can't learn about the Constitution without being introduced to some legal, political, and other jargon, but I do my best in this book to ease you into the constitutional vocabulary. If I use a term that I suspect may not be familiar to you, I put that term in italic and provide a definition or explanation nearby.

What You're Not To Read

This may seem like a strange topic to discuss — after all, I'd love for you to read every word that I've written! But the beauty of the *For Dummies* series is that I won't demand such commitment. If you're not interested in knowing every nitty-gritty detail about a certain subject, there are two types of text you can skim or skip altogether:

- **Paragraphs that have a Technical Stuff icon next to them:** In just a minute, I explain what the various icons in this book mean. This one means that the information in a given paragraph goes into detail that may be interesting to some readers but isn't essential to your understanding of the subject at hand.

- **Sidebars:** The text tucked into gray boxes is also optional. Sidebars contain in-depth historical information, somewhat technical explanations of legal or political situations, or just interesting stories that happen to be tangential to the topic at hand. Take them or leave them — it's your call.

How This Book is Organized

I've divided the book into six parts, each of which contains a series of related chapters. Here's a bird's-eye view of the way the book is arranged.

Part 1: Exploring Constitutional Basics

This part of the book explains the basic concepts underlying the Constitution and the motivating forces behind its creation. I present the basic concepts of the Constitution and where they came from. You may find a few surprises here. For example, the Constitution didn't originally establish a democracy — the word *democracy* doesn't appear even once in the entire document.

I also explain the different approaches to interpreting the Constitution and how those approaches can conflict. And I then show you how the Constitution has changed in the past 200-plus years in both formal ways (through relatively few amendments) and informal ways (as a result of the way the U.S. Supreme Court has interpreted and reinterpreted the Constitution).

Part 11: We the People: How the United States Is Governed

In this part, I first study who wields power in the United States, considering how that power is shared among "We the People," the President, Congress, the Supreme Court, and possibly other entities.

The *Framers* of the Constitution (the men who wrote and ratified it) were anxious to prevent the concentration of power in the hands of one person or one government institution, so they designed an elaborate structure to make sure that power was shared. They did so first by creating a *federal* government: one in which power is shared between the national and state governments. In Chapter 7, I explore how that power-sharing arrangement works.

In Chapter 8, I discuss another way in which power is shared: among the three branches of the federal government — the Executive (the President and his Cabinet), the Legislature (Congress), and the Judiciary (the Supreme Court and other federal courts).

Perhaps the biggest tug-of-war between the federal government and the states has centered on the power given to Congress in the Commerce Clause of the Constitution. In Chapter 9, I explain why this power is so important, how judicial interpretation has broadened it (and has recently reined it in slightly), and why the whole issue matters so much.

Part III: Balancing the Branches of Government: The President, Congress, and the Judiciary

This part tackles the three main parts of the U.S. government — the Executive, Legislative, and Judicial branches — as well as how members of those branches can be fired or removed.

I open this part by focusing on the President, covering such topics as how the President is elected, what it means to be commander in chief, how a president makes appointments, and whether (and when) a president is immune from lawsuits. I then turn my attention to Congress, explaining the membership and the important functions of the House of Representatives and Senate. Chapter 12, on the judiciary, explains how the justices of the Supreme Court and other federal judges are appointed, the powers of the Supreme Court, and how the Court operates.

I finish this part with a discussion of impeachment, explaining why it's possible to be impeached but not convicted (and therefore not removed from office), what the impeachment process is, and who has been impeached since the Constitution was ratified.

Part IV: The Bill of Rights: Specifying Rights through Amendments

Here I discuss the first ten amendments to the Constitution, which were all rati-fied together in 1791 (only three years after the main body of the Constitution). These amendments are commonly referred to as the *Bill of Rights* because they confer or guarantee fundamental civil rights, including the right to freedom of speech and assembly; the separation of church and state; the right to bear arms; the guarantee of a fair trial; the protection of private property rights; and the prohibition of "cruel and unusual punishments."

Part V: Addressing Liberties and Modifying the Government: More Amendments

In this part, I discuss the ragbag of amendments that have been ratified since 1791, including amendments that have reformed presidential elections, abol-ished slavery, ensured equal protection, prohibited alcohol and then made it legal again, given voting rights to women, and limited presidents to two elected terms.

Part VI: The Part of Tens

This part contains three short chapters: one that outlines ten landmark Supreme Court cases that have tackled constitutional issues; one that dis-cusses the influence of ten Supreme Court Justices who have served at vari-ous times in the country's history; and one that presents two sides of five sticky constitutional issues that are bound to be debated for years to come.

Icons Used in This Book

Throughout this book, you find small pictures in the margins. These *icons* highlight paragraphs that contain certain types of information. Here's what each icon means:

The Remember icon sits beside paragraphs that contain information that's worth committing to memory. Even if you're not studying for an exam on the Constitution, you may want to read these paragraphs twice.

This icon denotes material that may fall into the "too much information" category for some readers. If you like to know lots of details about a topic, the information in these paragraphs may thrill you. If details aren't your thing, feel free to skip these paragraphs altogether.

The Constitution is nothing if not controversial, and this icon highlights paragraphs that explain what all the debate is about. If you want to know why people can't seem to figure out what this document means even after 200-plus years, head toward these icons.

Where there's debate, there are opinions, and I won't pretend not to have some of my own. Where you see this icon, you'll know that I'm offering my perspective on the subject at hand, and I don't necessarily expect you to agree!

Where To Go from Here

That depends on why you're reading this book. If you're a student who needs help understanding how and why the Constitution was created, what it says, and why it's still so important, I'd suggest that you start at the beginning.

If you picked up this book because you want to understand the debate about a certain issue (such as gun rights), check the Table of Contents or Index and flip to the chapter where that debate is explored. (In the case of gun rights, that'd be Chapter 15.)

If you're planning to start a campaign to impeach a government official who rubs you entirely the wrong way, perhaps Chapter 13 will be your cup of tea.

If you want to very quickly get a sense of why constitutional issues can cause tempers to flare, flip to Chapter 25 and read about just five of the many debates that keep people talking.

Part I

Exploring Constitutional Basics

The 5th Wave   By Rich Tennant

George Washington: Father of the Country and first U.S. President. Presided over the Philadelphia Convention that drafted the United States Constitution in 1789 because of general dissent with the Articles of Confederation, and rewrote existing boating regulations to increase the number of occupants in a row boat from 5 to 12.

In this part . . .

These chapters give you a bird's-eye view of constitutional thought as a whole, starting with the ideas on which the Constitution was based and ending with a very brief summary of the Constitution as originally ratified in 1788 and of some of its amendments. Chapter 5 also explains how the Constitution has undergone some fundamental changes without formal amendment.

Chapter 1

Constitutional Law: The Framework for Governance

In This Chapter

▶ Understanding what a constitution is

▶ Finding out who created the U.S. Constitution, and why

▶ Gaining a bird's-eye view of the Constitution

▶ Introducing some constitutional problems

Most of the stuff written about the Constitution is boring and hard to understand. But it doesn't have to be. And frankly, it shouldn't be, because the Constitution is pretty important — yes, important to *you* in your daily life.

In this book, I do my best to explain the Constitution in simple language. And in this chapter, I offer a broad introduction to the Constitution: what it is, who created it, the principles it does and doesn't discuss, and the areas of controversy that keep it in the headlines even today.

Defining "Constitution"

First, what exactly *is* a constitution? Okay, here goes. A constitution is a sort of super-law that regulates the way a country or state is run. How helpful is that as a definition? Not very? So let's be more specific, and this time let's focus specifically on the Constitution of the United States.

The U.S. Constitution is the supreme law of the nation controlling the following main features (plus a few more):

✔ The functions and powers of the different branches of the government: the President, the Congress, and the courts

✔ The way in which the President and the Congress are elected and how federal judges are appointed

✔ The way government officials — including the President and the judges — can be fired

✔ The relationship between the federal government and the states

✔ Your rights as a citizen or inhabitant of the United States

Knowing When and Why the Constitution Was Created

The Constitution emerged from a meeting called the Philadelphia Convention, which took place in 1787. (That meeting has since come to be known also as the *Constitutional Convention.*) The Convention was held because the *Articles of Confederation* — the document that had been serving as the country's first governing constitution — were considered to be weak and problematic (see Chapter 2). The stated goal of the Convention was to revise the Articles of Confederation, but the outcome was much more than a mere revision: It was a new form of government.

The 55 delegates to the Philadelphia Convention came to be known as the *Framers* of the Constitution. They represented 12 of the 13 states (Rhode Island didn't send a delegate), and they included some familiar names, such as George Washington, Alexander Hamilton, and James Madison.

The Convention lasted from May 25 to September 17, 1787. In the end, only 39 of the 55 delegates actually signed the Constitution. Three delegates refused to sign it, and the rest had left the Convention before the signing took place.

In order for the Constitution to take effect, it had to be *ratified* — or confirmed — by nine states. Special conventions were summoned in each state, and the Delaware, New Jersey, and Georgia conventions ratified the Constitution unanimously. But some of the other states saw a pretty fierce battle for ratification. In New York, for example, the Constitution was ratified only by 30 votes to 27.

Ratification was achieved in 1788, and the Constitution took effect with the swearing in of President George Washington and Vice President John Adams on April 30, 1789.

Distinguishing the Founders from the Framers

The term *Founding Fathers* was (probably) coined by President Warren G. Harding about 100 years ago. *Founding Fathers,* or simply *Founders,* refers to the political leaders of the struggle for American independence against Britain. It includes the American leaders in the Revolutionary War, the signatories of the Declaration of Independence, and also the Framers of the Constitution.

The Founders include George Washington, Benjamin Franklin, Alexander Hamilton, John Jay, John Adams, Thomas Jefferson, James Madison, James Monroe, Patrick Henry, and Tom Paine.

The term *Founding Fathers* overlaps somewhat with the term *Framers of the Constitution,* but the two terms are not identical in meaning. The term *Founders* is much broader than the term *Framers* because it covers all the leaders in the fight for American independence, including all the delegates to the Philadelphia Convention that drafted the Constitution. So all the Framers were Founders, but not all the Founders were Framers!

Thomas Jefferson, for example, drafted the Declaration of Independence and was one of the leading Founders of the United States. But he was not involved in the drafting of the Constitution because he was on official business in France at the time. So Jefferson was a very prominent Founder, but he was not a Framer.

Summarizing the Main Principles of the Constitution

In broad strokes, here are the principles you find in the Constitution:

✔ **Liberty:** The Framers of the Constitution aimed to establish a form of government that gave the people as much individual freedom as possible, by guaranteeing them

- • Religious freedom

- • Freedom of speech

- • Freedom to defend themselves with arms

✔ **Federalism:** The United States started out as 13 separate British colonies, which banded together to throw off the British yoke. At first, in 1777, the colonies formed a loose alliance under the so-called *Articles of Confederation* (not to be confused with the similarly named Confederacy proclaimed by the seceding southern states in the 1860s). But the need for a stronger central government resulted in the drafting of the U.S.

Constitution, which was ratified in its original, unamended form in 1788. The Constitution established a *federal* system of government, which gave the central or federal government certain clearly defined and limited powers, reserving the remaining powers to the states or to the people.

✔ **Separation of powers:** The Framers of the Constitution were very anxious to prevent any one person or institution from becoming too powerful. So the Constitution keeps the three branches of government separate. These branches are the Executive (the President), Legislative (Congress), and Judicial (the law courts). But a system of "checks and balances" cuts across this separation. So, for example, Congress passes laws, but the President can veto them. Similarly, the President has the power to appoint Cabinet officers and federal judges, but his appointments are subject to the "advice and consent" of the Senate. And the Supreme Court can check any perceived abuse of the power of Congress by striking down laws that the court rules are unconstitutional.

✔ **Due process:** "Due process of law" is one of the main buzz-phrases of the Constitution — according to the Supreme Court. You may assume that this phrase would refer simply to *procedure,* or how things should be done, like whether or not you are allowed a jury trial. But the Supreme Court has widened its interpretation of the phrase greatly to include *substantive due process,* or what rights the Constitution actually confers or protects. As a result, the court has interpreted the Constitution as guaranteeing a bunch of controversial "fundamental rights," including

  • An expansion of the rights of those suspected or accused of crimes

  • An expansion of minority rights

  • Privacy

  • Abortion

Here are some of the principles you may assume are addressed in the Constitution, but aren't:

✔ **Democracy:** The words *democracy* and *democratic* don't figure anywhere in the text of the Constitution. In its original form, the Constitution was not democratic, and the House of Representatives was the only directly elected part of the federal government. The Constitution became democratic as a result of the rise of President Andrew Jackson's Democratic Party in the 1830s (see Chapter 6).

✔ **Equality:** Equality was also not one of the principles of the Constitution in its original form.

- Slavery formed an integral part of the Constitution until the Civil War. For example, Article IV, Section 2, Clause 3 provided in its original, unamended form that runaway slaves who escaped from a slave state to a free state had to be "delivered up" to their original owners. The whole structure of the House of Representatives also depended on slavery. In its original form, Article I, Section 2 of the Constitution apportioned the representation of the various states according to the numbers of their free population — plus three-fifths of their slaves. This "three-fifths rule" cynically used the slave population (who of course didn't have the right to vote) to give the slave states more representation in the House than they would otherwise have had.

- Women didn't have the right to vote until 1920.

- To this day, the interpretation of the anti-discrimination amendments to the Constitution remains highly controversial. The most controversial amendment is the Fourteenth, which can be invoked either in support of affirmative action or in opposition to it. Those Supreme Court justices who support affirmative action see it as a necessary part of the antidiscriminatory thrust of the Due Process Clause of the Fourteenth Amendment, while those justices who oppose affirmative action see it as itself just another form of discrimination.

The Federalist Papers

When the U.S. Constitution emerged from the Philadelphia Convention after being signed by delegates from each of the 12 participating states, it still had to be ratified, or confirmed, by the states, each of which summoned a special convention for this purpose. Fierce controversy reigned.

In October 1787, Alexander Hamilton, a leading member of the Convention and a dedicated upholder of the Constitution, started publishing a series of articles explaining and justifying the Constitution. Hamilton got James Madison, another leading Convention delegate, to join him. John Jay, another Founding Father (although not a Convention delegate) also contributed some articles.

The series of articles was titled *The Federalist* and was described as "a Collection of Essays written in favor of the New Constitution." Hamilton himself wrote 51 of the 85 articles, Madison contributed 27, and Jay wrote five.

Although they were written before the Constitution took effect, these essays show tremendous insight into the problems of government and have been cited ever since as embodying an authoritative interpretation of the Constitution.

Identifying Some Areas of Controversy

The whole text of the Constitution takes up just a few pages of print; see the Appendix if you don't believe me. So why do you need to read a book this long in order to understand it? The old-fashioned language of the Constitution sometimes needs to be explained. And there are a few — actually surprisingly few — genuine ambiguities in the text. But, for the most part, you can blame it on the lawyers and the judges — particularly the U.S. Supreme Court — who have made a major production out of a pretty simple, straightforward document.

How come there is such major disagreement about what the Constitution means? There are essentially three reasons:

✔ **Old-fashioned language:** The English language has changed since the horse-and-buggy era when most of the Constitution was written (but perhaps not as much as you may think). Consider the following examples:

  • Article III, Section 3 contains the phrase "Aid and Comfort" in connection with committing treason. Does this mean that you'll go to jail if you give the enemy milk and cookies? Not quite. The phrase was lifted straight out of the old English Treason Act of 1351. The word *comfort* comes from a Latin root meaning *to strengthen.* So, giving the enemy "Aid and Comfort" means actively assisting the enemy and strengthening him, whether by means of arms, money, or intelligence.

  • The biggest changes have occurred in punctuation. So, for example, the Fifth Amendment ends with this prohibition: *nor shall private property be taken for public use, without just compensation.* Some commentators have claimed to notice a smudge in the original handwritten version of the Bill of Rights, which they take to be a comma between "taken" and "for," making "for public use" a bracketed phrase. They conclude from this that the Constitution allows the government to take private property for purposes other than "for public use."

  Even if there's meant to be an additional comma in there, this interpretation is plainly wrong. First, in the 18th century commas were strewn around much more liberally than today, without affecting the meaning. Second, the idea that the government can just take private property whenever it feels like it goes clean against the whole tone and tenor of the Constitution.

✔ **Ambiguity:** There are a few passages in the Constitution where the meaning is genuinely in doubt. Here are two examples:

- **Do individuals have the right "to keep and bear Arms"?**
  The Supreme Court says yes, but the wording of the Second Amendment is not at all clear. I discuss this important question in Chapter 12 and Chapter 15.

- **If the President dies, does the Vice President become President or only Acting President?** Article II, Section 1 of the Constitution is genuinely ambiguous. The Twenty-Fifth Amendment, which came along only in 1967, says that in these circumstances the Veep does become President. But the problem was actually solved in practice by John Tyler, back in 1841. See Chapters 10 and 22 for all the details.

✔ **Interpretation:** Many of the disputes about the meaning of the Constitution arise out of different approaches to constitutional interpretations by justices of the Supreme Court. Some of these disagreements boil down to political differences between the members of the court. Here are just a few of the most controversial constitutional issues:

- **Can Congress pass any laws it likes?** The Supreme Court says no. But some commentators disagree with this interpretation and read Article I, Section 8 of the Constitution very widely. In particular, they interpret the power of Congress to "pay the Debts and provide for the common Defence and general Welfare of the United States" as meaning that Congress can pass any laws it likes. This reading is almost certainly wrong, and James Madison said so himself. I tackle this question particularly in Chapter 9.

- **Does the President have the power to lock up "enemy combatants" and deny them access to the U.S. courts?** In the 2008 case *Boumediene v. Bush,* by a majority of 5 to 4, the U.S. Supreme Court said no.

- **Is the death penalty kosher?** Yes, but it does depend on the method used. Lethal injection is now the favored method — and the Supreme Court says it's not "cruel and unusual punishment." But the Supreme Court has also held that it's unconstitutional to execute minors and the mentally ill.

- **Can a school district assign students to public high schools on the basis of race alone?** In 2007, by 5 votes to 4, the Supreme Court said no. Writing for the majority, Chief Justice John Roberts held that "The way to stop discrimination on the basis of race is to stop discriminating on the basis of race."

- **Is gay marriage unconstitutional?** Marriage doesn't figure in the U.S. Constitution at all. It's a matter for the states. Some states now allow same-sex marriages, but these unions are not recognized as marriages under federal law because of the Defense of Marriage Act (DOMA) of 1996. However, Article IV, Section 1 of the U.S. Constitution requires each state to give "Full Faith and Credit" to "the public Acts, Records, and judicial Proceedings of every other State." So, a gay marriage contracted in one state may have to be recognized by all other states as well. This question has not yet been decided by the U.S. Supreme Court. Watch this space.

- **Are states allowed to secede from the Union?** The Supreme Court says no. The last time secession was tried, it took a civil war to end it. Since that time a number of groups have advocated the secession of a state, a city, or a tribe, but no serious attempt has been made. (One such group, the Alaskan Independence Party, hit the news during the 2008 election campaign because of alleged links with Sarah Palin, the Republican vice presidential candidate.)

- **Is it okay to display the Ten Commandments in a courthouse?** In 2005, the U.S. Supreme Court decided in a 5–4 split that displaying the Ten Commandments on a Kentucky courthouse wall violated the First Amendment's requirement of separation between church and state. But a display of the Ten Commandments in the grounds of the Texas State Capitol in Austin, Texas, was held by the same margin to be permissible.

This is just the tip of the iceberg when it comes to constitutional controversies, and I devote a good deal of space in this book to sifting through them and offering my own humble opinions of the Supreme Court's interpretations. If the Constitution weren't a source of so much debate within the halls of government, perhaps it wouldn't be nearly as interesting to read and learn about. Luckily for you, that isn't the case!

Chapter 2

Framing the U.S. Constitution: Big Thinkers, Big Thoughts

● ●

In This Chapter

▶ Recognizing the influence of Magna Carta

▶ Adhering to the rule of law

▶ Noting influences on the Declaration of Independence

▶ Writing republicanism into the founding documents

● ●

*T*he United States started out as 13 British colonies that overthrew the British yoke — which was no joke at all! The American Revolution and the War of Independence led to the birth of a new nation and a new form of government enshrined in a written constitution — which, with a number of changes, has survived for more than 200 years.

Although the Unites States was born out of a bitter struggle with Britain, the leading citizens of the new nation — including the Framers of the Constitution (see Chapter 1) — were of British stock. They were educated men steeped in English law and familiar with British political institutions and philosophy.

No wonder, then, that the U.S. Constitution drew on these British sources — but no wonder either that it departed from British traditions in some major ways too, sometimes deliberately and sometimes accidentally.

In this chapter, I discuss some of the British constitutional documents, political writings, and doctrines that were most venerated by the Founders of the United States, including:

✔ Magna Carta

✔ Habeas corpus

✔ The rule of law

✔ Natural law

✔ The consent of the governed

✔ Republicanism

Building on Magna Carta

Magna Carta (Latin for "Great Charter") is a document dating back to the year 1215 containing a number of concessions made by King John of England to his rebellious barons.

What relevance could this kind of document possibly have to the United States nearly six centuries later? Magna Carta was used by the Founding Fathers as a justification for the Declaration of Independence and later as a precedent for some features of the U.S. Constitution.

Such is the veneration accorded this document in the United States that in 1957 the American Bar Association erected a memorial to Magna Carta in England. And a 1297 reissue of Magna Carta (recently sold at auction for $21.3 million!) sits in a glass case in the National Archives rotunda in Washington D.C. — right beside the original texts of the Declaration of Independence and the U.S. Constitution.

If you take the trouble to read Magna Carta, you'll probably find it just about as riveting as a phonebook — even if you speak Latin at home, because that is the language in which Magna Carta is written.

The good bits of Magna Carta are few and far between. Here's the most quoted provision:

> *No free man shall be arrested or imprisoned, or deprived of his rights or property, or outlawed or exiled . . . except by the lawful judgment of his equals or by the law of the land.*

Here are a few examples of ways Magna Carta may have influenced the Founding Fathers, as evidenced in the Declaration of Independence and the U.S. Constitution:

✔ **Taxation without representation:** Did Magna Carta prohibit taxation without representation? Clause 12 of the original promised "no scutage or aid shall be imposed on our kingdom, except by the common council of our kingdom." *Scutage* and *aid* were two feudal taxes on knights and barons alone. But did this mean that a tax could be imposed only with the consent of those subject to it? Possibly. The American patriots sure thought so. When in 1765 the British Parliament passed the Stamp Act taxing everything from newspapers to playing cards and dice, the Massachusetts Assembly declared the act "against the Magna Carta and the natural rights of Englishmen, and therefore . . . null and void." I discuss the concept of "the consent of the governed" in connection with the Declaration of Independence later in the chapter.

✔ **Trial by jury:** Did Magna Carta — in particular the clause quoted earlier in this section — guarantee trial by jury? The clause supposedly guaranteed everyone the right to be tried by their "equals," or fellow citizens. In fact, this right took a lot longer to be established in England — and it has now largely been lost there, except in cases of serious crime. But the right to a jury trial sure is alive and well in the United States and is enshrined in the Sixth and Seventh amendments to the Constitution, which I deal with in Chapter 18.

✔ **Habeas corpus:** Did Magna Carta guarantee *habeas corpus* — the right to take legal action to end unlawful detention? Not exactly, but Magna Carta was a trailblazer for this later right. The passage from Magna Carta quoted earlier in this section promises that nobody is to be imprisoned except after a proper trial. But this right didn't become available right away. As late as 1628, King Charles I had five knights imprisoned "by his majesty's special commandment." Habeas corpus became a major issue in the ensuing English Revolution, resulting in Charles I's execution. Habeas corpus was eventually incorporated into statute in 1679.

This important right is now enshrined in Article I, Section 9 of the U.S. Constitution: "The Privilege of the Writ of Habeas Corpus shall not be suspended, unless when in Cases of Rebellion or Invasion the public Safety may require it." Habeas corpus is a hot ticket issue as I write these words — in particular, with regard to detention in Guantanamo Bay.

Respecting the Rule of Law (Or the Rule of Lawyers?)

The rule of law is commonly regarded as a fundamental principle of the Western world, and of the United States in particular. The phrase *rule of law* sounds impressive. But what exactly does it mean?

At its simplest, the rule of law just means that nobody is above the law. This principle was used as a stick to beat the old absolute monarchs of Europe — like King Louis XIV of France, who famously boasted, "I am the state," or even the weak Louis XVI, who is reported as asserting, "It's legal because I wish it."

The counterblast to such exorbitant claims was put by the English political philosopher James Harrington as "the empire of laws and not of men." John Adams adapted this concept slightly and introduced it into the Massachusetts Constitution of 1780 as "A government of laws and not of men." In its most euphonious form, it became "A government not of men but of laws." This high-sounding ideal was echoed by Chief Justice John Marshall in the leading case of *Marbury v. Madison* (see Chapter 23).

But how can law rule? Laws are just words on paper. They are therefore subject to interpretation — by courts, judges, and lawyers (who argue their interpretations of laws to the courts and hope that their interpretations will be accepted). An anonymous wag put his finger on this truth and retorted that what the Founding Fathers were really likely to establish was "A government not of laws, but of lawyers."

This throwaway line has proved prophetic, and even some Supreme Court justices have admitted that the meaning of the U.S. Constitution changes in accordance with the changing views of the court. In the words of Chief Justice Charles Evans Hughes, "We are under a Constitution, but the Constitution is what the judges say it is."

This oft-quoted remark comes from a speech that Hughes gave as governor of New York in 1907, long before becoming a Supreme Court justice. But he was already pompous enough to add, "and the judiciary is the safeguard of our liberty and our property under the Constitution." Susette Kelo, who nearly lost her lovely salmon-pink Victorian cottage because of a particularly unjust decision by the U.S. Supreme Court in 2005, would probably not agree with Hughes's comment! (See my discussion of eminent domain in Chapter 17.)

The principle of the rule of law doesn't figure in the U.S. Constitution in so many words. The closest thing to the rule of law that appears in the Constitution is the Supremacy Clause in Article VI, which reads as follows:

> *This Constitution, and the Laws of the United States which shall be made in Pursuance thereof; and all Treaties made, or which shall be made, under the Authority of the United States, shall be the supreme Law of the Land; and the Judges in every State shall be bound thereby, any Thing in the Constitution or Laws of any State to the Contrary notwithstanding.*

This clause clearly places federal law above state law, but does it give the U.S. Constitution higher status than the rest of federal law? Article V sure makes it difficult to amend the Constitution, but that in itself doesn't prove that the Constitution trumps all other laws.

Chief Justice John Marshall, in the case of *Marbury v. Madison,* went to great lengths to show that the Constitution has higher status than any other law and that "a law repugnant to the Constitution is void." This was a new judge-made principle and enabled the Supreme Court to arrogate to itself the power of judicial review — which was to become its strongest weapon against the other branches of the federal government. See Chapter 23 for a full discussion of *Marbury v. Madison.*

The power of the Supreme Court to strike down laws found to be unconstitutional is now taken for granted. But was that the intention of the Founding Fathers? Thomas Jefferson objected strongly to the way the Supreme Court "usurped" the right "of exclusively explaining the Constitution," commenting that, "The Constitution on this hypothesis is a mere thing of wax in the hands of the judiciary, which they may twist and shape into any form they please."

A more accurate prediction about the Constitution would be hard to find!

Analyzing the Concepts Underlying the Declaration of Independence

The American colonists had an ambivalent attitude toward the British Constitution. Their leaders steeped themselves in the traditions of the British Constitution and generally identified with the revolutionary spirit that had led to the execution of one king — Charles I in 1649 — and the expulsion of another — James II in 1689. They regarded themselves as entitled to the same rights as natural-born Englishmen but found themselves treated at best as second-class subjects.

At first they appealed to King George III for redress of their grievances. But when their heartfelt pleas fell on deaf ears, they decided to throw off the British yoke altogether and declare their independence.

But on what basis could they justify this revolutionary step? Although they felt excluded from the British Constitution — because they were denied a voice in the British Parliament — they invoked the principles underlying Britain's embryonic democratic system, most notably the principles of "No taxation without representation" and "government by consent of the governed."

Thomas Jefferson took just 17 days to construct the case for American independence in the Declaration of Independence, whose rolling prose and unforgettable phrases were based on a blend of traditional British principles with some European ideas.

The Declaration of Independence, adopted on July 4, 1776 by the Second Continental Congress, marks the birth of the United States as a new nation — or does it? Upon closer inspection, the Declaration actually announces the birth of not one but 13 new nations — each of the former colonies being a separate nation. See Chapter 7 for more on this aspect of the Declaration.

But, whether the Declaration announced one birth or a litter of 13, it was a document essentially justifying the throwing off of British colonial rule.

The Founding Fathers were not natural revolutionaries. They were educated, well-to-do men of property and pillars of society who wouldn't normally have been mixed up in violence or war. So, what impelled these solid citizens to become involved in a bloody conflict that lasted six years?

The slogan that first rallied opposition to Britain was "No taxation without representation." The American colonies had elected legislatures, but the British parliament could override these colonial legislatures and pass laws without consulting them. The Stamp Act of 1765 was an example of this: It slapped a tax on everything from newspapers to playing cards and dice — without any consultation with the colonists. The high-handedness of this action rankled the colonists.

Did the colonists have a legal right to consent to decisions that affected them? Not under the British Constitution as understood at the time. So the colonists had to look elsewhere.

England had itself had a revolution — or two revolutions, to be precise — in the 17th century. The colonists naturally found themselves drawn to the rhetoric of those revolutionaries, who had relied a good deal on Magna Carta, to which they gave a very broad interpretation.

But Magna Carta wasn't enough on its own to justify throwing off the British colonial yoke. Magna Carta belonged to a bygone feudal age. Most of the rights contained in Magna Carta were concessions made by King John to the barons and didn't apply to ordinary people. During the English revolutions of the 17th century, the opponents of the Crown glamorized and reinterpreted Magna Carta in ways that were not always very convincing. The American Founders adopted the same expansive approach to Magna Carta, but they also used the following concepts that are reflected in the Declaration of Independence:

- ✔ Natural law
- ✔ "[U]nalienable Rights"
- ✔ Consent of the governed
- ✔ Republicanism

Invoking the law of nature

The Declaration of Independence opens with a claim on behalf of the American "people" to "the separate and equal station to which the Laws of Nature and of Nature's God entitle them."

The concept of the law of nature (or natural law) goes back to Ancient Greece and Rome, and it was commonly equated with the law of God (or divine law) and also with the law of nations.

Natural law theory said that man-made law — or *positive law* — was valid only if it conformed to the moral standards laid down by natural law, which was rational, universal, unchanging, and everlasting. The only problem with natural law was that there was no agreement about its content, as it was unwritten and existed only in the minds of its adherents. For example, was slavery in accordance with natural law? Some natural law advocates said yes, others no.

The Declaration of Independence claimed that the American states were entitled to independence from Britain on the basis of the supposed natural law principle that each nation, or "people," has the right to national self-determination. That supposed principle formed no part of the British Constitution — and was not even recognized in international law (with major modifications) until the 20th century.

Securing "unalienable Rights"

Natural law was popular among educated Americans in the late 18th century. But the problem with natural law was that those who supported it could disagree violently about its content. So, although natural law was relied on by the Founders, it provided a pretty shaky foundation for American independence. The Declaration of Independence is on firmer ground when it declares that it's the people's right — and even their duty — to overthrow a despotic government and to replace it with a government that will protect their "unalienable Rights."

This assertion is proclaimed in ringing tones:

> *We hold these truths to be self-evident, that all men are created equal, that they are endowed by their Creator with certain unalienable Rights, that among these are Life, Liberty and the pursuit of Happiness. That to secure these Rights, Governments are instituted among Men, deriving their just powers from the consent of the governed.*

These are just about the most sacred words of any American founding documents, but we need to delve just a little beneath their surface. Let's take a look at some of these rolling phrases:

- ✔ **We hold these truths to be self-evident:** This is an admission that these "truths" can't be proved.

- ✔ **All men are created equal:** How could this statement be reconciled with slavery? Thomas Jefferson himself, the author of the Declaration of Independence, was a slave owner, as were many other Founding Fathers. Similar wording in the Massachusetts Constitution of 1780 led to a legal challenge to slavery in the state courts, which effectively ended slavery in that state. But slavery was legally abolished throughout the nation only with the ratification of the Thirteenth Amendment in 1865 (see Chapter 20).

✔ **Creator:** Does the appearance of this word — and the appeal "to the Supreme Judge of the world" later on in the Declaration of Independence — mean that the United States is based on acceptance of religious belief? The last verse of the U.S. national anthem, "The Star-Spangled Banner," contains the words "And this be our motto: 'In God is our trust'." The motto "In God We Trust" has appeared on the penny since 1909, and since 1956 it has been the official national motto of the United States. But is this public display of religious belief in accordance with the First Amendment? I discuss this important subject in Chapter 14.

✔ **Unalienable Rights:** The word *unalienable* — in modern English, *inalienable* — refers to something that can't be taken away, or even given away. Inalienable rights are therefore fundamental rights that automatically belong to every human being. They can be seen as God-given rights or as rights conferred by natural law — similar therefore to what are commonly labeled *natural rights.* Not everybody believes that such rights actually exist. The British philosopher Jeremy Bentham famously declared, "The idea of rights is nonsense and the idea of natural rights is nonsense upon stilts."

✔ **Life, Liberty and the pursuit of Happiness:** This phrase is a variant on the phrase "lives, liberty, and property" that appeared in the Articles of Association of the First Continental Congress in 1774. *The pursuit of Happiness* is broader than *property* and harder to pin down. In the case of *Loving v. Virginia,* decided in 1967, the U.S. Supreme Court struck down a Virginia statute outlawing interracial marriage, on the ground that "The freedom to marry has long been recognized as one of the vital personal rights essential to the orderly pursuit of happiness by free men."

Even the term *Liberty* is hard to define. In *Meyer v. Nebraska,* the U.S. Supreme Court decided in 1923 that a Nebraska law banning the use of a foreign language as the medium of instruction to kids in grade school was unconstitutional and a denial of the "liberty" protected by the Due Process Clause of the Fourteenth Amendment. Justice Anthony Kennedy commented in 2000 that, had *Meyer*'s case been decided more recently, it would probably have been based not on the Fourteenth Amendment but rather on the First Amendment's protection of freedom of speech, belief, and religion.

"Deriving their just powers from the consent of the governed"

The Declaration of Independence goes on like this:

> [T]o secure these rights, Governments are instituted among Men, deriving their just powers from the consent of the governed.

REMEMBER

In other words:

✔ The purpose of government is to safeguard the rights of the people.

✔ The only legitimate type of government is one based on popular consent.

What exactly is meant by "consent of the governed"? By putting these words into the Declaration of Independence, Thomas Jefferson gave early notice that the government of the new United States was to be based on consent. New state constitutions soon followed suit, with elected governors and legislatures. And the government of the United States itself was designed on the same pattern, although it was at first confined, under the Articles of Confederation, to a Congress made up of delegates appointed by the state legislatures. (I discuss the Articles of Confederation later in this chapter.)

But how genuine was the claim that the governments set up by the American patriots did, indeed, govern by consent of the governed? It doesn't take much scrutiny to see that the American Revolution was not a democratic revolution. Instead, it was the overthrow of a colonial power by a wealthy elite, who then naturally stepped into the shoes of their former colonial masters.

In fact, the Framers never claimed to be democrats, and the word *democracy* doesn't appear anywhere in the U.S. Constitution (see Chapter 1). In establishment circles in the American colonies — as in England — *democracy* was a dirty word:

✔ John Adams, the future president, attacked the proposals of the radical Thomas Paine as "so democratical, without any restraint or even an attempt at equilibrium or counterpoise, that it must produce confusion and every evil work."

✔ James Madison, often described as "Father of the Constitution" and also a future president, was no fan of democracy either. Indeed, he attacked it in even stronger terms than the more conservative Adams. Here's what Madison said about democracy:

Democracy is the most vile form of government . . . democracies have ever been spectacles of turbulence and contention: have ever been found incompatible with personal security or the rights of property: and have in general been as short in their lives as they have been violent in their deaths.

The Founders just didn't trust the ordinary people and deliberately kept them at arm's length, as can be seen from the way they drafted the Articles of Confederation and then the U.S. Constitution. Keep reading to see what I mean.

Establishing a Republic

The Founding Fathers weren't democrats, so what were they? The concept that they embraced was *republicanism*. John Adams — the same John Adams who attacked democracy — waxed lyrical in his praise of republicanism. Here's how Adams defined it:

> *A government, in which all men, rich and poor, magistrates and subjects, officers and people, masters and servants, the first citizen and the last, are equally subject to the laws.*

As you start reading this definition, you get the impression that it's going to be egalitarian — based on the equality of all people. But the last phrase gives the game away. Republicanism, according to this definition, isn't about any power that the people *have* but about a power that they are *under*. In a republic, says Adams, everybody is equally under the law.

This definition of republicanism ties in with Adams's better-known statement of the goal aimed at by the newly independent states. As I note earlier in the chapter, this objective was so fundamental to Adams that he incorporated it into the Massachusetts state constitution: "A government of laws and not of men."

Adams's ideal was not one of people power at all. Rather, his ideal was one in which the people were subservient to laws made by an elite group (of which he was a prominent member) — with the last word on the interpretation of those laws going to judges drawn from the same elite group.

Democracy doesn't figure in the U.S. Constitution at all — but republicanism sure does. Article IV, Section 4 says:

> *The United States shall guarantee to every State in this Union a Republican Form of Government.*

There is no precise definition of *Republican*, but Adams's views on the subject are a reflection of the Framers' thinking (although Adams himself didn't attend the Constitutional Convention, as he was serving as U.S. ambassador to Britain at the time).

Getting rid of the king

The absence of a king is an important aspect of republicanism. The main body of the Declaration of Independence is taken up with a long list of grievances against King George III. Most of these grievances start with the word "He," referring to the King in person.

The truth is that King George did not call all the shots personally. He delegated a lot of his power to his ministers and, as I explain in the sidebar "Powerful Parliament, weak king," he just didn't have a great deal of power. (Later in life, after the American Revolutionary War, the poor guy was replaced by his son as Regent because King George suffered from serious mental illness.)

As a result, the King was in reality no longer head of government but only head of state — an increasingly purely ceremonial position in which the King represented the nation but was under pressure to become politically neutral.

This British model of government in which the head of state is separate from the head of government has spread around the world — not only among monarchies but also widely among republics, including Germany, Italy, Poland, India, and Israel.

But the American revolutionaries didn't understand these subtleties about British rule. As far as they were concerned, their main enemy was King George. For this reason, among others, the form of government of the United States of America wasn't about to be a monarchy; it would be a republic with a president who combined the positions of head of government and head of state — in other words, an executive presidency. The Framers never even realized that the separation between head of state and head of government was possible, let alone desirable.

Powerful Parliament, weak king

The British monarchy lost a lot of its power during the revolutions of the 17th century:

✔ The English Civil War between King Charles I and Parliament. The King lost the war and, after a show trial, he lost his head too, in 1649.

✔ The so-called "Glorious Revolution" of 1688–1689, in which King James II was deposed from the throne.

The Glorious Revolution enabled Parliament to consolidate its power by establishing the doctrine of the Sovereignty of Parliament as the most fundamental principle of the British Constitution. This doctrine meant:

✔ That Parliament could make or unmake any law it liked.

✔ That the King was obliged by convention — although not by strict law — to give his consent to any bill passed by both houses of Parliament. In fact, no king or queen of the United Kingdom has vetoed a bill since 1708.

✔ That a law passed by Parliament — known as an Act of Parliament — was the highest form of law under the British Constitution.

✔ That the validity of an Act of Parliament could never be challenged in any court of law nor declared unconstitutional.

Crafting the Articles of Confederation

Hot on the heels of the Declaration of Independence came the Articles of Confederation, adopted by the Second Continental Congress in 1777. These Articles were the first instrument of government of the fledgling United States of America, but they didn't really establish a single national government.

The Articles of Confederation didn't establish any national executive or any national judiciary. The Congress was the only national institution, and its powers were restricted to defense and foreign affairs.

 How democratic was the Congress? Not at all. The Congress was made up not of elected representatives but of delegates appointed by each of the state legislatures for just a year at a time. And the state legislatures themselves weren't that democratic either. The right to vote was restricted to adult white men of property.

Distinguishing *confederation, federation,* and *union*

The word *confederation* is not the same as *federation*. Let's take a moment to disentangle these terms.

Confederation: This is the weakest type of association between a number of independent regions, cantons, or states. The central government barely exists at all and is in control only of foreign affairs and defense. The best example of a confederacy or confederation in the modern world is Switzerland.

America has had two totally unconnected confederacies at two different times:

✓ The confederacy that lasted from 1777 until 1788, governed by the Articles of Confederation. However, the Articles stated at the beginning that "The Stile of this Confederacy shall be: 'The United States of America.'"

✓ The Confederate States of America, the 11 breakaway southern states that seceded

from the United States, resulting in the Civil War in 1861.

Federation: The U.S. Constitution established a federal system of government, in which quite extensive powers were delegated to the national, or federal, government. But any powers not delegated to the federal government were — and still are — retained by the states or by the people. See more on this topic in Chapter 19, which deals with the Tenth Amendment.

Union: The word *union* appears quite a few times in the U.S. Constitution in reference to the federal government, and it is still often used in that sense: for example, the President's annual "State of the Union" address. In fact, *union* is a misnomer as a description of a federal system. Strictly speaking, the word *union* refers to a much more centralized system of government where all power is concentrated in the national government, as in present-day France.

But this lack of democracy was not the reason the Articles of Confederation were eventually abandoned in 1788. The problem was that, in the absence of any proper national authority, the states started quarreling among themselves. George Washington and other leading figures felt the need for more central control. This resulted in the calling of a convention in Philadelphia to revise the Articles of Confederation. But, instead of merely tinkering with the Articles, the convention ended up drafting a whole new instrument of government: the U.S. Constitution.

Leaving democracy out of the U.S. Constitution

The U.S. Constitution in its original form wasn't a lot more democratic than the Articles of Confederation. Here's why:

✔ The Senate was not originally directly elected, but made up of members appointed by the state legislatures.

✔ The President was not elected by the people but by an Electoral College. The Electoral College system still exists, but, thanks to the rise of political parties, it has been short-circuited and is therefore more democratic than the Framers ever intended. (I discuss presidential elections in Chapter 10.)

✔ Even elections to the House of Representatives — the only body directly elected under the original version of the U.S. Constitution — were not truly democratic, because the right to vote was narrowly restricted in the early days of the Republic. It took more than a half century before the United States could be described as a democracy. The movement toward democracy was largely the achievement of a political party that started out by calling itself the Republican Party, then the Democratic-Republican Party, and later, under Andrew Jackson, — who was President from 1829 to 1837 — simply the Democratic Party (see Chapter 6).

Chapter 3

Debating the Constitution

The U.S. Constitution is only a few pages long (see the Appendix). It makes a pretty neat pocket-size pamphlet.

Why do you need to read this big book when you can just read the Constitution itself? One reason is that my publishers need to make a few bucks. (It's not for *my* benefit — we authors only get peanuts!)

Seriously, though, there are many reasons why everybody — and I do mean *everybody* — needs help to understand the Constitution. I explore these reasons in this chapter so you can begin to understand why this short document is such a source of confusion and debate.

Listing Some Sources of Confusion

Here are some of the key reasons the Constitution is such a difficult document to digest:

  ✔ **Technical language:** The Constitution is a statement of law, so it's not surprising that it contains some legal jargon. For example, *ratifying* an amendment is not the same thing as ratting on that amendment! To *ratify* an amendment means to confirm it. To change the Constitution, it's necessary for an amendment to be proposed and then ratified. (The Fifth Amendment deals with the process of amending the Constitution. For more on that subject, see Chapter 5.)

✔ **Old-fashioned language:** Most of the Constitution was written more than 200 years ago. The meanings of some words have changed a bit since then. For example, what is the meaning of the word *compact* — as in, "No State shall, without the Consent of the Congress . . . enter into any Agreement or Compact with another State, or with a foreign Power"? In modern English, *compact* often refers to something that occupies very little space. As a noun, *compact* can mean a small cosmetic case containing face-powder. But in the clause that I just quoted from Article I, Section 10 of the Constitution, *compact* means an agreement or an alliance. So, the quoted words mean that individual states are not allowed to pursue their own foreign policy. This provision gives the federal government a lock on foreign policy.

✔ **Old-fashioned ideas:** Just as a lot of the language of the Constitution is old-fashioned, so are some of the ideas and values that it expresses. For example, the Seventh Amendment guarantees a right to trial by jury in any civil suit "where the value in controversy shall exceed twenty dollars." In 1791, when the Bill of Rights (including the Seventh Amendment) was ratified, the average wage earner made only about $16 a week. Times have certainly changed. But in this case, the discrepancy is not important. If anything, it's good that the threshold for jury trial is so low, because that means that trial by jury is available for almost all civil suits.

✔ **Obsolete concepts:** The Constitution is based on old concepts and ideas. But does that mean the Constitution is no longer relevant to the present day? Some people have leveled this accusation against the Constitution. I examine this serious charge in this chapter (see the section "Discarding Out-of-Date Ideas?").

✔ **Ambiguity:** The Framers of the Constitution were educated, articulate men. But even these intellectual giants made a few boo-boos. I take a look at some of the unintended ambiguities in the Constitution in this chapter (see "Untangling Ambiguities").

✔ **Omissions:** Some of the most important constitutional concepts and institutions don't actually figure in the text of the Constitution at all. These missing features include democracy, political parties, the death penalty, privacy, and abortion. The death penalty does at least rate a couple of indirect mentions in the text of the Constitution. But the rest of these missing concepts don't get any mentions at all. I tackle this topic in the section "Giving Some Important Principles the Silent Treatment."

✔ **Interpretation:** The U.S. Supreme Court has made a lot of major changes to the Constitution — without altering a single word of the text. This is the most important reason why just picking up and reading the Constitution doesn't really tell you what it means. See the section "Interpreting the Constitution" to find out more.

Discarding Out-Of-Date Ideas?

It's easy to criticize the Constitution as being past its sell-by date. The Framers recognized the danger that later generations might want to keep changing the Constitution in accordance with shifting political fashions. That's why the Framers deliberately made the Constitution so difficult to amend. (See Chapter 5 for a discussion of the official and unofficial ways that the Constitution has been changed.)

Here are just three of the many constitutional provisions that have been singled out for attack as obsolete:

- **The right to bear arms,** contained in the Second Amendment, has always been controversial, but is it also obsolete? That depends on how it is interpreted. If you interpret the amendment as giving individuals the right to buy and use guns, the amendment appears obsolete to those people who view that right as part of a long-gone Wild West culture. But that same interpretation is seen as sensible and relevant to modern life if viewed from the perspective of human rights — and it is the inter- pretation now accepted by the Supreme Court. On the other hand, if you interpret the Second Amendment as protecting gun ownership and usage only by people who participate in state militias, the amendment may be seen as obsolete. That's because the National Guard, which is the modern successor to the militia, has since 1933 been a component of the U.S. Army (and its members sure don't have to provide their own weapons!). But *that* narrower interpretation is seen by its supporters as relevant to the need for gun control. See Chapter 15 for all the details and debates surrounding this amendment.

- **The right to trial by jury**, guaranteed for criminal trials by the Sixth Amendment and for civil trials by the Seventh Amendment, may be seen by some as anachronistic. Jury trial originated in England, but it has disappeared there from practically all civil trials, and even in criminal trials it is available in far fewer cases than it used to be. However, as a practicing trial lawyer, I would prefer to try a case in front of a bunch of ordinary folk than in front of any judge you could name.

- **The Electoral College system** for picking the President, as laid down by Article II, Section 1 of the Constitution and modified by the Twelfth Amendment, is often criticized as obsolete because it doesn't appear to be democratic. There is actually a confusion here between two different things: the *Electoral College* system on one hand and, on the other, the *winner-take-all* system.

  In most states these two systems are combined. That means that the winner of the presidential race in a particular state usually takes *all* the electoral votes of that state. So, if the Democratic candidate gets 60 percent of the votes in California and the Republican candidate gets

40 percent, all 55 of California's electoral votes go into the Democratic column. But the Constitution doesn't actually demand this approach. The Constitution only says that the electoral vote for a state is calculated by adding the number of representatives for that state in the House of Representatives to the number of senators (which is always two).

If California preferred, it could adopt a split vote system. For example, California could decide to split the electoral vote in the same proportion as the popular vote. So, if the Democratic candidate won 60 percent of the vote, that candidate would get 60 percent of California's electoral votes, which is 33 votes, and the Republican candidate would get the remaining 22.

If every state adopted this form of the Electoral College system, the Electoral College system would produce the same result as a straight popular-vote system calculated without reference to state boundaries — which is what most critics of the Electoral College system are angling for.

Whether a state goes for the *winner-take-all* system or for a *split vote* system is entirely a matter for that state to decide. At present, Nebraska and Maine are the only two states that operate a form of split vote. And that system did actually produce a split vote in the 2008 election, with Barack Obama getting one electoral vote from Nebraska while the other four electoral votes from that state went to John McCain.

Untangling Ambiguities

The Constitution has a reputation for being ambiguous at times. If it weren't, the members of the Supreme Court might have a lot more free time on their hands! Consider just two examples:

✔ Does the Second Amendment give individual citizens the right "to keep and bear Arms"? Or does it restrict the right to members of militias or their modern equivalent? James Madison, who drafted the amendment, must have known what he intended it to mean, but he didn't express it very clearly. As I explain in Chapter 15, proponents of both sides of the gun rights debate find support for their arguments within the murky structure of this one-sentence amendment.

✔ What happens if the Vice President takes the reins when the President dies or resigns? Is the Veep actually the President or just the acting President? Article II of the Constitution is clear as mud, and the issue became very real when William Henry Harrison died in 1841 and Vice President John Tyler took over as President. Tyler refused to be just an acting President, and he set a precedent that was followed by every subsequent Veep. But it was only in 1967 that the Twenty-Fifth Amendment finally settled the issue in crystal-clear language. For much more detail on this topic, see Chapter 4 and Chapter 22.

Giving Some Important Principles the Silent Treatment

The whole idea of a written constitution is to lay everything on the line. Chief Justice John Marshall famously remarked, "The government of the United States has been emphatically termed a government of laws, and not of men."

But how can this ambitious ideal ever be achieved if the Constitution omits all mention of some of the most important principles on which that constitution is based?

Here are some important principles and institutions that don't figure in the text of the Constitution at all:

✔ **Democracy:** As I explain in Chapter 1, the words *democracy* and *democratic* don't figure anywhere in the text of the Constitution. Is the United States a democracy? It sure wasn't in the early days of the Republic.

The Founders didn't trust the ordinary people. *Democracy* was a dirty word as far as they were concerned. Voting rights were restricted to property owners, and the House of Representatives was the only directly elected federal institution. Senators were appointed by the state legislatures, and the President was elected by an Electoral College. (The Electoral College system is still in place today, but it's now largely nominal. The existence of parties has short-circuited the Electoral College and democratized presidential elections. See my preceding discussion in the section "Discarding Out-Of-Date Ideas?")

The U.S. Constitution doesn't read as a blueprint for a democracy — simply because democracy wasn't on the agenda as far as the Founders were concerned.

✔ **Political parties:** The Constitution contains not a single reference to political parties, but political parties are the lifeblood of the Constitution. The competition between the parties has turned the United States into a democracy.

Parties started crystallizing quite early on, but the Framers didn't recognize their importance. As a result, the 1800 presidential election was a mess — and the Twelfth Amendment was needed to remedy the situation. (I discuss the Twelfth Amendment in Chapter 20.)

The United States has always had two main parties competing for power — at first Federalists and Democratic Republicans, then later Whigs and Democrats, and, since 1854, Republicans and Democrats. This two-party system gives voters a choice and prevents power from being concentrated in the hands of one group.

✔ **The death penalty:** The Constitution doesn't specifically allow or disallow the death penalty, but both the Fifth and the Fourteenth amendments refer to it. The Fifth Amendment opens with these words:

No person shall be held to answer for a capital, or otherwise infamous crime, unless on a presentment or indictment of a Grand Jury.

A *capital crime* means a crime carrying the death penalty. Which crimes were these? The amendment doesn't say, but it takes it for granted that such crimes exist. Murder is the most common capital crime, but it's usually a state crime rather than a federal crime — and the Fifth Amendment refers purely to federal law.

The Fourteenth Amendment does refer to state law, and the Due Process Clause in Section 1 of that amendment recognizes the death penalty:

nor shall any State deprive any person of life, liberty, or property, without due process of law.

For a state to deprive somebody of life by due process of law can only mean that execution was a recognized sentence in 1868, when the Fourteenth Amendment was ratified. So, how come the Constitution doesn't say in so many words that capital punishment is okay as long as certain due process is given? Because the Constitution doesn't restate the whole of the criminal law, which had always imposed the death penalty for murder, treason, and other "infamous" crimes.

The presence of these references to capital punishment in the Fifth and Fourteenth amendments, side by side with the ban on "cruel and unusual punishments" in the Eighth Amendment, makes it crystal clear that capital punishment *in itself* was not viewed as being cruel and unusual. However, the *mode* of execution could well make a difference as far as the Eighth Amendment is concerned. For example, execution by boiling in oil or by tearing the offender limb from limb would undoubtedly qualify as "cruel and unusual punishments."

Execution by lethal injection is acceptable, according to the 2008 U.S. Supreme Court ruling in the case of *Baze v. Rees*. The case arose out of a challenge by two men sentenced to death by lethal injection in Kentucky. Ralph Baze was convicted of murdering a sheriff and deputy sheriff who were trying to serve him with a warrant. Thomas Bowling was convicted of killing a husband and wife after ramming their car. The test used by the U.S. Supreme Court for "cruel and unusual punishments" is whether the punishment in question carries the risk of inflicting "unnecessary pain." In the words of Chief Justice John Roberts, writing for the majority on the court, "Kentucky has adopted a method of execution believed to be the most humane available, one it shares with 35 other States."

✔ **Privacy:** The word *privacy* also doesn't figure anywhere in the text of the Constitution. However, in the case of *Griswold v. Connecticut,* decided in 1965, Justice William O. Douglas, writing for the majority, found the right to privacy in the "penumbras" formed by "emanations" of guarantees contained in the First, Third, Fourth, and Fifth amendments. Concurring judgments cited also the Ninth and Fourteenth amendments.

Justice Potter Stewart disagreed, stating: "With all deference, I can find no such general right of privacy in the Bill of Rights, in any other part of the Constitution, or in any case ever before decided by this Court." But the powerful dissent by Stewart, joined by Justice Hugo Black, wasn't enough to block this far-reaching reinterpretation by the majority on the court. (For more on this subject, see Chapter 5.)

✔ **Abortion:** The new-found right to privacy served as the springboard to a right of abortion in certain circumstances. This controversial right was established by the court in *Roe v. Wade,* which I discuss in Chapter 5.

Interpreting the Constitution

Chief Justice Charles Evans Hughes famously remarked that, "We are under a Constitution, but the Constitution is what the judges say it is, and the judiciary is the safeguard of our liberty and our property under the Constitution." The Chief Justice was right to point out that the meaning of the Constitution keeps changing as a result of judicial interpretation and reinterpretation, without any change in the words on paper.

Hughes was not criticizing the courts for this process but was actually praising them. Not everyone would agree with this view. Here are some of the reasons for opposing judicial changes to the Constitution:

✔ Article V of the Constitution makes it clear that the only way that the Constitution can be changed is by formal amendment, which requires a two-thirds majority in both houses of Congress and ratification by three-fourths of the state legislatures.

✔ The Framers deliberately made amendment difficult, so that any change would command broad general support.

✔ The Supreme Court justices are unelected, are appointed for life, and are removable only by impeachment. This means that the justices are independent and not answerable to the electorate or to anybody else.

✔ Supreme Court justices who interpret the Constitution in ways that depart from the text are effectively rewriting that document by imposing their own views on it.

The reply to these points is along the following lines:

- The Constitution was mostly written more than 200 years ago. It's impossible to get back to the original intention of the Framers — even if we wanted to.

- To remain relevant and meaningful, the Constitution must be interpreted afresh by each new generation, as a "living Constitution."

- This process of interpretation in the light of changing political, social, and moral values does not amount to unauthorized amendment but is needed in order to make sense of the Constitution and to apply it to the modern age.

Comparing interpretations of "cruel and unusual punishments"

The Eighth Amendment's ban on "cruel and unusual punishments" provides a good example for comparing two different approaches to constitutional interpretation: on the one hand, the "living Constitution" approach coupled with judicial activism, and, on the other hand, strict constructionism coupled with judicial restraint.

During World War II, private Albert Trop was found guilty of desertion and was sentenced to three years' hard labor and a dishonorable discharge from the U.S. army. After serving his sentence, Trop applied for a passport. It was denied on the ground that he had lost his citizenship because of his conviction for desertion. The question before the Supreme Court in *Trop v. Dulles* was whether depriving Trop of his citizenship in this way amounted to unconstitutional "cruel and unusual punishments" under the Eighth Amendment.

By 5 votes to 4, the high court ruled that depriving Trop of his citizenship did indeed infringe on his Eighth Amendment rights. In the words of Chief Justice Earl Warren, writing for the majority, "The Amendment must draw its meaning from the evolving standards of decency that mark the progress of a maturing society."

The minority rejected this approach as a rewriting of the amendment departing from the meaning of "cruel and unusual punishments" as understood in 1791 — and also as an exercise in judicial activism, arrogating to the court more power than it was entitled to have.

Justice Felix Frankfurter's dissenting opinion, supported by three other justices, pointed out that desertion from the army in time of war had been a capital offense since the first year of independence. Can it be seriously urged, asked Frankfurter, "that loss of citizenship is a fate worse than death?"

Frankfurter went on to stress that the court should exercise "with the utmost restraint" the "awesome power" to strike down laws passed by Congress and approved by the President — "the two branches of our Government directly responsive to the will of the people and empowered under the Constitution to determine the wisdom of legislation."

Comparing interpretations of partial-birth abortion

In the past several decades, abortion has become a generally reliable litmus test to determine the approach to interpretation adopted by a Supreme Court justice. So let's take a look at the court's handling of the Partial-Birth Abortion Ban Act.

In 2003, President George W. Bush signed into law the Partial-Birth Abortion Ban Act, which makes it a criminal offense for a physician to carry out a partial-birth abortion. The act defines partial-birth abortion as

> *An abortion in which the person performing the abortion, deliberately and intentionally vaginally delivers a living fetus until, in the case of a head-first presentation, the entire fetal head is outside the body of the mother, or, in the case of breech presentation, any part of the fetal trunk past the navel is outside the body of the mother, for the purpose of performing an overt act that the person knows will kill the partially delivered living fetus; and performs the overt act, other than completion of delivery, that kills the partially delivered living fetus.*

The act was generally welcomed by *pro-life* opinion — people opposed to abortion — and opposed by *pro-choice* advocates — people in favor of abortion rights.

The constitutionality of the act was immediately challenged in *Gonzales v. Carhart,* which was heard by the U.S. Supreme Court in 2007. The result was a cliffhanger, with a 5–4 decision in favor of the act. The lineup showed the usual conservative–liberal split, with Justice Anthony Kennedy casting the swing vote. But the case shows just how extreme the polarization is between the different interpretative approaches on the court. Here's the breakdown of the three opinions that were delivered:

- ✔ A lengthy and unexciting majority opinion, written by Justice Kennedy, upheld the constitutionality of the act by steering a careful course between respect for a law passed by Congress and respect for previous pro-choice rulings by the high court.

- ✔ A very short and explosive concurring opinion written by Justice Clarence Thomas with the support of Justice Antonin Scalia — generally considered to be the most politically conservative members of the court — supported the majority opinion upholding the constitutional validity of the act. But the main thrust of this bombshell concurring opinion is a total rejection of the court's previous pro-choice rulings: "The court's abortion jurisprudence, including *Roe v. Wade,* has no basis in the Constitution."

- ✔ A dissenting opinion, penned by Justice Ruth Bader Ginsburg — probably the most politically liberal member of the court — described the majority decision as "alarming." She wrote, "The notion that the Partial-Birth Abortion Ban Act furthers any legitimate government interest is, quite simply, irrational."

Identifying methods of interpretation

The classification of the different schools of constitutional interpretation is messy, to say the least. But here's a bird's-eye view of the main divisions:

- ✔ **Living Constitution:** This school of thought sees the Constitution as a living and breathing document that must be interpreted and reinterpreted according to the changing needs of society. On the present Supreme Court, Justices Ginsburg, David Souter, and Stephen Breyer generally adhere to this approach. Justice Scalia has attacked this approach as undemocratic by wanting "matters to be decided not by the people, but by the justices of the Supreme Court."

- ✔ **Strict constructionism:** This label used to refer to a literal approach to constitutional interpretation. Thomas Jefferson favored this approach, which took a narrow view of the powers of the federal government as against the states. Chief Justice William Rehnquist was often described as a strict constructionist, as are Justices Clarence Thomas and Antonin Scalia. Scalia rejects the label, saying that he is "not a strict constructionist and no-one ought to be" — because the correct approach is to understand the words of the Constitution in their "ordinary" meaning and not only in their "strict" meaning.

- ✔ **Textualism:** Judges who are referred to by politicians and the media as strict constructionists nowadays tend to prefer to be regarded as *textualists, formalists,* or *originalists.* Although these three labels are not identical, we can lump them all together under the title of *textualists.* These judges believe that the Constitution should be interpreted in accordance with its original meaning.

These judges are also often regarded as conservatives, but there is some confusion here. Conservative judges normally have a certain reverence for *stare decisis* — the doctrine that courts should adhere to previous decisions. But what should a textualist do when his reading of the Constitution disagrees with a previous Supreme Court decision? In those circumstances, some of them, like Clarence Thomas, tend to jettison *stare decisis*.

✔ **Originalism:** This term is now applied to several different schools of thought, which share the view that the Constitution had a clear and definite meaning at the time it was drafted and that to interpret the Constitution a court must get back to that original meaning.

The most influential branch of this school of thought, claiming adherents such as Scalia, stresses *original meaning* at the expense of *original intent* — the meaning of the text as it would have been understood by a reasonable person at the time it was drafted, rather than some secret purpose that the Framers may have had. Critics of this approach have pooh-poohed as unrealistic the attempt to recapture the meaning of a text as it was understood more than 200 years ago.

The sight of judges beating one another over the head with old dictionaries can be entertaining. In 1994, Scalia, relying on a raft of dictionaries, ruled that the word *modify* meant no more than "to make minor changes." He rejected the argument, based on *Webster's Third New International Dictionary* published in 1976, that *modify* could also refer to the making of major or fundamental changes.

If this is the sort of mess a court can get into on the basis of word meanings of the late 20th century, how easy can it be to reach the original meaning of texts drafted in the late 18th century? Interpreting the Constitution on the basis of its meaning at the time it was written sure makes sense. The problem may be that neither Scalia nor any of the other high court justices is trained as a historian, a linguist, or a philologist.

✔ **Judicial activism:** Politically liberal judges are often identified as "judicial activists," while political conservatives are often assumed to be in favor of "judicial restraint." This is by no means always the case. For example, Felix Frankfurter, one of the most liberal Supreme Court justices of all time, was also noted for his loyalty to the federal government. So, in the 1944 case of *Korematsu v. United States,* he voted with the majority on the court to uphold a racially based executive order excluding Japanese-Americans from a designated military area in California. More recently, in 1995, conservative Chief Justice William Rehnquist wrote the majority opinion in *United States v. Lopez* — supported by conservative Justices Antonin Scalia and Clarence Thomas and vaguely conservative Justice Sandra Day O'Connor — striking down as unconstitutional a federal law prohibiting the knowing possession of a gun in a school zone. Opponents of this decision labeled it as an exercise in judicial activism, but it could also be characterized as an example of strict constructionism.

Chapter 4

Introducing . . . the Constitution! The Preamble and the Seven Articles

In This Chapter
▶ Explaining the Preamble
▶ Delving beneath the surface of the text
▶ Recognizing that the real story may not figure in the text at all

*I*s the Constitution complicated, hard to understand, and boring? You betcha! Okay, so don't read it yet. Read this chapter first.

In this chapter, I introduce you to the Preamble — the introduction — to the Constitution, as well as the seven articles. I deal with the subject matter of these seven articles in detail in later chapters.

My goal in this chapter is to look beneath the surface of the Constitution and identify what I consider the most important (and sometimes disputed) issues it addresses. I also reveal that some of the most important principles that formed the basis of the Constitution don't actually figure in the text at all.

Presenting the Preamble: "We the People . . ."

"We the People" are the best-known words of the U.S. Constitution. They are the opening words of the *Preamble* — the almost lyrical introduction to the Constitution:

We the People of the United States, in Order to form a more perfect Union, establish Justice, insure domestic Tranquility, provide for the common defence, promote the general Welfare, and secure the Blessings of Liberty to ourselves and our Posterity, do ordain and establish this Constitution for the United States of America.

The language of the Preamble is very different from that of the rest of the Constitution. The Constitution is essentially a legal document, but the Preamble reads more like a political statement. Let me examine the wording more closely:

- ✔ *We the People of the United States . . . do ordain and establish this Constitution for the United States of America:* Did "the people of the United States" really "ordain and establish" the Constitution? Yes and no. The delegates to the Philadelphia Convention that drafted the Constitution in 1787 were not directly elected; they were selected by their state legislatures. But the Constitution was then submitted for ratification to a directly elected convention in each state.

- ✔ *in Order to form a more perfect Union:* This clause refers to the perceived failure of the Articles of Confederation, the first American constitution, that had been in effect since 1777. The Philadelphia Convention drafted a Constitution that aimed "to form a more perfect Union" — a closer union than the loose association of sovereign states that existed under the Articles of Confederation.

- ✔ *[in Order to] establish Justice, insure domestic Tranquility, provide for the common defence, promote the general Welfare, and secure the Blessings of Liberty to ourselves and our Posterity:* This is an impressive list of objectives. The Articles of Confederation weren't able to deliver these goals. They didn't even set up any national law courts. The states were at one another's throats. And Congress wasn't able to offer protection against foreign enemies or the Native American tribes. But the Framers were confident that their new Constitution could secure these benefits for their own age and for the future. They turned out to be right!

Article 1: Setting up the Congress

Article I is by far the longest article of the Constitution (see the Appendix). Section 1 of that article reads as follows:

All legislative Powers herein granted shall be vested in a Congress of the United States, which shall consist of a Senate and House of Representatives.

At first sight this section looks as though it gives Congress total legislative power — the power to make any laws it likes. The very first word, "All," certainly contributes to this impression. But that impression is false.

The most important word in this section is not "All" but the easily-missed "granted." This important section can be rewritten like this:

✔ The Constitution grants the federal government certain limited legislative powers — the power to pass laws on certain matters, but not on just anything.

✔ The Constitution grants *all* these *limited* legislative powers to a Congress.

✔ The Congress shall consist of two houses: a Senate and a House of Representatives.

Sections 2 through 7 of Article I spell out who can run for election to each branch of Congress, how often those elections take place, how many members each branch has, and (in broad terms) how the business of Congress is to be run. I discuss these topics in Chapter 11.

But by far the meatiest sections of Article I are Section 8, which lists the powers of Congress, and Section 9, which details specific limits on congressional power. In the following sections, I explain two reasons that Section 8, in particular, deserves special attention.

Magnifying the commerce power

Over the years, the Constitution has been interpreted in such a way that the most important part of Article I, Section 8 is the *Commerce Clause,* which confers on Congress the power

> *To regulate Commerce with foreign Nations, and among the several States, and with the Indian Tribes.*

The U.S. Supreme Court has at times interpreted this clause — and particularly Congress's power over interstate commerce — so widely as to embrace virtually all economic activities. This interpretation is a far cry from what the Framers appear to have intended because the wording of the clause places interstate commerce slap bang between international trade and trade with the Native American tribes. This positioning can only mean that interstate commerce must be understood in the same limited way as the other two categories. I deal more fully with the Commerce Clause in Chapter 9.

(Mis)interpreting the "necessary and proper" clause

The "necessary and proper" clause of Article I, Section 8 is also important, but it too has suffered at the hands of greedy feds. This clause gives Congress the power

> *To make all Laws which shall be necessary and proper for carrying into Execution the foregoing Powers, and all other Powers vested by this Constitution in the Government of the United States, or in any Department or Officer thereof.*

Once again, it's easy to be unduly influenced by the opening words, "To make all Laws." But a close reading of the rest of the clause appears to indicate a serious limitation. The key words are "necessary and proper." Does this phrase apply to *all* congressional legislation? If it does, then it clearly acts as a limitation on the power of Congress.

In the leading case of *McCulloch v. Maryland,* decided in 1819, Chief Justice John Marshall disagreed with this interpretation and held that, far from restricting the power of Congress, the "necessary and proper" clause actually extended that power. My own view is that Marshall was wrong about this and that his interpretation of this clause is one of his many "twistifications" (a phrase that Thomas Jefferson coined). See my full discussion of this important decision in Chapter 8.

Article II: Hailing the Chief

Section 1 of Article II begins with these words:

> *The executive Power shall be vested in a President of the United States of America.*

Section 2 adds:

> *The President shall be Commander in Chief of the Army and Navy of the United States, and of the militia of the several states, when called into the actual service of the United States.*

In addition to his executive and military powers, the President's approval is needed for a Bill to become an Act of Congress. If the President doesn't approve a Bill, he is commonly said to *veto* it. The presidential veto kills the Bill concerned (but the veto can be overridden by a two-thirds majority in both houses of Congress). These legislative powers of the President are found in Article I, Section 7 of the Constitution.

The President is also Head of State of the United States, a position that isn't mentioned in the Constitution at all — because the Framers didn't recognize it as a separate position. I discuss this and the other powers of the President in Chapter 10.

Listing presidential powers and duties

Article II is surprisingly brief. The only presidential powers and duties that are specifically enumerated are the following:

- The power to make treaties — subject to confirmation by the Senate.
- The power — subject to confirmation by the Senate — to appoint "Ambassadors, other public Ministers and Consuls, judges of the supreme Court, and all other Officers of the United States, whose Appointments are not herein otherwise provided for."
- The power to fill casual vacancies in the Senate that occur during congressional recesses.
- The duty to report to Congress on the state of the union (the origin of the annual State of the Union Address).
- The power to recommend legislation to Congress.
- The power to call a meeting of one or both houses of Congress "on extraordinary Occasions" — a power that has been exercised by 16 presidents.
- The power to adjourn Congress "in Case of Disagreement" between the two Houses "with Respect to the Time of Adjournment."
- The right to "receive Ambassadors and other public Ministers" representing foreign nations.
- An obligation to "take Care that the Laws be faithfully executed" — a really important duty.
- The power to appoint all officers of the United States armed forces.

Finally, Article II, Section 4 contains one of the best-known features of the Constitution — the provision for the impeachment of "The President, Vice President and all civil Officers of the United States." I discuss impeachment in Chapter 13.

Identifying the real issues

This list of presidential powers and duties looks boringly straightforward. So how come different presidents have exercised such different degrees of power? You need only compare a weak president like James Buchanan with his immediate successor, Abraham Lincoln, to notice the difference — or, say, a strong president like Theodore Roosevelt with his weak hand-picked successor, William Howard Taft.

The reason for these contrasts is the divergent interpretations of the Constitution that these different presidents embraced. These days, the main areas of dispute include

- Presidential power in regard to war.
- Presidential power in regard to homeland security.
- The President's role in regard to healthcare.

I discuss all these topics in Chapter 10.

A drafting boo-boo

A big chunk of Article II deals with presidential elections. Most of these provisions were scrapped and replaced by the Twelfth Amendment, ratified in 1804, which I discuss in Chapter 20.

Article II had to be amended because, in drafting the rules for presidential elections, the Framers had totally ignored the role of political parties — which, in fact, aren't mentioned anywhere in the Constitution. This serious omission put the Framers in a delicate spot in the election of 1800.

The original version of Article II said that the members of the Electoral College had to vote for *two* candidates for President. The candidate with the most votes would then become President, and the candidate with the next highest number of votes would become Vice President.

This arrangement was naïve — because each political party naturally put up two candidates, one of them being the presidential candidate and the other his running-mate. But, because the Constitution didn't differentiate between a vote for President and a vote for Vice President, in the 1800 election Thomas Jefferson ended up with the same number of electoral votes as his running-mate, Aaron Burr. The result was a mess. Aaron Burr nearly became President. The outcome was decided by the House of Representative — after no fewer than 36 ballots!

Succeeding to the presidency

The provision for succession on the removal, death, or incapacity of the President is another defective piece of draftsmanship. The "Powers and

Duties" of the office of President were to "devolve on [pass on to] the Vice President." This provision appears clear enough. But, did it mean that the Vice President was to become President or only acting President?

After the death in 1841 of William Henry Harrison, the first President to die in office, Vice President John Tyler was referred to by his enemies as "His Accidency." But he took the presidential oath of office and was officially recognized by the Senate as President and not merely acting President. And to make a point, he returned unopened all mail addressed to the "acting President." He is counted as the tenth President on the official list.

All subsequent Vice Presidents who succeeded to the presidency were regarded as Presidents and not just as acting Presidents. But this status was not finally put on a constitutional footing until the ratification of the Twenty-Fifth Amendment in 1967 (see Chapter 22).

Article II also made no provision for the appointment of a new Vice President when the Vice President succeeded to the presidency. So, until the Twenty-Fifth Amendment came around, there was no Vice President during the presidency of a Vice President who had succeeded to the post.

Article III: Understating Judicial Power

Article III, which sets forth the power of the judiciary, looks pretty straightforward — and mind-numbingly dull. Here's Section 1:

> *The judicial Power of the United States shall be vested in one supreme Court, and in such inferior Courts as the Congress may from time to time ordain and establish. The judges, both of the supreme and inferior Courts, shall hold their Offices during good Behaviour.*

The provision allowing federal judges to hold office "during good Behaviour" is effectively the same as saying "for life." That's why the battle over who will receive a coveted appointment to a federal judgeship is often protracted and heated. Quite a number of Supreme Court justices — including most recently Chief Justice William Rehnquist — died in harness at an advanced age.

Article III, Section 2 lists the types of cases that the federal courts are empowered to hear. The U.S. Supreme Court is the most important court in the nation. The "inferior" federal courts include the U.S. courts of appeals, U.S. district courts, and also specialist courts such as the U.S. bankruptcy courts and the U.S. Tax Court.

There is only one surprise in the list of judicial functions in Article III: It includes cases "between a State and Citizens of another State," which were later excluded by the Eleventh Amendment (see Chapter 20).

The most important power of the Supreme Court doesn't figure in the text of the Constitution at all. This is the power of *judicial review,* which I discuss at length in Chapter 12. In brief, here's what judicial review means: It allows the U.S. Supreme Court to decide whether a federal or state law is in violation of the U.S. Constitution. If the court finds that a law conflicts with the Constitution, it declares the law unconstitutional. This means that the law (or the relevant part of the law) is *void,* or of no effect.

Because of judicial review, the Supreme Court is extremely powerful — arguably more powerful than either of the other two branches of government. The court can strike down a law that has been passed by both houses of Congress and signed by the President! In the words of Chief Justice Charles Evans Hughes, "the Constitution is what the judges say it is."

Two key questions come to mind, both of which I discuss in Chapter 12:

- **How come this great power of the Supreme Court isn't spelled out anywhere in the text of the Constitution?** The Framers of the Constitution may not have intended for the court to wield such power; the court arrogated the power of judicial review to itself. Chief Justice John Marshall started the ball rolling with a famous 1803 opinion in *Marbury v. Madison* — a case I discuss in Chapter 23.

- **Was the court's decision to give itself the power of judicial review wrong?** Probably. But nonetheless, the power remains intact today.

Article IV: Getting Along with the Neighbors — and Uncle Sam

The first sentence of Section 1 of Article IV is known as the *Full Faith and Credit Clause.* It reads as follows:

> *Full Faith and Credit shall be given in each State to the public Acts, Records, and judicial Proceedings of every other State.*

This clause appears to mean that every state has to recognize the laws and court decisions of every other state. But the Supreme Court established a "public policy" exception to the operation of this clause. In 1939, the court ruled that "there are some limitations to the extent to which a state may be required by the full faith and credit clause to enforce even the judgment of another state in contravention of its own statutes or policy."

Same-sex marriage is the latest issue to put the Full Faith and Credit Clause to the test. Is a state required under the Full Faith and Credit Clause to recognize a same-sex marriage, if that marriage was valid in the state where it was performed?

The opening sentence of Section 2 of Article IV, the Privileges and Immunities Clause, is less controversial. It reads as follows:

> *The Citizens of each State shall be entitled to all Privileges and Immunities of Citizens in the several States.*

But even this clause has had its problems — especially when it has come up against the clause modeled on it in the Fourteenth Amendment, which I discuss in Chapter 21.

Article V: Changing versus Amending the Constitution

Article V lays down the rather complicated procedure required for amending the Constitution — or, to be precise, four alternative routes that can be adopted for this purpose. With one exception — the Twenty-First Amendment, repealing Prohibition — the procedure adopted for every amendment has been the same, namely:

- ✔ Proposal by a two-thirds majority in both houses of Congress; and
- ✔ Ratification by three-fourths of the state legislatures.

The Framers deliberately (and cleverly) made the procedure for amending the Constitution as complicated and elaborate as possible — because they didn't want their handiwork undone by the shifting breezes of political fashion. On the face of it, the Framers appear to have achieved their objective: Since the ratification of the Bill of Rights (the first ten amendments) all at once in 1791, only 17 amendments have been made to the Constitution — in the space of more than two centuries.

Does this remarkable fact mean that, with the exception of these 17 amendments, the Constitution today is the same as it was in 1791? No, not at all. It means only that the wording of the Constitution hasn't been changed by formal amendment. There have been plenty of changes, accomplished by judicial interpretation. The power of the Supreme Court is such that it is able to "amend" the Constitution — sometimes quite radically — by interpreting a word or phrase. I discuss this topic in Chapter 5.

Article VI: Fudging Federalism

The most important part of Article VI is the Supremacy Clause, which reads as follows:

> *This Constitution, and the Laws of the United States which shall be made in Pursuance thereof; and all Treaties made, or which shall be made, under the Authority of the United States, shall be the supreme Law of the Land; and the judges in every State shall be bound thereby, any Thing in the Constitution or Laws of any State to the Contrary notwithstanding.*

This clause purportedly has the following effects:

- It sets federal law above state law.
- It makes the U.S. Constitution the highest law in the nation.
- It places international treaties above state law, and even above federal power.

I explore these effects, and the questions they raise, in Chapter 7.

Article VII: Ratifying the Constitution

A nice, easy one at last! Article VII of the Constitution, the last part of the original, unamended Constitution, sets out the requirement for ratifying the Constitution:

> *The Ratification of the Conventions of nine States, shall be sufficient for the Establishment of this Constitution between the States so ratifying the Same.*

In fact, all 13 of the original states ratified the Constitution — although North Carolina and Rhode Island didn't do so until after March 4, 1789, the date appointed "for commencing proceedings under the Constitution."

Article VII is purely of historical interest. It does not apply to the ratification of amendments, which is governed by Article V.

Chapter 5

Amending versus Interpreting the Constitution: Taking Time for Change

*H*ow does the Constitution change? Only with difficulty. The Framers of the Constitution believed that they'd hit the jackpot. They had thought and debated long and hard about the best form of government, and they wanted to make sure that future generations wouldn't mess up their perfect construction by adding or subtracting bits arbitrarily. Benjamin Franklin, one of the Framers, described the Constitution as creating a system of government that was "near to perfection." So the Framers deliberately made the Constitution very hard to change — not impossible, just very complicated.

I'm talking here about *amendments*: official, formal changes to the Constitution. But there is another, less formal kind of change — through decisions of the U.S. Supreme Court *interpreting* the Constitution. You won't find that type of change even mentioned in the Constitution because the Framers never imagined change could come about in that way. It simply wasn't supposed to happen.

Some of the most important changes to the Constitution have been made as a result of Supreme Court decisions. These include:

- Banning racial segregation
- Expanding the rights of people charged with crimes
- Declaring a right to privacy
- Establishing a (limited) right to abortion

I come back to judge-made changes later in the chapter. But first I discuss the type of change allowed by the Constitution: *amendment.*

Noting the Four Paths to an Amendment

Article V of the Constitution provides for no fewer than four different ways of amending the Constitution. Ready for some fancy footwork?

- Congress proposes an amendment — passed by a two-thirds majority of both houses. This amendment is then *ratified* (confirmed) by the legislatures of three-fourths of all the states.
- Congress proposes an amendment — passed by a two-thirds majority of both houses. This amendment is then ratified by special conventions in three-fourths of the states.
- Two-thirds of the state legislatures ask Congress to call a national convention. This convention proposes an amendment, which is then ratified by the legislatures of three-fourths of the states.
- Two-thirds of the state legislatures ask Congress to call a national convention. This convention proposes an amendment, which is then ratified by special conventions in three-fourths of the states.

Whew! A lot of this technical detail is of academic interest only. The first of the four ways of amending the Constitution has by far the greatest practical significance. This method has been used for 26 of the 27 amendments ratified so far. The second method was used once — for the Twenty-First Amendment, which repealed the Eighteenth Amendment (Prohibition). And the third and fourth routes for amendment provided by the Constitution have never been used.

The President is not involved in the amendment process at all. He can neither propose an amendment nor veto it. This is surprising, to say the least, because Article I, Section 7 of the Constitution gives the President the right to approve or disapprove "Every Order, Resolution, or Vote" needing the agreement of the House and the Senate. Doesn't this cover amendments as well? On the basis of Article I, Section 7, it sure looks like it. But Article V, the article that deals with amending the Constitution, doesn't mention the President at all.

No President has ever tried to muscle in on the amendment process. But the question of his involvement was raised before the U.S. Supreme Court early on in *Hollingsworth v. Virginia*, decided in 1798. Hollingsworth claimed that the Eleventh Amendment was invalid because it had not been presented to the President in accordance with Article I, Section 7 of the Constitution. The court rejected the claim and accepted the literal wording of Article V, meaning that the President had no say in regard to amendments, and this is still the position today. Presidents have occasionally signed proposed amendments nevertheless, in order to give them extra support. In 1861 President James Buchanan signed a pro-slavery proposed amendment for this reason, and in 1865 Abraham Lincoln followed his example by signing the Thirteenth Amendment abolishing slavery.

Explaining What Happens in Practice

As is so often the case, the words of the Constitution raise more questions than they answer. Let me tackle a few of these questions:

- ✔ **Two-thirds of both houses of Congress can propose an amendment. Does this mean two-thirds of all members?** No. Only two-thirds of those present and voting at the time — provided there is a *quorum* (more than half of the members) present in each house.

- ✔ **What exactly is meant by a *convention*?** A convention is a meeting of delegates, and Article V provides for two different kinds of conventions: a national convention for proposing amendments, and state conventions for ratifying amendments.

- ✔ **Who gets to be chosen as a member of a national convention?** The only national constitutional convention in U.S. history was the initial Philadelphia Convention that drafted the U.S. Constitution in 1787. The 55 delegates were not elected, but selected by the state legislatures. More than 500 requests for a national convention have recently been made by states, but Congress has remained resistant to all such requests. The method of choosing delegates to any future convention is undecided.

- ✔ **What powers would a national convention have?** A national convention would be permitted to propose amendments but not to ratify them. Why? Because Article V of the Constitution leaves the "Mode of Ratification" up to Congress. But a national convention would in practice have unlimited power to propose amendments or even a radical rewriting of the Constitution — which is probably why Congress is reluctant to agree to another national convention.

- ✔ **Who gets to be chosen as a member of a state convention?** The only time state conventions were ever called was in 1933, in order to ratify the Twenty-First Amendment. Different states had different arrangements. But a common method was for the voters in the state concerned to elect delegates from a list chosen by the state governor in consultation with other state officials.

   ✔ **What powers does a state convention have?** State conventions can ratify proposed amendments but can't themselves propose any amendments. The Twenty-First Amendment is the only one that has been ratified by this method.

In the 200-plus years that the Constitution has been in force, no fewer than 5,000 — that's right, 5,*000* — amendments have been introduced in Congress. Of these, only 33 have gotten over the two-thirds hurdle to be formally proposed, and of these just 27 have made it through the ratification process to become part of the Constitution. This figure of 27 includes the first ten amendments, which were all ratified together on December 15, 1791, and are collectively known as the *Bill of Rights*. This leaves the amazingly small total of 17 amendments in the whole period from 1791 to the present day.

Listing the Amendments

Here is a rundown of all 27 amendments that have made it into the U.S. Constitution:

   ✔ First Amendment: Freedom of speech, religion, and assembly

   ✔ Second Amendment: Right to bear arms

   ✔ Third Amendment: Ban on quartering of soldiers

   ✔ Fourth Amendment: Unreasonable search and seizure

   ✔ Fifth Amendment: Grand juries, double jeopardy, self-incrimination, due process, and the taking of private property for public use

   ✔ Sixth Amendment: Jury trial and other rights of defendants in criminal trials

   ✔ Seventh Amendment: Trial by jury in civil suits

   ✔ Eighth Amendment: Cruel and unusual punishments

   ✔ Ninth Amendment: Rights retained by the people

   ✔ Tenth Amendment: Powers reserved to the states or to the people

   ✔ Eleventh Amendment: Ban on lawsuits brought by citizens of one state against another state

   ✔ Twelfth Amendment: Electing the President and Vice President

   ✔ Thirteenth Amendment: Abolishing slavery

   ✔ Fourteenth Amendment: Rights of citizenship, obligations of the states, due process

   ✔ Fifteenth Amendment: Ban on racial discrimination in voting

   ✔ Sixteenth Amendment: Income tax

- Seventeenth Amendment: Direct election of senators

- Eighteenth Amendment: Prohibition

- Nineteenth Amendment: Women's right to vote

- Twentieth Amendment: Fixing new term dates for the President and Congress

- Twenty-First Amendment: Repealing Prohibition

- Twenty-Second Amendment: Presidential term limits

- Twenty-Third Amendment: Voting rights for Washington D.C.

- Twenty-Fourth Amendment: Banning poll tax as a bar to voting rights

- Twenty-Fifth Amendment: Death, removal, resignation, or incapacity of the President

- Twenty-Sixth Amendment: Voting age reduced to 18

- Twenty-Seventh Amendment: No pay increases for Congress until after the general election

I give each amendment its due in Parts IV and V of this book.

Rating the Ratification of the Fourteenth Amendment

The Fourteenth Amendment is one of the most important parts of the U.S. Constitution. But was the Fourteenth Amendment properly ratified? This is an important question. If the amendment was not properly ratified, then it's not part of the Constitution.

The problem is that the Fourteenth Amendment was the product of the Civil War, which ended in 1865. Congress proposed the Fourteenth Amendment in June 1866, and the amendment was ratified in July 1868.

The main objections to the constitutionality of the Fourteenth Amendment are twofold:

- **The Congress that proposed the Fourteenth Amendment was an unconstitutional body because 80 representatives and 28 senators from the 11 former Confederate states were excluded from it.** It is true that the two-thirds majority of both houses of Congress required to propose the Fourteenth Amendment was obtained in this way. Eight state legislatures objected to this procedure at the time on the ground that Article V of the Constitution guarantees all states "equal Suffrage in the Senate."

✔ **The Fourteenth Amendment was not ratified by three-fourths of the states.** This objection is even stronger than the previous one. The United States was made up of 37 states in 1868. Ratification therefore required the approval of 28 states. However, no fewer than 15 states specifically rejected the Fourteenth Amendment in 1866 and 1867, including 4 states that had remained in the Union during the Civil War.

This rejection of the amendment by well over one-fourth of the states should have meant that the amendment was dead in the water. However, Congress then passed — over the veto of President Andrew Johnson — the Reconstruction Acts, which placed 10 of the 11 former Confederate states under military rule and made their readmission to the Union conditional on their ratifying the Fourteenth Amendment. Ratification by five of these states — three of which had previously rejected the amendment — was necessary for the Fourteenth Amendment to become part of the Constitution.

In short, the Fourteenth Amendment became part of the Constitution only by coercion. Does this important fact invalidate the amendment? It probably should have that effect, but the moral of the story is that, in practice, war and politics trump strict law.

Reviving a Forgotten Amendment

The Twenty-Seventh Amendment, the most recent addition to the Constitution, took more than 200 years to be ratified. It was passed by a two-thirds majority in Congress in 1789, together with 11 other proposed amendments — ten of which went on to become the Bill of Rights.

This particular proposed amendment prohibited members of Congress from voting themselves a pay raise without the approval of the electorate. By 1791 this proposal had been ratified by 6 of the 11 state legislatures that were needed. Then, after a few flurries, it just languished and was completely forgotten until 1982.

Its resuscitation came from an unlikely source. In 1982, Gregory Watson, a Texas college student, recognized that if Congress did not set a deadline for the ratification of a particular amendment, there was no time limit. No deadline had been set for this particular proposal.

Watson embarked on a frantic letter-writing campaign, which resulted in the ratification of the proposal by 38 states (the requisite three-fourths of the 50 states) and its formal certification as the Twenty-Seventh Amendment to the Constitution in 1992. But, as is so often the case, its effect has been blunted or even nullified by judicial interpretation. This happened in 1994, when the U.S. Court of Appeals for the District of Columbia Circuit ruled that the amendment has no effect on annual cost of living adjustments (COLAs), which are really just pay-raises by another name!

Calling Time on an ERA

The fate of the Equal Rights Amendment (ERA) has been less happy than that of the Twenty-Seventh Amendment. The ERA's wording mirrors that of the Fifteenth, Nineteenth, and Twenty-Sixth amendments. The first and main section of the ERA says,

> Equality of rights under the law shall not be denied or abridged by the United States or by any state on account of sex.

The ERA got off to a flying start in 1972 with overwhelming support in Congress, which gave it a seven-year deadline for ratification. At first it looked as though that was not going to be a problem, as 22 states fell over one another to ratify it. But the enthusiasm for it cooled, and Congress extended the time limit to 1982. At that point, the ERA was still 3 states short of the 38 needed for ratification, and in the meantime, 5 states that had ratified the ERA changed their minds. A federal court held that these states had the right to reverse their previous decisions but that Congress had acted unlawfully in extending the deadline! Before this rather strange decision could be appealed to the U.S. Supreme Court, the extended ratification period expired, killing off the ERA. (There have been more recent attempts to revive it in Congress but without the requisite two-thirds majority.)

Reviewing Other Unratified Proposed Amendments

The ERA differs from the other unratified proposed amendments because Congress imposed a deadline for the ratification of the ERA but not for any of the others. Here's a brief rundown of these other proposed amendments:

✔ **The Congressional Apportionment Amendment:** This was the very first amendment ever proposed, in 1789. After being ratified by 11 states through June 1792, this proposal died. The whole question of Congressional representation is now satisfactorily dealt with by ordinary legislation. There is no chance that this proposed amendment will ever be revived.

✔ **Titles of Nobility Amendment (TONA):** Article I, Section 9 of the Constitution doesn't allow any U.S. officeholder to accept any foreign title of nobility without the permission of Congress. TONA goes further and strips of his or her citizenship any U.S. citizen who accepts any foreign title of nobility.

TONA was proposed by Congress in 1810 and was ratified by 12 states at a time when only 13 were needed. It was long thought that TONA had indeed been ratified, and many 19th-century printings of the Constitution show it as the Thirteenth Amendment. It would now need to be ratified by an additional 26 states, making a total of 38 (three-fourths of the present complement of 50 states). If you've been offered a foreign title of nobility, better grab it now before those 26 states ratify it! But don't worry, that's not going to happen any time soon.

✔ **The Corwin Amendment:** This proposed amendment is an historical relic. It prohibits any amendment ever to be made to the Constitution abolishing slavery! Yet it was passed by a two-thirds majority in both houses of Congress in 1861, just weeks before the outbreak of the Civil War. Outgoing President James Buchanan endorsed the proposed amendment. Amazingly, the new President, Abraham Lincoln, also expressed his support for it in his first inaugural address. However, the proposal was soon overtaken by events. It can't stand with the Thirteenth Amendment abolishing slavery, which was ratified in 1865.

✔ **Child Labor Amendment:** This proposal gives Congress the power to regulate and even prohibit the labor of children under 18. Proposed in 1924, it has so far been ratified by 28 states. It needs to be ratified by an additional ten states if it's ever to make it into the Constitution. In 1939, the U.S. Supreme Court held that this amendment was still pending business before the state legislatures because Congress had not placed a deadline on ratification.

Debating the Need for Judge-Made Law

Article V of the Constitution lays down pretty clear procedures for amending the Constitution, providing a choice of four routes. Isn't this enough? The objections to limiting constitutional change to the methods set out in Article V are as follows:

✔ The Article V procedures are cumbersome and slow.

✔ As a result, we are stuck with a constitution that is largely the product of a bygone age.

✔ This situation makes it difficult for the Constitution to respond to changes in society and politics.

✔ The old-fashioned language of the Constitution has to be interpreted and made relevant to modern society.

✔ The U.S. Supreme Court is very well-suited to making the Constitution relevant to modern society.

On the other side are people who argue that we should stick to the proper Article V procedure for amending the Constitution. They believe that it's just plain wrong for judges to rewrite the Constitution. Here are some of the reasons supporting this view:

✔ The Article V procedures ensure that changes to the Constitution are made only after due consideration and with wide support.

✔ The principles enunciated in the Constitution are timeless.

✔ The Constitution should not become the plaything of changing fashions.

✔ The language of the Constitution does have to be interpreted, but that is not the same thing as changing its meaning.

✔ If judges rewrite the Constitution according to their own predilections, this can only lead to disagreement over what the Constitution means.

✔ The U.S. Supreme Court — made up of unelected judges — is not entitled to change the Constitution.

✔ It's simply undemocratic, or even anti-democratic, for judges to rewrite the Constitution according to their own likes and dislikes.

Which of these two points of view is right? You're welcome to make up your own mind, but my own view is that it's wrong for judges to try to amend the Constitution. To help you make up your mind on this question, let's take a look at a key example of a judge-made constitutional amendment: the right to privacy.

Reading a Right to Privacy into the Constitution

The word *privacy* doesn't appear anywhere in the Constitution, yet there is now supposedly a constitutional right to privacy. How could this change have come about?

Using a sledgehammer to crack a nut: Griswold v. Connecticut

The right to privacy stems from the Supreme Court decision in *Griswold v. Connecticut,* decided in 1965. An old Connecticut law prohibited the use of contraceptives. Was this law unconstitutional? That was the question facing the U.S. Supreme Court.

By a majority of seven to two, the court found that the Connecticut statute was indeed unconstitutional. But on what basis? The Bill of Rights contains no specific right of privacy, so the majority on the court relied on a less direct approach. They located the right to privacy in some pretty vague phrases:

- ✔ "Penumbras" (shadowy surrounds) of specific guarantees in the Bill of Rights "formed by emanations from those guarantees"

- ✔ The (vague) Due Process Clause of the Fourteenth Amendment (which I discuss in Chapters 17 and 21)

- ✔ The (extremely vague) Ninth Amendment (which I discuss in Chapter 19)

Now let's take a look at the dissenting opinions in *Griswold.*

Disliking a law versus declaring it unconstitutional

It's important to remember that the question before the justices was *not* whether they agreed or disagreed with the Connecticut birth-control law, but only whether the law was constitutional or not.

Justice Potter Stewart, in his dissent, held that the Connecticut law was *not* unconstitutional. But Stewart made no secret of his disdain for the state law. He described it as "an uncommonly silly law" and "obviously unenforceable." Was Stewart contradicting himself, then? Not at all. He recognized the fundamental difference between not liking a law and declaring it unconstitutional.

Stewart examined all the claims made by the majority on the court. He concluded, "I can find no such general right of privacy in the Bill of Rights, in any other part of the Constitution, or in any case ever before decided by this Court." Pretty powerful stuff, eh?

So, should Connecticut be stuck with this "uncommonly silly law," then? No. Stewart pointed to the correct, democratic solution: If the people of Connecticut didn't agree with the birth-control law, they should persuade their state legislature to repeal it. As Stewart put it, "That is the constitutional way to take this law off the books."

Was it really necessary to find a right of privacy lurking between the lines of the Constitution in order to knock a ridiculous old state law on the head? No — and especially not if it meant allowing judges to usurp the democratic right to amend the Constitution.

Embarking on the road to Roe v. Wade

When the Supreme Court makes a decision adopting a certain position, that decision becomes a precedent that is then followed in later decisions. And precedents are not just followed — they are often expanded. That is what happened with *Griswold:* It became the basis of a constitutional right of privacy, which was then expanded to include a constitutional right to have an abortion. Quite a stretch. Hold on to your hat!

The Supreme Court decided *Roe v. Wade* in 1973. The question before the court was whether Texas antiabortion laws were constitutional. The Supreme Court declared the Texas laws unconstitutional. But in so doing, the court also struck down many other state and federal antiabortion laws.

Justifying abortion rights

What is the justification for such a major judge-made change to the Constitution? The Supreme Court split seven to two in favor of abortion rights. Justice Harry Blackmun wrote for the majority. Here are the main legal points in his opinion:

- ✔ "The Constitution does not explicitly mention any right of privacy."

- ✔ However, "the Court has recognized that a right of personal privacy . . . does exist under the Constitution." (Justice Blackmun here listed a number of Supreme Court decisions, including *Griswold* and some search and seizure cases.)

- ✔ This right of personal privacy is based largely on the Due Process Clause of the Fourteenth Amendment.

- ✔ This right of personal privacy includes a pregnant woman's right to terminate her pregnancy — an absolute right up to the end of the first trimester (weeks 1 to 12). After that time, the right to an abortion continues when it's necessary to protect a woman's health.

Denying abortion rights

Obviously, not everyone agrees with the majority opinion in *Roe V. Wade*. Here are some of the arguments against it:

- Having read a right of privacy into the Constitution in *Griswold,* the U.S. Supreme Court took a huge leap beyond it in *Roe v. Wade*.

- If there is a constitutional right of privacy, this right no doubt gives everyone the right over his or her own body. So, nobody has the right to cut off your hand or to take your kidney and give it to someone else.

  But is a fetus just another part of the pregnant woman's body? Or is it a separate life with its own rights? This is a highly charged moral, religious, and political question.

- Even if a fetus is not considered as having any rights — at least in the first trimester — why should the right to terminate it belong solely to the mother? Does the father have no rights?

- For the Supreme Court to decide this important issue according to the personal beliefs of the majority on the court was, in the words of Justice Byron White (dissenting), "an exercise of raw judicial power." White added, "I find nothing in the language or history of the Constitution to support the Court's judgment."

Even Justice Ruth Bader Ginsburg, a strong pro-choice advocate, has criticized *Roe v. Wade* as "heavy-handed judicial intervention" in an issue that should rather have been left to the democratic political process.

On the other hand, Justice Harry Blackmun, who wrote for the majority in *Roe v. Wade,* firmly believed in abortion rights as fundamental to the equality of women.

Part II

We the People: How the United States Is Governed

AFTER SEVERAL TANKARDS, DELEGATES TO THE CONSTITUTIONAL CONVENTION DISCUSS THE SEPARATION of POWERS

Okay, the judiciary shall have the power of flight but not invincibility, which shall belong to the executive branch, and the legislative shall have the power to read minds and shape shift during a full moon.

In this part . . .

This part provides an analysis of some of the biggest constitutional topics: sovereignty (who really rules the United States?); federalism (the power-sharing arrangement between the national government and the states); the separation of powers between Congress, the President, and the courts; and the Commerce Clause (probably the most important power wielded by Congress). No need to be terrified of these big beasts anymore!

Chapter 6

Scrutinizing Sovereignty: Who Rules America?

In This Chapter

▶ Figuring out who "We the People" were and are

▶ Measuring the power of the President, Congress, and the Supreme Court

▶ Recognizing states' influence

▶ Testing some conspiracy theories

"**W**e the People" rule the U.S. of A. Right? Ummm, well, maybe not. The President and a few other big hitters are involved too. Here are the main contenders for the title of ruler of the United States:

- ✔ We the People
- ✔ The President
- ✔ The Congress
- ✔ The U.S. Supreme Court
- ✔ The Council on Foreign Affairs, the Trilateral Commission, and the Bilderberg Conference

I examine the claims of each of these contenders in turn. My conclusion is that sovereignty isn't held by any one single person or institution — sovereignty is shared among the first four institutions that I have just listed. But that doesn't mean that all four institutions have an equal share. They do not, but the degree of dominance that any one institution enjoys at any one time varies in accordance with circumstances and with the personalities concerned.

Introducing "We the People"

The phrase "We the People" entered history when it appeared in the Preamble (or introduction) to the U.S. Constitution (see Chapter 4). The Preamble is a fanfare proclaiming the nature and purpose of the Constitution. It doesn't form part of the Constitution as a legally enforceable instrument. But courts sometimes cite the Preamble as evidence of the Framers' intentions in drafting the Constitution as a whole.

Does the use of the phrase "We the People" mean that the Framers claimed to be establishing a democracy? Not at all. Ancient constitutions and legal systems claimed to have been handed down by a god, a king, or some semi-divine lawgiver. The Framers tacitly rejected these models and claimed a popular basis for the U.S. Constitution — but that is not the same as claiming that the system of government established by that constitution was a democracy. Indeed, neither the word *democracy* nor the word *democratic* figures anywhere in the text of the Constitution (see Chapter 1).

Ordaining and establishing a Constitution

The Preamble claims that "We the People . . . do ordain and establish this Constitution for the United States of America." Is this claim true? The Constitution was drafted by the Philadelphia Convention made up of 55 delegates from 12 of the 13 states. (Rhode Island refused to participate.) The 55 delegates included most of the Founding Fathers of the nation, with the notable exceptions of John Adams and Thomas Jefferson, who were both serving in Europe at the time. Jefferson described the Convention as "an assembly of demigods" but regretted their decision to conduct their deliberations behind closed doors.

Who picked these demigods? *Not* "We the People." They were selected by the state legislatures, which in turn were elected. But only about 15 percent of the adult white male population had the right to vote. So "We the People" rings a bit hollow as far as the drafting of the Constitution is concerned.

But "We the People" at least ratified (confirmed) the Constitution, right? Not exactly. Ratification was entrusted to a specially elected convention in each of the 13 states (except Rhode Island). So "We the People" had only an indirect say on ratification.

The Constitution did not aim to establish a democracy. Instead, the Framers were aiming to establish "a *Republican* Form of Government" — which was not the same thing at all. See Chapter 2 for a full explanation.

Making democracy fashionable

The acceptability of democracy as a political ideal can be gauged from the use of the word *democratic* as a party political label.

Historians often refer to the political party founded in 1791 by Thomas Jefferson and James Madison as the Democratic-Republican Party, but in fact both Jefferson and Madison referred to themselves simply as Republicans and to their party as the Republican Party down to 1823. (That party had nothing to do with the modern Republican Party, by the way.)

Adherents of the party of Jefferson and Madison were sometimes called *democrats* — not by themselves but as an insult by their opponents, who equated *democrats* with *Jacobins,* the most extreme French revolutionaries. Ex-President George Washington himself said of a "professed Democrat" that "he will leave nothing unattempted to overturn the Government of this Country."

At the party's first national convention, held in 1832, it was still calling itself the Republican Party. It officially changed its name to the Democratic Party only in 1844. By this time *democratic* had become a positive political label — thanks largely to Andrew Jackson, who was instrumental in extending voting rights to all adult white males.

Resolving to preserve democracy

The first six presidents were all members of a wealthy elite. The election of Andrew Jackson to the presidency in 1828 broke with that aristocratic tradition.

Andrew Jackson's form of democracy

Jackson was an unabashed populist. The first plank in the program of *Jacksonian democracy* was the extension of voting rights to all white men, sweeping away property qualifications. Jackson also repeatedly called for a constitutional amendment to abolish the Electoral College system, which he saw as an undemocratic way of electing the President.

But Jackson was no liberal. His populism extended only to the white population; he was himself a slave owner. And his belief in the *Manifest Destiny* of the United States to expand westward and control the whole of North America from the Atlantic to the Pacific Ocean resulted in a less than sympathetic attitude toward Native Americans.

As a result of Jackson's two-term strong presidency followed by the single term of the skillful Democratic Party organizer, Martin Van Buren, and that of the much underrated James K. Polk, populist democratic ideals became widely accepted in the 1840s.

Abraham Lincoln's vision of democracy

By the time of Abraham Lincoln, who was first elected President in 1860, democracy had become quite respectable. Lincoln concluded his famous Gettysburg address with a solemn pledge that has echoed down the years:

> We here highly resolve that these dead shall not have died in vain — that this nation, under God, shall have a new birth of freedom — and that government of the people, by the people, for the people, shall not perish from the earth.

This is pretty heady stuff. But what exactly does it mean? Lincoln delivered his speech on November 19, 1863, just a few months after the bloody battle of Gettysburg. The occasion was the dedication of the Soldiers' National Cemetery in Gettysburg, Pennsylvania.

Abraham Lincoln doesn't use the word *democracy,* but his three rhythmical phrases — "government of the people, by the people, for the people" — are commonly taken as a definition of democracy.

Was Lincoln holding up democracy as an ideal for the future? Yes, but he also seems to have thought that it already existed. Indeed, the theme of his two-minute address was that the cause of the Union in the Civil War was the cause of democracy.

But did Lincoln really have the right to cast himself as the spokesman for democracy? His own election to the presidency in 1860 was anything but a landslide. Although he won a majority of electoral votes, he carried only 18 states out of 33 and got less than 40 percent of the popular vote. His election to the presidency was the most divisive in American history. When Lincoln was declared the winner of the 1860 presidential election, seven southern states seceded even before his inauguration.

Lincoln's identification with democracy also has another problem, because government "by the people" looks very much like *direct democracy,* which has never existed in the United States.

Defining democracy

The word democracy comes to us from the Greek *demokratia,* meaning the "power of the people."

But can the people ever rule themselves? Well, it did happen in ancient Athens — sort of. The citizens all met together in the *Ekklesia,* or Assembly, and deliberated. But only adult males had the rights of citizenship. Women, slaves, and resident aliens had no civic rights. Athens had about 30,000 citizens at its height — about 10 percent of the population.

Athenian democracy was *direct democracy.* That form of government would be impossible in the United States today with a population of around 300 million! Instead, the type of democracy that exists now is *indirect* or *representative democracy* — in which the people don't run the government themselves but pick other people to do it for them.

So, how does an indirect democracy stand up to Lincoln's three-part test?

- **Government of the people:** This is the easy one. Any government is automatically a government *of* the people. It doesn't have to be a democratic form of government. A monarchy, a dictatorship, an oligarchy — all are governments *of* the people, but they aren't governments *by* the people.

- **Government by the people:** This is the elusive one. Government *by* the people has never existed in the United States — and could never exist. So what was Abe Lincoln thinking of? Or did he just figure that it had a nice ring to it as part of a threesome?

- **Government for the people:** Every government of every kind everywhere in the world always maintains that it governs in the interests of its people — or *for* the people. This is not a specifically democratic feature at all.

In fairness to Abe, he probably figured that the sort of indirect, representative democracy that we have in the United States was actually government *by* the people — a pretty dangerous assumption to make by a guy who got into the White House with just 39.8 percent of the popular vote.

Testing for democracy today

But what about today? Is the United States a true democracy in the 21st century? Yes and no.

Here are some points **in favor of** and *against* classifying the United States as a democracy:

- **Everybody over the age of 18 has the right to vote.** *The voters are usually presented with a choice of one out of only two candidates — if that. The really important election often is not the general election but the Democratic or Republican primary.*

- **Voters can also pick the candidates for the political party of their choice by participating in the primaries.** *But the choice in primaries is usually among a bunch of millionaires because primary candidates have to fund their own ad campaigns.*

✔ **Office-holders are mostly restricted to comparatively short terms, like four years for the President and two years for members of the House of Representatives.** *Presidents are limited to two elected terms, but representatives can be reelected indefinitely — and quite often are!*

✔ **More posts are filled by popular election than in most other countries — often including state judges, mayors, school boards, and (previously) even dogcatchers.** *Most elective positions are at the state level. It's a pity federal judges aren't elected too!*

✔ **Popular or citizens' initiatives or referenda are the closest thing in the United States today to ancient direct democracy. They allow the voters a direct say in no fewer than 24 states plus the District of Columbia.** *But initiatives are just votes on specific issues — a far cry from decision-making on a day-to-day basis. Also, initiatives exist purely at the state level. Moves to allow national initiatives have never gotten very far.*

✔ **The United States has a healthy two-party system that guarantees competition.** *But quite a number of districts — and even whole states — are routinely in the red or blue column.*

✔ **The views represented in U.S. political institutions span a wide range.** *But third parties and independents have little chance of being elected — largely because of the winner-take-all electoral system.*

So, do "We the People" rule the roost? No, because the power of the people is indirect. But We the People must certainly be regarded as having *some* share of sovereignty at least. Let us now turn to the power of the President, which I examine in more detail in Chapter 10.

Hailing the Chief

The President of the United States is commonly said to be the most powerful person in the world, but how much power does he exercise in the United States?

From the beginning, critics of the Constitution were afraid that the President would become too monarchical. For example, Patrick Henry, the radical revolutionary, characterized the Constitution as "squinting towards monarchy." To counter these fears, George Washington discouraged people from addressing him as "Your Excellency," preferring the more republican appellation, "Mr. President."

The Framers were careful to incorporate into the Constitution the principle of the *separation of powers* coupled with a system of *checks and balances*. The purpose of this arrangement was to prevent any one of the three branches of government — Executive, Legislative, and Judicial — from becoming too powerful.

Here are the points **in favor of** and *against* regarding the President as sovereign:

- **The President combines the position of head of state with executive power, so his dominance over the federal government is guaranteed.** *Not so. Periods of strong presidential power have alternated with periods when the President was pretty insignificant compared to Congress and the Supreme Court. Abraham Lincoln was a strong President, but the Presidents who preceded and succeeded him were mostly pretty weak. After the strong presidencies of Theodore Roosevelt and Woodrow Wilson, Congress became dominant again, until the so-called "imperial presidency" of Franklin D. Roosevelt. In 1973, Watergate dealt a severe blow to presidential power, but Ronald Reagan put the presidency on a strong footing again, which benefited Bill Clinton and George W. Bush.*

- **The President has control over foreign affairs and defense, especially in times of war.** *Sure, but the War Powers Act allows Congress to limit presidential war powers. The Senate also has the power to block presidential appointees. And the Supreme Court can clip the President's wings too, as happened with President George W. Bush in regard to Guantanamo Bay.*

- **The President can veto bills that have passed Congress, and a presidential veto can be overridden only by a two-thirds majority in both houses of Congress.** *True, but vetoes can backfire, as President Bill Clinton found out when his deadlock with Congress over the budget twice paralyzed the federal government for months.*

At the time of this writing, the power of the President is great but certainly not unchallenged. I turn now to Congress, which I examine more closely in Chapter 11.

Congress: Flexing Its Lawmaking Muscle

With the exception of the presidencies of Andrew Jackson, James K. Polk, and Abraham Lincoln, the first century of the republic was dominated by Congress — so much so that when in 1884 a young Woodrow Wilson wrote a book about the U.S. constitutional practice, he titled his book *Congressional Government*. He wrote, "The actual form of our present government is simply a scheme of congressional supremacy."

Grover Cleveland, who ended up as both the 22nd and 24th president, broke the pattern of weak presidents who were subservient to Congress. He was succeeded by several other strong presidents: William McKinley, Theodore Roosevelt, and Woodrow Wilson himself. But then came another period of congressional dominance — until FDR's "imperial presidency," which, with a few hiccups along the way, still survives today.

But the conflict between the President and Congress has recently paled in comparison with the conflict between the Supreme Court and Congress. Here are just a few recent examples:

- In 1995, the Supreme Court struck down the Gun-Free School Zones Act of 1990. This was the first time since the New Deal that the court challenged Congress's power under the Commerce Clause of Article I of the Constitution (see Chapter 9).

- In 1997, the Supreme Court struck down part of the Religious Freedom Restoration Act of 1993.

- In 1999, the Supreme Court struck down a federal law allowing citizens to sue a state without that state's consent.

- In 2000, the Supreme Court struck down parts of the Violence Against Women Act of 1994.

- In the 2008 decision *Boumediene v. Bush* concerning the lawfulness of detaining "enemy combatants" at Guantanamo Bay, the Supreme Court struck a blow not only at the President but also declared the Military Commissions Act of 2006 unconstitutional.

What has this judicial challenge done to the power wielded by the legislature? It has undoubtedly weakened Congress to some extent, but not enough to have deprived Congress of a share of sovereignty.

The High Court: Saying What the Law Is

The Supreme Court certainly deserves to be up there with the President and the Congress as a sharer in sovereignty.

This idea would have come as a shock to the Framers. The Constitution establishes the principle of the separation of powers, in which the three branches of government — the Executive, Legislative, and Judicial branches — are all equal, and each acts as a check and balance against the others.

However, one of the leading Framers of the Constitution, Alexander Hamilton, was convinced that, with separation of powers, the judiciary "will always be the least dangerous" to the other two branches of government. He contrasted the powers of the three branches:

> *The Executive not only dispenses the honors, but holds the sword of the community. The legislature not only commands the purse, but prescribes the rules by which the duties and rights of every citizen are to be regulated. The judiciary, on the contrary, has no influence over either the sword or the purse; no direction either of the strength or of the wealth of the society; and*

can take no active resolution whatever. It may truly be said to have neither FORCE nor WILL, but merely judgment; and must ultimately depend upon the aid of the executive arm even for the efficacy of its judgments.

Hamilton drew this conclusion:

It proves incontestably, that the judiciary is beyond comparison the weakest of the three departments of power; that it can never attack with success either of the other two; and that all possible care is requisite to enable it to defend itself against their attacks.

From a present-day vantage point, Hamilton's view of the judiciary as a shrinking violet seems almost laughable. For example, Hamilton speaks of the power to "prescribe the rules by which the duties and rights of every citizen are to be regulated." This is a perfect description of one of the many powers exercised by the Supreme Court — but Hamilton attributes it to Congress!

Hamilton wrote the words that I have just quoted in 1788. Hamilton could not have known how completely the role of the Supreme Court was to be transformed by Chief Justice John Marshall, who held office from 1801 to 1835. In the famous case of *Marbury v. Madison,* decided in 1803, Marshall said,

It is emphatically the province and the duty of the judicial department to say what the law is.

These words are so important and so often quoted that they can now be seen inscribed on the wall of the Supreme Court building behind John Marshall's statue.

But where in the Constitution does it say that the Supreme Court has this huge power? Nowhere. So, where did Marshall get this idea from? It was one of his many *twistifications* — Thomas Jefferson's word to describe the way in which Marshall's mind worked. (And Jefferson ought to have known, as the two men were distant cousins and lifelong foes.)

The word "emphatically" in Marshall's quotation is a dead giveaway. If the courts really had the power that Marshall says they had, there would have been no need to use the word *emphatically* at all. *Emphatically* is a word of argument, of debate. Marshall puts it in to underline the claim that he is making for the court — a claim that goes way beyond anything that the Constitution envisioned.

Jefferson, the third President, recognized the danger of judicial activism. He wrote these words during his presidency in 1804, the year after *Marbury v. Madison:*

But the opinion which gives to the judges the right to decide what laws are constitutional, and what not, not only for themselves in their own sphere of action, but for the legislature and executive also, in their spheres, would make the judiciary a despotic branch.

Charles Evans Hughes, Chief Justice from 1930 to 1941, famously said, "We are under a Constitution, but the Constitution is what the judges say it is." This looks like a cynical recognition of the power of the Supreme Court. But Hughes then went on to say, "and the judiciary is the safeguard of our liberty and our property under the Constitution." So, he recognized the power of the judges but saw it as a power for good.

It's impossible to disagree with Hughes's assessment of the power of the Supreme Court, but not everyone would agree with his characterization of that power as benign.

I deal with the judiciary in Chapter 12. Here I list just a few of the issues in regard to which the Supreme Court has recently reinterpreted the law:

- ✔ The death penalty
- ✔ Gun law
- ✔ The rights of "enemy combatants"
- ✔ Affirmative action
- ✔ Police powers

Giving the States Their Due

Do the states have a share in the sovereignty of the United States? Absolutely. The history of the United States could easily be written in terms of the tensions between state and federal power.

I deal with the power of the states in Chapters 7 and 20. But here are just a few of the landmarks in the interaction between federal and state power:

- ✔ The Articles of Confederation, in force between 1777 and 1789, were the first instrument of government of the United States. They provided for a loose association of 13 sovereign states (which proved unsatisfactory).

- ✔ The Philadelphia Convention of 1787 was called in order to provide the United States with a stronger central government. The Constitution was drafted, as the Preamble says, "in Order to form a more perfect Union" (plus to accomplish a few other objectives).

- ✔ Slavery posed a problem right from the start because some states entered the Union as slave states and others as free states. The problem did not go away. As new territories were taken over and became states, it had to be decided whether slavery was to be allowed in each one or not.

✔ Did states have the right to secede from the Union? This question was never conclusively answered before 1861. Then in 1861 came the Civil War, or the War between the States, in which 11 southern states seceded and formed the Confederate States of America, or the Confederacy.

✔ The victory of the North over the South in 1865 ushered in a period of Reconstruction in which all but one of the secessionist states were placed under military governors.

✔ The victory of the Union also led to the Fourteenth Amendment, which extended to the states many of the obligations of the federal government.

✔ The passing of the Sixteenth Amendment in 1913, which legalized federal income tax, placed citizens more directly under federal power than before.

✔ The Great Depression leading to FDR's "New Deal," followed by World War II, placed more power in the hands of the federal government than ever before.

✔ The so-called *Dixiecrats,* a breakaway movement from the Democratic Party in the South, fought unsuccessfully for more states' rights, especially in the interests of segregation.

✔ The rise of the Civil Rights movement in the 1950s and 1960s and its support by the Democratic Party at the federal level drove many conservative southern Democrats into the arms of the Republican Party.

✔ The U.S. Supreme Court under Chief Justice William Rehnquist broke with long tradition and started supporting states' rights increasingly from 1995 onward in what is sometimes called the *new federalism.* This trend has continued to some extent under Chief Justice John Roberts, who was appointed in 2005.

Uncovering Conspiracies

Conspiracy theories have been around forever. Any organization or group of people that was a bit separate from the rest of society, a bit different, or a bit secretive was likely to find itself targeted as holding the controlling power behind the scenes. The theory behind this kind of thinking is that the Constitution is just a front for the exercise of power by some group or groups. Groups that have been targeted in this way include the Jews, the Catholic Church, and the Freemasons.

Three associated organizations — the Council on Foreign Relations, the Trilateral Commission, and the Bilderberg Conference — have been attacked in recent years as being the secret power-brokers not only over the United States but also internationally. Here's a brief rundown on these three organizations:

- ✔ **The Council on Foreign Relations** is a private, U.S.-based organization established in 1921 and dedicated to a study of foreign policy. Its members include Republicans, Democrats, and independents. It is widely believed to have had considerable influence on U.S. foreign policy, including the normalization of relations with Red China.

- ✔ **The Trilateral Commission** is a private association of about 350 members established in 1973. The idea behind it was to develop closer economic cooperation between North America, Europe, and Japan. Its membership is said to include former Secretary of State Henry Kissinger; former U.S. presidents Jimmy Carter, George H.W. Bush, and Bill Clinton; former Vice President Dick Cheney; and Senator John McCain.

- ✔ **The Bilderberg Group, Club, or Conference** is the strangest of the three associated organizations, as its 130 members meet only once a year. The group was founded in 1954 to counter growing anti-American sentiment in Western Europe by fostering mutual understanding between Europe and the United States. There are generally two invitees from each participating nation: one conservative and one liberal. The membership of this club overlaps to quite a marked extent with that of the Trilateral Commission and to some extent also with that of the Council on Foreign Relations.

The membership of the three organizations includes a lot of influential names. But are they influential because of their membership, or are they members because they were already influential? The latter seems to be the case.

The three organizations have been accused of aiming to establish a single world government or "New World Order," in which the United States would lose its separate identity and become absorbed into an international state ruled by a small elite. But if that is the plan, it doesn't appear to have made much headway so far.

Chapter 7

Federalism: Forming One out of Many

- -

In This Chapter

▶ Tracing the history of U.S. federalism

▶ Evaluating John Marshall's contribution to federal power

▶ Placing the "new federalism" under the microscope

▶ Asking the big questions about states' rights

- -

The United States has a federal system of government, right? Right. Any time anybody doesn't like what the federal government is doing, he blames "the feds." And when you come across a government acronym starting with the letter "F", chances are it stands for *Federal* (think FBI, FCC, FDIC . . .).

The United States has a federal system of government, but the word *federal* doesn't figure anywhere in the text of the Constitution. This fact raises some pretty important questions, which I tackle in this chapter:

✔ What is federalism?

✔ How do we know that the United States has a federal system of government?

✔ Has U.S. federalism changed over time and, if so, how?

Tracing the Origins of U.S. Federalism

A federal system of government is one in which power is shared between the *federal* government — the central or national government — and the state, provincial, or regional governments. The United States is the oldest federal nation in the world, but it sure isn't the only one. Just a few of the other countries that also have federal systems of government are Argentina, Australia, Austria, Brazil, Canada, Germany, India, Mexico, and Nigeria.

Analyzing the founding documents

The United States began life as 13 separate British colonies, which united in opposition to their treatment by the British government of the day — particularly against the imposition of taxes by the British Parliament, on which the American colonies were not represented. This opposition was expressed in the slogan "No taxation without representation."

The Declaration of Independence

The Declaration of Independence of July 4, 1776, was headed "The unanimous Declaration of the thirteen united States of America." We are now used to using the term "The United States of America" as referring to one single country. But that phrase didn't have the same meaning back in 1776 — as can be seen from a close reading of the text of the Declaration. The concluding part of the Declaration is particularly revealing. It declares

> *That these United Colonies are, and of Right ought to be Free and Independent States; . . . and that as Free and Independent States, they have full Power to levy War, conclude Peace, contract Alliances, establish Commerce, and to do all other Acts and Things which Independent States may of right do.*

The Declaration of Independence is commonly taken to mark the beginning of the existence of the United States of America as a nation. The Declaration certainly severed all ties with Britain, but it did not create a single new country. Instead, it created 13 separate new countries. Notice that the language of the Declaration is all in the plural. The key to its meaning lies in the last sentence that I have quoted. Each of the states, says the Declaration, has the power to make war and peace! And the end of the quoted passage contains an assertion that the 13 colonies are "Independent States."

The Articles of Confederation

The Articles of Confederation, passed by Congress in 1777 and formally ratified in 1781, served as the constitution of the United States from 1777 until 1788.

A *confederation* is a weaker form of association between states than a *federation*. The best-known confederation today is Switzerland, which has a very weak — almost nonexistent — central government. Power resides with the governments of the 26 cantons that together form the Swiss Confederation.

The American Articles of Confederation recognized the sovereignty of each of the 13 states. Article II of this document made the position quite clear:

> *Each state retains its sovereignty, freedom, and independence, and every power, jurisdiction, and right, which is not by this Confederation expressly delegated to the United States, in Congress assembled.*

The Congress was the only central institution established by the Articles of Confederation. The Congress was not an elected body but was made up of delegates appointed by each of the state legislatures for a year at a time. Congress had power only over foreign affairs and defense. The Articles of Confederation did not establish any form of central executive or any national courts. The Articles established not a single country but merely "a firm league of friendship" among the 13 sovereign states.

Forming "a more perfect Union"

The form of government set up under the Articles of Confederation was hopelessly weak, and conflicts among the states arose. George Washington and some other leading figures recognized the need for a new constitution "to form a more perfect Union." So a "Grand Convention" was called to meet in Philadelphia in May 1787. Its original purpose was to revise and amend the Articles of Confederation, but the Convention ended up drafting a whole new instrument of government: the U.S. Constitution.

The first printed draft of the Constitution, dated August 6, 1787, is significantly different from the final version approved by the Convention only a few weeks later, on September 17, 1787. Instead of the now-familiar "We the People of the United States" in the Preamble, the earlier draft had a list of all the states:

> *We the People of the States of New-Hampshire, Massachusetts, Rhode-Island and Providence Plantations, Connecticut, New-York, New-Jersey, Pennsylvania, Delaware, Maryland, Virginia, North-Carolina, South-Carolina, and Georgia, do ordain, declare and establish the following Constitution for the Government of Ourselves and our Posterity.*

The change from this formulation to "We the People of the United States" signals a last-minute shift in emphasis from the states to the national government.

However, both versions of the Constitution assert the supremacy of the U.S. Constitution and federal law over the state constitutions and laws. In the final version of the Constitution, this fundamental principle is found in the so-called "Supremacy Clause" in Article VI:

> *This Constitution, and the Laws of the United States which shall be made in Pursuance thereof; and all Treaties made, or which shall be made, under the Authority of the United States, shall be the supreme Law of the Land; and the judges in every State shall be bound thereby, any Thing in the Constitution or Laws of any State to the Contrary notwithstanding.*

Does the Supremacy Clause mean that the federal government can simply ride roughshod over the states and do whatever it likes? No. The Supremacy Clause gives supremacy to the federal (or union) government subject to the limits imposed upon it by the Constitution. The Tenth Amendment makes the position clear:

> *The powers not delegated to the United States by the Constitution, nor prohibited by it to the States, are reserved to the States respectively, or to the people.*

This amendment, ratified in 1791 together with the other nine amendments that form the Bill of Rights, sets out the true historical perspective of the way the Constitution came into existence:

- ✔ Power originated with the people of each individual state.

- ✔ In each state, the people delegated some of their power to their state government.

- ✔ In the U.S. Constitution, the states then delegated some of these powers to the federal government — for example, the power to make war and peace with foreign countries.

Banking on McCulloch v. Maryland

McCulloch v. Maryland, decided in 1819, was one of the earliest Supreme Court cases — and by far the most important — to deal with the relationship between the federal and state governments. Chief Justice John Marshall wrote the unanimous opinion of the court. The two main questions before the court were these:

- ✔ "Has Congress power to incorporate a bank?" (in the words of Chief Justice Marshall).
- ✔ If so, do the states have the right to tax such a bank?

In 1816, Congress incorporated the second Bank of the United States by granting it a charter. The federal government owned only 20 percent of the bank stock, so the bank was essentially a privately owned corporation. But there was a lot of opposition to the whole idea of a bank that could open branches in any state without a charter from that state.

The state of Maryland imposed a tax on all banknotes issued by the Bank of the United States. This tax was apparently intended as a punitive measure against the federal government.

Testing the limits of federal power

"Has Congress power to incorporate a bank?" asked Chief Justice Marshall. This was not an easy question for Marshall, a dyed-in-the-wool Federalist who believed in upholding federal power at the expense of the states.

Marshall desperately wanted to find in favor of the federal government, but he was forced to recognize that federal power was limited under the Constitution. Referring to the Supremacy Clause in Article VI, Marshall said:

> *If any one proposition could command the universal assent of mankind, we might expect it would be this — that the government of the Union, though limited in its power, is supreme within its sphere of action.*

"Supreme within its sphere of action"? Okay. But this formulation begs the question: "What *is* its sphere of action?" Maryland struck a potentially killer blow by invoking the last clause of Article I, Section 8, which provided that

> *The Congress shall have Power . . . To make all Laws which shall be necessary and proper for carrying into Execution the foregoing Powers, and all other Powers vested by this Constitution in the Government of the United States, or in any Department or Officer thereof.*

Maryland argued that the phrase "necessary and proper" places a severe restriction on the legislative power of Congress, because it must mean that Congress can pass only those laws that are "necessary and proper" for implementing the powers listed in Article I, Section 8.

But Marshall didn't accept this apparently unanswerable point. He was in a characteristically combative mood, and he constructed an argument in support of the federal government.

Expanding the definition of "necessary"

Marshall redefined the word "necessary" to suit his purpose. This is one of Marshall's most unpersuasive "twistifications" (Thomas Jefferson's phrase). Marshall first correctly distinguished *necessary* from *absolutely necessary*. But he then proceeded to equate *necessary* with "convenient, or useful, or essential." The first two of these, from a purely linguistic or semantic point of view (whether in 1819 or today), are just plain wrong.

But this twistification enabled him to conclude that "To employ the means necessary to an end is generally understood as employing any means calculated to produce the end, and not as being confined to those single means without which the end would be entirely unattainable."

Marshall was now practically home and dry. Having destroyed the force of the "necessary and proper" clause, he was able to greatly widen the powers of the federal government and, in so doing, to curb those of the states.

Skirting the question of Congress's scope of power

Marshall had now established to his own satisfaction that "There is nothing in the Constitution of the United States . . . which exclude[s] incidental or implied powers."

Sidestepping the "necessary and proper" clause enabled Marshall to propound another grandiose principle: "If the end be legitimate, and within the scope of the Constitution, all the means which are appropriate, which are plainly adapted to that end, and which are not prohibited, may constitutionally be employed to carry it into effect."

Realizing the repercussions

Why is *McCulloch v. Maryland* considered a landmark case? Because it established some fundamental constitutional principles. The fact that some of these principles are based on very dubious twistifications has not affected the continued acceptance of the principles themselves.

Following are the principles established in *McCulloch v. Maryland.* Not all the principles that Marshall put forward in that case are wrong. The principles that I consider to be true constitutional principles are printed in **bold**; those principles that are more likely to be true than not are printed in plain text; and the principles based on twistifications are shown in *italic.* So, here goes:

- ✔ **Federal law is superior to state law.**

- ✔ The U.S. Constitution is the highest form of law.

- ✔ **The federal government possesses only those powers that are delegated to it by the U.S. Constitution.**

- ✔ *But these powers must be broadly interpreted.*

- ✔ *In particular, the "necessary and proper" clause in Article I, Section 8 of the Constitution must be read not as limiting congressional power but as expanding it.*

Navigating the Commerce Clause with John Marshall

After Marshall effectively knocked the "necessary and proper" clause on the head in the case of *McCulloch v. Maryland,* the conflict between federal and state power shifted to the interpretation of the Commerce Clause, which remains to this day a potential battleground between the feds and the states.

The Commerce Clause appears in the long list of powers granted to Congress in Article I, Section 8. The clause grants Congress the power

> *To regulate Commerce with foreign Nations, and among the several States, and with the Indian Tribes.*

The case of *Gibbons v. Ogden,* decided by the U.S. Supreme Court in 1824, was a lot easier for Chief Justice Marshall to handle than the rather tricky case of *McCulloch v. Maryland.*

Both Aaron Ogden and Thomas Gibbons had a supposedly exclusive license to operate a ferry service between New York and New Jersey. Ogden's license was issued by the State of New York, while Gibbons was licensed by Congress. The question before the U.S. Supreme Court was this: Did the grant of navigation licenses fall within the Commerce Clause? If it involved the regulation of interstate commerce, then it did fall within the Commerce Clause. If this was indeed the case, then navigation was a matter for Congress and not for the states.

Marshall had no trouble finding that navigation was a branch of commerce and that the ferry service in question was a matter of interstate commerce, the regulation of which was reserved by the Constitution to Congress. This clear decision set the tone for subsequent Commerce Clause disputes between the feds and the states for a long time to come. See the next section of this chapter and also Chapter 9 for later twists and turns in this saga.

Riding the Federalism Rollercoaster

The United States has had a rollercoaster ride along the federalism highway — including a serious detour in the shape of the Civil War. Here are just a few of the major milestones viewed from a constitutional standpoint:

- 1819: *McCulloch v. Maryland,* discussed earlier in this chapter.
- 1824: *Gibbons v. Ogden,* discussed in the previous section.

✔ 1851: *Cooley v. Board of Wardens.* John Marshall was succeeded in 1835 as Chief Justice by Roger Taney, a Jacksonian Democrat who was much more favorable to states' rights than Marshall. The *Cooley* case was remarkably similar to *Gibbons v. Ogden,* but an opposite conclusion was reached. A Pennsylvania law required all ships entering or leaving a Philadelphia harbor to hire a local pilot. The question before the Supreme Court was whether this law violated the Commerce Clause of the Constitution. The court said no — a result that could never have been reached on the Marshall court!

✔ 1861–1865: The Civil War. I discuss this crucial time later in this chapter.

✔ 1869: *Texas v. White.* In this case, decided during the so-called Reconstruction period that followed the Civil War, the Supreme Court ruled that states were not allowed by the Constitution to secede from the Union, and that any legislation passed by a secessionist state was "absolutely null."

✔ 1877: *Pensacola Telegraph Co. v. Western Union Telegraph Co.* The Civil War and Reconstruction — when the South was occupied by Union troops — strengthened the hand of the federal government against the states. The growing industrialization of the country intensified this development still further. The *Pensacola* case provides a good example of this fact. The court ruled that Congress's power under the Commerce Clause to regulate interstate commerce included the right to establish telegraph lines, and that states could not interfere with this federal power.

✔ 1886: *Wabash, St. Louis & Pacific Railroad Company v. Illinois.* Illinois passed a law regulating interstate transportation contracts. The U.S. Supreme Court ruled that this law violated the Commerce Clause. This decision marked a major departure from the *Cooley* case. *Wabash* led to the creation in 1887 of the Interstate Commerce Commission (ICC), which survived until 1995, when its functions were transferred to the Surface Transportation Board. The ICC was the first of the so-called independent agencies of the U.S. government, of which there are now several hundred. Although independent, these agencies are mostly run by appointees of the federal government, and their rules or regulations have the force of federal law. *Wabash* and the establishment of the ICC therefore mark a major turning point in favor of federal power.

✔ 1895: *The Sugar Trust Case.* The feds' big victory of 1886–1887 was put on hold by the rise of a new breed of Supreme Court justices, who placed the principle of freedom of contract ahead of most anything else. Under the Sherman Antitrust Act of 1890, the federal government asked for the cancellation of some contracts that gave the American Sugar Refining Company a monopoly of sugar manufacture in the United States. But the Supreme Court refused to play ball with the feds. The court ruled that manufacture did not fall within the Commerce Clause. Interstate commerce, it held, does not begin until goods "commence their final movement from their State of origin to that of their destination."

✔ 1905–1937: This period is often termed the *Lochner* era, named for a controversial U.S. Supreme Court decision striking down a New York labor law that limited the number of permissible hours of work in bakeries — on the basis that the state law violated the freedom of contract of employers and employees alike. *Lochner* itself clearly didn't favor the states any more than it assisted the feds. The doctrine of freedom of contract opposed government interference in the economy in general. It didn't distinguish between state and federal government intervention.

In the 1930s, the doctrine of freedom of contract was used to strike down program after program of FDR's New Deal. This opposition to the President's policies came to a sudden end in 1937, and in the period after that the Supreme Court handed the economy, bound hand to foot, over to the federal government. I discuss this topic in depth in Chapter 9.

✔ 1951: *Dean Milk Co. v. City of Madison.* The doctrine of the "Dormant Commerce Clause" is sometimes used to strike down state laws. This doctrine has been traced to a couple of throwaway remarks made by Chief Justice John Marshall back in the 1820s, but it really came into its own only in the latter half of the 20th century. The Dormant Commerce Clause doctrine says that a state law violates the Commerce Clause if it interferes with interstate commerce — even if Congress hasn't already legislated on the particular product or issue concerned. The *Dean Milk Co.* case is a typical example of the cases decided under the Dormant Commerce Clause.

The case dealt with a municipal law that required all milk sold in Madison, Wisconsin, to have been pasteurized within 5 miles of the city, a law justified by its proponents as being necessary for the health of the consumers. The Supreme Court struck the law down, even though Congress had never legislated milk issues, because it discriminated against out-of-state milk producers (even though it also discriminated against Wisconsin milk producers who happened to be more than 5 miles from Madison!).

The Dormant Commerce Clause is a highly controversial judge-made doctrine, which is rejected by some Supreme Court justices.

✔ 1995: *United States v. Lopez.* Such was the power of the federal government over the economy between 1937 and 1995 that during the whole of that period the U.S. Supreme Court didn't strike down a single federal law as being an unconstitutional exercise of power under the Commerce Clause. But in *Lopez,* the court did declare a federal statute unconstitutional, and it also set aside part of a federal law five years later in *United States v. Morrison.* These decisions were hailed by some as a sign of the "new federalism" heralded by Chief Justice William Rehnquist. But then in 2005 came *Gonzales v. Raich,* which was a step backward. For more on these developments, see Chapter 9.

Ignoring the Elephant in the Room: The Question of State Sovereignty

The U.S. Constitution is not at all clear about the status of the states and their relationship with the federal government. Above all, are the states sovereign? And what is the meaning of *sovereignty* anyway?

Defining sovereignty

A *sovereign* state is one that has complete legal independence. For example, the United Kingdom is a sovereign state, but Scotland is not. Scotland forms part of the United Kingdom and enjoys a high degree of *autonomy,* or self-rule, but Scotland does not have complete legal independence.

The United States started out as 13 British colonies that declared themselves individually independent as 13 sovereign states. In 1777, these 13 sovereign states banded together under the Articles of Confederation, which recognized each of the states as sovereign.

This loose association of sovereign states didn't work out too well, which is why the U.S. Constitution was created. But the Constitution didn't directly address the question of whether the 13 states were still sovereign or whether they had surrendered some of their independence to the federal government.

A sovereign state automatically enjoys *sovereign immunity,* meaning that it can't be prosecuted for any crime or sued in a civil court unless the sovereign state itself gives permission for that to happen. (That's why cars belonging to the representatives of foreign nations can ignore parking tickets — a serious problem in Washington, D.C. and New York City!)

Are the states of the United States sovereign, and do they enjoy sovereign immunity? The Eleventh Amendment, which was intended to settle this issue, can be interpreted in four different ways! The most generally accepted, though vague, answer to these tricky questions is that the states are *not* sovereign in the fullest sense of that term and that they therefore enjoy only partial immunity from suit. For more on this discussion, see Chapter 20.

Testing state sovereignty: Chisholm v. Georgia

The question of sovereignty arose early in the history of the U.S. Supreme Court, in the leading case of *Chisholm v. Georgia,* decided in 1793. Alexander Chisholm of South Carolina filed suit against the state of Georgia for breach of contract, seeking payment for goods supplied to Georgia during the War of Independence.

Georgia refused to enter an appearance before the U.S. Supreme Court, arguing that, as a state, it possessed sovereign immunity from suit and could be sued only if it gave its consent. The court found in favor of Chisholm and held that Article III, Section 2 of the Constitution took away the states' sovereign immunity because in the list of cases that could be heard by the U.S. Supreme Court that section included "Controversies . . . between a State and Citizens of another State."

Such was the outcry against this decision that the Eleventh Amendment was passed to stop any such suits from being brought in the future. I discuss this amendment in Chapter 20.

Can a state secede from the union?

Can a state lawfully secede from the United States of America? The Constitution doesn't provide an answer to this crucial question.

When 11 southern states did in fact secede in 1860–1861and constituted themselves into the Confederate States of America, — or the *Confederacy,* as it's commonly known — their action was condemned as "rebellion," and a bloody civil war ensued.

Would it have made any difference if secession had been clearly permitted under the U.S. Constitution? Probably not. But the legal position remains unclear to the present day.

Dredging up the Articles of Confederation

In the 1869 case of *Texas v. White,* the U.S. Supreme Court ruled that Texas had remained a state throughout the Civil War, that its secession from the Union was unconstitutional, and that the laws passed by its secessionist state government were "absolutely null." Amazingly, the court based its conclusion *not* on the U.S. Constitution but on its predecessor, the Articles of Confederation, which were in effect from 1777 until 1788.

The argument put forward by Chief Justice Salmon P. Chase was as follows:

- ✔ The Articles of Confederation, passed in 1777 and ratified in 1781, described themselves as "perpetual," meaning eternal and unchangeable.

- ✔ The Articles of Confederation were found to be "inadequate to the exigencies of the country," so "the Constitution was ordained 'to form a more perfect Union.'"

- ✔ "It is difficult to convey the idea of indissoluble unity more clearly than by these words. What can be indissoluble if a perpetual Union, made more perfect, is not?"

On the face of it, this argument looks persuasive, but it falls apart on closer scrutiny. Chief Justice Chase based his argument primarily on the Articles of Confederation. But the key fact is that the Articles were no longer in force in 1869. They ceased to have any legal effect the moment they were replaced by the U.S. Constitution in 1788. Couldn't the Constitution also have expressed itself as creating a *perpetual union*? Sure, but it didn't. Why not? We just don't know — and we can't call James Madison to ask.

What about Chase's argument regarding "a more perfect Union"? His point is that the Constitution actually goes even further than the Articles of Confederation — because the Articles created a perpetual union and the Constitution built on it and made it "more perfect."

Chase's argument is flawed because the concept of a perpetual union is a matter of *time,* whereas the concept of a "more perfect Union" is a matter of *degree of closeness.* The Articles are talking apples, while the Constitution is talking pears. You can't add apples and pears together. The one doesn't build on the other.

But it's easy enough to see why Chief Justice Chase was anxious to conclude that secession was unconstitutional:

- ✔ The year was 1869, and Texas and the other secessionist states were in the throes of Reconstruction.

- ✔ Chase himself had been Secretary of the Treasury in President Abraham Lincoln's cabinet.

- ✔ Chase and four other justices who sat on *Texas v. White* were appointed to the Supreme Court bench by Abraham Lincoln.

So, did the Supreme Court have an ulterior political motive for declaring that secession was unconstitutional? You betcha!

Chapter 8

Separation of Powers:
To Each His Own

. . . .

In This Chapter

▶ Understanding the meaning of this doctrine

▶ Giving each branch its own membership and function

▶ Bringing checks and balances into the mix

. . . .

*T*he separation of powers is one of the fundamental principles of the U.S. Constitution — right up there with federalism, democracy, the rule of law, and judicial review. And like these other principles, the separation of powers is not specifically mentioned in the text of the Constitution.

What exactly is the meaning of *separation of powers*? At its simplest, this doctrine refers to separation between the three branches of government:

✔ **Legislative:** Congress, the lawmaking branch of government

✔ **Executive:** The President, who has the duty under Article II, Section 3 of the Constitution to "take Care that the Laws be faithfully executed"

✔ **Judicial:** The Supreme Court justices and other judges who interpret and enforce the law through the courts

We must examine separation of powers from four angles:

✔ The membership of the three branches of government

✔ The functions of the three branches of government

✔ The purpose of separation of powers

✔ Checks and balances between the three branches

I discuss each of these topics in this chapter, but first I trawl the text of the Constitution for any cryptic references to separation of powers.

No Moonlighting for the President

Although the Constitution never uses the phrase *separation of powers*, it does contain some oblique references to that principle. This fact is significant, because it shows that separation of powers was embedded in the Constitution from the beginning but the Framers took the principle for granted.

Here are the references to separation of powers in the Constitution:

- Article I, Section 1 gives Congress "all legislative Powers" under the Constitution. This means that the other two branches of government are not allowed to be involved in legislation. (In reality, they both *are* involved, as we see when we look at the workings of checks and balances later in this chapter.)

- Article III, Section 1 similarly reads, "The judicial Power of the United States shall be vested in one supreme Court, and in such inferior Courts as the Congress may from time to time ordain and establish." Although this section doesn't say "All judicial Power," the phrase "The judicial Power" makes it clear that the courts are to have *all* judicial power, excluding the other two branches of government from judicial activities.

- Article II, Section 1 forbids the President from receiving any payment from the United States or any of the states besides his salary as President. This means that the President isn't allowed to moonlight as a senator or a judge. Here's the actual wording: "The President shall, at stated Times, receive for his Services, a Compensation . . . and he shall not receive within that Period any other Emolument from the United States, or any of them."

Tracing the origins of separation of powers

The Framers of the Constitution constantly had before their eyes the examples of Britain and Europe. They adopted what they liked from these systems, modified the features that they thought needed tweaking, and rejected the rest.

In France, Spain, and other so-called absolute monarchies, a great deal of power was concentrated in the hands of the King. King Louis XIV of France famously remarked, "I am the state."

The American Founding Fathers greatly admired the writings of Baron de Montesquieu, an 18th-century French aristocrat who praised the British Constitution for its supposed separation of powers. In fact, Montesquieu had an exaggerated impression of the degree of separation of powers that actually existed in the British Constitution.

The Framers of the U.S. Constitution had no firsthand experience of the workings of the British Constitution. They simply accepted Montesquieu's analysis of the British Constitution, together with his theoretical framework.

Keeping the Branches Apart

Would it be possible to have strict separation between the members of the three branches of government without strict separation of functions? Yes, it would — and that is the case with the U.S. Constitution. For example, the President can never be a member of the legislature or the judiciary, but he does exercise some legislative functions and actually appoints the federal judiciary. (To be more precise, the President nominates the federal judges, who must be confirmed by the Senate. If they are confirmed, the President appoints them as federal judges.) The sections that follow explore the membership and functions of each branch of the U.S. government.

Membership

Separation of powers is strictly observed in regard to membership of the three branches of government:

- No member of the legislature — Congress — is allowed to hold an executive position at the same time.

- No member of Congress is allowed to hold a judicial post — as a Supreme Court justice or other judge — at the same time.

- Neither the President — the executive head of the nation — nor any member of his Cabinet is allowed to combine that position with a seat in Congress.

- Neither the President nor any member of his Cabinet is allowed to combine that position with a judicial post.

- No justice of the Supreme Court or any other judge is allowed to combine that judicial position with a Cabinet post or a seat in Congress.

The President comes to Congress every year to give the State of the Union address, but he or she is not a member of Congress. That is why the Congress generally goes wild when the President arrives, with everyone wanting to shake his hand or even get his autograph — and why large numbers of normally staid legislators jump to their feet every few minutes during the President's speech.

It's unthinkable that the President could be a member of Congress while serving as President, even though that kind of combination is quite normal (even obligatory) in many other countries, like Britain, Ireland, and Germany. But where in the U.S. Constitution does it say that the President is not allowed to combine these two positions? The only reference to this rule is the oblique prohibition that we've already looked at in Article II, Section 1:

The President shall, at stated Times, receive for his Services, a Compensation . . . and he shall not receive within that Period any other Emolument from the United States, or any of them.

Does this mean that it's okay for an incumbent President to serve as a member of Congress as long as he doesn't get a paycheck for doing so? Ummm, no.

The same rule applies to the President's Cabinet, to whom the President delegates some of his executive power. Neither the Secretary of State, nor the Secretary of the Treasury, nor the Attorney General, nor any other Cabinet member is allowed to combine that position with a seat in Congress.

But why doesn't the Constitution spell out this prohibition more directly?

The Philadelphia Convention that passed the Constitution recognized the need for strict separation between the three branches in their *membership* while retaining flexibility of *function.* But the Convention stopped short of putting this two-pronged rule into words — except in the oblique manner that I have already mentioned.

The reason for this omission is unknown, but the rule of strict separation among the membership of the three branches has nevertheless been religiously followed at all times.

Not only is it unconstitutional to hold office in more than one branch of the government at the same time, but it is also illegal under state law in many states even to *run* for more than one office at the same time. When Lyndon Johnson was picked as John Kennedy's vice presidential running mate in the 1960 presidential race, Johnson also ran for a third term in the U.S. Senate — just in case the Kennedy–Johnson ticket lost the election.

Johnson had to get Texas law changed in order to be permitted to run for both offices at the same time — in what came to be called "Lyndon's law." Johnson won both elections, but he made no attempt to hold down both positions. As soon as his second term in the Senate ended on January 3, 1961 — and before being inaugurated as Vice President — Johnson resigned his Senate seat, and with it his position as Senate majority leader. (He soon regretted having to give up this powerful position because as Vice President he was almost totally sidelined by President Kennedy!)

Functions

Strictly speaking, the Legislative branch should legislate, the Executive branch should "take Care that the Laws be faithfully executed," and the Judicial branch should interpret and enforce the law through the courts — and each branch should stay away from the functions of the other two branches. But there are two problems with this theory:

✔ In practice, overlap between the functions of the three branches can't be entirely avoided — and in some important situations, overlap is quite deliberate.

✔ If each of the three branches kept religiously to its own specific functions and didn't stray into the preserve of the other branches, the branches couldn't act as checks and balances on one another.

I discuss the first problem here and the second in the next section, "Checking and Balancing."

Some of the overlap between the three branches of government is the result of a genuine desire of one branch to help out another. For example, after Congress has passed a law, the Executive branch must enforce it. Sometimes, enforcing a law may involve making additional rules. But this practice has come under attack. A Supreme Court ruling in 1825 established what's called the *non-delegation doctrine*. Chief Justice John Marshall in *Wayman v. Southard* held that "important" matters can't be delegated, but Congress may delegate the power to one of the other branches of government "to fill up the details." For example, Congress delegates to executive agencies, such as the Food and Drug Administration and the Internal Revenue Service, the power to make detailed regulations in the areas that they cover.

The U.S. Supreme Court has given its blessing to Congress's delegation of power to other government bodies. Here's the test that the court applies in deciding whether a particular delegation is kosher or not:

> *Congress simply cannot do its job absent an ability to delegate power under broad general directives. Accordingly, this Court has deemed it "constitutionally sufficient if Congress clearly delineates the general policy, the public agency which is to apply it, and the boundaries of this delegated authority."*

The Supreme Court has only rarely struck down Acts of Congress delegating power to the other branches of government. An exception to this trend was the 1998 case *Clinton v. City of New York,* in which the Supreme Court struck down the Line Item Veto Act of 1996, which allowed the President unilaterally to delete individual items of expenditure approved by Congress. The idea behind the act was to allow the President to cut *pork barrel spending* — government spending that benefits a particular region rather than the nation as a whole. Most state governors have long had this power. President Ronald Reagan asked for a line item veto in his State of the Union address in 1986, saying, "Give me the authority to veto waste, and I'll take the responsibility, I'll make the cuts, I'll take the heat."

Surprisingly, perhaps, the Line Item Veto Act of 1996 originated not with the Democratic President but with his Republican opponents, who had just won control of both houses of Congress in the 1994 midterm elections. President Bill Clinton then also eagerly embraced the idea of a line item veto. So, what was wrong with the act? In a nutshell, the objection to the line item veto is that it allows the President to legislate, contrary to the principle of the separation of powers.

Muscling in on the other branches of government

Since the United States was founded, the three branches of government have jockeyed for position, with each trying to get one over on the other branches. Here are a few examples:

✔ **Legislative courts:** From an early date, Congress tried to break the courts' lock on litigation by setting up its own courts for certain purposes. The U.S. Supreme Court hit back by narrowly restricting the scope of the power of these legislative courts. In *Murray's Lessee v. Hoboken Land & Improvement Co.*, decided in 1856, the court ruled that a legislative court couldn't hear "a suit at the common law, or in equity, or admiralty" — in other words, any regular lawsuit. This left only "public rights" determinations to the legislative courts — cases between a citizen and the government.

✔ **The Supreme Court strikes back:** In a 1982 case called *Northern Pipeline Co. v. Marathon Pipe Line Co.*, a plurality of the Supreme Court struck down an Act of Congress that had set up bankruptcy courts with wide jurisdiction. The main objection to these bankruptcy courts was that they posed a "serious threat that the exercise of the judicial power would be subject to incursion by other branches." Not that the Supreme Court had ever heard many bankruptcy cases!

✔ **Jurisdiction stripping:** Article III, Section 2 of the Constitution says, "[T]he supreme Court shall have appellate Jurisdiction . . . with such Exceptions . . . as the Congress shall make." Justice Felix Frankfurter commented,

"Congress need not give this Court any appellate power: it may withdraw appellate jurisdiction once conferred." Was Frankfurter right? Absolutely. The Illegal Immigration Reform and Immigrant Responsibility Act of 1996 provides a good example of Congress's exercise of the power to restrict the power of the courts. Under this act, if the Immigration and Naturalization Service (INS) refuses to grant a particular person asylum, no federal court — including the high court — is permitted to review that decision.

✔ **Guantanamo Bay:** Could Congress exclude the jurisdiction of the courts in regard to detention in Guantanamo Bay? The Military Commissions Act (MCA) of 2006 did just that. The MCA established special "military commissions" to try "alien unlawful enemy combatants engaged in hostilities against the United States." In the 2008 case *Boumediene v. Bush,* the U.S. Supreme Court ruled 5 to 4 that the MCA was unconstitutional and that foreign detainees held in Guantanamo Bay *did* have the right to challenge their detention in the ordinary U.S. courts. Justice Antonin Scalia, in his dissenting opinion, held that the majority's "analysis produces a crazy result."

It's important to distinguish these examples of competition among the different branches of government from the checks and balances between them that the Framers deliberately inserted into the Constitution in order to prevent concentration of power in too few hands.

Checking and Balancing

Here's what James Madison said in the *Federalist Papers* in support of separation of powers:

> *The accumulation of all powers, legislative, executive, and judiciary, in the same hands, whether of one, a few, or many, and whether hereditary, selfappointed, or elective, may justly be pronounced the very definition of tyranny.*

Madison and the other Framers considered separation of powers essential in order to avoid "tyranny." But the Constitution went much further than the mere separation of powers — it also established an elaborate system of checks and balances.

The concept of checks and balances is in one sense a natural extension of separation of powers, but in another sense the two concepts — separation of powers and checks and balances — are actually in opposition to each other.

On its own, separation of powers should just mean that each branch of government would go its own merry way without interference from any other branch. But this arrangement isn't practical, because the boundaries between the three branches of government aren't clear-cut. Plus, the Framers deliberately introduced overlaps between the functions of the three branches so that they could act as checks and balances on one another.

Keeping each branch in line

Here are the most important checks and balances built into the Constitution. I look first at checks on Congress, then at checks on the President, and lastly at checks on the judiciary. Here are the checks on Congress:

- ✔ **The President's veto power:** Under Article I, Section 7 of the Constitution, the President has the power to veto — or block — any bill passed by both houses of Congress. This is a really powerful tool against the legislature in the hands of the executive. A presidential veto can be overridden by Congress, but only by a two-thirds majority in both houses, which is notoriously difficult to achieve.

- ✔ **The Veep:** The Vice President is a member of the executive branch of government, and he is also President of the Senate by virtue of Article I, Section 3 of the Constitution. But, although he has the right to preside over the Senate, the Vice President is not a member of that legislative body, cannot participate in debates there, and cannot vote except to

break a tie. So, his potential to keep the Senate in check is very limited —
especially since most Veeps don't spend a lot of time presiding over the
Senate. They tend to leave that to the *president pro tem* of the Senate, the
senior senator of the day.

✔ **Judicial review:** The most serious check on Congressional power
doesn't appear in the text of the Constitution at all but was read into
it by Chief Justice John Marshall in the famous 1803 case of *Marbury v.
Madison,* which I discuss in Chapter 23. Marshall's highly controversial
ruling is still accepted today. It gives the Supreme Court the power to
strike down any law passed by Congress or any of the state legislatures
if the court finds that law unconstitutional. I discuss the effect of this
ruling later in this chapter and also in Chapter 12.

Now for the main checks on the President:

✔ **Impeachment:** Impeachment is the best-known check on the President
because it can result in his or her removal from office. But impeachment has been used only twice — against Andrew Johnson in 1869, and
against Bill Clinton in 1999. Neither Johnson nor Clinton was removed
from office, but Richard Nixon's resignation in 1974 was in reaction to a
serious threat of impeachment.

In impeachment proceedings, the House of Representatives prosecutes
and the Senate sits as a jury and decides the case. A two-thirds majority is needed for a conviction. The Chief Justice presides over the trial,
which represents a further check on both the President and the Congress
on the part of the judiciary. I discuss impeachment in Chapter 13.

✔ **"Advice and Consent":** Article II, Section 2 of the Constitution gives
the President the "Power, by and with the Advice and Consent of the
Senate, to make Treaties, provided two thirds of the Senators present
concur." This provision seriously cramps the President's style in foreign
policy matters. Similarly, the President's power to appoint ambassadors,
Supreme Court justices, and other federal officials is exercised "by and
with the Advice and Consent of the Senate" — which translates in practice into sometimes quite lengthy and acrimonious confirmation hearings. I deal with the presidency in Chapter 10.

✔ **Commander in Chief:** Article II, Section 2 of the Constitution makes the
President Commander in Chief of the armed forces. But under Article I,
Section 8, Congress has the power "to declare War." The precise relationship between the President and Congress in regard to war remains
the subject of intense debate. I discuss this issue in Chapters 10 and 11.

✔ **Choosing the President:** If no candidate running for President obtains
a majority (more than 50 percent) of the electoral votes, the Twelfth
Amendment provides that "the House of Representatives shall choose

immediately, by ballot, the President" — with each state having one vote. This provision has been used twice. The Senate has the same power in regard to choosing the Vice President.

✔ **Judicial review:** The Supreme Court has a similar power in regard to decisions of the President and other members of the executive branch as it has in regard to Congress. The court can set aside an executive decision as unconstitutional. This derives from the power of the Supreme Court to interpret the Constitution — a right that doesn't figure in the text of the Constitution, but which derives from Chief Justice John Marshall's ruling in *Marbury v. Madison,* which I discuss in Chapter 23.

What about checks on the judiciary by the other two branches? There are remarkably few:

✔ **Impeachment:** The main check on the judiciary is impeachment. Many more judges have been impeached than presidents. Only one of these judges was a Supreme Court justice, and he was acquitted. But no fewer than 13 other federal judges have been impeached, seven of them being removed from the bench and a couple others choosing to resign. As with presidents, the threat of impeachment can be as effective as a successful impeachment conviction. Justice Abe Fortas — nominated by President Lyndon Johnson to become Chief Justice — is reliably thought to have resigned rather than face impeachment. As with presidential impeachments, the House of Representatives prosecutes and the Senate tries the case. But the Vice President presides — not the Chief Justice as in the impeachment of a President.

✔ **Appointment:** Supreme Court justices and other federal judges are appointed by the President subject to confirmation by the Senate. But Article III, Section 1 of the Constitution allows them to "hold their Offices during good Behaviour" — in other words, for life, subject only to removal by impeachment.

✔ **Pardons:** Article II, Section 2 of the Constitution gives the President the "Power to grant Reprieves and Pardons for Offences against the United States, except in Cases of Impeachment." Is this power a check on the judiciary? Yes, in a sense, because a pardon cancels the sentence without cancelling the conviction.

Considering the judiciary's special position

The judiciary has fewer checks on its power than either of the other two branches of government because, once appointed, a federal judge is there for life unless he really steps out of line sufficiently to be impeached.

The judiciary also exercises more control over the other two branches than those branches have over the judiciary. Judicial review is the killer weapon in the hands of the U.S. Supreme Court, which can use it against the President as well as against Congress, and also against the states.

Interestingly enough, this nuclear weapon doesn't figure anywhere in the text of the Constitution. The Supreme Court arrogated this power to itself back in 1803 in the case of *Marbury v. Madison,* and it has clung to this power ever since. That ruling is doubly worrying in regard to the doctrine of the separation of powers, for two reasons:

- ✔ It gave the judiciary the exclusive right to interpret the Constitution, a power that the Constitution itself doesn't confer on them. Such was the skill of Chief Justice John Marshall that his "twistifications of the law" (Thomas Jefferson's term) have become accepted as valid constitutional law. Jefferson's own take was quite different:

    My construction of the Constitution is . . . that each department [or branch of government] is truly independent of the others and has an equal right to decide for itself what is the meaning of the Constitution in the cases submitted to its action; and especially where it is to act ultimately and without appeal.

- ✔ It gave the judiciary the power to add to its own power simply by means of a high court decision — which is also nowhere to be found in the Constitution, and is in any case contrary to the whole principle of the separation of powers.

Above all, the effect of *Marbury v. Madison* is to give a group of unelected justices the power to strike down as unconstitutional any laws passed by a democratically elected Congress. Here's Jefferson's take on that ruling:

The Constitution . . . meant that its coordinate branches should be checks on each other. But the opinion which gives to the judges the right to decide what laws are constitutional and what not, not only for themselves in their own sphere of action but for the Legislature and Executive also in their spheres, would make the Judiciary a despotic branch.

Right away in 1804, Jefferson recognized the danger of runaway power in the hands of the Supreme Court. He was President at the time yet was powerless to stop that development — even though it was not sanctioned by the Constitution. And none of his successors has been able to stop the inexorable growth of judicial power either. For more on this subject, see Chapter 12.

Chapter 9

Doing Business: The Commerce Clause

Congress is the legislative branch of the federal government — the branch that makes laws. But Congress can't pass just any laws it likes. Its lawmaking powers are limited by the Constitution as part of the delicate balancing act that the Constitution performs between the federal government and the states.

Article I, Section 8, of the Constitution lists the powers of Congress. It's a pretty long list — but don't worry, I'm not going to bore you with it here. (You can turn to the Appendix if you're dying with curiosity.)

Article I, Section 8, Clause 3 — known as the *Commerce Clause* — contains probably the most important of these listed powers. Here is what the Commerce Clause says:

> *The Congress shall have Power . . . To regulate Commerce with foreign Nations, and among the several States, and with the Indian Tribes.*

As usual, there's more to these few words than meets the eye.

How the Commerce Clause Was Born

The Commerce Clause owes its existence to the economic conflicts between the states during the period under the Articles of Confederation, which were in force from 1781 until the ratification of the U.S. Constitution in 1788.

Under the Articles of Confederation, the national government was extremely weak and had no power to regulate the economy. The states were essentially independent of one another. In 1787 James Madison wrote to George Washington in exasperation at the way the states continued "to harass each other with rival and spiteful measures dictated by mistaken views of interest." Examples of this problem were the taxes imposed by New York and Pennsylvania on imports from abroad destined for landlocked New Jersey.

Madison — often called the "Father of the Constitution" — recognized that the only way to put an end to this economic conflict among the states was by establishing a stronger national government. This was the main objective of the Philadelphia Convention that crafted the U.S. Constitution.

In the same letter to Washington, Madison wrote that "the national Government should be armed with positive and compleat authority in all cases which require uniformity; such as the regulation of trade, including the right of taxing both exports & imports."

But how far does the Commerce Clause reflect Madison's view on this important subject? The poor little guy (he was only 5 foot 3 3/4 inches tall) was often thwarted in the Constitutional Convention.

Interpreting the Commerce Clause

The courts have pored over practically every word in the Commerce Clause. Here are some of the issues associated with the definitions of certain words and phrases:

- ✔ **Power:** The question here is whether the Commerce Clause gives Congress *exclusive* power to regulate commerce — particularly over interstate commerce — or whether the states have a *concurrent* power (a power running parallel to that of Congress). I discuss this tricky question in the next section.

- ✔ **Commerce:** Two hundred years ago, *commerce* referred primarily to the buying and selling of goods and commodities. But, in the leading case of *Gibbons v. Ogden,* decided in 1824, Chief Justice John Marshall held that it also included navigation. Since then, the term *commerce* has been narrowed and widened at different times, according to the changing views of the Supreme Court justices.

- ✔ **Regulate:** *To regulate* was defined by Marshall as meaning "to prescribe the rule by which commerce is to be governed."

- ✔ **"Commerce with foreign Nations":** It is not at all surprising that Congress was given the power to regulate foreign trade, because foreign affairs generally were the concern of the national government and not of the states.

- ✔ **"among the several States":** As Marshall put it, this phrase "may very properly be restricted to that commerce which concerns more states than one" — now generally called *interstate* commerce. The definition of this term has fluctuated in accordance with the views of the justices of the Supreme Court over time. The ruling definition of *interstate commerce* is now very broad, covering the movement of pretty much any goods or services — or even people — across state lines.

- ✔ **"with the Indian Tribes":** Native Americans were recognized from the foundation of the Republic as being separate from the United States. However, in an 1831 case the Supreme Court decided that the Cherokee nation was not an independent state but a "denominated domestic dependent nation." By referring to Native Americans separately from foreign nations, the Commerce Clause supports this high court view.

Hunting Down the Dormant Commerce Clause

The Commerce Clause gives Congress the power "to regulate Commerce." Does this mean that Congress has *exclusive* power to regulate commerce, or does it mean that the states have *concurrent* power with Congress in this area — power running parallel to that of Congress?

Neither of these interpretations is entirely satisfactory. Let's take a look at each of them in turn.

Assuming Congress has exclusive power

I first examine the view that the Commerce Clause gives Congress exclusive power. If Congress has exclusive power over this vast area, then these conclusions must follow:

- ✔ The states can't regulate interstate commerce at all — even on matters that Congress hasn't legislated about. Adherents of the *Dormant Commerce Clause* theory take this line. The theory can be traced back to a remark made by Chief Justice John Marshall in a case decided in 1829, but it really came into its own in the second half of the 20th century. The idea behind this misnamed theory is that, even when Congress hasn't legislated on a particular aspect of interstate commerce, its power is only sleeping — so the states aren't allowed to make laws affecting this aspect anyway.

- ✔ Any attempt by a state to regulate interstate commerce in any way must be struck down as unconstitutional. On this basis, in 1997 the U.S. Supreme Court struck down a Maine statute that imposed tax penalties on organizations catering mainly to out-of state customers. A summer camp run by the Christian Science Church had to pay more than $20,000 per year in local property taxes just because it catered mainly to out-of-state campers. Justice John Paul Stevens, writing for the majority, held that the state law infringed on the Dormant Commerce Clause and was therefore unconstitutional. Despite the wide definition of the Commerce Clause that the majority on the court applied in this case, the outcome was probably fair. This was an important decision, affecting many charitable organizations across the nation.

✔ The interests of the Federal government predominate over those of the states. The Supreme Court justices who support the Dormant Commerce Clause tend to favor federal power over state power.

Giving concurrent powers to the states

The Dormant Commerce Clause theory is a bit like a flying saucer. Those who believe in it are passionate in its support, while skeptics are dismissive of the whole idea.

Having examined the implications of a valid Dormant Commerce Clause, let's turn to the alternative theory: that the states retain a concurrent commerce power, which is subject to the Supremacy Clause of the Constitution. The Supremacy Clause, which I discuss in Chapter 7, subordinates all state laws to the U.S. Constitution and all federal laws "made in Pursuance thereof."

Here's a hypothetical example of how the concurrent commerce power theory works in practice:

✔ Texas makes a law stipulating that out-of-state cowboy boots sold in that state must be colored pink with purple spots.

✔ This law clearly concerns interstate commerce, so Congress has the power to regulate this trade.

✔ But Congress hasn't passed any laws about cowboy boots.

✔ So the Texas law is valid — until or unless Congress decides to pass a law prohibiting discrimination against out-of-state cowboy boots.

✔ Any such Congressional legislation automatically makes the Texas law unconstitutional.

This scenario is hardly more satisfactory than the one based on the Dormant Commerce Clause theory because it means that state laws concerned with interstate commerce are always teetering on the brink of unconstitutionality.

So, which theory is right?

Poking holes in the Dormant Commerce Clause

Is the Dormant Commerce Clause actually part of the Constitution at all? It sure doesn't appear in the text of the Constitution. It's a judge-made interpretation of the Commerce Clause — but one that now has an apparently respectable pedigree simply because so many Supreme Court justices have accepted it over the years.

IN MY OPINION

In my view, the arguments against the Dormant Commerce Clause theory are far stronger than this vague aura of respectability. Here are some of the arguments against this theory:

✔ Article I, Section 10, of the Constitution lists a lot of things that the states are not permitted to do. Among these prohibitions on the states is the right to "lay any Imposts or Duties on Imports or Exports" except with the consent of Congress. Import and export duties are of course connected with commerce, but they are only one small part of commerce and are concerned solely with foreign trade. What about the exercise by the states of other powers involving the regulation of commerce? These are not prohibited in the Constitution. So we can only conclude that these other powers *may* be exercised by the states — unless Congress decides to step in.

✔ During the period of the Articles of Confederation, from 1781 to 1788, the weak central government had no commerce power at all; the states had complete power to regulate all aspects of commerce. If the U.S. Constitution intended to take this major power away from the states and hand it exclusively to Congress, it would have had to spell out that change really carefully. But there is no sign of this change in the wording of the Constitution.

✔ Chief Justice John Marshall did use the term *dormant* in reference to the Commerce Clause a couple of times, but it's a mistake to think that he was thinking of anything like the Dormant Commerce Clause theory. Marshall made his view on the subject crystal clear in *Gibbons v. Ogden* in 1824, when he said, "It is perfectly settled, that an affirmative grant of power to the United States does not, of itself, devest the States of a like power." In other words, just because the Constitution gives Congress a particular power doesn't strip the states of a similar power. The states therefore enjoy a *concurrent* power with Congress to regulate interstate commerce.

✔ Marshall reasserted his position on the Dormant Commerce Clause theory in the case of *Willson v. Blackbird Creek Marsh Co.*, decided in 1829. A company was authorized by a Delaware state law to build a dam, which blocked the passage of a ship licensed under federal law. Was the building of the dam a violation of the Commerce Clause? The Supreme Court, speaking through Chief Justice Marshall, said no — simply because Congress had not "passed any act which bore upon the case."

Tracing the Changing Meaning of the Commerce Clause

The commerce power is one of the most important powers that the Constitution entrusts to Congress. So, Supreme Court justices favoring the federal government have tended to adopt a broad interpretation of the clause, while justices favoring states' rights have generally taken a narrow view of the clause.

In 1824, there was debate about whether even a commercial activity like navigation fell within the commerce power. But within half a century the high court had greatly widened its interpretation of the Commerce Clause. In 1877, Chief Justice Morrison Waite ruled that, as the power to regulate commerce was "intrusted to the general government for the good of the nation, it is not only the right, but the duty, of Congress to see to it that intercourse among the States and the transmission of intelligence are not obstructed or unnecessarily encumbered by State legislation."

Protecting freedom of contract

The next phase in the life of the Commerce Clause was a restrictive interpretation by the high court of government power — state as well as federal — to regulate commerce.

The period between 1905 and 1937 is often termed the *Lochner* era, named for the controversial Supreme Court decision striking down a New York labor law that limited the number of permissible hours of work in bakeries. The majority on the court held that the state law violated the *freedom of contract* of employers and employees alike. They also ruled that freedom of contract was an integral part of the liberty protected by the Due Process Clause of the Fourteenth Amendment. So, by infringing on this right, the New York law was unconstitutional. (I discuss the Due Process Clause and the Lochner case in more detail in Chapter 17.)

The *Lochner* decision itself was not based on the Commerce Clause. But the principle of freedom of contract soon became a useful weapon against the commerce power of Congress.

Introducing the Four Horsemen and the Three Musketeers

The stage was set for a major battle in the Supreme Court between the supporters of federal regulation of the economy and the champions of freedom of contract.

The doctrine of freedom of contract was still dominant when Franklin Delano Roosevelt (FDR) was elected President in 1932. FDR's New Deal took the form of a series of radical programs embodied in congressional legislation. Four justices on the Supreme Court — nicknamed the Four Horsemen (of the Apocalypse) — were staunch conservatives who fought the New Deal tooth and nail. Luckily for the Horsemen, they found an ally in Justice Owen Roberts, who often provided the swing vote giving the Horsemen a majority on the court. The liberal wing of the court — nicknamed the Three Musketeers — was no match for the Horsemen when they had Roberts in tow.

Between 1935 and 1937 the conservative majority struck down one after another of the New Deal programs as unconstitutional.

Finding that mining and manufacture are not commerce

Carter v. Carter Coal Co. is a typical example of the approach adopted by the Four Horsemen. The case was about the so-called Guffey Coal Act of 1935, which regulated prices, wages, and "fair practices" in the coal industry. The question before the court was whether this federal law was constitutional or not. The Four Horsemen had Justice Owen Roberts in harness and declared the law unconstitutional.

Here is a summary of the arguments that the Horsemen used to reach this conclusion. I have added my comments in italic.

- ✔ The federal government "can claim no powers which are not granted to it by the Constitution, and the powers actually granted must be such as are expressly given or given by necessary implication." *This "cardinal rule" is not in dispute. It is quoted from an important 1816 high court decision.*

- ✔ The Commerce Clause of the Constitution gives Congress the power to regulate commerce. *No problem with this either!*

- ✔ But manufacture is not the same thing as commerce. Commerce means "intercourse for the purpose of trade." However, "Mining is not interstate commerce, but like manufacturing, is a local business subject to local regulation and taxation." *Yeah? But, as Justice Benjamin Cardozo*

> said in his dissent: *"Mining and agriculture and manufacture are not interstate commerce considered by themselves, yet their relation to that commerce may be such that, for the protection of the one, there is need to regulate the other."* The Horsemen's narrow view of the commerce power inevitably led to the desired conclusion. No surprises here. Check the next bullet.
>
> ✔ So the Guffey Act is unconstitutional. *Whew! That wasn't too difficult, now, was it?*

Showing how a switch in time saved nine

FDR was sick of the way the Four Horsemen thwarted him repeatedly in the court by, as he put it, "reading into the Constitution words and implications which are not there, and which were never intended to be there."

Not a single vacancy on the Supreme Court bench opened up during FDR's first term, so the President wasn't able to name any new justices. But, bolstered by two landslide victories and an overwhelming majority in both houses of Congress, FDR decided to play the Horsemen at their own game — the game of constitutional interpretation.

Article III of the Constitution establishes a Supreme Court, but nowhere does the Constitution say how many members that court should consist of. Roosevelt therefore proposed a law giving the President the power to appoint an additional Supreme Court justice for every sitting member of the court who had reached the age of 70½. This measure would immediately have allowed FDR to appoint six more justices, which would have given him indirect control over the court — something that even some of his staunchest supporters opposed as an abuse of presidential authority.

In the end, Roosevelt didn't need his court-packing scheme in order to get the Supreme Court on his side. The threat of it was enough. The turning point came when Justice Owen Roberts switched sides — the famous "switch in time that saved nine" (justices) in *West Coast Hotel v. Parrish*, decided in 1937, which I discuss in Chapter 23. (There is still some doubt whether Roosevelt's plan really was the reason for Roberts's sudden switch, because it appears that Roberts had written his opinion before the President even announced his proposal.)

West Coast Hotel v. Parrish signaled the end of the *Lochner* "freedom of contract" era. With a pro-New Deal majority on the court, it was inevitable that federal power under the Commerce Clause would grow exponentially.

Signaling the feds' control of the economy

The first sign of this growth in federal power came in *National Labor Relations Board (NLRB) v. Jones & Laughlin Steel Corporation,* decided in 1937. The

NLRB, set up under a New Deal law, found Jones & Laughlin guilty of discriminating against employees of theirs who wanted to join a labor union. The NLRB ordered the corporation to rehire ten employees whom it had fired and to give them back pay. The corporation refused to comply with the NLRB ruling on the ground that the act setting up the NLRB was unconstitutional under the Commerce Clause.

The high court ruled in favor of the NLRB, holding that the Commerce Clause gave Congress the power to regulate labor relations. The court cast to the four winds the previous restrictive interpretation of the Commerce Clause.

But this decision was by no means the most extreme manifestation of the control over the economy that the federal government had now obtained. That honor probably goes to a 1942 case about a small farmer and his small allotment: *Wickard v. Filburn*.

Controlling the production of wheat that never left its home farm

The Agricultural Adjustment Act of 1938 — part of FDR's vast New Deal program — restricted the area that farmers could use for growing wheat. The idea was to keep wheat prices stable by controlling production.

Roscoe Filburn was a small farmer in Ohio. He produced 239 bushels more wheat than his federal quota allowed him. So he was hit with a penalty amounting to 57 percent of the market value of his excess production.

Roscoe pointed out that he didn't sell any of his excess wheat production. Not only did none of his wheat crop enter interstate commerce, but also none of it ever left his farm. All his wheat was consumed right there by himself, his family, his poultry, and his livestock. Roscoe figured that this explanation gave him an ironclad case against the feds — but he hadn't reckoned on the new pro-government approach of the Supreme Court.

The question before the high court in the case of *Wickard v. Filburn* was quite simple: Was the law setting production quotas in keeping with the Commerce Clause — even when the wheat crop in question never left the state where it was grown?

Amazingly, the high court ruled unanimously in favor of the federal legislation. It held that if Filburn had not grown and consumed his excess wheat, he would have had to buy it from someone else — which is commerce. In the words of Justice Robert H. Jackson, writing for the court, "Even if [Filburn's] activity be local, and though it may not be regarded as commerce, it may still, whatever its nature, be reached by Congress if it exerts a substantial economic effect on interstate commerce."

Justice Jackson was not noted as a comedian, but was this a joke? Did he really say *"though it may not be regarded as commerce"*? Yep, he sure did. So, that must mean that even something that's not commerce at all — let alone *interstate* commerce — can still be regulated by the feds under the Commerce Clause! But that's not all he said. How about the phrase *"if it exerts a substantial economic effect on interstate commerce"*? Seriously, how could 239 bushels of wheat exert a substantial effect on anything?

Using the Commerce Clause to advance civil rights

The high court's decision in Filburn's case was a signal that allowed the feds to muscle in on pretty much any economic activity. Not surprisingly, the feds took the opportunity to use their economic power to further their political program — including, above all, civil rights. Federal legislation outlawed segregation, and the Supreme Court under Chief Justice Earl Warren was quick to support this legislation in any way it could, including using the Commerce Clause. One leading example of this kind occurred in a case involving an Atlanta motel.

The Heart of Atlanta Motel in Atlanta, Georgia, offered accommodation only to white people. This policy was directly contrary to federal law. The Civil Rights Act of 1964 specifically outlawed racial discrimination "in any place of public accommodation" if its operations "affect commerce."

The owner of the motel filed suit in federal court arguing that, in passing this provision, Congress exceeded its powers under the Commerce Clause. A unanimous Supreme Court ruled that the ban on racial discrimination in public accommodations was well within Congress's powers under the Commerce Clause. The court also noted that three-fourths of the motel's guests came from outside Georgia, so the business clearly affected interstate commerce.

Turning back the federal tide?

The *Heart of Atlanta* case was no isolated example. The Commerce Clause was a convenient tool in the hands of the Supreme Court to bring the states to heel. But the court itself was beginning to change, most notably after the appointment of William Rehnquist as Chief Justice in 1986. Rehnquist was a conservative who tended generally to favor states' rights in what came to be called "the new federalism."

In *United States v. Lopez,* decided in 1995, the Supreme Court at last struck down a federal law on the ground that it went beyond the permissible limits of the Commerce Clause. This was the first high court decision since 1937 to restrict congressional authority to legislate under the Commerce Clause.

The legislation in question, the Gun-Free School Zones Act of 1990, made it "unlawful for any individual knowingly to possess a firearm at a place that the individual knows, or has reasonable cause to know, is a school zone."

Alfonso Lopez, a twelfth-grader, walked into his high school in San Antonio, Texas, carrying a concealed .38-caliber handgun and five bullets. He was convicted under the 1990 federal law and was sentenced to six months in prison.

On appeal, Lopez claimed that the provision under which he had been convicted was unconstitutional because it exceeded Congress's power to legislate under the Commerce Clause.

The high court agreed with him. Chief Justice William Rehnquist, writing for the majority, held that the relevant section of the 1990 law "is a criminal statute that by its terms has nothing to do with 'commerce' or any sort of economic enterprise, however broadly one might define those terms."

This decision is undoubtedly right — although the idea of keeping guns away from schools is not a bad one. Mass school killings have been all too frequent in recent years.

Lopez was first charged under a Texas law. It's not clear why those charges were dropped in favor of federal charges. If Congress had not mistakenly assumed that it had the power to legislate gun control, Lopez would probably have been duly convicted and sentenced under a perfectly valid state law.

"Appropriating state police powers under the guise of regulating commerce"

United States v. Morrison, decided in 2000, was another case in which the high court struck down part of a well-intentioned federal statute. The law in question was the Violence Against Women Act (VAWA), and the relevant provision allowed female victims of gender-based violence to file civil suits in federal court.

Here are some of the arguments used by the majority on the court, speaking through Chief Justice Rehnquist:

✔ Violent crime has only a minimal effect on interstate commerce.

✔ "No civilized system of justice" could fail to provide a remedy for indecent assault or rape, but under our federal system that remedy must be provided by the states and not by federal law.

✔ The scope of the commerce power must not "embrace effects upon interstate commerce so indirect and remote that to embrace them . . . would effectually obliterate the distinction between what is national and what is local and create a completely centralized government." (Here, Rehnquist is pointing back to the *NLRB* New Deal case that I discuss earlier in the chapter.)

✔ The economic effects of crimes against women are indirect and don't therefore fall under the commerce power — even if a whole lot of incidents are "aggregated" together. (This "aggregation principle" supposedly comes from *Wickard v Filburn,* but it's not actually mentioned there.)

Justice Clarence Thomas, concurring with Rehnquist, charged Congress in the VAWA with "appropriating state police powers under the guise of regulating commerce." This statement puts the majority decision in a nutshell.

It's important to note that the high court did not invalidate the whole of VAWA but only the part allowing a civil remedy in federal court. The rest of VAWA — mainly providing funding for the investigation and prosecution of sexual violence in the *criminal* courts — is still alive and well. It was reauthorized by Congress in 2005 and signed into law by President George W. Bush in 2006 — with the addition of relief for male victims of domestic violence and indecent assault.

Taking a step backward

After the successful check on the feds in *United States v. Morrison,* we find ourselves back in 1942. In *Gonzales v. Raich,* decided in 2005, the high court upheld a federal law banning the use of marijuana for medicinal purposes — although a California state law allowed such use. Angel Raich, who brought the case, used only in-state marijuana. In the words of Justice Clarence Thomas, dissenting, Raich's "local cultivation and consumption of marijuana is not 'Commerce . . . among the several states'." The result of this sad case was the same as that in the remarkably similar case of *Wickard v. Filburn* — victory for the feds over the little person, over the states, and over the correct interpretation of the Commerce Clause.

Part III

Balancing the Branches of Government: The President, Congress, and the Judiciary

The 5th Wave   By Rich Tennant

THE JUSTICES RULE ON
PAPER vs SCISSORS vs STONE

In this part . . .

Want to know what the different branches of the federal government can and can't do? It's all here, starting with the President, then moving on to Congress and the judiciary. If you're not satisfied with their performance, you may want to fire them. Chapter 13 tells you how to impeach the President and the judges. (Members of Congress can only be voted out.)

Chapter 10

Looking at the Role of Commander in Chief

*T*he President of the United States is commonly described as the most powerful person in the world. So it's pretty important to understand how the President is chosen and exactly what powers and responsibilities the President has under the Constitution. That's what this chapter is all about.

Being "Eligible to the Office of President"

Thinking about running for president? Want to know if you qualify? Article II, Section 1 of the Constitution lays down the requirements for eligibility:

No person except a natural born Citizen, or a Citizen of the United States, at the time of the Adoption of this Constitution, shall be eligible to the Office of President; neither shall any Person be eligible to that Office who shall not have attained to the Age of thirty five Years, and been fourteen Years a Resident within the United States.

In other words, to be eligible for the office of President, you have to be

- "[A] natural born" U.S. citizen — but see the discussion that follows.
- At least 35 years old.
- A U.S. resident for at least 14 years.

Do you really need to have been born a citizen of the United States in order to become President? A close reading of the quoted section shows that you don't — provided you became a U.S. citizen by June 21, 1788. The only snag is that you'd have to be more than 220 years old to qualify under that rule!

Does the term "natural born Citizen" mean that you have to be born in a state of the United States? Or is it good enough if you were born in a U.S. territory? Barry Goldwater, the Republican presidential nominee in 1964, was born in Arizona Territory before it became a state, but his right to run for President was never seriously questioned. The same applied to John McCain, who was born to U.S. parents (his father was an admiral) at a U.S. military base in the Panama Canal Zone, which was a territory of the United States at the time.

The phrase "eligible to the Office of President" has been the subject of a lot of recent debate. Some people have suggested that a former two-term President of the United States could lawfully run for election as Vice President, and then, if the President resigned, become President for a third term!

It's a two-party system

In order to run for President, it helps to be a billionaire. It also helps to have been nominated as the candidate of one of the two major political parties, Democratic or Republican. Nomination can be achieved only by winning enough *primary elections* — contests within one of the major parties — to ensure the support of a majority of pledged delegates at the party convention.

These are not constitutional requirements, but in practice it's almost impossible for a third-party candidate to be elected President. In 1912, ex-President Theodore Roosevelt, running on a Progressive Party (or "Bull Moose") ticket, made a strong showing as a third-party candidate. He received 88 electoral votes, far superior to incumbent Republican President William H. Taft's 8 electoral votes. But what Roosevelt really accomplished was putting Democratic nominee Woodrow Wilson into the White House (with 435 electoral votes).

More surprisingly, in 1992, Ross Perot, a 62-year-old billionaire who had never held public office, picked up 18.9 percent of the popular vote. Although Perot got no electoral votes because he didn't get a majority in any one state, he arguably cost incumbent President George H.W. Bush the election and put Bill Clinton into the White House.

This is no abstract discussion. It was motivated by the desire to see Bill Clinton back in the White House. The suggestion is preposterous because the Twenty-Second Amendment states categorically that "No person shall be elected to the office of the President more than twice." The pro-Clintonites argue that this amendment is a prohibition only on being *elected* President, but not on becoming President by some other route, like being elected as Veep and then succeeding to the Presidency on the resignation of the President. For a discussion on the Twenty-Second Amendment see (appropriately enough) Chapter 22.

"[E]ligible to the Office of President" just means "able to be *elected* to the office of President." This phrase in Article II, Section 1 dovetails with the Twenty-Second Amendment, and also with the Twelfth Amendment, which provides that "no person constitutionally ineligible to the office of President shall be eligible to that of Vice-President of the United States." In short, if you can't be elected President, you also can't be elected Vice President. Reading the three constitutional texts together, we get this: *A former two-term President can't be elected to a third term as President, and he also can't be elected as Vice President.*

Picking a President

The Constitution goes into great detail on presidential elections — but much of what it says on that subject is obsolete or misleading.

The biggest problem in regard to the constitutional rules for presidential elections is the Framers' total disregard of the existence of political parties, which they scorned as "factions" but which came to play a major role in elections.

Paying the price for passing over political parties

Article II, Section 1 of the original, unamended Constitution contains a long spiel about presidential elections. The system of presidential elections set out there was applied in the elections of 1796 and 1800 — with disastrous consequences. In 1796, John Adams emerged as President with his political opponent, Thomas Jefferson, as his Vice President! In 1800, the election ended up with a contest for the top spot between Jefferson and his intended running-mate, Aaron Burr. Luckily, Jefferson won — but only after a lot of backstairs intrigue and horse-trading. For more on these early boo-boos, see Chapter 20.

Why did the Framers flunk so badly on the issue of presidential elections? The problem was their failure to recognize the importance of political parties. Parties were in an embryonic state when the Constitution in its original form was ratified in 1788, so the Framers can't really be blamed.

Rescuing the situation with the Twelfth Amendment

After the fiasco of the 1800 election, reform of the electoral system was urgently needed. The Twelfth Amendment, which was ratified just in time for the 1804 election, prevented the earlier anomalies from recurring. The Twelfth Amendment still didn't refer to political parties, but it tacitly recognized the role that parties played in the electoral process.

The system for electing the President is still governed by Article II, Section 1, subject to the Twelfth Amendment — at least in theory. The Framers of the Constitution didn't trust the ordinary people. So the system they set up was indirect election of the President by *electors,* whose title indicates their intended function: picking the President. The Twelfth Amendment didn't change this feature.

Examining the modern electoral system

Let's take a look at how the President gets elected today:

- **How many electors does each state get?** Each state chooses electors equal in number to the total of the representatives from that state plus the two senators from that state. So, for example, at present Florida has 27 electors because that state has 25 representatives and 2 senators. A state with a small population, like Wyoming, may have only one representative but, like all states, has two senators. So Wyoming is entitled to three electors.

- **Who elects the electors?** The Constitution leaves it up to each state legislature to decide how the electors for that state are chosen. Today, the electors are always directly elected. I discuss this point more in a minute.

- **What is the Electoral College?** The term *Electoral College* is commonly used to refer to the electors of all the states together. But the phrase *Electoral College* doesn't figure in the text of the Constitution. And the

Electoral College never meets together as a national body — only as 51 separate groups of electors (one for each state plus one for Washington, D.C., which has three electors).

✔ **What about the popular vote?** The real election — the vote by the people — doesn't rate a mention in the Constitution! The reason for this omission is that in the early days the people didn't get to vote for the President at all. The state legislatures would often choose the electors themselves, and the electors would then pick the President according to their own personal preferences. Democracy triumphed only through the rise of the party system, under which the voters in each state were presented with a slate of electors for each party. Voters picked the slate of the political party of their choice. The electors were *pledged* to support the presidential candidate of one or the other particular party. So, in choosing, say, the Republican slate, a voter was actually voting for the Republican presidential candidate.

✔ **What is the short ballot?** Nowadays, the whole Electoral College system is usually short-circuited. Most states use the so-called *short ballot,* which just shows the names of the presidential candidates themselves. Anonymous slates of electors still lurk behind the candidates' names, but the voters are given the impression — which is almost invariably correct — that they are picking the President directly themselves.

✔ **What happens when the electors meet?** The electors then meet in their respective states and formally cast their votes. They vote separately for the President and for the Vice President. But the whole of this stage of the election is a charade because the electors almost always vote for the candidates to whom they have pledged their support. Can an elector step out of line and refuse to vote for his pledged candidate? Sure, but it doesn't happen all that often. (In Chapter 20, I discuss the so-called *faithless elector.*)

✔ **Who tallies the formal vote count?** Each state certifies the number of votes cast by its electors for the different candidates. These certificates are sent to Washington, D.C. and are opened at a joint sitting of both houses of Congress. The electoral votes from all the states are then tallied up, and the official result is formally announced.

✔ **What happens if a candidate gets a majority?** If the presidential candidate with the most votes has more than 50 percent of the total number of electoral votes cast, that candidate becomes President. The same applies to the candidates for Vice President.

✔ **What happens if no presidential candidate gets a majority?** If the top-scoring presidential candidate doesn't receive a majority of electoral votes, or if two candidates tie, the election is thrown into the House of Representatives, which chooses the President from the three top-scoring candidates. Here each state has only one vote. To become President, a candidate needs 26 states to vote for him. This procedure has been used twice, in 1800 and 1824 — and should probably also have been used in 2000. This arrangement gives a great advantage to the smaller states. For example, it gives Alaska the same say as California, although under the normal Electoral College system Alaska has only 3 electoral votes to California's 55.

✔ **What happens if no vice-presidential candidate gets a majority?** If no vice-presidential candidate gets the requisite majority in the normal Electoral College process, the Senate picks the Vice President. Support from 51 out of the 100 senators is needed for victory.

Exploding some myths about the Electoral College

Presidential elections are so important that it would be surprising if they weren't surrounded by a few myths. The commonest myth is that the Electoral College system is by its very nature undemocratic. This fallacy is based on the assumption that the *winner-take-all* system, or plurality voting system, is a necessary part of the Electoral College system.

The winner-take-all arrangement sure is unfair because a difference of one vote out of millions can switch all the electoral votes of a state from one party's column to the other. Here's how the system works.

Let's take a hypothetical state with 12 electoral votes. In a presidential election, let's assume that 2,000,000 votes are cast for the Democratic ticket in that state and that the Republican ticket garners 1,999,999 votes — just one vote less. The winner-take-all arrangement dictates that in those circumstances all 12 electoral votes for that state stand in the Democratic column.

In that scenario, the winner at least has a majority — more than 50 percent — of the votes. But the same rule applies where the winner has only a *plurality*: less than 50 percent but more votes than any other candidate.

This doesn't look like a very fair outcome — and it also makes disputed elections and recounts much more likely. The close vote in Florida in the 2000 election is an excellent example of this problem.

The election result in our hypothetical state appears unsatisfactory, to say the least. But is that outcome the fault of the Electoral College system, as is generally assumed? No, the problem is caused not by the Electoral College system itself but by the winner-take-all arrangement that is associated with it. But, isn't winner-take-all part and parcel of the Electoral College system? The two systems are generally found together, but that isn't necessarily so.

The winner-take-all arrangement is

- ✔ Not a necessary part of the Electoral College system
- ✔ Not laid down by the Constitution
- ✔ Not used by all states

Explaining the Nebraska and Maine "district method"

Can you really have the Electoral College system without winner-take-all? Sure. Two states have already taken the step of separating these two features. These states are Nebraska and Maine, which allow the electoral vote to be shared between the parties in accordance with the proportion of the vote each party gets.

Maine has four electoral votes, based on its two congressmen plus its two senators. The state is divided into two congressional voting districts. Let's assume the following results in a hypothetical presidential election:

- ✔ Statewide vote: Democrat 60%, Republican 40%
- ✔ District 1: Democrat 80%, Republican 20%
- ✔ District 2: Democrat 40%, Republican 60%

In this hypothetical situation, the Nebraska–Maine "district method" gives two electoral votes to the Democratic ticket for winning the statewide popular vote, plus a third electoral vote for winning in District 1, while the Republicans pick up one electoral vote for winning in District 2. The overall result is then a 3:1 split of the electoral vote, instead of the winner-take-all approach which would give all four electoral votes to the Democrats.

Until 2008, neither Nebraska nor Maine had ever actually split its electoral votes because Nebraska was normally overwhelmingly Republican, while the Democrats have always had big majorities in Maine since the system was introduced there in 1972. However, in the 2008 presidential election, Senator Barack Obama, the Democratic Party candidate, was awarded one of Nebraska's five electoral votes, with the remaining four electoral votes going to Senator John McCain, the Republican flag-bearer.

A simpler version of this system was proposed for Colorado in 2004, but it was roundly rejected by an almost two-thirds majority of the voters. The proposal was for the state's electoral votes to be split in proportion to the votes cast for each ticket. So, if the Democrats received 55 percent of the votes and the Republicans received 45 percent, Colorado's nine electoral votes would have been split 5:4.

Those campaigning against the change argued that, because presidential elections in Colorado tend to be close, 4 of Colorado's 9 electoral votes would always go to the loser, so that Colorado's influence on the election would amount to only one electoral vote — 5 minus 4. The logic of this argument may be flawed, but it played well with Colorado voters.

On the basis of the Colorado experience, the winner-take-all method of calculating electoral votes looks set to survive as the dominant system for the foreseeable future.

But what about scrapping the Electoral College altogether and going to a pure nationwide popular vote system?

Picking the President by popular vote?

The biggest objection to the Electoral College system is that it has on four occasions — most recently in 2000 — denied victory to the winner of the popular vote. I must stress once again that these supposedly "stolen elections" were the product not of the Electoral College system itself but of the winner-take-all arrangement that is usually, but not necessarily, associated with it.

In the 2000 election, for example, George W. Bush *would* have been elected President with 273 electoral votes to 264 electoral votes for Al Gore if the electoral vote in each state had been split in proportion to the popular vote in that state. This was very much the same result as was finally certified in the actual election of 2000 — but it would have been done without the intervention of the U.S. Supreme Court!

Instead of the legal circus that actually occurred in 2000, under the Constitution the election ought to have been thrown into the House of Representatives. In that scenario, Bush would have won hands-down because he had 30 states in his column as against only 20 (plus the District of Columbia) for Gore.

However, on the basis of the popular vote alone, Gore would have won because he ended up with about 543,000 votes more than Bush. Scrapping the Electoral College altogether and replacing it with a pure popular vote system would require an amendment to the U.S. Constitution. What chance such an amendment would have of being adopted is hard to say, but it would face concerted opposition from those favoring states' rights, from the smaller states generally, and probably from most conservatives.

Although pure popular election looks simple, democratic, and modern, it has problems of its own. For example, would a plurality of the popular vote be enough to win the election, or would the winning candidate need to have a majority? If the latter, would there have to be a runoff election — or would the House of Representatives have to decide, as under the present system? I discuss the arguments for and against popular election in Chapter 20.

Canning the President

Firing a President — known as *impeachment* — is just as important as picking a President in the first place. So how come impeachment gets only this itsy-bitsy paragraph here dedicated to it? In fact, impeachment has a whole chapter of its own in this book: Chapter 13. Check it out.

Signing, Vetoing, and Pocketing Legislation

Article I, Section 7 of the Constitution gives the President an important power against Congress: the power to stop any bill passed by both houses of Congress from becoming law. This is known as the *presidential veto power,* although the word *veto* doesn't appear anywhere in the Constitution.

Here's a summary of how the President's veto power works.

- ✔ Every *bill* (proposed law) has to pass both the Senate and the House of Representatives by a majority in each house.
- ✔ After passing both houses, a bill is sent to the President for his approval.
- ✔ If the President approves the bill, he signs it, which makes it law — he *signs it into law.*
- ✔ If the President doesn't approve a bill, he can veto it by returning it unsigned to Congress with his objections.
- ✔ Congress then reconsiders the vetoed bill. A two-thirds majority in both houses is needed to override the President's veto.
- ✔ If the President has not returned a bill within ten days of it being sent to him, it becomes law anyway, without the President's signature.
- ✔ If the President doesn't sign the bill, and if Congress adjourns before the ten-day period is up, the bill doesn't become law. This provision is called the *pocket veto.*

A pocket veto is better for the President than an ordinary veto because a pocket veto kills a bill stone-dead. If Congress still wants the bill passed, the bill must start life again in the next session and go through the whole procedure from the beginning.

In the 1938 case of *Wright v. United States,* the Supreme Court approved the possibility of Congress appointing agents to send and receive messages on behalf of Congress during an adjournment, in order to stop the President from taking unfair advantage of the pocket veto rule. That practice is now routinely used. The agent is usually either the Clerk of the House of Representatives or the Secretary of the Senate, depending on the house where the bill originated.

Appointing Key Positions

Article II, Section 2 of the Constitution says that the President

> *shall nominate, and by and with the Advice and Consent of the Senate, shall appoint Ambassadors, other public Ministers and Consuls, judges of the supreme Court, and all other Officers of the United States, whose Appointments are not herein otherwise provided for, and which shall be established by Law.*

This provision gives the President the power to make a lot of important appointments: Supreme Court justices, other federal judges, Cabinet officers, and diplomats, to mention but a few. But all appointments are subject to the confirmation of the Senate. The Senate has blocked presidential appointments so frequently that the phrase "Advice and Dissent" is now often jocularly used instead of the phrase "Advice and Consent" that appears in the Constitution.

The Senate has sometimes exercised its power to advise and consent in such a way as to amount to a veto over the President's power to appoint qualified officials. This power has been exercised more savagely in recent times than previously. Besides actually voting a nomination down, the Senate can tie a nomination up in committee for so long that it has to be withdrawn, or senators seeking to block a nomination can keep talking indefinitely to stop a vote on the nomination from being taken — a technique known as a *filibuster*. Here are a few examples of these tactics:

- ✔ The Senate started blocking presidential appointments very early on. In 1795, by 14 votes to 10, the Senate voted down George Washington's nomination of John Rutledge as Chief Justice of the United States. This rebuff to Washington appears to have been motivated by a combination of opposition to Rutledge's political views and a feeling that he was mentally unstable.

- ✔ The degree of support enjoyed by a President in the Senate is an important factor determining how that body is likely to react to any particular nomination. Vice President John Tyler, who succeeded to the presidency on the death of the Whig President William Henry Harrison in 1841, had more of his nominees to the Supreme Court rejected by the Senate than any other President — four nominees, some of whom were rejected twice. The reason for this was that the Senate had a majority of Whigs, whom Tyler had angered by vetoing all their proposed legislation. He was then expelled from the Whig party and became known as "the man without a party."

✔ In 1987, the Senate rejected President Ronald Reagan's nomination of Judge Robert Bork by 58 votes to 42. Bork was extremely well-qualified for the appointment in terms of knowledge, intellect, and integrity. He was rejected because of his extremely conservative views on politics and on the role of the judiciary.

✔ Justice Clarence Thomas, nominated to a seat on the Supreme Court by President George H.W. Bush in 1991, was subjected to probably the most embarrassing hearings of any presidential nominee ever. Thomas faced opposition both on the grounds of his conservative views and because of allegations of sexual harassment leveled against him by Anita Hill, a former colleague of his at the U.S. Equal Employment Opportunity Commission. Thomas managed to weather the storm, and he was confirmed by the Senate by 52 votes to 48.

✔ The nomination by President George W. Bush of John Bolton, an outspoken conservative, as the Permanent U.S. Representative to the United Nations, was blocked in May 2005 by a Democratic Party filibuster in the Senate. The President appointed Bolton anyway while the Senate was in recess — which is specifically allowed under the Constitution as a temporary measure. Bush then renominated Bolton in 2006, but opponents kept a vote from being taken in the relevant Senate committee. Eventually, Bolton decided to step down when his recess appointment expired in December 2006.

Hailing the Chief: The President's Administration

Article II, Section 1 of the Constitution says, "The executive Power shall be vested in a President of the United States of America." *Executive power* means the power to enforce the law and to administer — or run — the government on a day-to-day basis. This provision gives the President power over all aspects of the federal government: financial issues, domestic affairs, and foreign affairs (not to mention military matters, which I discuss separately a little later in this chapter).

The Constitution is silent on the way that the President is expected to perform this mammoth task. In practice, the President operates through a vast administrative machine — hence the description of a President's period in office as his *administration*.

Faithfully executing the laws?

A throwaway clause tucked away in Article II, Section 3 of the Constitution requires that the President "shall take Care that the Laws be faithfully executed." What exactly does this mean? The President does not *make* law: His job is to *execute,* or enforce, the laws made by Congress.

Abraham Lincoln claimed that his duty as president to "take Care that the Laws be faithfully executed" allowed him to suspend *habeas corpus* — the right of a detained person to ask a court to release him or her from detention.

Lincoln also based his decision to suspend habeas corpus on the presidential oath of office, as laid down in Article II, Section 1 of the Constitution, in which the new President swears that he "will to the best of my Ability,

preserve, protect and defend the Constitution of the United States."

In the leading case known as *Ex parte Merryman,* decided in 1861, Chief Justice Roger Taney (sitting as a federal circuit judge) ruled that Lincoln's suspension of habeas corpus was unconstitutional. Lincoln ignored the ruling.

Article I, Section 9 of the Constitution provides, "The Privilege of the Writ of Habeas Corpus shall not be suspended, unless when in Cases of Rebellion or Invasion the public Safety may require it." But who has the right to suspend habeas corpus? The fact that this section forms part of Article I, which deals with Congress, probably means that the power to suspend habeas corpus can be exercised only by Congress, with presidential consent, and not by the President alone.

Uncovering the secrets of Cabinet secretaries

The President's chief lieutenants in running his huge empire are his Cabinet secretaries, including the Secretary of State, Secretary of Defense, Secretary of the Treasury, Secretary of the Interior, and Secretary of Homeland Security.

What's with this title of *secretary*? It makes these high officers of state sound like jumped-up typists. The title of *secretary* originated in England, where the Secretary of State was originally the King's private secretary — and the word *secretary* reflected the fact that this office-holder really was the keeper of confidential information.

The secret about U.S. Cabinet secretaries is that their activities are not secret. The President *does* also have some more personal and more confidential advisers — in the Executive Office of the President, which I discuss a bit later in this chapter.

The Tenure of Office Act

In 1867, Congress passed the Tenure of Office Act over the veto of President Andrew Johnson. This act required the President to obtain the consent of the Senate for the removal of any Cabinet officer — which had never been the case before.

The reason for the passing of this law was that President Johnson and Congress didn't see eye to eye. Johnson succeeded to the presidency on the death of Abraham Lincoln in 1865 and kept Lincoln's Cabinet in place. But Johnson soon fell out with Cabinet members, in particular with Secretary of War Edwin Stanton.

Johnson attempted to fire Stanton in breach of the Tenure of Office Act. Stanton barricaded himself in his office with the support of the radical Republicans in Congress, who proceeded to impeach Johnson. The President was acquitted by a single vote in the Senate. The Tenure of Office Act was repealed in 1887, and a similar law was declared unconstitutional by the U.S. Supreme Court in 1926.

Article II, Section 2 contains the only reference to the Cabinet officers in the original, unamended Constitution:

> [The President] may require the Opinion, in writing, of the principal Officer in each of the executive Departments, upon any Subject relating to the Duties of their respective Offices.

This cryptic provision raises more questions than it answers. Does this brief clause envision a Cabinet at all, or just several separate government departments doing their own thing? And what's with "may require the Opinion, in writing"? Is that the only way that the President can communicate with his own Cabinet secretaries? What about Cabinet meetings? And can't the President give instructions to his Cabinet officers?

The Framers were probably in a hurry to go out to lunch when they drafted this baffling snippet, which is both too vague and too precise at the same time — if that makes any sense!

In practice, presidents have not been hamstrung by this curious clause. Some Presidents have given their Cabinet officers a free hand, while others have tried to micromanage the whole enchilada.

Cabinet officers — and in particular Secretaries of State — were much more important in the early days than they are today. In the first 60 years of the Republic, no fewer than six Secretaries of State made it to the presidency, starting with Thomas Jefferson and ending with James Buchanan. Since then, not a single President has come from the ranks of the Secretaries of State.

Here's a quick rundown of some important facts about Cabinet officers, most of whom (fortunately!) don't hit the headlines that often:

- ✔ **How do you become a Cabinet officer?** The President can appoint whomever he likes to his Cabinet — subject to confirmation by the Senate. The Senate doesn't usually give the President as hard a time over Cabinet appointments as over his nomination of Supreme Court justices.

- ✔ **How do Cabinet officers get fired?** The President doesn't have to consult the Senate or anybody else if he wants to fire a Cabinet secretary. This has not always been the legal position, as I explain in the nearby sidebar "The Tenure of Office Act."

- ✔ **What do Cabinet officers do?** Each Cabinet officer heads up a department of the federal government. For example, the Secretary of State, the most important Cabinet member, is in charge of foreign affairs. He or she is the boss of all ambassadors and ministers representing the United States in foreign countries. The Secretary of Defense is responsible for the whole defense establishment.

- ✔ **Where do Cabinet officers figure in the presidential succession?** The importance of Cabinet officers is recognized by their presence in the order of succession on the death, resignation, or removal of the President. The Presidential Succession Act of 1947 places the Vice President in first position, followed by the Speaker of the House of Representatives and the President Pro Tempore of the Senate. But then comes the Secretary of State and all the other Cabinet secretaries in the order of seniority of their offices — so the Secretary of Homeland Security is last in line, because that office was created only in 2003. I discuss the question of succession to the presidency more fully in Chapter 22.

Unmasking the imperial presidency

The Founders took a lot of flak for creating what some critics saw as a monarchy. George Washington was often addressed as "Your Excellency," although he preferred the simpler, more republican-style "Mr. President," which became the normal form of address for all later Presidents — except when they were being mocked. (John Adams was referred to as "His Rotundity" for being short and fat, and John Tyler was ridiculed as "His Accidency" for being the first Vice President to succeed to the Presidency as a result of the previous President's death.)

With a few notable exceptions — Andrew Jackson, Abraham Lincoln, and Theodore Roosevelt — the President's power rarely outmatched that of Congress in the period before the election of Franklin Delano Roosevelt in 1932. But then the power of the presidency rapidly escalated. On the basis of the Great Depression followed by World War II, FDR established what is sometimes called an "imperial presidency": a presidency with far greater powers than were envisioned by the Framers of the Constitution.

Unlocking the Executive Office of the President

The Executive Office of the President (EOP) first came into existence in 1939 and now comprises a staff of about 1,800 people who are directly responsible to the President. Staff in the EOP have the title "Assistant to the President" or "Special Assistant to the President." Senior officials in the EOP include the White House Chief of Staff and the White House Press Secretary. Most staff on the EOP don't have to be confirmed by the Senate — which is a great boon to presidents.

For national security and foreign policy matters, presidents now rely to a great extent on the National Security Council (NSC), which is part of the EOP. The NSC was first set up during the presidency of Harry Truman in 1947. The President chairs this august body himself. Meetings of the NSC are regularly attended by Cabinet officers such as the Secretary of State, the Secretary of Defense, and the Secretary of the Treasury, as well as by the Vice President. However, the NSC, together with the White House Situation Room, is run by the National Security Adviser, who is directly responsible to the President. (This position's formal title is Assistant to the President for National Security.)

The Secretary of State as policy-maker

Some Presidents have allowed their Cabinet officers more latitude and independence than others. Secretaries of State who stand out as major policy-makers include:

✔ William Henry Seward, who served under presidents Abraham Lincoln and Andrew Johnson.

✔ Elihu Root, who served under presidents William McKinley and Theodore Roosevelt as Secretary of Defense and later as Secretary of State, and who was awarded the Nobel Peace Prize in 1912.

✔ Cordell Hull, who served as FDR's Secretary of State for 11 years, making him the longest-serving Secretary of State in U.S. history. Despite being blamed for denying 900 Jewish refugees entry into the United States in 1939, Hull was awarded the Nobel Peace Prize in 1945.

✔ General George Marshall, who served as Secretary of State and later as Secretary of Defense under Harry Truman. He was the author of the European Recovery Program— known as the *Marshall Plan*—in the immediate aftermath of World War II. He was awarded the Nobel Peace Prize in 1953.

✔ John Foster Dulles, Secretary of State under President Dwight D. Eisenhower. He is the only Cabinet officer to have an airport named for him — the Washington Dulles International Airport.

✔ Henry Kissinger, who served as Secretary of State under presidents Richard Nixon and Gerald Ford — a colorful and rather controversial character who was awarded the Nobel Peace Prize in 1973.

The Homeland Security Council (HSC) was established by President George W. Bush in the wake of the 9/11 terrorist outrages in 2001. It mirrors the NSC on the domestic front. Like the NSC, the HSC forms part of the EOP and is chaired by the President himself. As with the NSC, the HSC is under a non-Cabinet official, in this case the Assistant to the President for Homeland Security and Counterterrorism.

Why aren't the NSC and the HSC under Cabinet officers, the Secretary of State and the Secretary of Homeland Security respectively? Because it suits the President to keep more direct control of these important bodies by chairing their meetings himself and by placing their day-to-day running under hand-picked "Assistants to the President" — who, if need be, can also be used as counterweights to overambitious or unduly independent Cabinet secretaries.

Selling the President's legislative program

In spite of the separation of powers, the President is inevitably involved in legislation. The President's approval is needed for a law to be passed by Congress. But modern presidents do not just wait around for Congress to propose legislation: The President has his own legislative program as well.

The President used to connect with Congress through the Bureau of the Budget or the Office of White House Counsel. However, in 1953 President Dwight Eisenhower formalized the relationship between the executive and legislative branches by establishing a Legislative Affairs Office in the White House.

This arrangement still survives today, with a permanent Legislative Affairs Office of about 12 members under the Office of Management and Budget, which forms part of the Executive Office of the President. One of the tasks of the Legislative Affairs Office is to produce Statements of Administration Policy (SAPs) addressed to a house of Congress that set out the President's views on a particular bill or issue. During the second session of the 110th Congress alone, in 2008–2009, no fewer than 88 SAPs were issued.

Most modern presidents have recognized the importance of liaison with Congress for the implementation of the President's legislative program. Even before taking office, President Barack Obama named Phil Schiliro as Assistant to the President for Legislative Affairs, or simply the Director of Legislative Affairs.

Presidents have also employed more direct methods of persuasion in respect to policies dear to their hearts. The use of President Lyndon Johnson's famed "Johnson Method" of twisting the arms of recalcitrant lawmakers came into its own in the push to have the Civil Rights Act signed into law in 1964. Bill

Clinton appointed an "Intensive Care Unit" to promote the President's abortive healthcare reform package in Congress. President George W. Bush had a hard time selling what became the Medicare Modernization Act to lawmakers in 2003.

At the time of this writing, healthcare reform is a top priority with the Obama administration, second only to ending the war in Iraq and tackling the economic recession. The direct involvement of the President in healthcare reform is now taken for granted.

President Obama's financial "bailout" plan — an extension of one first proposed by President George W. Bush in 2008 — and a major economic stimulus package together represent the closest involvement a President has had in legislation regulating the economy since FDR's New Deal in the 1930s. It remains to be seen what effect, if any, this development has on the relative power exercised by the President and by Congress.

Battling Executive Privilege

The President has long claimed *executive privilege,* the right to withhold information from the courts or from Congress. The expressed ground for this claim is national security, or else the need for confidentiality within the executive branch. The claim of executive privilege is ultimately based on the doctrine of the separation of powers, under which the three branches of government — the executive, the legislature, and the judiciary — are kept separate in terms of membership. (But there is a certain amount of overlap in function for the purpose of checks and balances.) I discuss the separation of powers in Chapter 8.

Claiming executive privilege in the early days

The Constitution doesn't say anything about executive privilege. The term "executive privilege" was coined by President Dwight D. Eisenhower in the 1950s, but the right was first claimed by President George Washington himself.

Washington invoked this right in 1796 by denying a request from the House of Representatives for documents relating to the so-called Jay Treaty with Britain. Washington gave the documents to the Senate but not to the House, on the ground that the Constitution gives the Senate, but not the House, the power to ratify treaties.

The next attempt to use executive privilege resulted in a presidential climb-down. This occurred when the U.S. Supreme Court ordered President Thomas Jefferson to produce private letters about former Vice President Aaron Burr, who was tried for treason in 1807. Jefferson reserved "the necessary right of the President of the United States to decide, independently of all other authority, what papers coming to him as President the public interest permits to be communicated, and to whom." Jefferson expressed willingness to turn over the letters in question, but not in response to a court order, because, under the principle of the separation of powers, the President was independent of the courts.

Chief Justice John Marshall, who was Jefferson's spiteful distant cousin, ruled that the President had to obey the court order. Jefferson did so, and in so doing allowed Marshall to strike a major blow in favor of the power of the court. Marshall turned the knife yet further with one of his characteristic "twistifications of the law" (Jefferson's phrase) by defining treason so narrowly that Burr — another of Jefferson's enemies — had to be acquitted.

Achieving a total blowout against President Nixon

The most serious blow to executive privilege was administered by the Supreme Court against President Richard Nixon. In 1972, seven White House aides were indicted in connection with a break-in at the Democratic National Committee offices in the Watergate building in Washington D.C. Special Watergate prosecutor Leon Jaworski subpoenaed the tape recordings of 64 of Nixon's conversations. The President contended that the special prosecutor couldn't sue him and that the request was for "confidential conversations between a President and his close advisers that it would be inconsistent with the public interest to produce."

A unanimous Supreme Court (without Justice William Rehnquist, who recused himself because of his friendship with Richard Nixon) ordered the President to hand over the tapes. Chief Justice Warren Burger, writing for the court, rejected the absolute privilege claimed by Nixon but admitted the existence of a qualified executive privilege: "The President's need for complete candor and objectivity from advisers calls for great deference from the courts." But, added Burger, executive privilege had to be based on "a claim of need to protect military, diplomatic, or sensitive national security secrets."

Balancing recent claims of justice against executive privilege

President Bill Clinton crossed swords with the courts over his affair with intern Monica Lewinsky. Clinton unwisely invoked executive privilege in refusing to allow his aides to be called to testify about the affair. Clinton lost. A federal judge ruled that the aides could be called.

Clinton later agreed to waive executive privilege and testify before a grand jury himself — but only under certain conditions. In the words of independent counsel Kenneth W. Starr, "Absolutely no one is above the law." On the basis of evidence collected by Starr, Clinton became only the second President to be subjected to impeachment proceedings. (However, he was acquitted and served out the remainder of his second term. He left office in January 2001 with a 65 percent approval rating, the highest end-of-term rating of any President since Dwight D. Eisenhower 40 years earlier.)

President George W. Bush's administration also got involved in some battles over executive privilege. For example, the administration claimed executive privilege in declining to disclose information about Vice President Dick Cheney's energy taskforce. In the 2004 case *Cheney v. U.S. District Court for the District of Columbia,* the Supreme Court ruled in favor of the administration. Here's an extract from the 7-to-2 ruling:

> *While the President is not above the law, the Judiciary must afford Presidential confidentiality the greatest possible protection, recognizing the paramount necessity of protecting the Executive Branch from vexatious litigation that might distract it from the energetic performance of its constitutional duties.*

President George W. Bush also invoked executive privilege over the firing of eight federal prosecutors. The administration refused to comply with a Senate Judiciary Committee subpoena requiring presidential advisers to testify before the committee. However, quite a number of Justice Department officials resigned — including Attorney General Alberto Gonzales.

The Bush administration also claimed executive privilege in relation to the death in Afghanistan — by "friendly fire" — of popular football player Pat Tillman, who had passed up a football contract offer of $3.6 million over three years to enlist in the U.S. army.

Supreme Court Justice Anthony Kennedy identified the central problem in regard to claims of executive privilege:

> *Once executive privilege is asserted, coequal branches of the Government are set on a collision course. The Judiciary is forced into the difficult task of balancing the need for information in a judicial proceeding and the Executive's Article II prerogatives. This inquiry places courts in the awkward position of evaluating the Executive's claims of confidentiality and autonomy, and pushes to the fore difficult questions of separation of powers and checks and balances.*

This statement recognizes executive privilege as lurking within Article II of the Constitution. But the bottom line is that the Supreme Court has given itself the right to decide the limits of the President's powers — and of its own powers. Can that be what the Framers of the Constitution intended? See Chapter 12 on the judiciary for more discussion.

Making War versus Declaring War

The Founders clearly intended to split responsibility for national defense between the President and Congress. Article II, Section 1 gives the President total executive power. This broad power links up with Article II, Section 2, which says:

> *The President shall be Commander in Chief of the Army and Navy of the United States, and of the Militia of the several States, when called into the actual Service of the United States.*

The problem is how the two passages relate to Article I, Section 8, which gives Congress the Power

> *To declare War . . .;*
>
> *To raise and support Armies, but no Appropriation of Money to that Use shall be for a longer Term than two Years;*
>
> *To provide and maintain a Navy;*
>
> *To make Rules for the Government and Regulation of the land and naval Forces;*
>
> *To provide for calling forth the Militia to execute the Laws of the Union, suppress Insurrections and repel Invasions;*
>
> *To provide for organizing, arming, and disciplining the Militia, and for governing such Part of them as may be employed in the Service of the United States, reserving to the States respectively, the Appointment of the Officers, and the Authority of training the Militia according to the discipline prescribed by Congress.*

Don't forget, the Founders were well-bred 18th-century gentlemen who would have regarded war between nations as a sort of polite parlor game played by the rules of international diplomacy. So, step 1 must be a formal declaration of war by Congress. Step 2 is the raising of an army, again by Congress. Step 3 is the calling out of the militia. It's only when you get to Step 4, the actual conduct of the war, that the President becomes involved as Commander in Chief by deciding on strategy and tactics and leading the troops into battle.

The first five full-scale international wars that the United States was involved in were all initiated with a formal declaration of war passed by Congress. These wars are the following:

- ✔ The War of 1812 against Great Britain
- ✔ The Mexican–American War of 1846–1848
- ✔ The Spanish–American War of 1898
- ✔ World War I, in which the United States was involved from 1917 to 1918
- ✔ World War II, which for the United States lasted from 1941 to 1945

Controlling the President through the War Powers Act of 1973

After World War II, the United States became involved in the Korean War in 1950 without any declaration of war. President Harry Truman relied on United Nations resolutions as a justification for U.S. involvement and never sought congressional authorization.

Some members of Congress weren't happy about this bypassing of Congress on the part of the President. The Vietnam War, which lasted from 1964 to 1973, aroused much fiercer resentment in Congress.

So, in 1973 Congress passed the War Powers Act, providing that

> *The constitutional powers of the President as Commander-in-Chief to introduce United States Armed Forces into hostilities, or into situations where imminent involvement in hostilities is clearly indicated by the circumstances, are exercised only pursuant to (1) a declaration of war , (2) specific statutory authorization, or (3) a national emergency created by attack upon the United States, its territories or possessions, or its armed forces.*

If any troops are already engaged, the President must pull them out within 60 days

> *unless the Congress (1) has declared war or has enacted a specific authorization for such use of United States Armed Forces, (2) has extended*

by law such sixty-day period, or (3) is physically unable to meet as a result of an armed attack upon the United States.

The Act goes on to say that, "notwithstanding" the 60-day rule,

any time that United States Armed Forces are engaged in hostilities outside the territory of the United States without a declaration of war or specific statutory authorization, such forces shall be removed by the President if the Congress so directs by concurrent resolution.

It's worth noting that this act was vetoed by President Richard Nixon, but his veto was overridden by a two-thirds majority in both houses of Congress.

Every President since 1973 has declared the War Powers Act unconstitutional — yet they have all been careful to comply with its requirements.

Preventing presidential precedents?

If every President has recognized the War Powers Act in practice while rejecting it as unconstitutional, who has the correct interpretation of the Constitution in this respect, the President or Congress? The answer is that both are partly right.

And, if presidents for the past 35 years have all complied with the Act, why do they need to reject its validity? In order to free themselves from a law that limits presidential power. If the President admits that the act is constitutional, then all presidential actions complying with it since 1973 automatically become legally binding precedents subordinating the President to Congress.

Congress's case in favor of the constitutionality of the War Powers Act is, as is stated in Section 2(a) of the act itself, that the act fulfills "the intent of the framers of the Constitution of the United States" to "insure that the collective judgment of both the Congress and the President will apply to the introduction of United States Armed Forces into hostilities."

The President's position is exactly the opposite. Here is a statement of the constitutional position as seen from the President's point of view, taken from a 2003 legal brief from the administration of President George W. Bush:

The Constitution vests the President with full "executive Power," and designates him "Commander in Chief" of the Armed Forces. Together, these provisions are a substantive grant of broad war power that authorizes the President to unilaterally use military force in defense of the United States' national security.

The main difference between the President's position and that of Congress is that the President interprets his constitutional powers as Commander in Chief broadly, while Congress adopts a narrow interpretation of these powers.

The President's role as Commander in Chief must surely mean that the President is in charge of military operations. To that extent the presidential approach is correct.

But the power of the Commander in Chief appears from the Constitution to be triggered by a declaration of war, the deployment of troops, and the summoning of the militia (or nowadays, of the National Guard) — all of which are functions entrusted by the Constitution to Congress and not to the President.

Perhaps the most important provision in the War Powers Act is the recognition that insisting on a declaration of war or even congressional authorization is unrealistic and unnecessary in the event of "a national emergency created by attack upon the United States."

Chapter 11

Giving Everyone a Voice: The House of Representatives and Senate

- -

- -

*T*he United States may be a democracy, but that doesn't mean that "We the People" get to directly elect every branch of the government. Citizens don't vote for Supreme Court justices, for example, and even the President is elected indirectly through that thing called the *Electoral College* (which I discuss in Chapter 10).

Where your vote has the most direct effect is in the legislative branch of government: the House of Representatives and the Senate. But I'd bet serious money that the vast majority of U.S. citizens can't name both senators currently representing their state plus the House representative elected from their district. Can you?

In this chapter, I explore the responsibilities of both houses of Congress. By the time I'm done, I hope you'll have a better understanding of just how important your vote can be and why, if you couldn't tick off the names of your senators and representative just now, you may want to get to know these folks a little better.

Making the Laws That Govern the Land

Article I, Section 1 of the Constitution states:

> *All legislative Powers herein granted shall be vested in a Congress of the United States, which shall consist of a Senate and House of Representatives.*

In a nutshell, this means that Congress has the power to create all federal laws. It can't do so in a vacuum — the President gets a say as well — but all laws are birthed in the two houses of Congress. Later in the chapter, in the section "Passing Legislation," I explain in detail the steps Congress takes to draft a bill, debate and modify it, and pass it into law.

One function, two houses

The fact that there are two houses of Congress means that it is *bicameral* — a word you probably learned in middle school. The Senate is sometimes referred to as the *upper house* and the House as the *lower house,* but the Constitution doesn't use these designations.

Why a bicameral legislature? George Washington supposedly explained the reasoning like this to Thomas Jefferson, who was pouring his tea into a saucer before drinking it. "Why did you do that?" Washington asked. "To cool it," came the reply. "Exactly so," explained Washington. "We pour the House legislation into the Senatorial saucer to cool it." The implication was that the House tended to be more partisan while the Senate was more of a deliberative body. Washington's observation still holds true today (because there are fewer senators than representatives, because senators serve longer terms than representatives, and because Senate rules are somewhat more relaxed).

Strictly speaking, the term *congressman* or *congresswoman* should apply to a member of either house, but in practice it is used only for members of the House, who are also referred to as *representatives.* Members of the Senate are referred to only as *senators.* Each house is a bit coy when referring to the other. Each stops short of ignoring the other house altogether but never refers to it by name, calling it instead "the other body."

Keeping the President in the loop

Do the two houses of Congress have the power to pass any laws as long as they both agree? A federal law is known as an *Act of Congress,* and every Act of Congress starts with the formula "Be it enacted by the Senate and House of Representatives of the United States in Congress assembled."

Who gets to elect the House?

Since the day the Constitution was enacted, "the People" have had the right to elect the House of Representatives. But which people have that right? The Constitution isn't particularly helpful on that point. All it says is this, in Article I, Section 2:

The House of Representatives shall be composed of Members chosen every second Year by the People of the several States, and the Electors in each State shall have the Qualifications requisite for Electors of the most numerous Branch of the State Legislature.

This seems a surprisingly vague and roundabout provision. But there is a reason for the murkiness. The right to vote in federal elections is based on the right to vote in state elections, and this right is left to the states to decide.

In the early days, voting rights were not uniform across the country; they varied from state to state. Hence the provision that the right to vote for the House of Representatives would go to everyone entitled to vote for "the most numerous Branch of the State Legislature." (This is the lower house in those states — all except Nebraska — that have a *bicameral* or two-house legislature. In 41 states, the lower house is called the House of Representatives, in five states it's called the Assembly, and in three it's called the House of Delegates.)

Today, voting rights for the upper house, or state senate, are exactly the same as those for the lower house, but this was not always the case. Originally, voting rights for the lower house were more liberal.

What about the President? Doesn't he play a role in legislation? Yes, he most certainly does. His approval is needed before a *bill* (a proposed law) can become an Act of Congress. He must respond to a bill within ten days (not counting Sundays) because if he doesn't the bill becomes law automatically. The President can veto any bill, and Article I, Section 7 states that his veto can be overridden only by a two-thirds majority of both houses. Also, in practice many bills nowadays originate from the White House rather than from the *Capitol* (the building occupied by Congress). So it turns out that Congress does not have *all* legislative power after all.

Visiting the People's House

The two houses of Congress are equal under the Constitution, and both are needed for a law to be made, but each house has special features and functions that are not shared with the other. In this section, I walk you through the particulars of the House of Representatives.

Representing the U.S. population

The House of Representatives has always been directly elected by the people (unlike the Senate, as I explain later in the chapter). Therefore, it's known as "the people's house." Since 1911 (except for the period from 1959 to 1963), the *House* (as it's commonly referred to) has had 435 voting representatives. The present makeup of the House is

- ✔ 435 representatives from the 50 states
- ✔ Non-voting delegates (one each) from Washington, D.C. and the territories of American Samoa, Guam, and the U.S. Virgin Islands
- ✔ A Resident Commissioner from Puerto Rico

There's roughly one representative for every 647,000 U.S. residents (based on the census of the year 2000). Keep in mind I'm talking about *population* here, not the number of voters.

Because representation is based on a state's population, it's possible for a state to gain or lose representatives as its population changes. These gains or losses take place during the *reapportionment* of House seats, which happens every ten years based on the U.S. Census. In 2000, for example, four states gained an extra two representatives each, two states lost two seats each, and quite a few states either gained or lost one seat.

Although House seats are based on population, each state is entitled to at least one representative, no matter how small it is. Wyoming has way below 647,000 inhabitants but still has one representative in the House.

Respecting the power of the Speaker

The Framers of the Constitution make only one mention of the important office of Speaker of the House: "The House of Representatives shall chuse their Speaker and other Officers." They probably didn't think it was necessary to write a job description because the position was already familiar from colonial times and from the British Constitution, which says that the Speaker presides over debates without being allowed to participate in them.

The Speaker of the British House of Commons remains studiously neutral and has practically no political power. By contrast, the Speaker of the House of Representatives has an armory of powers, just about the least of them being the right to participate in debate and to vote — which is rarely exercised, except on constitutional amendments or other really important issues.

The Speaker comes immediately after the Vice President in the line of succession to the presidency. This chain of succession isn't in the Constitution itself but in the Presidential Succession Act of 1947. Some people have questioned the constitutionality of this provision, but it has never been tested because no Speaker has ever succeeded to the presidency.

Redistricting and gerrymandering

Each of the 435 representatives in the House represents a voting district, referred to by state and number. For example, Speaker Nancy Pelosi represents the eighth Congressional District of California, which covers most of San Francisco. As populations shift, congressional voting districts sometimes have to shift as well. Otherwise, a district may be home to too many or too few residents to be represented by a single member of the House.

In 36 states, redistricting is done by the state legislature, mostly subject to the approval of the governor. Seven states have handed this important power to an independent bipartisan commission, though in two of these states the state legislature has the final say. The remaining seven states have only one representative each, so the problem doesn't arise.

The term *gerrymander* is the dubious legacy of Elbridge Gerry, who was governor of Massachusetts from 1810—1813 and Vice President from 1813—1814. Gerry proposed a redistricting bill for Massachusetts that blatantly favored his own Democratic-Republican party. One narrow, elongated district so resembled a lizard that it prompted someone to remark "Salamander?" To which a wag retorted, "No, gerrymander." The name stuck, and Gerry went down to defeat for reelection as state governor.

There has been no shortage of charges of gerrymandering over the years. The object is to maximize the number of seats won by your own party without wasting too many votes. Two techniques of gerrymandering have been identified:

✔ Where the opposition party has a comfortable majority in a particular district, you add more opposition-dominated counties to it so that the opposition has, if possible, an 80 percent or 90 percent majority in that district. This strategy is called *packing*. The opposition party would carry that district anyway, but now a lot of its votes are wasted because it needs only a simple majority (50+ percent) to win. By packing an opposition-controlled district, you don't waste too many of your own party's votes.

✔ Next comes *cracking,* which is redistricting so that your party has a comfortable but not overwhelming majority in as many seats as possible. You *crack* a minority of opposition voters into those districts so that those votes are wasted without wasting too many of your own party's.

The Supreme Court has found that the Fourteenth Amendment, which I discuss in Chapter 21, provides some protection against gerrymandering. However, in a 2004 decision, the Supreme Court found that claims related to political (but not racial) gerrymandering cannot be resolved by the court.

Presiding over debates, or not

The role of Speaker of the House has developed into one of the most powerful in the U.S. system of government. As is so often the case, the Speaker's true position is attributable more to party politics than to constitutional law. The Speaker is the presiding officer of the House, but that's just the start.

The function of actually presiding over debates is usually delegated to a representative of the Speaker's choosing. During debates, whoever is presiding is addressed as "Mr. Speaker" or "Madam Speaker," except when the House resolves itself into a *Committee of the Whole* — which is a fancy way of saying that the House considers itself to be a committee for the purpose of making changes (*amendments*) to bills. When that happens, the Speaker passes the gavel to another presiding officer, who is addressed as "Mr. Chairman" or "Madam Chairman." For important debates, the presiding officer will be a senior member of the majority party, but for routine debates it could be quite a junior representative.

The presiding officer decides who to *recognize,* meaning who to allow to speak in debates. He or she also rules on points of order, though such rulings can be appealed to the whole House. (Joseph Gurney Cannon, who served as Speaker from 1903 to 1911, ruled the House with an iron fist and supposedly recognized only the representatives he liked.)

Leading the House's majority party

The Speaker's most important role is as leader of the majority party in the House. (The House Majority Leader, who is subordinate to the Speaker, assists the Speaker in persuading the representatives of the majority party to support the party's legislative program.) Because the Constitution doesn't recognize the existence of political parties (see Chapter 10), it's not surprising that the Speaker's true role isn't even mentioned. But from this strong partisan base, the Speaker's power and influence flow.

The Speaker's chief concern is to make sure that the majority party's program is passed into law. The Speaker's influence extends to deciding which bill is considered when. Subject to the approval of the majority party's *conference* or *caucus* (a body made up of all representatives belonging to that party), the Speaker chooses 9 of the 13 members of the powerful Rules Committee (the other 4 coming from the minority party). The Rules Committee controls amendments, debate, and timetabling. Here's what I mean:

- ✔ **Amendments** are changes to a bill on its way to becoming an Act of Congress, or a law. These changes can be very important, and no bill goes through unchanged. Representatives propose amendments to bills. The Rules Committee sifts through these proposals and decides which amendments should be allowed to be considered by the whole House.

- ✔ **Debate,** or discussion, on a bill happens before the House votes on it. Representatives try to persuade their fellow members to vote either in favor of a bill or against it. Debate in the House is not unlimited (in contrast with the Senate, which I discuss later in this chapter). The Rules Committee decides on the limits in the scope and time available for debate on any particular bill.

✔ **Timetabling** is important because the fate of a bill may depend on the amount of time allowed for its debate. If the majority party leadership wants a bill passed quickly and without much publicity, the Rules Committee may allocate little or no debate time to it. But if the majority party leadership wants to create a big publicity campaign in favor of a bill, they are more likely to arrange a liberal debate schedule for it.

So by controlling the Rules Committee, the majority party and the Speaker have a stranglehold over the House.

Dancing with the President

When the White House is occupied by a president of the same party as the Speaker, the Speaker tends to defer to the President. But when the Speaker and President are from opposite parties, the Speaker can become essentially the leader of the opposition. For example, Speaker Tip O'Neill openly opposed President Ronald Reagan's domestic and defense policies; President Bill Clinton came up against a formidable foe in Speaker Newt Gingrich; and Speaker Nancy Pelosi took a strong line against President George W. Bush.

But being members of the same party doesn't guarantee harmony either. At the start of the 20th century, Speaker Joseph ("Uncle Joe") Gurney Cannon didn't get on well with fellow Republican President Teddy Roosevelt, who was described by the Speaker as having "no more use for the Constitution than a tomcat has for a marriage license."

Controlling the nation's purse strings

The House is in charge of the nation's finances — an enormous responsibility in a nation whose budget is in the trillions, and reason enough for you to get familiar with the person representing your home district. You wouldn't just hand your wallet over to a stranger in the grocery store and say, "I need some food. Can you buy it for me?" The U.S. government buys lots of things on your behalf — infrastructure, public education, the military — so it makes sense to know who's collecting your money to make those purchases.

Here's what Article I, Section 7 of the Constitution says about this responsibility:

All Bills for raising Revenue shall originate in the House of Representatives; but the Senate may propose or concur with Amendments as on other Bills.

The first half of this provision means that the House alone can originate tax legislation, but the second half ensures that the Senate has influence as well.

Why does the House get first dibs at crafting tax-related legislation? The Framers of the Constitution didn't forget the slogan that led to U.S. independence in the first place: "No taxation without representation." For the Senate to initiate tax bills would be unfair because in the Senate small states are over-represented in terms of their population and big states are underrepresented. The Framers knew that "the people's house" should have the principal voice in deciding how much of the people's money the government can claim.

But just because the House gets it paws on revenue legislation first doesn't mean the Senate is in a weak position. The power to add amendments to legislation is crucial. The reality is that when the Senate receives revenue legislation, it can add new provisions, change tax rates — alter it as much as its members (at least a majority of them) deem appropriate.

The flip side of raising money is spending it, which occurs thanks to *appropriation* bills: bills authorizing the spending of federal funds. The Constitution doesn't specify that the House is solely responsible for originating those bills, so in theory, they could originate in the Senate as well. And sometimes they do. However, the House wants to keep the upper hand in all financial legislation, so when the Senate does send it an appropriations bill, that bill usually gets ignored.

Deciding disputed presidential elections

The House also has another special power that the Senate doesn't: the right to decide disputed presidential elections. The Twelfth Amendment, ratified in 1804, states that if no candidate has a majority of electoral votes, the election is taken to the House of Representatives. As I explain in Chapter 10, it's not enough for a winning candidate to have a plurality of electoral votes; that person must receive an absolute majority of more than 50 percent.

The House has exercised this power on two occasions: in 1800 (to elect Thomas Jefferson) and in 1824 (to elect John Quincy Adams). In 1876, in the midst of highly disputed election results, it delegated its power to an Electoral Commission, which ushered Rutherford B. Hayes into power.

Some people think the House should have been asked to decide the election of 2000, which instead was decided by the U.S. Supreme Court. The House gets involved in deciding a presidential election only after all the states have certified their election results. But in 2000, the presidential candidates rushed to court over the Florida election result before it was certified. So the House never got a look-in.

A couple of flaws exist with the House's power to decide a disputed election:

✔ Each House member gets one vote. That may seem fair because the number of representatives in a state is determined by the state's population. The problem is that this system differs from the Electoral College system, which lets each state have as many votes as it has senators and representatives. In other words, a state with a small population (and only one representative in the House), like Alaska or Vermont, gets three votes in the Electoral College. But that same state gets only a single vote if the disputed election goes to the House.

✔ The House has the power to choose the President, but the Senate has the power to choose the Vice President. If the two houses are controlled by different parties, this could result in having a Republican President and a Democratic Vice President, or vice versa.

Why does this flaw exist? The Framers of the Constitution failed to appreciate the importance of political parties. As a result, Thomas Jefferson served as Vice President under John Adams, who belonged to a different party. Difficult as that situation was 200 years ago, it would be a serious problem in today's extremely partisan political environment. In my opinion, a better solution would be to throw disputed elections to both houses of Congress together, which would choose both the President and the Vice President.

Impeaching the President and other civil officers

The Constitution gives the House of Representatives "the sole Power of Impeachment." It then gives the Senate "the sole Power to try all Impeachments." This language means that in impeachment cases, the House of Representatives acts as the prosecutor and is empowered to bring the charges, and the Senate acts as the jury and decides the outcome or verdict. This is such an important function of the two houses of Congress that I devote an entire chapter to it: Chapter 13.

Declaring war

The Constitution splits war powers between the President and Congress. The President is Commander in Chief , but in Article I, Section 8, Congress is given the power to "declare War" and to "raise and support Armies."

Congress has exercised its power to declare war only five times during the whole history of the United States. The last time Congress declared war was in World War II. Congress didn't declare war in any of these major conflicts:

- The Korean War
- The Vietnam War
- The Persian Gulf War
- The war in Afghanistan
- The Iraq War

Congress did "authorize" all these military engagements, but that isn't the same thing as a declaration of war. Critics of presidential power say that all these wars were illegal because a legal war requires a Congressional declaration of war. Those who defend the President's war powers say that Congress's constitutional power to "declare War" isn't the same as a power to commence or initiate war. The people who take this line of argument believe that the President as Commander in Chief can initiate a legal war without the need for a Congressional declaration of war.

The War Powers Resolution (or Act) of 1973 says that, "in the absence of a declaration of war," the President has to submit a written report to Congress within 48 hours of sending U.S. troops into action in any foreign country. The Act goes on to say that the President must withdraw these troops from the foreign country concerned within 60 days unless Congress has in the meantime either declared war or specifically authorized the President's decision to send the troops into the foreign country.

Can you run for the House or Senate?

If you plan to run for a seat in the House of Representatives, keep these requirements in mind:

- You have to be at least 25 years old.
- You have to have been a citizen of the United States for at least seven years.
- When elected you must be living in the state where the voting district that you represent is situated.

The Senate gets its name from a similar body in the Roman Republic. The name comes from the Latin word *senex*, which means "old man." So it's not surprising that senators have to be a little older than representatives. Here's the scoop on becoming a senator:

- You have to be at least 30 years old.
- You have to have been a citizen of the United States for at least nine years.
- When elected you must be living in the state that you represent.

Is the War Powers Act constitutional? Presidents have generally taken the view that the 1973 law is unconstitutional. So, every time a President has drafted a report required by that Act, he has said that his report was "consistent with" the War Powers Act — not that it was "pursuant to" the Act. Writing a report "pursuant to" a particular law means that the writer is acting in obedience to that law. But writing a report that is "consistent with" a particular law doesn't entail recognition of the validity or constitutionality of that law. The question of the constitutionality of the War Powers Act has not yet been tested in court. I tackle the serious and topical question of the President's war powers in Chapter 10.

Getting to Know the Senate

The Senate is an august body made up of just 100 members (two from each state) who serve six-year terms — longer than those of any other elected officeholders in the federal government. The Senate has two ancestors:

- The Senate of Ancient Rome
- The British upper house, the House of Lords

The Senate is the embodiment of *federalism*: a political system in which national and state governments share power. Hence the words emblazoned above the Dirksen Senate Office Building: "The Senate is the Living Symbol of Our Union of States."

If the House of Representatives is "the people's house," the Senate is the states' house. James Madison wrote that "the government ought to be founded on a mixture of the principles of proportional and equal representation." The House of Representatives provides proportional representation: States are represented according to the size of their populations. The Senate provides equal representation for each state.

For example, California has 53 representatives for its 36 million inhabitants, and Wyoming has just one representative for its population of 515,000. But in the Senate, Wyoming and California get two members each. So in the House, the biggest states are dominant, but in the Senate, the smallest states have equal influence.

So important is this principle that Article V of the Constitution protects it in a way that no other provision is protected: "No State, without its Consent, shall be deprived of its equal Suffrage [right to vote] in the Senate." For example, say a constitutional amendment was proposed that said Alaska was henceforth to have only one seat in the Senate. Even if this amendment was ratified by the requisite three-fourths of all state legislatures, it would not take effect unless Alaska (through its elected officials) gave its consent.

Electing a senator

Originally, the Constitution called for senators to be chosen by each state's legislature rather than by popular vote. This arrangement worked okay at first, but it broke down under bitter party rivalries in the 19th century, which sometimes left senate seats vacant for years at a time.

In the late 19th century, some states started using a type of referendum that effectively allowed the direct election of senators. Popular pressure built up in favor of a constitutional amendment for the direct election of senators nationwide. About two-thirds of the states had already introduced direct election to the U.S. Senate by the time this reform became part of the Constitution through the ratification of the Seventeenth Amendment in 1913 (see Chapter 22). Unlike members of the House of Representatives, who are elected by their individual voting districts, each senator is elected by the state as a whole.

Direct popular election gave the Senate democratic credibility that it had lacked before, and with it came enhanced prestige. Senators now tend to refer to themselves not by their official designation as "senator *from* New Mexico" but rather as "senator *for* New Mexico," which sounds more democratic.

Senators with higher aspirations

After 1913, when the Seventeenth Amendment called for senators to be elected by popular vote, senators became much more likely to be nominated for higher office. Here are some recent examples:

✔ Both Barack Obama and John F. Kennedy were sitting senators who were elected President without ever being a state governor or Vice President.

✔ Harry Truman and Richard Nixon were elected to the Vice Presidency immediately after serving in the Senate, and both of them later became President.

✔ Senator Hubert H. Humphrey was elected Vice President in 1964 and ran for President on the Democratic ticket in 1968.

✔ In 1992, Democratic Senator Al Gore was elected Vice President. After serving two terms, he ran for President in 2000 with Senator Joe Lieberman as his running mate.

✔ In 1996, the Republicans chose Senator Robert Dole as their presidential candidate.

✔ In 2004, the Democratic ticket was made up of two senators: John Kerry for President and John Edwards as his running mate.

✔ In 2008, senators really came into their own. Not only were the two main party nominees — Barack Obama and John McCain — sitting senators, but the contenders for the Democratic Party nomination were mainly drawn from the ranks of the Senate as well. They included Joe Biden, Hillary Clinton, Christopher Dodd, and John Edwards.

Of the two senators from a particular state, the one with the longer unbroken tenure is known as the *senior senator* from that state, and the other is known as the *junior senator*. But these titles don't reflect any difference in status. The official title of a senator takes this form: "The Honorable John Doe, the junior senator from Wyoming." But nowadays, we generally just write "Senator John Doe."

Elections to the Senate are staggered. A *class*, made up of roughly one-third of the Senate, is up for election every two years. Senators' terms of office are arranged so that both seats from a particular state are never contested at the same time. And while senators enjoy longer terms than any other elected federal officials (six years), they can also run for reelection as many times as they like.

Presiding over the Senate

The Constitution gives the Vice President the job of presiding over the Senate. Here's what Article I, Section 3 of the Constitution says:

> *The Vice President of the United States shall be President of the Senate, but shall have no Vote, unless they be equally divided.*

In practice, the Veep doesn't often preside over the Senate. He's likely to have more important things to do, and in any case, he doesn't have an active role to play in the Senate. He can't participate in debate and can cast a vote only to break a tie. For this reason, the Constitution provides for the election of "a President pro tempore, in the Absence of the Vice President."

The position of *president pro tempore* ("president for the time being") usually goes to the most senior senator of the majority party. Election to this position is a great honor, and the president pro tempore ranks immediately after the Speaker of the House of Representatives in the line of succession to the presidency. But the president pro tempore of the Senate wields a lot less power than the Speaker of the House.

The functions of the office of president pro tempore are not fixed. Each holder of the office molds it in his own image. When he chairs the Senate, the president pro tempore has full authority to administer oaths and to sign legislation on behalf of the Senate. In the absence of the Vice President, the president pro tempore presides together with the Speaker of the House when both houses of Congress sit together in joint sessions. The president pro tempore presides over the Senate as frequently or infrequently as he likes and quite often names other senators, sometimes even freshmen senators, to chair meetings of the Senate in his absence.

The president pro tempore forms part of the leadership of his party in the Senate, but his role in the party is subordinate to that of the majority leader. (In the House, by contrast, the Speaker is the leader of the majority party, as I explain earlier in this chapter.)

Advising and consenting

The Senate has some important powers not shared by the House of Representatives, most notably the power of "Advice and Consent." Here's what Article II, Section 2, Clause 2 says about this power:

> [The President] shall have Power, by and with the Advice and Consent of the Senate, to make Treaties . . . ; and he shall nominate, and by and with the Advice and Consent of the Senate, shall appoint Ambassadors, other public Ministers and Consuls, judges of the supreme Court, and all other Officers of the United States, whose Appointments are not herein otherwise provided for . . .

There has been some disagreement about what this provision means in practice. The text indicates that the President is meant to have both the power to nominate and the power to appoint. Some people argue that the Senate was intended to question or prevent those nominations and appointments only in cases of favoritism, incompetence, or fraud. But from the beginning, partisan politics influenced the Senate's power to advise and consent.

For example, George Washington's 1796 nomination of John Rutledge as the second Chief Justice was blocked by the Senate at least partly for political reasons (though Rutledge also had some mental problems). Since then, a lot of presidential nominations have been blocked by the Senate on a party political basis, including Judge Robert Bork's nomination to the U.S. Supreme Court by President Ronald Reagan.

Judges up for confirmation are now routinely asked questions about their views on privacy and abortion, which are just as much political as legal questions. Another technique favored by both parties in recent years is simply to delay the holding of hearings, which has left a good number of vacancies among federal circuit and district court judges, who form the backbone of the federal judiciary.

The views of the senators from a nominee's home state are often weighted in the Senate. The term *blue slip process* refers to this situation. The blue slip system has lately been expanded, giving a senator virtual veto power over appointments of judges not only from her home state but also from any other state in the circuit to which her home state belongs. (The states are grouped into 11 circuits for the federal court system.)

Passing Legislation

The main function of Congress is to make laws, and Congress is the federal lawmaking body in the United States. A law passed by Congress is known as an *Act of Congress,* which starts life as a bill. No fewer than 14,000 bills were introduced during the 110th Congress of 2007–2009, but only 449 of these were actually passed (and of those, 144 just renamed some federal buildings). But where do all these bills come from? There are several possible sources:

- **Lobbyists.** There are now almost 35,000 registered Congressional lobbyists, double the number that there were in 2000. Lobbyists may even prepare the text of a bill for a sympathetic member to introduce.

- **Election campaign promises or party platforms.**

- **Petitions from citizen groups.**

- **State legislatures.** They may pass *memorials* asking Congress to pass certain laws.

- **Executive communications.** These may come from the President, a Cabinet member, or an independent agency.

An alternative way of proposing legislation is by *joint resolution,* which is practically indistinguishable from a bill except that it normally begins with a preamble explaining the need for the legislation. Like a bill, a joint resolution must be passed by both houses of Congress and must be accepted or vetoed by the President. And like a bill, it becomes a law. Joint resolutions are used to authorize minor government expenditures, to create commissions and other bodies, and for other fairly technical legislation. But they can also be used for some pretty important stuff, like admitting new states into the Union (a power specifically reserved to Congress by Article IV, Section 3 of the Constitution) and proposing an amendment to the Constitution.

Tracking a bill's progress

A bill may start its life either in the House or in the Senate. (As I explain earlier in the chapter, if the bill raises taxes, it must originate in the House, which has power over revenue.) The way in which bills are proposed differs between the two bodies:

- In the House, a member wishing to introduce a bill places it in the *hopper,* a wooden box next to the rostrum. The bill, or at least its title, used to be read out before the whole House, but this practice is no longer followed.

- In the Senate, the procedure may be more formal, with the sponsor introducing his bill from the floor. But the bill can also simply be left with the clerk without any comment.

The bill is referred to the appropriate standing committee, of which the House has 20 and the Senate 16. Each committee is led by a chairman belonging to the majority party and a "ranking member" of the minority party. The committee may hold hearings and collect relevant evidence. I explain the committee process in detail in the next section.

If the committee is in favor of the bill, it is reported out of the committee and reaches the floor of the chamber concerned. (If the committee doesn't favor the bill, it can be killed without ever reaching the floor.) The House or Senate may then debate the bill and amend it. The debate process differs between the two houses.

Debating in the Senate

In the Senate, the presiding officer must recognize the first senator who rises to speak about a bill, but the majority and minority leaders are generally given first dibs. Senate speeches aren't required to be relevant to the bill being debated, and senators may usually speak for as long as they like.

To delay or block a vote on a bill, senators can use a special tactic not available in the House: the *filibuster*. Essentially, to filibuster means to talk so long that the Senate can't actually vote on a bill. The record is held by Senator Strom Thurmond, who filibustered the Civil Rights Act of 1957 by talking continuously for more than 24 hours.

Since 1917, it has been possible to end a filibuster by passing a *cloture* (French for "closure") motion. This tactic isn't often used because it needs a three-fifths majority to pass or, if it involves changing Senate rules, a two-thirds majority. Plus, cloture doesn't stop debate immediately; it allows 30 more hours of debate — a number that can be increased by another three-fifths majority.

Debating in the House

In the House, debate is much more tightly controlled. The presiding officer has a good deal of freedom to decide whom to recognize. The Rules Committee determines whether amendments to a particular bill are going to be allowed or not. Debate is normally limited to one hour: a half hour for each party. Each party appoints a *floor manager,* who allocates time to members who wish to participate in the debate. If a lot of members want to have their say, a member may be allocated 2 minutes or even just 30 seconds.

Voting

After the debate, the bill is put to a vote. The House uses several different forms of voting but nowadays generally uses an electronic vote. The Senate shuns such modern gadgetry. In that body, the typical manner of voting is by *roll call*: The clerk calls out the name of each senator in alphabetical order, the member votes "Aye" or "No," and the clerk repeats the member's vote. It's a time-consuming process. (Thank heavens there are only 100 senators.)

Moving to the other body

After a bill is passed by one house of Congress, it is sent to the other chamber, which may pass, reject, or amend it. If the bill is amended by the second house, a conference committee made up of members of both houses meets to reconcile the differences. Conference committees have, on occasion, departed from both versions in producing a composite bill. President Ronald Reagan once remarked, "If an apple and an orange went into conference consultations, it might come out a pear." For the bill to pass, both houses have to agree to the conference committee's version.

Landing on the President's desk

The bill is then ready to be presented to the President. The President may either sign it into law or veto it, and he offers a message giving the reasons for either action. A presidential veto can be overridden only by a two-thirds majority of both houses.

If the President does nothing, the bill automatically becomes law after ten days (excluding Sundays). However, if Congress adjourns during that ten-day period, the bill fails. This situation is known as a *pocket veto* because it's as if the President just puts the bill in his pocket and forgets about it. Unlike a regular veto, a pocket veto can't be overridden by Congress because the bill is not returned to Congress.

The pocket veto has recently attracted some controversy. If a President tries unsuccessfully to exercise a pocket veto on a bill, then the President's non-response allows that bill to become law automatically. To avoid this outcome, recent presidents have started using a so-called *protective return veto*. The President exercises a pocket veto but then returns the vetoed bill to Congress. President George H.W. Bush and President Bill Clinton both used this tactic. If it is successful, this type of veto kills the bill in question without any chance of a Congressional comeback. But, just in case this tactic doesn't work, the President can at least be sure that he has vetoed the bill in the ordinary way and that it will not automatically become law.

Examining congressional committees

In his 1885 book on *Congressional Government,* future President Woodrow Wilson wrote, "It is not far from the truth to say that Congress in session is Congress on public exhibition, whilst Congress in its committee rooms is Congress at work." There are no fewer than 200 congressional committees and subcommittees. Although the first committees were established in 1789, the present committee system dates from 1946.

Types of committees

There are three main types of congressional committees:

- ✔ **Standing:** Permanent committees within the House and the Senate.
- ✔ **Select, or special:** Committees created by the House or Senate to do work not covered by existing standing committees.
- ✔ **Joint:** Committees with members from the House and the Senate that tackle issues relevant to both. Most of these are standing committees, but a select committee can also be a joint committee.

There's a standing committee for most every branch of government, including Armed Services, Budget, Foreign Affairs (which in the Senate is called the *Foreign Relations Committee*), Judiciary, and Homeland Security. As I note earlier in the chapter, a powerful standing committee in the House is the Rules Committee. (Its counterpart in the Senate, known as the *Committee on Rules and Administration,* is much less powerful.)

At present there are only two select committees in the House:

- ✔ The Select Committee on Energy Independence and Global Warming
- ✔ The Permanent Select Committee on Intelligence

In the Senate, there are three select committees:

- ✔ Ethics
- ✔ Intelligence
- ✔ A Special Committee on Aging

Committee powers

Congressional committees have very wide powers, including the power to investigate and keep a check on the President, his Cabinet, and other executive branch officials. Committees may look into the effectiveness of laws that have been passed, the need for new legislation, and the performance of the executive (and to some extent of the judiciary).

Committees may hold hearings and can compel a witness to testify or to produce certain documents by issuing a subpoena. Witnesses who ignore a subpoena can be cited for contempt of Congress, which is similar to contempt of court. The penalty for this offense is a maximum of 12 months in jail.

A debate has long raged about whether Congress can subpoena executive officials and compel their testimony. People who take this line are likely to reject executive privilege while upholding congressional privilege (which I explain in a nearby sidebar). For more on this topic, see Chapter 8 on the separation of powers.

Chapter 12

"During Good Behaviour": The Judicial System

. . . .

. . . .

The legislature, the executive, and the judiciary are the three branches of government. The legislature, or Congress, passes laws. The executive, or the President, must "take Care that the Laws be faithfully executed." But what is the function of the judiciary? It's more complex than you may imagine, and I start this chapter with a brief discussion of that function.

With the function of the judiciary defined, I then delve into discussions of how someone becomes a judge, why judges aren't subject to the same types of term limits as presidents and members of Congress, and how the courts have assumed greater powers than the Founding Fathers ever imagined.

Examining the Courts' Function

Section 1 of Article III of the Constitution says:

> *The judicial Power of the United States shall be vested in one supreme Court, and in such inferior Courts as the Congress may from time to time ordain and establish.*

But what exactly does this judicial power consist of? Section 2 of Article III was drafted to answer this question, and it's a mouthful. I'll let you turn to the Appendix if you're brave enough to read it, but here are the key points:

- ✔ The U.S. Supreme Court has *original jurisdiction* over cases involving ambassadors and other diplomats, and cases in which a state is a party. This means that in these two types of cases alone the Supreme Court can hear the case from the beginning, as a court of first instance.

- ✔ In all other cases, the Supreme Court has only *appellate jurisdiction* — the power to act as an appeal court from lower federal courts or, in regard to certain matters, from state courts.

Defining jurisdiction

The appellate jurisdiction of the Supreme Court (and all other federal courts) is made up of two main categories: *federal question jurisdiction* and *diversity jurisdiction.* These terms don't actually appear in the text of the Constitution; they are a form of modern shorthand for what Article III, Section 2 says. Both of these categories are pretty technical, but here are the basic concepts involved:

- ✔ *Jurisdiction* refers to the power of a court to hear a particular case or type of case. For example, if a citizen of Florida sues a citizen of Ohio in a dispute over real estate situated in Texas, the state courts of Florida, Ohio, and Texas all have jurisdiction to hear the case, but the courts of New Jersey would have no jurisdiction to hear it.

- ✔ *Federal question jurisdiction* and *diversity jurisdiction* are the two main types of jurisdiction possessed by the federal courts:

  - *Federal question jurisdiction* essentially covers cases involving federal law.

  - *Diversity jurisdiction* covers cases where the plaintiff and the defendant are from different states, provided the amount of money in controversy is above a certain threshold, which is now set at $75,000 and is periodically adjusted to keep up with the times. The question here is what law is applicable. Should it be the law of the plaintiff's state, the law of the defendant's state, or federal law? Under the so-called *Erie Doctrine,* adopted by the high court in 1938, the Supreme Court (and other federal courts) must apply the substantive law of the state where the cause of action arose.

Applying the law

How do Supreme Court justices and other federal judges decide cases in practice? To put it at its simplest, they apply the law to the facts of the case. Trial courts spend a lot of time sorting out the facts, but the Supreme Court doesn't hear any live evidence, so it concentrates on the law.

Here are some of the important questions that the Supreme Court has to ask about the law:

- What is the relevant law that is being challenged?
- How should it be interpreted?
- What are the relevant constitutional provisions?
- How should they be interpreted?
- Is the challenged law in keeping with the Constitution, or is it unconstitutional?
- What previous relevant cases are there?
- Should these cases be followed, distinguished, or overruled?

Appointments and Elections: Becoming a Judge

Federal judges are appointed by the President, subject to confirmation by the Senate. Supreme Court justices, District Court judges, and judges of the federal Courts of Appeals are appointed "during good Behaviour" — meaning, for life. Other federal judges are appointed for long terms — for example, 15 years in the case of bankruptcy judges.

State court judges, by contrast, are mostly chosen by popular election. No fewer than 39 states elect at least some of their judges, and 87 percent of all state judges in the nation are elected. In some states, judges are initially appointed by elected officials but can then be reappointed by means of retention elections. These elections may take the form of a "Yes" or "No" vote, where the judge in question is not running against anybody else. Yet, even in such cases, unpopular judges have been voted out. Chief Justice Rose Bird of California is an example. She was removed from office in 1986 on the basis of a sweeping vote against her.

Judging the election process

Here are some of questions to consider about popularly elected judges:

- **Can anybody run for election as a judge?** No. In most states with elected judges, you have to be a member of the state bar in order to qualify.

- **How does a lawyer become a judge?** Whenever a vacancy occurs between elections, the state governor appoints someone to fill the office temporarily. At election time, these appointees run as incumbents (and usually get elected).

- **For how long do elected judges serve?** Terms vary from state to state, but a six-year term is common for the lower courts. Judges can run for reelection as many times as they want.

- **How do voters pick a judge?** Here's how elections usually work:

  - State bar associations sometimes rate the candidates. This may be helpful to voters, but it may also favor the more establishment-minded candidates or those who have been members of the local bar association for a long time.

  - The candidates usually finance their campaigns using their own funds or by soliciting contributions, and they put out their own campaign literature.

  - In most states, candidates for judgeships must run as individuals without party labels, but they often hint at their party affiliation.

  - Candidates are not normally allowed to make specific campaign promises, but some give an indication that they are going to be tough on crime.

- **Can candidates for judicial election announce their views on disputed political and legal issues?** Yes. That was the answer that the U.S. Supreme Court gave in the 2002 case known as *Republican Party of Minnesota v. White.* The Minnesota Supreme Court prohibited judicial candidates from revealing their views on most issues. By 5 votes to 4, the high court ruled that the Minnesota prohibition violated the First Amendment guarantee of freedom of speech. Justice Ruth Bader Ginsburg, writing for the minority, opined, "Judges are not politicians, and the First Amendment does not require that they be treated as politicians simply because they are chosen by popular vote."

Considering whether elections taint the judiciary

Justice Ginsburg's remark goes to the heart of the matter. She seems to have assumed that judges are above politics and that they decide cases purely on the basis of law. In fact, judges have political views just like anybody else — and their political views cannot help but color their legal decisions. Most judges are not too difficult to pigeonhole in terms of their political preferences — on the basis of which it's usually quite easy to predict how they are likely to rule.

This fact applies just as much to unelected U.S. Supreme Court justices as to elected state court judges. Justice Ginsburg is herself a prime example of a judge whose views on any given case can usually be predicted. She is one of the most politically liberal members of the court, and her voting record on the court matches her political outlook.

Justice Sandra Day O'Connor formed part of the majority in the *White* case, but she later said that she regretted her vote. O'Connor had herself started out as an elected judge in Arizona but favored the switch from elected to appointed judges that took place there in the 1970s. She said, "I watched the improvement of the judiciary in that state." Her preference? "If I could wave a magic wand . . . I would wave it to secure some kind of merit selection of judges across the country."

Even in her concurring opinion in *White,* Justice O'Connor took some side-swipes at elected judges. As she put it, "I am concerned that, even aside from what judicial candidates may say while campaigning, the very practice of electing judges undermines" the state interest in having an impartial judiciary.

O'Connor made the following attacks on elected judges (and my responses are in italic):

> ✔ Elected judges are less likely to be impartial, because they "cannot help being aware that if the public is not satisfied with the outcome of a particular case, it could hurt their reelection prospects." *Maybe. But is this necessarily a bad thing? It means that elected judges' rulings are more likely to be in tune with public opinion — in contrast with the decisions of U.S. Supreme Court justices, who do not answer to the people and can remain in office until they drop dead.*

> ✔ "Contested elections generally entail campaigning. And campaigning for a judicial post today can require substantial funds . . . Even if judges were able to refrain from favoring donors, the mere possibility that judges' decisions may be motivated by the desire to repay campaign contributors is likely to undermine the public's confidence in the judiciary." *This sure looks bad. But should the whole system of elected judges be thrown out because of it? That would be throwing the baby out with the bathwater. Instead, why not introduce some campaign finance reform? North Carolina has already done that with the Judicial Campaign Reform Act, which mandates using public money to pay for judicial election campaigns.*

Understanding Judicial Independence without Accountability

The independence of the federal judiciary is enshrined in the Constitution. It's easy to miss because the relevant section doesn't actually include the word *independence* at all. Instead, the relevant provision is buried in this throwaway clause in Article III, Section 1:

> *The Judges, both of the supreme and inferior Courts, shall hold their Offices during good Behaviour, and shall, at stated Times, receive for their Services a Compensation, which shall not be diminished during their Continuance in Office.*

Bypassing term limits and salary concerns

What exactly is meant by "during good Behaviour"? Convicted criminals in jail are usually allowed time off for good behavior. Does that phrase have the same meaning as it does here? No.

"During good Behaviour" is the guarantee of judicial independence. It means that Supreme Court justices, federal district judges, and appeals court judges can't be fired by the President or anybody else for any reason — unless they are impeached and found guilty of "Treason, Bribery, or other high Crimes and Misdemeanors." I discuss impeachment in Chapter 13.

So, unless removed from office after impeachment, these top judges are appointed for life. Many of them resign of their own accord when they feel no longer able to cope with the demands of the job. But some have stayed in office until they dropped dead, like Chief Justice William Rehnquist, following the example of his idol, John Marshall, who died in office after serving as Chief Justice for 34 years.

The "during good Behaviour" provision is linked with a prohibition on reducing a judge's salary after his or her appointment. Justices and judges protected by these two provisions can certainly afford to be independent. No matter what views on law and politics they may espouse at the time of their appointments, they can change their minds as much as they like afterward.

Is that a bad thing? Not necessarily, but it means they can decide cases entirely according to their personal predilections — or "the whim of the gavel." This situation is particularly dangerous in the U.S. Supreme Court, which decides many highly sensitive political issues. The independence of the Supreme Court justices is independence without accountability. Nine unelected and unaccountable people can decide the fate not only of individuals but also of the nation as a whole. And all too often the decision is in the hands not of nine but of one — the swing vote. (I discuss the swing vote in detail later in this chapter.)

Chief Justice William Rehnquist termed judicial independence "one of the crown jewels of our system of government." Supreme Court justices owe their appointments to the President, but once in office they can take whatever line they like.

Consider some examples:

- Chief Justice Earl Warren was picked for the top spot by President Dwight Eisenhower in 1953 on the assumption that he was a conservative. When Warren turned out to be one of the most liberal justices of all time, Eisenhower famously remarked that Warren's appointment was "the biggest damned-fool mistake I ever made." But there was nothing Eisenhower nor any other President could do about that.

- More recently, Justices Harry Blackmun, John Paul Stevens, and David Souter also turned out to be much more liberal on the bench than was anticipated. Souter, appointed in 1990, was widely expected to adopt extremely conservative positions. The National Organization for Women held a rally to oppose his confirmation, and the then-president of that organization actually testified at Souter's confirmation hearing that his appointment would "end . . . freedom for women in this country." Souter's confirmation was also opposed by the NAACP, which asked its members to write their senators to block his appointment to the court. Yet Justice Souter has emerged as one of the most liberal justices on the court.

Grappling with issues the Constitution doesn't address

Such examples are what judicial independence is all about — or is it? Independence from direct political pressure is one thing. But what about independence from *indirect* political, social, and intellectual currents?

Some of the most contentious recent constitutional battles concern affirmative action, abortion, gay rights, and same-sex marriage. What did Benjamin Franklin, Alexander Hamilton, or James Madison think about these issues? The answer is nothing. None of these issues were in the air when the Constitution was being drafted, nor for a very long time afterward.

So, what does the Constitution have to say on these issues? The Constitution doesn't address any of them, precisely because the Framers weren't aware of them. Justices who adhere to the *living Constitution* school of thought read into the Constitution the broad doctrines that they claim to have found there by way of extrapolating from the words that actually figure in the text. On the other hand, *textualists, originalists,* and other justices loosely described as *strict constructionists* generally refuse to speculate on how the Framers would have reacted to the modern problem issues but claim to stick to what the Constitution actually says. In the upcoming section "Labeling Supreme Court Justices," I explain each of these approaches to the Constitution.

Examining the abortion litmus test

Why did Harry Blackmun, who wrote for the majority in *Roe v. Wade,* espouse abortion rights? Nobody put a pistol to his head to force him to do so. It was an exercise of free will on his part — and it formed part of a pattern of liberal beliefs that he had come to hold after his appointment to the high court. These beliefs included women's rights generally, gay rights, and the rights of convicted prisoners.

Blackmun concluded his concurring opinion in a 1992 abortion case, *Planned Parenthood of Southeastern Pennsylvania v. Casey,* on a personal note: "I am 83 years old. I cannot remain on this Court forever, and when I do step down, the confirmation process for my successor well may focus on the issue before us today. That, I regret, may be exactly where the choice between the two worlds will be made." The phrase "the choice between the two worlds" is telling. Based on what we have seen in subsequent confirmation hearings for Supreme Court justices, Blackmun was absolutely right in identifying abortion rights as a litmus test for future appointments to the high court.

Blackmun's choice of one world rather than the other was the product of complex factors — including his social and economic background, his psychology, and his temperament — which led him to adopt ideas and doctrines that would be labeled *liberal.* Similar but opposite forces made Justice William Rehnquist consistently oppose liberal ideas, which is why he dissented in *Roe.*

Were Blackmun and Rehnquist independent in choosing these two different worlds? Independent, yes, but maybe not *autonomous* — a term which is often used loosely as a synonym for *independent* but is not quite the same.

Blackmun and Rehnquist, just like all of us, were conditioned by innumerable factors to be influenced by opposing social, political, and legal stimuli. Justices are human, after all, and cannot block out influences that affect the rest of the population.

So, how does the judicial independence of unelected judges and justices differ from that of elected judges? Probably only in this regard: that unelected judges have independence without accountability while the independence of elected judges is tempered by political accountability. Is there anything wrong with that? In my opinion, no, as long as elected judges don't allow themselves to be bought by campaign donors and wealthy backers.

Making the Judiciary Paramount: Judicial Review

In *Marbury v. Madison,* decided in 1803, Chief Justice John Marshall claimed the power of judicial review for the courts, and in particular for the U.S. Supreme Court. I discuss this landmark case throughout the book and particularly in Chapter 23. (The nearby sidebar "John Marshall's conflict of interest" provides some background.)

Understanding the nature of judicial review

Almost all the cases heard by the Supreme Court today fall under the court's *appellate jurisdiction,* which I discuss earlier in the chapter. Since the passing of the Judiciary Act of 1925, the great majority of cases heard by the high court under this head are cases of judicial review — which, strictly speaking, are not appeals at all.

An *appeal* is normally an application to a higher court contesting the decision of a lower court. In contrast, in a *judicial review,* the appellate court concerned reviews the lawfulness of a law passed by Congress or a state legislature, or a decision or other executive action taken by the President or a state.

Application for judicial review is made by filing a petition for a *writ of certiorari* with the appropriate appellate court. If the court agrees to hear the case, it is said to grant *certiorari.* This phrase does not mean that the court agrees with the petitioner — only that the court is prepared to hear the petitioner's case. An appellate court exercising the power of judicial review doesn't get to hear any live witnesses, and there is no jury — only a bench of judges. In the

U.S. Supreme Court, the decision whether *certiorari* is to be granted or not is decided by four justices. Every case in which *certiorari* has been granted is then heard by all nine justices sitting together — which places a huge burden on them.

Judicial review doesn't figure in the wording of the Constitution. Yet early in the country's history, it became the mainstay of the power of the Supreme Court. Today, judicial review is more important than ever.

Judicial review gives the U.S. Supreme Court the power to decide whether a federal or state law is in violation of the U.S. Constitution. If the court finds that the law in question conflicts with the Constitution, the court declares the law unconstitutional. This ruling means that the law (or the relevant part of the law) is *void,* or of no effect. Another way of describing this situation is to say that the court *strikes the law down,* because the effect of the court's decision is to strike the law (or the relevant part of the law) from the record as if it never existed in the first place.

John Marshall's conflict of interest

One of the key problems with the case of *Marbury v. Madison* relates not to the decision itself but to the circumstances surrounding it.

The case arose out of lame-duck President John Adams's attempt to appoint a whole bunch of "midnight judges" — 16 circuit judges and 42 justices of the peace — the day before his term was due to end. These were all political appointees. Adams, a Federalist, had been deprived of a second term by his defeat at the hands of his own Vice President, Thomas Jefferson, a Democratic-Republican, in the 1800 election. So Adams decided to take his revenge by ensuring that the judiciary remained Federalist-dominated well beyond his presidency.

All these "midnight" appointments were rushed through the Senate. But the *commissions,* or official letters of appointment, still had to be delivered to each of the new appointees. Time ran out on Adams's presidency before all the commissions had been delivered — and without an official commission, an appointment could not take effect.

William Marbury was one of Adams's "midnight" justices of the peace whose commission was not delivered in time. President Thomas Jefferson ordered the new Secretary of State, James Madison, to withhold the commissions that hadn't been delivered, including Marbury's. So Marbury petitioned the U.S. Supreme Court to order Madison to deliver his commission to him.

Madison was the named defendant because delivering commissions to new appointees was one of the duties of the Secretary of State. Marbury's beef was with Madison for not delivering the commission to him. But the guy who really let Marbury down wasn't Madison — it was Madison's predecessor as Secretary of State, John Marshall. Yes, that's the very same John Marshall who presided over the case as Chief Justice. If ever there was a blatant example of a conflict of interest, this had to be it!

But that didn't stop Marshall from going on to expand the power of the Supreme Court — and of himself as Chief Justice — by means of judicial review.

Judicial review is more important today than ever before because:

✔ The U.S. Supreme Court has expanded the scope of the Constitution to cover issues that the Framers never intended it to cover, such as abortion, affirmative action, and gay rights.

✔ The high court has narrowed down the *political question* doctrine, which says that the courts should keep its hands off questions that are entrusted by the Constitution to one of the other branches of government, either the President or the Congress. A good example of this development is the Supreme Court's determination of the presidential election of 2000 in *Bush v. Gore.*

✔ The high court has interpreted the Due Process Clause of the Fourteenth Amendment so widely as to make practically the entire Bill of Rights applicable to the states as well as to the federal government — giving the court far more control over the states than the Framers ever envisioned.

Tracing the origins of judicial review

If the high court wasn't given the power of judicial review by the Constitution, where did this power come from? There is considerable disagreement on this question. Here are some possible answers:

✔ **Although judicial review isn't specifically mentioned in the Constitution, it's implied.** This position was taken by Alexander Hamilton in the *Federalist Papers* even before the Constitution was ratified. (Note that the *Federalist Papers* were published precisely in order to win enough support for the Constitution to be ratified.) Hamilton's argument runs as follows:

   • The Constitution is "fundamental law."

   • Any law that conflicts with the Constitution is therefore void.

   • Who should decide the constitutionality of a particular law? It's "rational to suppose" that the courts were intended to have this power because "The interpretation of the laws is the proper and peculiar province of the courts."

The problem with this explanation is that judicial review is so important a power of the Supreme Court that, if the Framers really intended to give the court this power, it's hard to understand why they didn't actually spell it out. The omission of any mention of judicial review from the text of the Constitution is unlikely to be accidental and may well indicate a deliberate decision not to give the court this awesome power.

✔ **The existence of a written constitution with the status of fundamental law makes judicial review necessary. Somebody has to decide whether any federal or state law is in conflict with the fundamental law — and who more appropriately than the courts?** How convenient! Why can't such conflicts be decided by the legislature? This solution is what the Virginia constitution of 1776 provided for that state. (See the upcoming section "Considering alternatives for solving Constitutional conflicts.")

✔ **Judicial review was invented by John Marshall in *Marbury v. Madison.*** Judicial review was discussed long before *Marbury* at the Constitutional Convention and in the state ratifying conventions — and it also figures in the *Federalist Papers.* But all this discussion makes it more rather than less likely that its omission from the Constitution was deliberate — which can only mean that judicial review was feared as likely to give the judiciary too much power. That certainly was the view of certain individual Framers. Here, for example, is what Charles Pinckney of North Carolina had to say in 1799:

> *On no subject am I more convinced, than that it is an unsafe and dangerous doctrine in a republic, ever to suppose that a judge ought to possess the right of questioning or deciding upon the constitutionality of treaties, laws, or any act of the legislature. It is placing the opinion of an individual, or of two or three, above that of both branches of Congress, a doctrine which is not warranted by the Constitution, and will not, I hope, long have many advocates in this country.*

So if some of the Framers held such strong views against judicial review, why didn't they specifically ban it in the Constitution? As I explain above and in the upcoming section "Considering alternatives for solving Constitutional conflicts," Alexander Hamilton was one Framer who *did* support the idea of judicial review. But, though Hamilton was influential, he recognized the fears that the prospect of judicial review aroused even before the Constitution came into force (at a time when Hamilton was desperately trying to ensure the Constitution's ratification). Hamilton's state, New York, ratified the Constitution by the narrow margin of 30 votes to 27. In that situation, Hamilton wisely did not press for judicial review to be spelled out in the text of the Constitution — and those who opposed judicial review could take comfort from its omission.

✔ **John Marshall didn't cite any precedents for judicial review in his opinion in *Marbury v. Madison.* So this must mean that no such power existed before.** No. In fact, there were some earlier Supreme Court precedents. Why did Marshall not mention them? Probably because of the ginger approach adopted in them. In two of them, while striking down congressional legislation, Justice Samuel Chase shrank from laying claim to the right to judicial review: "It is unnecessary, at this time, for me to determine, whether this court constitutionally possesses the power to declare an act of Congress void, on the ground of its being made contrary to, and in violation of, the constitution." Here are the relevant precedents:

- *Hayburn's Case* of 1792, which declared an Act of Congress void because it required high court justices to undertake some nonjudicial work.

- *Hylton v. United States,* decided in 1796, in which the high court set aside an Act of Congress.

- *Ware v. Hylton,* decided in 1796, in which a Virginia law was struck down. As it happens, the future Chief Justice John Marshall appeared as counsel in this case and argued in favor of upholding the Virginia law.

- *Calder v. Bull,* decided in 1798, affirming the decision in *Ware v. Hylton.*

Noting Jefferson's response to Marbury v. Madison

Thomas Jefferson, a distant cousin and sworn enemy of John Marshall, was President at the time of *Marbury v. Madison.* Jefferson rejected what he called Marshall's "twistifications of the law" in claiming the power of judicial review for the Supreme Court. Here's what he wrote shortly after the *Marbury* ruling:

> *The opinion which gives to the judges the right to decide what laws are constitutional and what not, not only for themselves in their own sphere of action but for the Legislature and Executive also in their spheres, would make the Judiciary a despotic branch.*

Jefferson's fears proved well-founded. Judicial review gave the Supreme Court power over Congress and the President that was contrary to the whole idea of three coequal branches under the doctrine of separation of powers.

What did Jefferson do to counter Marshall's twistifications? He first set in motion the impeachment of Justice Samuel Chase. This move was blatantly political. Chase, like Marshall, was a staunch member of the opposition Federalist Party. Jefferson was hoping to use Chase's impeachment as a springboard to impeaching Marshall. Chase was impeached but was acquitted on all counts — and Jefferson gave up any hope of going after Marshall.

But what about challenging the decision in *Marbury*? Not even Jefferson could figure out a way of doing so — despite the glaring conflict of interest involved (see the sidebar "John Marshall's conflict of interest").

Considering alternatives for solving Constitutional conflicts

The real problem was a practical one. If judicial review was abolished, how would conflicts between the Constitution and other laws be resolved? The 1776 Constitution of Virginia suggested an alternative approach. Section 7 of that Constitution's Bill of Rights read as follows:

> *That all power of suspending laws, or the execution of laws, by any authority, without consent of the representatives of the people, is injurious to their rights, and ought not to be exercised.*

We should not be surprised to learn that the Constitution of Virginia was mainly drafted by none other than Jefferson himself.

The section in question clearly takes away from the judiciary the power of "suspending" and, therefore, also of setting aside any law. In other words, judicial review was not permitted under the Virginia constitution. This power was given instead to the popularly elected legislature. This is not a bad solution and is much more in keeping with democratic principles than judicial review exercised by unelected judges.

The legislature would presumably take its time in deliberating whether any particular law should be suspended — but the courts are not exactly noted for their speed of action either.

So, why didn't Jefferson try to introduce the same ban on judicial review into the federal Constitution? Jefferson was abroad and didn't attend the Philadelphia Convention that drafted the U.S. Constitution, but there was no reason a prohibition on judicial review couldn't have been included in the Bill of Rights. Jefferson returned from France in 1789. The Bill of Rights was drafted in 1789 and ratified in 1791. There would have been ample opportunity to add a prohibition on judicial review.

If Jefferson had tried to prevent judicial review, he would have found himself up against a formidable adversary, Alexander Hamilton, one of the leading Framers of the Constitution. In the influential and authoritative *Federalist Papers,* Hamilton in 1788 described the judiciary as "the least dangerous to the political rights of the Constitution" and as "beyond comparison the weakest of the three departments of power." On this basis, Hamilton actually specifically advocated judicial review — before the Constitution was even in force. (Keep in mind that the very possibility of conflict between the Constitution and other laws was in 1788 purely hypothetical, and most people did not give it much thought at all.)

Watching the Supreme Court's power seep into politics

Like Alexander Hamilton, James Madison saw judicial review as implied by the Constitution. But Madison's take on this possibility was very different from Hamilton's. Instead of justifying judicial review like Hamilton, Madison foresaw and deplored the danger of judicial review. Here's what Madison wrote on October 15, 1788:

> *In the State Constitutions, and, indeed, in the Federal one also, no provision is made for the case of a disagreement in expounding them; and as the Courts are generally last in making their decision, it results to them, by refusing or not refusing to execute a law, to stamp it with its final character. This makes the Judiciary Department paramount in fact to the Legislature, which was never intended and can never be proper.*

The problem has turned out in practice to be far more serious than Madison could have predicted, largely because of the bold intrusion of the high court into politics.

The *political question* doctrine is potentially one of the most valuable constitutional doctrines. It springs from the fundamental doctrine of the separation of powers. The doctrine requires the courts to decline jurisdiction in a case which the Constitution has entrusted to either the executive or the legislature.

Here are a couple of recent examples of the application of this doctrine:

- In *Goldwater v. Carter,* decided in 1979, Senator Barry Goldwater and other members of Congress challenged President Jimmy Carter's right to break a treaty with Taiwan — thereby favoring Red China — without consulting the Senate. The U.S. Supreme Court threw out the application on the ground that it raised a political question "because it involves the authority of the President in the conduct of our country's foreign relations." The court left open the question of the constitutionality of the President's action.

- In *Nixon v. United States,* decided in 1993, a federal judge, Walter Nixon (no relation to the former president), challenged the handling of an impeachment trial by the Senate. Nixon had been convicted of perjury before a grand jury but refused to resign from office even after he had been jailed. The Senate then impeached and removed him from office. The Supreme Court unanimously threw out his application on the ground that impeachment was under the control of Congress and the court had no right to get involved.

Cases like these are obvious political questions. But what about all the other issues in which the court gets involved, like abortion, gay rights, or the election of the President? Aren't these actually political questions too? That argument has never been used in relation to those issues. Yet other countries around the world have laws about abortion and gay rights that are decided by legislators, not judges.

For the courts to become embroiled in such highly fraught political debates could easily be interpreted as judicial activism at its worst, usurping the role of the other branches of government. On the other hand, the very existence of a written constitution makes it likely that almost any issue of importance is likely to find its way sooner or later into a high court docket.

Justice Ruth Bader Ginsburg has recognized that for the court to have made abortion a constitutional issue could also have harmed the pro-choice cause that she favors. Here's what she said about *Roe v. Wade* long before she took her seat on the Supreme Court: The court's ruling terminated "a nascent democratic movement to liberalize abortion law." And: "Heavy-handed judicial intervention was difficult to justify and appears to have provoked, not resolved, conflict."

Casting the Swing Vote

With judicial review as its main weapon against the President, Congress, and the states, the power of the Supreme Court grew unchecked. For nine unelected judges to exercise this kind of power has often been criticized as undemocratic. But at certain times, the power has been exercised not by nine judges but by one — the wielder of the swing vote. If judicial review is by its very nature undemocratic, then unbridled judicial review power exercised by a single judge can only be regarded as anti-democratic in the extreme. In this section, I present some key examples of the power of the swing vote.

Recalling "the switch in time that saved nine"

In the 1930s, Franklin D. Roosevelt found his New Deal programs blocked at every turn by a 5–4 majority on the Supreme Court — made up of four conservative judges (the so-called "Four Horsemen") plus Justice Owen Roberts, exercising a swing vote. As I discuss in Chapter 9 and Chapter 23, Roberts was so influential that his decision to switch sides in 1937 was hailed as "the switch in time that saved nine." (The "nine" were the high court justices.)

Roosevelt had proposed naming additional justices to the Supreme Court (because the Constitution doesn't limit the number of justices), but Roberts's decision to switch sides made that proposal unnecessary.

Wielding the swing vote under Rehnquist and Roberts

Under Chief Justices William Rehnquist and John Roberts, Justices Sandra Day O'Connor and Anthony Kennedy were able to flex their muscles by casting swing votes. Since O'Connor's retirement in 2005, Kennedy has exercised disproportionate influence by holding in his hands the determination of a number of sensitive cases — which also often gave him the right to write the majority opinion for the court. For example,

- Kennedy's swing vote put George W. Bush into the White House in the 2000 decision in *Bush v. Gore.*

- His vote also gave victory to the conservatives on the court in *Boy Scouts of America v. Dale,* which allowed the Boy Scouts to exclude gays from membership as scoutmasters. But in *Lawrence v. Texas,* decided in 2003, he joined O'Connor and the liberals on the court to strike down a Texas law criminalizing homosexual intercourse.

- On abortion, Kennedy has taken the side of the liberals. In *Planned Parenthood of Southeastern Pennsylvania v. Casey,* decided in 1992, his vote produced a controlling plurality that struck down a Pennsylvania law requiring a husband to be notified before an abortion could be performed. In this case, Kennedy initially supported the four conservative justices — thus producing a majority — in favor of striking down *Roe v. Wade.* However, at the last minute Kennedy switched his swing vote to save *Roe v. Wade.*

- The debate on partial-birth abortion in *Stenberg v. Carhart* in 2000 saw Kennedy on the side of the conservative minority.

- Kennedy has generally adopted a liberal line on capital punishment. In *Roper v. Simmons,* decided by 5 votes to 4 in 2005, Kennedy wrote the opinion for the majority, ruling that it was unconstitutional to execute Christopher Simmons for a murder committed when he was under 18.

Despite the horrendous nature of the murder, Kennedy ruled that "The Eighth and Fourteenth Amendments forbid imposition of the death penalty on offenders who were under the age of 18 when their crimes were committed." His opinion was that no exceptions are allowed to this blanket ruling, which effectively strikes down provisions in the death penalty laws of 20 states. I discuss the *Simmons* case in more detail in Chapter 21.

✔ However, in *Kansas v. Marsh,* decided in 2005, Kennedy gave the conservatives a 5–4 majority in another capital punishment case. The issue here was whether a defendant could be sentenced to death where the mitigating factors and aggravating factors were of equal weight. A Kansas law said yes. The question before the high court was whether this law was unconstitutional. As a result of Kennedy's swing vote, the court upheld the Kansas law.

✔ Kennedy wrote for the 5–4 liberal majority in the 2008 case *Kennedy v. Louisiana,* which ruled that state laws imposing the death penalty for child rape are unconstitutional. In crimes against individuals, Kennedy held, "the death penalty should not be expanded to instances where the victim's life was not taken."

✔ The very next day after handing down this liberal ruling, Kennedy gave a 5–4 victory to the conservative wing of the court in the important gun-rights case *District of Columbia v. Heller* (see Chapter 15).

✔ In yet another historic case decided in 2008, *Boumediene v. Bush,* Kennedy wrote for the liberal 5–4 majority that he had created, ruling that foreign detainees at Guantanamo Bay had the right to challenge their detention according to the principles of habeas corpus under the U.S. Constitution.

✔ Kennedy also gave a 5–4 victory to the more liberal wing of the court in the highly contentious 2005 case of *Kelo v. City of New London* about "eminent domain" under the Fifth and Fourteenth amendments. I discuss this case in Chapter 23.

These examples are merely a selection of *some* of the important cases whose outcome has been determined by Justice Kennedy's views. I pick on him only because he has managed to place himself in a pivotal position on the current court.

Can it be right that a single unelected judge should have this kind of power? Since John Kennedy's election to the presidency, there has been much speculation about the power of the Kennedy clan. But in fact Justice Kennedy — no relation to the former president — has for well over 20 years exercised more power and influence than all the members of the Kennedy clan put together, and can probably expect to do so for many more years to come.

The reason for this concentration of power in the hands of a single judge is twofold:

✔ The tremendous power wielded by the U.S. Supreme Court, in particular in regard to judicial review

✔ The absence of any agreed-upon approach to constitutional interpretation, resulting in the division of the court into two opposed ideological blocs

If the members of the high court could agree on a common approach to the Constitution, the amount of power possessed by the court as an institution would be less frightening than it is now, where all that power can often be controlled by just one person.

Chief Justice Roberts clearly recognizes this problem, because he has made it a priority to promote unanimity and collegiality on the court — but so far to no effect. On the contrary, the disagreements on the court appear more acrimonious than ever, and there is no solution in sight.

Labeling Supreme Court Justices

Supreme Court justices can be classified in a number of different ways, which can sometimes cut across one another. Following are discussions of the basic divisions.

Conservative/liberal

Political conservatives generally favor states' rights over federal power. But when it comes to individual rights, the position is less clear. Liberals tend to favor women's rights, gay rights, and affirmative action, which conservatives largely oppose. But conservatives tend to be more *libertarian* than liberals — in the sense of favoring small government, low taxes, and generally allowing individuals to live their lives with as little interference from government as possible. Liberals, by contrast, are more likely to favor big government, welfare programs, and government involvement in healthcare and other facets of life in the interests of what they see as socially desirable goals.

Political conservatives are much more likely than liberals to support individual gun rights, while liberals are more likely to support gun control. That dichotomy is well illustrated by the Supreme Court's 2008 decision on the Second Amendment, *District of Columbia v.Heller,* which I discuss in Chapter 15. In that case, the lineup of liberal justices — Stevens, Breyer, Souter, and Ginsburg — faced the conservative lineup — Scalia, Roberts, Thomas, and Alito — together with swing-vote Justice Anthony Kennedy. But the justices don't always line up so predictably.

Strict constructionism/living Constitution

Politically conservative justices are more likely to adopt a conservative approach to constitutional interpretation by seeking to get back to the original meaning of the Constitution — *originalism* — or by sticking closely to the meaning of the text — *textualism*. Both approaches are commonly lumped together under the label of *strict constructionism*. Justices who reject this approach view the Constitution as a living and growing organism that must be interpreted in accordance with social change and with "the evolving standards of decency." Strict constructionists retort that judges who support the "living Constitution" doctrine are guilty of *judicial activism* (which I discuss momentarily).

Stare decisis/free exercise of power

Stare decisis, or the doctrine of *precedent,* means that judges are expected to follow previous decisions on the same legal issues. The U.S. Supreme Court pays lip service to this ancient doctrine but is not formally bound by it and has, in fact, overruled its own decisions in well over 100 cases in the past half-century. In general, *stare decisis* is a conservative doctrine — both politically and judicially conservative.

But what is a strict constructionist judge to do when his own view of what the Constitution means is contradicted by a longstanding high court precedent? Does he go with his own view of what the text of the Constitution means, or does he follow the precedent, even though he thinks it's wrong? Justices Antonin Scalia and Clarence Thomas — both conservatives — differ in this respect. As Scalia put it, Thomas "doesn't believe in *stare decisis,* period. If a constitutional line of authority is wrong, he would say let's get it right. I wouldn't do that."

What about believers in a "living Constitution"? Such justices wouldn't regard it as a big deal to break with precedent when they thought it was wrong. For example, in *Brown v. Board of Education,* decided in 1954, the liberal-dominated Supreme Court under Chief Justice Earl Warren had no trouble departing from the 1896 high court ruling in *Plessy v. Ferguson,* which had accepted racial segregation.

Judicial activism/judicial restraint

The term *judicial activism* is almost always used as a derogatory or negative label to refer to the exercise of judicial power that goes beyond its proper limits. Judges pilloried by critics as guilty of judicial activism are typically accused of

- ✔ Making law instead of applying and interpreting it
- ✔ Legislating from the bench
- ✔ Ruling by the whim of the gavel
- ✔ Deciding cases on the basis of their own political predilections

Nobody ever claims to be a judicial activist. This label is pinned on judges by their critics — including other judges. Chief Justice William Rehnquist expressed himself anxious "to prevent judges from roaming at large in the constitutional field guided only by their personal views." By what, then, should judges be guided? Rehnquist opined, "It is impossible to build sound constitutional doctrine upon a mistaken understanding of constitutional history."

Justice Harry Blackmun is a likely candidate for consideration as a judicial activist. In 1972, he dissented in *Furman v. Georgia,* which declared the capital punishment laws of a number of states to be unconstitutional. Blackmun specifically rejected the majority opinion on the ground that it was an exercise in judicial activism. However, in subsequent cases Blackmun himself came out against the constitutionality of the death penalty. And Blackmun also was the author of the majority opinion in *Roe v. Wade,* the highly contentious 1973 abortion rights case, which has often been characterized by its opponents as a prime example of judicial activism.

Judicial restraint is the opposite of judicial activism and refers to the doctrine that the judiciary should show due deference to the elected branches of government and, in particular, should be slow to strike down laws as unconstitutional. Judicial restraint is a judicially conservative doctrine and is often associated with political conservatives as well. Chief Justice Roberts, a conservative, has identified himself with judicial restraint, saying "Judges are like umpires. Umpires don't make the rules; they apply them."

Judicial restraint can also restrict the *scope* of the subject matter that the high court is prepared to accept as falling within its purview. For example, in 1964 Justice John M. Harlan II, attacked what he called

> *a current mistaken view of the Constitution and the constitutional function of this court. This view, in short, is that every major social ill in this country can find its cure in some constitutional principle and that this court should take the lead in promoting reform when other branches of government fail to act. The Constitution is not a panacea for every blot upon the public welfare nor should this court, ordained as a judicial body, be thought of as a general haven of reform movements.*

Harlan is generally regarded as a conservative. But liberals also lay claim to judicial restraint. For example, Justice John Paul Stevens, widely regarded as the most liberal member of the present-day court, has also claimed to be an adherent of judicial restraint. In 1983, he declared that a policy of judicial restraint "enables this Court to make its most effective contribution to our federal system of government."

Chapter 13

You're Fired! Investigating the Impeachment Process

The key to democracy is people power. And the most important power the people have is to hire and fire their own government. This is normally done by means of elections, but there is a problem here: Presidential elections are held only every four years. Does this mean that a president can't be fired between elections? No. The Framers of the Constitution took care of that. They wrote into the Constitution an alternative way of getting rid of a president: impeachment.

This chapter looks at what impeachment is, who can be impeached, and how the process works. I also discuss another method for removing an unwanted politician from office: recalling a state governor.

There's Nothing Peachy about Impeachment

Election campaigns have something of a carnival atmosphere about them, accompanied as they are by hoopla, wild rallies, and raucous music. Impeachment has its own brand of exuberance but more in the nature of a lynching. A president who fails to be reelected is just a loser in the high-stakes game of politics and can come back to run again. (Grover Cleveland did so successfully in 1892.) But a president who lost his job as a result of impeachment would be finished. He would be also probably be barred from running for any federal office again, and his name would be mud forever. That has never happened, but there have been a couple of near misses.

Impeachment is nothing like an election; it's really a trial. Most people think of impeachment as a peculiar form of torture reserved for presidents. Not so. The Constitution says that impeachment can be used to remove the President, Vice President, or any other "civil Officers of the United States." (Note that members of the armed services cannot be impeached. However, they can be removed by court martial.)

Only two Presidents have been impeached, and both were acquitted. These were Andrew Johnson in 1868 and Bill Clinton in 1999. (I devote a section to each later in this chapter.) Many people think that Richard Nixon was impeached too, but he wasn't. He jumped before he could be pushed; he was the only President in history to resign. (More on this topic later in the chapter as well.) Another 14 federal office-holders have been impeached, 7 of them successfully. All 14 were federal judges, and all were removed from office. Their names are not well-known, even though three of these impeachments took place less than 20 years ago.

"High Crimes and Misdemeanors": *What Impeachment Is and Isn't*

The Constitution is a pretty short document, yet it contains no fewer than seven mentions of impeachment. Article II, Section 4 states:

> *The President, Vice President and all civil Officers of the United States, shall be removed from Office on Impeachment for, and Conviction of, Treason, Bribery, or other High Crimes and Misdemeanors.*

Following are a few other mentions of impeachment:

- Article I, Section 2, Clause 5: "The House of Representatives . . . shall have the sole Power of Impeachment."

- Article I, Section 3, Clause 6: "The Senate shall have the sole Power to try all Impeachments. When sitting for that Purpose, they shall be on Oath or Affirmation. When the President of the United States is tried, the Chief Justice shall preside: And no Person shall be convicted without the Concurrence of two thirds of the Members present."

- Article I, Section 3, Clause 7: "Judgment in Cases of Impeachment shall not extend further than to removal from Office, and disqualification to hold and enjoy any Office of honor, Trust or Profit under the United States: but the Party convicted shall nevertheless be liable and subject to Indictment, Trial, Judgment and Punishment, according to Law."

Defining impeachment

Despite the impressive rolling phrases, these provisions raise more questions than they answer. For example,

- ✔ Is impeachment a purely political offense?
- ✔ Can you be impeached for something that isn't a crime?
- ✔ If you're impeached for something that *is* a crime, and then you're prosecuted for that crime, isn't that double jeopardy?

Congress has never tried to second-guess the Framers of the Constitution by defining impeachment — not officially, anyway. But maybe Congressman (later President) Gerald Ford's 1970 definition isn't so far from the mark (and he wasn't walking and chewing gum when he delivered this pearl of wisdom):

> *What, then, is an impeachable offense? The only honest answer is that an impeachable offense is whatever a majority of the House of Representatives considers it to be at a given moment in history; conviction results from whatever offense or offenses two-thirds of the other body [i.e. the Senate] considers to be sufficiently serious to require removal of the accused from office. . . . There are few fixed principles among the handful of precedents.*

Can you be impeached for something that isn't a crime at all?

Not one of the 11 articles of impeachment hurled at Andrew Johnson by his accusers amounted to a crime under the ordinary law. But that doesn't necessarily mean that Johnson's enemies were wrong; the Constitution itself seems to support the view that "high crimes and misdemeanors" don't necessarily have to be crimes in the ordinary sense.

To arrive at this conclusion, we need to consider what the Constitution has to say about the punishment for impeachable offenses. Article I, Section 3, Clause 7 says that the only punishment for impeachment is removal from office and disqualification to hold office in the future. That's a pretty stiff penalty in anybody's language, but it's not the end of the story. The same clause says that even if you've been convicted on impeachment, you will still "be liable and subject to Indictment, Trial, Judgment, and Punishment, according to Law."

In other words, if the offense that leads to impeachment also involves breaking a law, the person under the microscope can be both impeached and prosecuted. After being impeached, tried, found guilty, and deprived of office (by Congress), that person can still be hauled up before a judge and jury and maybe do some jail time.

How many times can someone be punished for the same thing? After all, being punished twice for the same thing just isn't allowed — that's called *double jeopardy* and is strictly forbidden by the Fifth Amendment (see Chapter 17).

The point is that being impeached is *not* the same thing as being punished under the law. That's why double jeopardy doesn't apply. With this understanding in mind, we can deduce that the Framers of the Constitution distinguished between impeachable offenses and illegal behaviors. It's certainly possible that one action can be both impeachable and illegal, but it's also possible that an action can be impeachable without being illegal.

What would qualify someone for impeachment without being illegal? See the sections on Andrew Johnson and Bill Clinton later in this chapter for the two prime examples in U.S. history. And consider what Alexander Hamilton wrote about impeachment in the *Federalist Papers,* an influential series of 85 articles written by Hamilton, James Madison, and John Jay in 1787 and 1788 advocating the ratification of the newly drafted Constitution:

> *The subjects of its jurisdiction are those offenses which proceed from the misconduct of public men, or, in other words, from the abuse or violation of some public trust. They are of a nature which may with peculiar propriety be denominated POLITICAL, as they relate chiefly to injuries done immediately to the society itself.*

Not bad for a description written before the Constitution even came into effect!

Tracking the Impeachment Process

The Constitution says that "The House of Representatives shall have the sole Power of Impeachment." But it doesn't specify how the House shall use that power. Does that mean that the procedure is fluid and can change any time the House likes? Yes and no.

On the one hand, the basic procedure is hundreds of years older than the U.S. Constitution. The House's role derives from that of the British House of Commons, which used to prosecute impeachments before the House of Lords, and the Lords' function as a trial jury has come down to the U.S. Senate. On the other hand, both the House of Representatives and the Senate have their own detailed "Rules of Procedure and Practice," which change from time to time. The Senate revised its rules in 1974 after Watergate. The current version of the Senate rules dates from 1986.

Playing grand jury and prosecutor: The role of the House

Any member of the House can propose an impeachment resolution, and in fact the initial complaint can even come from outside Congress. President Clinton's impeachment, for example, was set in motion by Independent Counsel Ken Starr, who dumped 36 boxes of evidence on the House, together with a 453-page report citing 11 possible impeachable offenses allegedly committed by the President.

As with most things in the House, the Rules Committee gets to see any impeachment proposal first. From there, the proposal generally goes to the House Judiciary Committee, which may conduct its own hearings. (I explain these committees in Chapter 11.)

In the Clinton impeachment, the full House voted 258–176 to authorize a full impeachment inquiry. The Judiciary Committee then began holding televised hearings. The Committee drafted four articles of impeachment, all of which it approved essentially along party lines. The first three articles alleged perjury and obstruction of justice in regard to Paula Jones, a woman who had accused the President of sexual harassment, and in connection with his relationship with intern Monica Lewinsky. The fourth and last article of impeachment alleged that Clinton had "misused and abused his office by making perjurious, false and misleading statements to Congress."

The next stage is for the articles of impeachment to return to the full House for a debate, possibly in closed session, followed by a vote on whether to impeach or not to impeach. In the Clinton case, two of the four articles were passed by the full House. (The fourth article was rejected by a whopping 285–148.)

The impeachment process doesn't end here — the Senate must then try the case and decide whether to convict, as I explain in the next section. However, if the House approves one or more articles of impeachment, the person is officially "impeached."

The role of the House in impeachments is as the prosecutor. At first it acts as a grand jury, deciding whether the case should go to trial. Then, if it decides that the case should move forward, the House appoints managers to act as prosecuting counsel at the trial. (In the Clinton impeachment, 13 Republican members of the House Judiciary Committee served as managers under the chairmanship of Representative Henry Hyde of Illinois.)

Trying the articles of impeachment: The role of the Senate

After passing the House, an impeachment is ready for trial by the Senate. The Senate acts as the trial jury but, unlike a jury, has the freedom to ask questions and debate the issues. The Senate hears all the legal arguments and evidence and then decides the outcome by a roll-call vote. A simple majority vote cannot convict; the Constitution states that a two-thirds vote is required.

The trial process can take weeks or even months. Andrew Johnson's trial in 1868 took almost three months, but Clinton's in 1999 took only about five weeks. In the Clinton case no live witnesses were called, but videotape evidence was presented. In both the Johnson and Clinton trials there was a majority vote for impeachment, but both of them got off — Johnson by a single vote — because the prosecutors failed to convince a two-thirds majority, as is needed for conviction.

The Framers of the Constitution were careful to appoint the Chief Justice of the U.S. Supreme Court to preside over an impeachment when the President is on trial. All other impeachment trials of lesser officials are presided over by the Vice President, who is the president of the Senate. (In practice, the *president pro tempore* — the highest-ranking senator — or a deputy will often preside.) The Vice President couldn't very well be allowed to preside over the impeachment trial of the President because he'd have a conflict of interest: The conviction of the President would turn the presidency over to the Vice President!

Understanding the Implications of Impeachment

Impeachment is one of the sexiest aspects of the Constitution. It's a fun thing — except of course for the person being impeached. And when it happens to a president, everybody has an opinion. But there are a lot of misconceptions about it too.

Impeaching isn't the same as convicting

The words "impeach" and "impeachment" sound pretty bad. When we hear "A.B. was impeached," this seems to imply that he was found guilty of something. In fact, all it means is that A.B. was formally charged and tried. It says nothing about the outcome, which would either be a *conviction* (a guilty verdict) or an *acquittal* (a not guilty verdict).

It's quite correct to say that Andrew Johnson and Bill Clinton were impeached, though both were acquitted. That's why the Constitution uses the clumsy phrase "impeachment for, and conviction of . . ." — because impeachment and conviction are two different things.

Keeping Congress out of the fray

According to the Constitution, any "civil officer of the United States" can be impeached. But what exactly is a civil officer? Does the term include members of Congress? This question was put to the test early in U.S. history.

In 1797, Senator William Blount of Tennessee was impeached by the House of Representatives. The Senate decided that it didn't have the right under the Constitution to try him. The arguments by which it reached that conclusion were far from clear, but the gist may have been that senators are not regarded as "civil officers of the United States" who alone are subject to impeachment.

An important practical consideration was the fact that Blount had already been expelled from the Senate for being guilty of a "high misdemeanor" inconsistent with his duty as a senator. (This decision was based on Blount's involvement in a military conspiracy to take Florida and Louisiana from Spain and hand them over to Britain.)

So does this mean that a person can escape impeachment if he is no longer a "civil officer" at the time? The punishment laid down for impeachment by Article I, Section 3, Clause 7 is not only removal from office but also "disqualification to hold and enjoy any Office of honor, Trust or Profit under the United States." This language seems to indicate that even somebody who is no longer in office can be impeached because, if found guilty, he can still be disqualified from holding office in the future. But in practice, after a person has jumped ship it is most unlikely that he will still be pursued for impeachment. (Richard Nixon is a good example of this fact, as I discuss in a sidebar in this chapter.)

No member of Congress has been impeached since Blount, and it's unlikely that any ever will be.

Impeaching for poor private conduct

The Constitution doesn't specify whether someone can be impeached only for acts carried out in his or her official capacity. In 1881, a Minnesota judge was removed from office in a state impeachment for being found guilty of "frequenting bawdy houses and consorting with harlots." The question of whether private conduct can be the basis of an impeachment is still very much a live issue, as President Clinton's case proves.

The Constitution allows for impeachment in cases of treason and bribery, which seems clear enough. But it also allows impeachment for "High Crimes and Misdemeanors" — a strange combination. "High Crimes" sounds solemn and serious, but "Misdemeanors" usually refers to pretty insignificant offenses like jaywalking. Presumably, we need to read this phrase to mean "High Crimes and *High* Misdemeanors." But a "High Misdemeanor" sounds like a contradiction in terms, something like "grand jaywalking" or "aggravated jaywalking." Or maybe "Misdemeanor" here refers to something that is not really a crime at all but essentially means "misconduct."

The phrase "High Crimes and Misdemeanors" found its way into the Constitution as the result of compromise. George Mason, one of the delegates to the Constitutional Convention, wanted to include "maladministration" as a ground for impeachment, but James Madison felt that this word was too vague. Mason then came up with "High Crimes and Misdemeanors" to cover what he called "attempts to subvert the Constitution."

"High Crimes and Misdemeanors," then, seems to be a formula to represent political rather than purely legal offenses. This interpretation agrees with Alexander Hamilton's view of impeachment that I quote earlier in the chapter. Andrew Johnson's impeachment falls into this category. As I explain in a moment, his real crime was that he wasn't Abraham Lincoln, and he opposed everything (except the Union) that Lincoln stood for.

Pardoning is not an option

Article II, Section 2 of the Constitution gives the President a general "Power to grant Reprieves and Pardons for Offences against the United States, except in Cases of Impeachment." This wording is another recognition of the special (political) nature of impeachment.

Didn't Richard Nixon get a presidential pardon from his successor, Gerald Ford? Yes. But keep in mind that Nixon wasn't impeached; he quit. The pardon protected Nixon from any criminal charges or civil lawsuits in the ordinary courts but had nothing to do with impeachment.

Impeachment in Action: Johnson, the Judges, and Clinton

Impeachment is a British invention, but it hasn't been used there for more than two centuries because it was perceived as essentially political. Plus, it was very time-consuming. The celebrated trial of Warren Hastings on corruption charges lasted seven years (from 1788 to 1795), took up 145 sittings of the House of Lords, and resulted in a unanimous acquittal on all charges!

Similar issues hover over U.S. impeachments. As I explain here, Andrew Johnson's impeachment was clearly politically motivated — as was Bill Clinton's. Clinton's sexual exploits and his alleged perjury should have been dealt with through the ordinary courts. Impeachment is a valuable constitutional tool and should not be misused.

Andrew Johnson: "Let them impeach and be damned"

"His faith in the people never wavered" reads the epitaph on Andrew Johnson's grave in Greenville, Tennessee. History mostly remembers the seventeenth President differently. If he's remembered at all, it's for being the first President to be impeached.

Abraham Lincoln was assassinated in 1865 only six days after the end of the Civil War and six weeks after his second inauguration. He was succeeded by his Vice President, Andrew Johnson, a pro-slavery southerner who was not even a member of Lincoln's Republican Party; he was a Democrat.

Not only was Johnson not a Republican; he had a visceral hatred of the Republican Party and all it stood for (except the Union, which he supported passionately). After he was installed as President, he was determined to put his own political program into effect. A clash with Congress loomed large on the horizon from the moment he took the Presidential oath of office. When Johnson vetoed the Civil Rights Bill granting citizenship to blacks, Congress not only overrode his veto but also went on to propose the Fourteenth Amendment to the Constitution guaranteeing "due process" and "equal protection of the laws" to all.

Johnson loudly opposed the amendment and, in the 1866 midterm elections, campaigned for conservative Democrats who felt the same way he did. But his efforts backfired badly, especially when he likened himself to Jesus Christ and claimed that the divine purpose behind Lincoln's assassination was to make Andrew Johnson the President.

The President's trial before the Senate — the first in U.S. history — was the high point of the Washington social season. It was open to the public, and tickets were in great demand. Scalpers had a field day! After a rather boring, technical trial lasting almost three months, the Senate voted 35–19 against the President. Though this was a majority, it was just one vote short of the two-thirds majority required for conviction and removal from office. So Andrew Johnson was saved by the skin of his teeth to serve out the rest of his term.

What were the "High Crimes and Misdemeanors" for which Andrew Johnson was impeached? The source of his problem was the Tenure of Office Act, which made it unlawful for the President to remove any member of his own Cabinet without the approval of the Senate. Johnson believed that this law was unconstitutional, so he ignored it and dismissed his Secretary of War anyway. (History has proven him right: In *Myers v United States,* the U.S. Supreme Court declared the Tenure of Office Act unconstitutional. But that was in 1926 — a bit too late to help Johnson!)

Johnson's impeachment was really a power struggle between the President and Congress. His main accuser told the House of Representatives that "Andrew Johnson must learn he is your servant and that as Congress shall order he must obey." This same Congressman also referred to the Constitution as "a worthless bit of old parchment." (The Constitution, based as it is on the concept of the separation of powers, makes it clear that the President is not subordinate to Congress any more than Congress is subordinate to the President. For more on the separation of powers see Chapter 8.)

If Johnson had been convicted, not only would he have been out of a job, but every President after him would have been the servant of Congress.

Judging the judges

Thomas Jefferson called impeachment a "scarecrow" because the threat of impeachment is often enough to deter an official from pursuing an unacceptable course of conduct. But in some cases the threat of impeachment isn't enough: It's necessary to initiate an impeachment prosecution. Judges are the officials who are most likely to face impeachment proceedings. A total of 14 federal judges have been impeached, and 7 of them were found guilty and removed from office.

The most recent of these cases was Judge Walter Nixon (no relation to the former President), who was impeached in 1989 for committing perjury before a grand jury. He was convicted by the Senate and removed from office. This impeachment, which was based on perjury, served as a precedent for impeaching President Clinton in 1999.

Bill Clinton: "I did not have sexual relations . . ."

Like Andrew Johnson more than a century earlier, President Clinton was impeached but not fired — there were not enough votes in the Senate to convict him. Unlike all previous impeachments, Clinton's case arose out of his sex life.

Richard Nixon: Close, but no impeachment

Some people are under the impression that Richard Nixon was impeached. He wasn't. Instead, he resigned — the only U.S. President ever to do so. But did he jump before being pushed?

Nixon remains one of the most controversial and enigmatic figures in U.S. history. He first made his name as a right-wing Republican political "gut fighter," as he called himself, dedicated to exposing politicians and government officials who were "soft on communism." After serving as a congressman and then briefly in the Senate, Nixon was picked as Dwight D. Eisenhower's running mate in 1952 and again in 1956. Two landslide victories and eight years as Vice President made Nixon a shoo-in for the Republican nomination for President in 1960. He lost to John Kennedy in one of the closest and most questionable elections ever.

Nixon's presidential moment eventually came in 1968, and he was reelected in 1972 by more than 60 percent of the popular vote. Yet it was in the run-up to this election that the fateful Watergate break-in took place. The aptly named CREEP (Committee to RE-Elect the President) hired a band of "plumbers," as they were referred to, to bug the offices of the Democratic National Committee in Washington's Watergate building. An address book left on the scene by one of the "plumbers" pointed to a White House connection. Was Nixon privy to this burglary? He always steadfastly denied it. But, even if he only found out about it afterward, was he involved in the cover-up? This question opened up a can of worms, or, to be more precise, hundreds of cans of audiotapes containing voice-activated recordings of every conversation that had ever taken place in the oval office throughout the Nixon presidency.

Claiming executive privilege, Nixon refused to hand the tapes over to the special prosecutor appointed by the Senate. Nixon then ordered his Attorney General to fire the special prosecutor, Archibald Cox, but the Attorney General refused to do so and was therefore himself obliged to resign. The Deputy Attorney General followed suit. The President's instruction was passed down to the Solicitor General, Robert Bork, who duly fired Cox in what came to be known as the "Saturday Night Massacre."

When the House of Representatives started moving toward impeachment, Nixon surrendered some of the tapes, but they turned out to have been edited. One of the tapes contained a 1972 conversation in which Nixon told the FBI to butt out of investigating the Watergate burglary, as this was a "national security" operation. Did this instruction amount to an obstruction of justice?

A new special prosecutor appointed by the Senate called for more of the tapes. Nixon again refused to disclose them on the basis of "executive privilege." In July 1974 the Supreme Court decided against the President. The House Judiciary Committee then voted to recommend that Nixon be impeached on three counts, alleging obstruction of justice, abuse of executive power, and failure to comply with Congressional demands for the tapes.

Nixon was not prepared to take a chance on the outcome of an impeachment. He resigned, and a month later he was granted a full presidential pardon by Gerald Ford. Since he had never been formally charged, the pardon was a broad one rather than for specific offenses.

Was Nixon involved in the Watergate break-in? We'll never know for sure. It may seem strange that he felt the need to bug the Democratic Party's offices in the run-up to an election that, as it turned out, he won by a landslide. Nixon always felt insecure and constantly under threat, which made him extremely suspicious and in general very cautious — so cautious that (if he *was* directly involved in the break-in) it impelled him into a senseless rash act that brought him down. As he said in an interview given to David Frost a few years later, "I brought myself down. I gave them a sword and they stuck it in. And they twisted it with relish."

It all started with a federal lawsuit filed against the President by Paula Jones in 1994. Her story was that back in 1991 when Clinton was governor of Arkansas and Jones was an Arkansas state employee, she was approached by a state trooper bearing a note reading "The Governor would like to meet with you in Suite no. XXXX." Jones claimed she had never met or spoken to Clinton before and had no idea what the note was all about. When asked, the state trooper said, "It's okay. We do this all the time for the Governor." Reassured by this response, Jones allowed the state trooper to escort her to Clinton's hotel suite. After a few flattering remarks about her hair and her figure, she claimed, he exposed his erect penis and invited her to "kiss it." According to her testimony, she recoiled in horror and left. Paula Jones sued Bill Clinton for $700,000 for sexual discrimination in his alleged unwanted advances and subsequent unfair treatment of her as a state employee.

Was it right for a President to have to face a lawsuit like this while still in office? Clinton's lawyers argued that it was unconstitutional. But the U.S. Supreme Court, after putting the lawsuit on hold till after the 1996 election, allowed it to go ahead. Clinton eventually got Jones to drop her suit by paying her $850,000 but without issuing any apology or admission of guilt or legal liability.

So ended the Paula Jones saga — or so we thought. The problem was Clinton's videotaped deposition in the Paula Jones case. It was the first time that a sitting President had ever been required to give evidence as a defendant. It was here that Clinton came out with the remark "I have never had sexual relations with Monica Lewinsky" in sworn testimony. (He later repeated that claim in a slightly paraphrased form that became notorious.)

This comment, which was later proven to be untrue and therefore perjurious, enabled Special Prosecutor Kenneth Starr to expand his investigation of the President (originally confined to the Whitewater real estate venture in Arkansas) to include Clinton's sex life and, in particular, his relationship with White House intern Monica Lewinsky. This investigation led directly to his impeachment.

How could the President's sexual conduct in private possibly amount to "High Crimes and Misdemeanors"? Clinton's supporters pooh-poohed the whole thing as too trivial for impeachment. But his critics made the point that if he lied under oath, how could you trust him as a leader?

Clinton was confronted with two charges:

- ✔ Perjury, on the ground that the President had lied under oath during the Paula Jones case before Kenneth Starr's grand jury.

- ✔ Obstruction of justice, on the ground that the President tried to hide some evidence relating to the same case.

Courting justice for Supreme Court justices

Richard Nixon was not the only public figure who jumped before he could be pushed (see the other sidebar in this chapter). Justice Abe Fortas, appointed to the Supreme Court bench by President Lyndon Johnson, was hounded by the media after accepting $20,000 for becoming a consultant to a charitable foundation headed up by a former client. Johnson, himself embattled over Vietnam, had already announced that he would not be seeking reelection. As a lame-duck President he could do nothing to help his longtime friend. In 1969, with the threat of impeachment hanging over his head, Abe Fortas resigned from the Supreme Court in disgrace.

Several Supreme Court justices have been confronted with calls for their impeachment, notably Chief Justice Earl Warren and Justice William O. Douglas. In Douglas's case a resolution calling for his impeachment was sponsored by 110 congressmen and introduced into the House of Representatives in 1970 by (future President) Gerald Ford. But that is as far as it got. The only Supreme Court Justice who was ever actually impeached was Samuel Chase, back in 1805 — and he was acquitted.

On Article I, the vote in the Senate was 55 for acquittal and only 45 for conviction. On Article II, the Senate was split 50–50. A two-thirds majority was needed for conviction, so the impeachment managers were 17 votes short of a firing squad. Bill Clinton remained in office and left with a 65 percent approval rating — the highest of any retiring President since Dwight D. Eisenhower.

Removing State Officials from Office

Impeachment is not confined to federal officials. It applies equally to state officials in 49 of the 50 states. The one exception is Oregon, where "public officers" charged with "incompetence, corruption, malfeasance, or delinquency in office" are tried in the ordinary courts, which have the power to strip them of their office as well as to punish them in other ways. In the remaining 49 states, impeachment is a possibility, though the form it takes may differ slightly from the federal model.

Many state constitutions mirror the language of the U.S. Constitution, but the language is varied. There is a procession of "malfeasance," "malpractice," "misconduct," and even the vague term opposed by James Madison, "maladministration." Four states cite "moral turpitude" or "moral turpitude in office" as grounds for impeachment. (Had this language been in the U.S. Constitution, would President Clinton have been fired?)

Impeaching governors

Governors are the equivalent of the President at the state level, so they are liable to impeachment. Twelve state governors have been impeached over the years. Eight were convicted and removed from office, and one resigned.

In 2008, Governor Eliot Spitzer of New York resigned in the face of impeachment threats arising out of a scandal involving a prostitute. In 2009, Governor Rod Blagojevich of Illinois was impeached for allegedly trying to sell the Senate seat vacated by President Obama. His whirlwind impeachment trial before the Illinois State Senate ended with a unanimous 59–0 vote against him. He was immediately removed from office and disqualified from ever again holding any "office of honor or trust" in Illinois. Blagojevich's impeachment conviction did not exempt him from facing criminal charges in a regular criminal court.

Total recall, or terminating a governor

Some states have devised an even more ingenious way of ridding themselves of elected public officials between elections: *recall*. The best-known example of a recall occurred in California in 2003, when Governor Gray Davis, who had been reelected for a second term only the previous year, was recalled and replaced by Arnold Schwarzenegger.

Recall has been available to Californians since 1911. To set the process in motion requires the signatures of 12 percent of the number of votes cast in the previous election. In the 2003 case this meant that the signatures of 897,158 registered California voters were needed!

A recall election ballot has two parts:

- ✔ In the first part you vote "Yes" or "No" to recall the incumbent.
- ✔ If "Yes" wins, there is a second round, in which you select the replacement candidate of your choice.

It's pretty easy to get on the ballot. All you need is 65 nomination signatures and a $3,500 filing fee.

In the 2003 California recall ballot, there was a 55.3 percent vote to recall Gray Davis, with Arnie taking 48.7 percent of the vote in part two, a remarkable feat considering that there were no fewer than 131 candidates on the ballot, 41 of them Republicans!

Without a superstar candidate to galvanize public support, recall elections are clearly not the easiest way to remove a governor from office, but they are an interesting safety valve. Above all, they are a form of direct democracy.

Part IV
The Bill of Rights: Specifying Rights through Amendments

The 5th Wave   By Rich Tennant

Guard! Order those people to stop talking! We're trying to write the First Amendment up here!

In this part . . .

Here's where you get the lowdown on your constitutional rights. The Bill of Rights may have been an afterthought as far as the Framers of the Constitution were concerned, but for most people these first ten amendments are crucial. Read all about them here.

Chapter 14

The First Amendment: Freedom of Religion, Speech, and Assembly

▶ Establishing freedom of religion

▶ Protecting freedom of speech responsibly

▶ Guarding against obscenity

▶ Protecting freedom of assembly and association

The First Amendment forms part of the *Bill of Rights* — the name we give to the first ten amendments. The First Amendment is arguably the most important part not only of the Bill of Rights but also of the Constitution as a whole because it guarantees some pretty fundamental rights:

✔ Freedom of religion and belief

✔ Freedom of speech

✔ Freedom of the press

✔ Freedom of assembly and association

✔ Freedom to petition the government

In this chapter, I explain each of these rights and how they've been interpreted through the years.

Considering the Amendment's Wording

Here's what the First Amendment says:

> *Congress shall make no law respecting an establishment of religion, or prohibiting the free exercise thereof; or abridging the freedom of speech, or of the press; or the right of the people peaceably to assemble, and to petition the Government for a redress of grievances.*

Prohibiting Congress from taking away rights

Notice the unusual wording. The whole amendment is governed by the opening phrase "Congress shall make no law . . ." No other amendment starts that way. How come the First Amendment differs from all the other amendments in this important respect?

The answer is that in this amendment the Framers were not granting new rights to the people. They assumed that those rights already existed. The amendment was clearly designed to stop Congress from taking away rights that already existed.

Applying the amendment to the states

The opening word of the First Amendment makes it clear that the amendment applies only to Congress, which is part of the federal government. There is no indication that it applies to the states. Should we conclude that the First Amendment doesn't apply to the states? You may assume that's the simple, logical conclusion. But the U.S. Supreme Court in its wisdom has decided otherwise.

As I explain in Chapter 17, the high court has expanded its interpretation of the famous Due Process Clause in the Fourteenth Amendment to incorporate much of the Bill of Rights — including the First Amendment — and apply it to the states. In other words, the high court has ruled that based on the Fourteenth Amendment, states must adhere to much of the Bill of Rights, just as the federal government does.

The First Amendment is considered *completely incorporated.* That means all the rights spelled out in the amendment must apply at the state level, as well as at the federal level.

Separating Church and State

The first two clauses of the First Amendment are about religion. The first of these clauses — *Congress shall make no law respecting an establishment of religion* — is commonly referred to as the Establishment Clause. Let's break down the wording of this clause:

✔ **Congress shall make no law:** The word *shall,* even in more modern legal documents, means "must." So "Congress shall make no law respecting an establishment of religion" means "Congress must not make any law about the establishment of religion."

✔ **establishment:** In England there was (and still is) an established religion and state church, known as the Church of England. Opposition to this state church was one of the most important motivating forces leading the early settlers to leave England and come to America. A number of the colonies replaced the Church of England with their own favored brand of Protestantism, and this situation continued after independence. The intention of the Establishment Clause was to prevent Congress from establishing a national church — and also to stop Congress from interfering with existing state establishments. The only high court justice who ever showed any sign of understanding this important latter point was the much underrated Justice Potter Stewart (the judicial hero of Justice John Paul Stevens).

✔ **respecting:** The phrase "respecting an establishment of religion" just means "about an establishment of religion."

Testing, testing

The high court has formulated the *Lemon* Test for legislation concerned with religious matters — named for the 1971 case *Lemon v. Kurtzman,* in which a legal challenge was mounted against Pennsylvania and Rhode Island statutes providing state aid to church-related schools. Chief Justice Warren Burger, writing for the majority, set out the test in these terms:

✔ *First, the statute must have a secular legislative purpose;*

✔ *Second, its principal or primary effect must be one that neither advances nor inhibits religion;*

✔ *Finally, the statute must not foster "an excessive government entanglement with religion."*

In *Lee v. Weisman,* heard in 1992, the high court supplemented the *Lemon* test with Justice Anthony Kennedy's "coercion test," which ruled as unconstitutional the giving of a nonsectarian benediction by a clergyman at a public school graduation ceremony — on the dubious basis that this religious feature placed the graduating students under subtle religious "coercion."

Justice Sandra Day O'Connor's "endorsement test" makes it even easier for a law or government action to "run afoul" of the Establishment Clause. This test asks whether the government action in question "conveys a message of endorsement or disapproval" of religion — either of which is unconstitutional.

If the Establishment Clause was intended to prevent the establishment of *any* official church at either the national or state level, why didn't it say so? The Establishment Clause raises more questions than it answers. Here are some of those questions:

✔ **Is it okay for a state to authorize the recitation of a voluntary, non-denominational prayer at the start of each school day?** The prayer in question, introduced by the school district of New Hyde Park, New York, read as follows: *Almighty God, we acknowledge our dependence upon Thee, and we beg Thy blessings upon us, our parents, our teachers, and our Country.* In the 1962 case *Engel v. Vitale,* the high court ruled that the use of the prayer "breaches the constitutional wall of separation between Church and State." Justice Potter Stewart, in his lone dissent, made some trenchant points against this ruling, notably:

  • The majority placed too much reliance on the phrase "wall of separation between Church and State," quoted from a letter written by Thomas Jefferson in 1802 — "a phrase nowhere to be found in the Constitution."

  • Both houses of Congress open their daily sessions with prayer.

  • The President's oath of office ends with "so help me God" (added to the official wording in the Constitution by George Washington and every one of his successors).

  • The National Anthem, "The Star-Spangled Banner," contains the verse, "And this be our motto 'In God is our Trust.'"

  • "Since 1865, the words 'IN GOD WE TRUST' have been impressed on our coins."

  • Since 1954, the Pledge of Allegiance to the Flag has contained the words "one nation *under God . . .*" (Several so-far indecisive legal challenges have been launched against this wording.)

  • The Supreme Court itself starts each day with the invocation by the court crier, "God save the United States and this Honorable Court."

✔ **Is it okay for a state to provide tuition vouchers for use in public or private schools, including religiously affiliated schools?** In the 2002 case of *Zelman v. Simmons-Harris,* the majority on the court said yes — provided the vouchers went to parents and not to the schools, and provided the parents had a choice of nonreligious as well as religious schools.

✔ **Is it okay for the Ten Commandments to be displayed in a courthouse?** In 2003, the Chief Justice of Alabama, Roy Moore, was fired for refusing to remove a granite monument of the Ten Commandments from the central rotunda of the Alabama Judicial Building. Moore's removal from office followed a ruling by a federal District Court declaring that the monument violated the Establishment Clause of the First Amendment and was therefore unconstitutional. In 2005, the U.S. Supreme Court decided in a 5–4 split that displaying the Ten Commandments on a Kentucky courthouse wall violated the First Amendment's requirement of separation between church and state. But a display of the Ten Commandments on the grounds of the Texas State Capitol in Austin, Texas, was held by the same margin to be permissible!

Guaranteeing the Free Exercise of Religion

The second clause of the First Amendment says that [*Congress shall make no law*] *prohibiting the free exercise [of religion]*. This clause is known as the Free Exercise Clause.

In the 1879 case of *Reynolds v. United States,* the Supreme Court divided the exercise of religion into two parts: belief or opinion on the one hand and, on the other hand, practice. The court ruled that the law can't interfere with "mere religious beliefs and opinions," but it may interfere with religious practices.

The *Reynolds* case was about polygamy, as practiced at that time by some Mormons. Could religion be a defense to illegal actions? No, said Chief Justice Morrison Waite, writing for the court; otherwise, even religiously based human sacrifice would have to be allowed.

Adopting a strict scrutiny test

In the 1963 case *Sherbert v. Verner,* the Supreme Court adopted a *strict scrutiny* test to determine whether a person's rights under the Free Exercise Clause have been violated. Adell Sherbert was a Seventh Day Adventist who was fired from her job because she refused to work on Saturdays. She couldn't find another job, so she applied for unemployment compensation. But her unemployment claim was denied by the Employment Security Commission, by a South Carolina trial court, and by the South Carolina Supreme Court. Sherbert's claim for unemployment compensation eventually reached the U.S. Supreme Court.

The high court established the following criteria for the *Sherbert* Test, as it was quickly dubbed:

- ✓ **Whether the plaintiff's religious belief was sincere:** Adell Sherbert's religious sincerity was not in doubt.

- ✓ **Whether the government action imposed a "substantial burden" on the plaintiff's ability freely to exercise her religion:** The Supreme Court found that this requirement had been met in the Sherbert case.

If these two criteria are satisfied, then the government has to prove

- ✓ **That there was "a compelling state interest" justifying the government's action:** In the *Sherbert* case, no compelling state interest was found that denied Adell Sherbert unemployment compensation.

- ✓ **That it could not have pursued its compelling interest in a way that did not infringe on the plaintiff's freedom of religion:** In the *Sherbert* case, this point didn't arise.

So Adell Sherbert won her case in the Supreme Court — and in the process established a sensible *strict scrutiny* test that protected the free exercise of religion of others.

However, in 1990 the Supreme Court abandoned the need for strict scrutiny in cases involving the free exercise of religion. This change meant that freedom of religion was no longer accorded the same protection as under the *Sherbert* Test. To restore the *Sherbert* Test, Congress passed the Religious Freedom Restoration Act (RFRA) with overwhelming bipartisan support.

But RFRA put the high court's nose out of joint because it looked as though Congress was not just *enforcing* the Constitution but *interpreting* it — a privilege that the court had long ago arrogated to itself (see Chapter 12). In the words of Justice Anthony Kennedy, writing for the majority on the court, "Congress does not enforce a constitutional right by changing what the right is." Come again? Wasn't it the Supreme Court that changed the test in the first place — and, in so doing, changed the right also?

Witnessing judicial gyrations: Jehovah's Witnesses and the Supreme Court

No religious group has been given a rougher rollercoaster ride by the Supreme Court than the Jehovah's Witnesses. As has happened so often in the history of the court, it keeps changing its mind.

In the 1940 case *Minersville School District v. Gobitis,* Jehovah's Witnesses challenged the right of public schools to compel students to salute the flag and recite the Pledge of Allegiance. Justice Felix Frankfurter, writing for the majority on the court, ruled against the Jehovah's Witnesses. He held that "the flag is the symbol of the nation's power, the emblem of freedom in its truest, best sense."

Three years later, the high court changed its mind in *West Virginia State Board of Education v. Barnette*, an almost identical case to *Gobitis.* During the three-year interval, some Jehovah's Witness children were threatened with expulsion from public schools, and a spate of physical attacks on Jehovah's Witnesses occurred. This situation undoubtedly factored into the high court's change of heart — as did a change in the composition of the court itself.

In *Barnette,* it seemed clear that Jehovah's Witnesses were not refusing to salute the flag because of any lack of patriotism but purely on the basis of a deeply-held faith according to which saluting the flag amounted to idolatry. In the words of Hugo Black and William O. Douglas, two of the justices who changed sides, "Words uttered under coercion are proof of loyalty to nothing but self-interest."

Guaranteeing Freedom of Expression

After religion, the First Amendment turns to freedom of expression. Here are the relevant words:

> *Congress shall make no law . . . abridging the freedom of speech, or of the press.*

Flag burning: Protecting unspoken speech

In the 1989 case of *Texas v. Johnson,* a 5–4 majority on the court characterized flag burning as protected "speech" under the First Amendment. Interestingly, the conservative Chief Justice William Rehnquist and the liberal Justice John Paul Stevens both strongly dissented for different reasons. Stevens highlighted the illogicality of the majority ruling by pointing out that if a protestor had "chosen to spray-paint his message of dissatisfaction on the façade of the Lincoln Memorial, there would be no question about the power of the Government to prohibit his means of expression."

This provision looks pretty straightforward. But let's look at it as little more closely:

- The whole provision is couched in negative terms and is governed by the words "Congress shall make no law." Why? Because the First Amendment is not *granting* any new rights. It's only *guaranteeing* rights that already existed.

- The right to freedom of speech already existed in colonial times — but subject to certain exceptions, notably defamation and obscenity.

- The amendment draws a distinction between freedom of speech and freedom of the press. But doesn't the term "freedom of speech" cover freedom of the press? Sure, but press freedom was considered important enough to deserve separate protection.

- However, press freedom can also sometimes actually conflict with individual freedom of speech. A good example of this occurred in the run-up to the 2008 presidential election, when *The New York Times* refused to print an op-ed piece by John McCain responding to one by Barack Obama.

Denying protection to speech creating a "clear and present danger"

Congress has passed a number of laws that prohibit certain types of expression, particularly in regard to revolutionary speeches or writings. And the high court has addressed many questions relating to such types of expression. Here are a few:

- **Can speech lose its First Amendment protection if it creates a "clear and present danger"?** The court answered yes (until 1969 — see the last bullet of this list). Charles Schenck, a Socialist, published a leaflet urging young men to refuse to serve in World War I if drafted. In *Schenck v. United States,* heard in 1919, the high court rejected Schenck's claim that his publication was protected by the First Amendment. Justice Oliver Wendell Holmes, writing for a unanimous court, held that the leaflets created a "clear and present danger" that draftees would refuse to serve in the armed forces, which was a "substantive evil" that the government had the right to prevent. Holmes based this doctrine on a shaky parallel: "The most stringent protection of free speech would not protect a man in falsely shouting fire in a theatre and causing a panic."

- **How clear and how present does the "clear and present danger" have to be?** According to the Supreme Court, not very clear and not very present. In *Gitlow v. New York,* decided in 1925, the majority on the court greatly widened the "clear and present danger" test, upholding Benjamin Gitlow's New York conviction for advocating the violent overthrow of the government. Oliver Wendell Holmes, the originator of the "clear and present danger" test, dissented. He held that the publication of Gitlow's revolutionary writings did not create any such danger, as his views were shared by only a small minority of people — and Gitlow was only calling for a revolution at some "indefinite time in the future."

✔ **Is the "clear and present danger" test still in force?** No. The high court unanimously replaced it, in the 1969 case of *Brandenburg v. Ohio,* with a new, more liberal test, allowing First Amendment protection even to advocacy of the use of force — "except where such advocacy is directed to inciting or producing imminent lawless action and is likely to incite or produce such action."

Allowing obscenity to be seen?

Are pornography and obscene publications protected under the First Amendment?

Justice Thurgood Marshall, writing for the court in the 1964 case *Stanley v. Georgia,* famously held that "If the First Amendment means anything, it means that a State has no business telling a man, sitting alone in his own house, what books he may read or what films he may watch."

In a nutshell, here's where the court stands on protections related to obscene materials: The possession of obscene material is protected under the First Amendment. The sale and distribution of obscene material, on the other hand, does not enjoy First Amendment protection (although the American Civil Liberties Union [ACLU] successfully challenged parts of the Communications Decency Act of 1996 that made it a crime to use the Internet to send or display to anyone under the age of 18 any communication that is "patently offensive, obscene or indecent").

The possession protection does not extend to child pornography. The law on child pornography has been tightened through the years, including with the PROTECT Act of 2003. (PROTECT is an acronym for Prosecutorial Remedies and Other Tools to end the Exploitation of Children Today.) The constitutionality of this act was unsuccessfully challenged in the 2008 case of *United States v. Williams.*

This whole discussion begs the question, what is the definition of obscenity? The high court had a major problem with this question until, in 1973, it hit upon a definition that is still generally accepted. This definition, formulated in the case of *Miller v. California,* restricts the label *obscene* to

> *works which, taken as a whole, appeal to the prurient interest in sex, which portray sexual conduct in a patently offensive way, and which, taken as a whole, do not have serious literary, artistic, political, or scientific value.*

What a mouthful!

Using and abusing the right to freedom of the press

In the early days of the United States, anybody could set up a printing press in a back room of his or her house. The Framers regarded press freedom as something very precious because it gave the little person a voice against big government.

In the early 20th century, the state of Minnesota challenged freedom of the press with a state law that provided for the gagging of any "malicious, scandalous and defamatory newspaper, magazine or other periodical." *The Saturday Press,* a particularly scurrilous rag, was prosecuted under this law. But, in the 1931 case of *Near v. Minnesota,* the U.S. Supreme Court struck down the state law as unconstitutional. Chief Justice Charles Evans Hughes, writing for the majority, held that "Liberty of speech and of the press, is not an absolute right, and the State may punish its abuse" — but only after publication, not before.

The high court gave a great boost to press freedom in the landmark 1964 case of *New York Times Co. v. Sullivan*. Sullivan was a police chief in Montgomery, Alabama. *The New York Times* ran an advertisement that Sullivan claimed was defamatory of himself. Sullivan was awarded damages of $500,000 by an Alabama court. The U.S. Supreme Court took this money away from him and created a new rule applicable to public officials bringing a defamation or libel suit concerning their official conduct. To win a libel suit, a public official needs to prove not only that the words he objects to are untrue but that they also involve *actual malice* — meaning that the person who published those words knew that they were false or didn't care whether they were true or false.

What if the published falsehood is deliberate but intended to be satirical? The well-known 1988 case of *Hustler Magazine v. Falwell* concerned a spoof interview with the Rev. Jerry Falwell in which Falwell "admitted" that his "first time" was drunken incest with his mother in an outhouse. Falwell was awarded $150,000 for emotional distress. But the high court found in favor of the magazine because the purported claims contained in the offending article were so extreme that nobody could be expected to take them seriously.

In 1971, *The New York Times* led another notable, but somewhat dubious, triumph for press freedom. The case centered on the Pentagon Papers — a 14,000-page top-secret government report about the handling of the Vietnam War. The report was leaked to *The New York Times* by Daniel Ellsberg, who was involved in a study of the documents originally commissioned by Defense Secretary Robert McNamara. The *Times* at once began publishing excerpts from these top-secret documents in serialized form.

The majority on the high court found in favor of the newspaper's right to publish the excerpts, arguing that except when the nation was actually at war, the First Amendment guarantee of freedom of speech is absolute. In the words of Justice William Brennan:

> *The entire thrust of the Government's claim has been that publication of the material sought to be enjoined "could," or "might," or "may" prejudice the national interest in various ways. But the First Amendment tolerates absolutely no prior judicial restraints of the press predicated upon surmise or conjecture that untoward consequences may result.*

Chief Justice Warren Burger dissented, describing the published information as "purloined documents." Justice Harry Blackmun, who also dissented, concluded that publication of the Pentagon Papers "could clearly result in great harm to the nation." Blackmun set the First Amendment against the background of the Constitution as a whole:

> *The First Amendment, after all, is only one part of an entire Constitution. Article II of the great document vests in the Executive Branch primary power over the conduct of foreign affairs, and places in that branch responsibility for the Nation's safety.*

Protecting the Right to Assemble and Petition

The right to march to Washington D.C. and make your feelings known to the government is still an important one, but probably less important than it was in the early days of the nation, before the rise of the party system, before radio, before television, and before the Internet.

The connection between the right to assemble and the right to petition can easily be seen, and so can the connection between the right to assemble and the right to free association — which has been interpreted to allow membership of labor unions and other associations.

United States v. Cruikshank, decided in 1875, is one of the few leading cases on this aspect of the First Amendment. An armed white mob clashed with a large gathering of African Americans at the courthouse in Colfax, Louisiana, at the time of a gubernatorial election. Some whites were charged under a Louisiana law that made it a felony for two or more persons to "combine, conspire, and confederate together, with the unlawful purpose of depriving United States citizens of African descent" of their civil rights. The U.S. Supreme Court threw out the indictments for vagueness. But the most important part of the ruling in *Cruikshank* was to refuse to apply the First Amendment to the states. In other words, the high court did not regard the First Amendment as "incorporated" by the Fourteenth Amendment's Due Process Clause. The court held that the First Amendment applied only to the national government.

However, the U.S. Supreme Court now regards the whole of the First Amendment as "incorporated" — including the right to petition and freedom of assembly. So the states are now subordinate to the feds in regard to these rights also.

In the 1937 decision in *De Jonge v. Oregon,* a unanimous U.S. Supreme Court overturned the conviction of a Communist leader for addressing a meeting allegedly advocating "criminal syndicalism and sabotage." The high court declared the interpretation of the Oregon law by the state Supreme Court to be "repugnant" to the First Amendment as incorporated into the Due Process Clause of the Fourteenth Amendment.

National Socialist Party of America v. Village of Skokie is an interesting and highly controversial 1978 case illustrating the conflicting forces at work. A neo-Nazi group wanted to stage a march through the village of Skokie, Illinois, a largely Jewish area. The local authorities wanted to keep the neo-Nazis out. The Illinois Supreme Court, upheld by the U.S. Supreme Court, refused to ban the march. The Illinois Supreme Court even specifically refused to ban the display of the swastika emblem — using the rather dubious parallel of permission given to war protesters in another case to wear black armbands. In the end, the neo-Nazis didn't march through Skokie, but they had won a legal victory without doing so.

Chapter 15

The Second Amendment: Bearing Arms

*T*he Second Amendment is one of the shortest — and one of the most controversial — of all the amendments. Here's how the amendment reads, according to the handwritten version of the Bill of Rights now hanging in the U.S. National Archives in Washington D.C. (as painstakingly inked on parchment by congressional clerk William Lambert back in 1789):

> *A well regulated Militia, being necessary to the security of a free State, the right of the people to keep and bear Arms, shall not be infringed.*

But the version of the amendment that was actually passed by Congress and ratified by the states is worded this way:

> *A well regulated militia being necessary to the security of a free State, the right of the people to keep and bear arms shall not be infringed.*

This version looks more modern. The difference between the two versions is two extra commas in the Lambert version: one after "Militia" and another after "Arms." Do the commas really matter? Probably not. Punctuation was more arbitrary 200 years ago than it is today. A comma could just indicate a pause without any grammatical significance.

But the interpretation of this single sentence — with or without the two extra commas — is the focus of heated debate. In this chapter, I introduce the arguments surrounding this amendment and explain the impact of a recent Supreme Court decision about gun rights.

Debating Interpretation: Individual versus State Rights

Two main schools of thought do battle over the Second Amendment: the individual (or personal) rights school of thought and the states' (or collective) rights school of thought. In a nutshell, here's how the two differ:

- ✓ **Individual rights:** The individual rights school interprets the amendment as giving people the right to buy guns and use them for sport, self-protection, or any other lawful purpose. This school believes that every person has the same right, not just members of the military, the National Guard, or any other kind of militia.

- ✓ **States' rights:** This school sees the amendment as giving states the right to establish militias like the National Guard but not giving any rights to individuals.

A range of intermediate views exists, of course, which fall somewhere between these two schools of thought. For example, some people believe that the amendment

- ✓ Restricts the right to possess firearms to members of some sort of militia but allows such members to use their arms for their own personal protection as well as for national defense.

- ✓ Allows any law-abiding and responsible citizen to possess firearms after undergoing a background check.

- ✓ Grants individual citizens the right to have firearms for their personal use, provided the firearms are of a standard military type.

If you pay any attention to politics, you probably realize that people who define themselves as conservative tend to fall on one side of the debate between individual and states' rights, and people who call themselves liberal often fall on the other side. In case you opt not to pay attention to politics at all (which means you probably get less heartburn than the rest of us), here's the general breakdown:

- ✓ **Conservatives:** Broadly speaking, conservatives favor the right of U.S. citizens to arm themselves if they so wish. Conservatives tend to oppose placing restrictions on the purchase or possession of guns because they assume that criminals can gain access to firearms anyway. By clearing away legal restrictions, they argue, the law favors law-abiding citizens over the criminal element.

- ✓ **Liberals:** Liberals tend to fall into the states' rights camp. Many liberals fear the possibility of individuals taking the law into their own hands and are more inclined to support restrictions on buying and carrying guns.

Obviously, these are generalizations, and you probably wouldn't have too much trouble finding exceptions to the rule.

Breaking Down the Amendment's Clauses

Why, exactly, do people debate the Second Amendment so heatedly? After all, the entire Second Amendment is contained in a single sentence. The problem is that the two halves of that sentence seem to point in opposite directions:

- ✔ The first half — *A well regulated Militia, being necessary to the security of a free State* — appears to place an emphasis on collective rights and obligations.

- ✔ The second half — *the right of the people to keep and bear Arms, shall not be infringed* — places the emphasis on individual rights.

To understand the true meaning of the Second Amendment, we must take both its clauses into account. But the two schools of thought on this amendment each emphasize one clause at the expense of the other. The individual rights school emphasizes the second clause, while the states' rights school concentrates on the first.

In terms of English grammar, the second half of the amendment is the main clause, while the first half is a subordinate clause. This structure seems to support the individual rights interpretation, but nothing about this amendment is quite clear-cut. As I show in the next section, states' rights supporters have a different way of interpreting the sentence structure.

Understanding the states' rights interpretation

The Second Amendment is the only part of the U.S. Bill of Rights that has a preamble or prefatory clause. I have enough faith in the amendment's authors to believe that the sentence structure is not accidental, but what does the first clause tell us?

Finding meaning in "Militia"

To get an answer, consider that the word *militia* also appears in Article I, Section 8 and Article II, Section 2 of the Constitution and in the Fifth Amendment. (See the nearby sidebar "'Militia' in other parts of the Constitution.") I believe that the word *militia* means the same thing in all these passages.

The Framers of the Constitution had markedly different feelings about armies than about militias. The Framers didn't trust standing armies, which you can see from the fact that Article I, Section 8 of the Constitution prohibits Congress from financing an army for more than two years at a time. The function of keeping order and even of repelling invasions is entrusted to "the Militia" rather than the army.

Moreover, although the President is designated as Commander in Chief of the militia as well as of the army and navy (in Article II, Section 2), that chain of command applies only when the militia is "called into the actual Service of the United States." Under normal circumstances, the militia is under the control of the individual states, not of the federal government. This fact was explained by President Thomas Jefferson in a letter to Destutt de Tracy in 1811, in which Jefferson writes that the governor of each state is "constitutionally the commander of the militia of the State."

Jefferson was very concerned that the young Republic should have an efficient and effective militia. He referred to it frequently in his annual messages to Congress. For example, in 1808 he said:

> *For a people who are free, and who mean to remain so, a well-organized and armed militia is their best security. It is, therefore, incumbent on us, at every meeting to revise the condition of the militia, and to ask ourselves if it is prepared to repel a powerful enemy at every point of our territories exposed to invasion.*

Why the sharp contrast between the attitude toward militias and toward armies? Keep in mind that in the 18th century, police as we know them did not exist, so law and order had to be kept by soldiers. But if those soldiers were formed into a standing (permanent) army, the executive government would have tremendous power. A standing army owed its loyalty to the government, and in Europe governments had often used their troops as a repressive police force. Militias, by contrast, were the citizenry under arms (and generally carried their own arms).

By the time the Second Amendment was ratified in 1791, the original part of the Constitution had been in force for about three years. It would have been strange, therefore, if "the well regulated Militia" of the Second Amendment referred to anything other than the type of militia that had been given such prominence elsewhere in the Constitution.

Its presence in the Constitution has invested the term *militia* with a certain sanctity. Not surprisingly, a number of self-proclaimed militias exist in the United States, some of which are really no more than vigilante groups. By using this label, they wrap themselves in the flag and claim a specially protected status. But are they entitled to it? Not unless they are militias in the sense intended by the Second Amendment.

TECHNICAL STUFF

"Militia" in other parts of the Constitution

The term *militia* appears in several places in the Constitution. Its usage in other passages helps us determine how the Framers intended it to be interpreted in the Second Amendment.

Article I, Section 8 of the Constitution contains two clauses dealing with the militia and one dealing with armies. It gives power to Congress

> *To raise and support Armies, but no Appropriation of Money to that use shall be for a longer Term than two Years;*

> *To provide for calling forth the Militia to execute the Laws of the Union, suppress Insurrections and repel Invasions;*

> *To provide for organizing, arming, and disciplining, the Militia, and for governing such Part of them as may be employed in*

> *the Service of the United States, reserving to the States respectively, the Appointment of the Officers, and the Authority of training the Militia according to the discipline prescribed by Congress.*

Article II deals with the presidency. Section 2 starts:

> *The President shall be Commander in Chief of the Army and Navy of the United States, and of the Militia of the several States, when called into the actual Service of the United States.*

The Fifth Amendment says that nobody is to be charged with "a capital, or otherwise infamous crime" unless indicted by a grand jury "except in cases arising in the land or naval forces, or in the Militia, when in actual service in time of War or public danger."

Interpreting the second clause with states' rights in mind

The states' righters like the first clause of the amendment better than the second, but they can't get away from the fact that the second clause is the main clause. So how do they interpret it — in particular the words "the right of the people to keep and bear arms"?

They start by recognizing that a militia is made up of ordinary citizens under arms that they provide for themselves. They then focus on the word "bear."

In 1840, the Tennessee Supreme Court in *Aymette v. The State* was adamant that the word "bear" had a distinctly military connotation:

> *The words 'bear arms' have reference to their military use, and were not employed to mean wearing them about the person as part of the dress.*

> *A man in the pursuit of deer, elk, and buffaloes might carry his rifle every day for forty years, and yet it would never be said of him that he had borne arms; much less could it be said that a private citizen bears arms because he has a dirk or pistol concealed under his clothes, or a spear in a cane.*

This passage was fully endorsed by the Ninth Circuit Court of Appeals in *Silveira v. Lockyer* in 2002.

Interpreting "the right of the people"

Now that we have a sense of how states' rights advocates interpret the two clauses of the Second Amendment, let's turn our attention to the individual rights school of thought. To start, keep in mind that individual rights advocates focus on the second half of the amendment, which is the main clause: *the right of the people to keep and bear Arms, shall not be infringed.*

The Second Amendment is not the only one to contain the phrase "the right of the people." This same expression also appears in the First and Fourth amendments (see Chapters 14 and 16), where it clearly refers to individual rights.

If the Second Amendment gives rights to individuals, what exactly are those rights and what lawful restrictions can be placed on them? For example, does the right apply to any kind of firearm, or are there some justifiable restrictions? As I show later in this chapter, the U.S. Supreme Court in *United States v. Miller* recognized the right as being a personal or individual one but held that it had to be exercised in accordance with "the security of a free State."

What are the nature and scope of the rights claimed by pro-gun advocates? Most of them insist that the purpose of the Second Amendment was not to grant any new rights but to preserve and guarantee rights that were already in existence. Some take the view that these rights are absolute, or unlimited. They're afraid of the "slippery slope" — the danger that apparently minor restrictions are likely to lead to the eventual disappearance of gun rights altogether.

Others are prepared to accept restrictions on the purchase of certain types of firearms, such as automatic and semiautomatic weapons, and don't object to background checks before buying a gun. Sportsmen are sometimes prepared to accept a ban on handguns, as long as they can still buy shotguns and hunting rifles. But gun rights activists reject this approach as defeatist and insist that the amendment doesn't protect only hunting but is intended primarily for self-defense.

Upholding Individual Rights: D.C. v. Heller

In 2008, in the case *District of Columbia v. Heller,* the Supreme Court for the first time actually decided on the meaning of the Second Amendment. The court was finally able to get its teeth into this important question because of a challenge to a Washington, D.C. law.

The law in question totally banned the possession of handguns in the home. It also made it a crime to carry any unregistered firearm and required any lawful firearm in the home to be bound by a trigger-lock.

Those opposed to the D.C. law portrayed it as completely preventing home-owners and other residents from defending themselves against intruders. The law banned handguns, the firearm of choice for home protection, and disabled all other firearms by insisting that they have a trigger-lock on.

The question before the high court was therefore quite simple: Was the D.C. law in keeping with the Second Amendment, or did it violate rights under that amendment?

To answer that question, it was necessary for the court to interpret the meaning of the amendment. As I explain earlier in the chapter, there are two main interpretations of the Second Amendment: the individual rights inter-pretation and the states' rights interpretation.

In its ruling, the Supreme Court divided along traditional lines, with two of the court's big hitters slugging it out:

✔ The heavyweight conservative standard-bearer Justice Antonin Scalia did battle in favor of individual rights.

✔ The agile 88-year-old liberal Justice John Paul Stevens (on the court since 1975) gave as good as he got on the states' rights side.

Stevens emphasized the first clause of the amendment, while Scalia argued that the second clause was the really important one. Scalia won a narrow but decisive 5–4 victory. So it's official: You *do* have an individual constitutional right to own and use a gun.

Concentrating on the D.C. law's ban on handguns and its requirement that licensed firearms in the home be kept inoperable at all times, the majority ruled that "This makes it impossible for citizens to use firearms for the core lawful purpose of self-defense and is hence unconstitutional." The court therefore struck the D.C. law down as unconstitutional.

The minority on the court sought to uphold the D.C. law, relying on the fact that *some* regulation of the possession and use of firearms had always been allowed and the D.C. law's restrictions did not go beyond proper limits.

Justice Stephen Breyer, in an additional dissent, opined:

> *The protection the Amendment provides is not absolute. The Amendment permits government to regulate the interests that it serves. . . . The majority's view cannot be correct unless it can show that the District's regulation is unreasonable or inappropriate in Second Amendment terms. This the majority cannot do.*

Considering an earlier Supreme Court decision

Although *Heller* was the first Supreme Court case to offer a comprehensive interpretation of the Second Amendment, the amendment was considered in several earlier Supreme Court cases. The most important of these was *United States v. Miller,* decided in 1939. Two suspected robbers and moonshiners were charged with transporting an unregistered sawed-off shotgun across state lines in violation of the National Firearms Act of 1934. The question before the Supreme Court was whether this law violated the Second Amendment. The law didn't prohibit the possession or transportation of any kind of firearm. It just required certain classes of firearms, including sawed-off shotguns, to be registered at a cost of $200.

Justice James McReynolds, writing for a unanimous high court, ruled that the 1934 act did not conflict with the Second Amendment. McReynolds held that the Second Amendment "must be interpreted and applied" with the view of maintaining a "militia." A sawed-off shotgun didn't have any "reasonable relationship to the preservation or efficiency of a well regulated militia," so the restriction on such firearms by requiring them to be registered didn't violate the Second Amendment.

Taking two sides on what Miller meant

The minority in *Heller* expressed great respect, even reverence, for the unanimous opinion in *Miller,* which Justice John Paul Stevens summarized as holding that the Second Amendment "protects the right to keep and bear arms for certain military purposes, but . . . does not curtail the legislature's power to regulate the nonmilitary use and ownership of weapons."

Antonin Scalia for the majority rejected this interpretation of *Miller* out of hand:

> *Miller did not hold that and cannot possibly be read to have held that. Miller stands only for the proposition that the Second Amendment right, whatever its nature, extends only to certain types of weapons. It is particularly wrongheaded to read Miller for more than what it said, because the case did not even purport to be a thorough examination of the Second Amendment.*

The conservative majority therefore effectively distinguished *Miller* — sidelined it as irrelevant — while the liberal minority strongly believed that it should have been followed and applied to *Heller.*

Considering the Future of the Debate

The Second Amendment is one of the most topical and controversial of all parts of the Constitution — and that is not going to change any time soon in spite of the Supreme Court's ruling in *Heller.* But the debate is likely to be narrower than before.

The high court says that individuals have the right to own and use guns — but Justice Scalia, writing for the majority, freely admitted that the right is not unlimited. It is not "a right to keep and carry any weapon whatsoever in any manner whatsoever and for whatever purpose."

Scalia identified the following as lawful restrictions on individual gun rights:

- "prohibitions on carrying concealed weapons"
- "prohibitions on the possession of firearms by felons and the mentally ill"
- "laws forbidding the carrying of firearms in sensitive places such as schools and government buildings"
- "laws imposing conditions and qualifications on the commercial sale of arms"
- Prohibitions on "the carrying of 'dangerous and unusual weapons'"

Arguments about the definition and scope of these restrictions are likely to open up a whole new can of worms — making the Second Amendment as controversial as ever.

The Protection of Lawful Commerce in Arms Act of 2005 is another likely source of controversy. This law essentially prevents anyone from bringing a lawsuit against a gun dealer because of the "misuse" of a gun. But when does use become "misuse"?

Yet another source of controversy is the question whether the Second Amendment binds the states as well as the federal government by being "incorporated" into the Due Process clause of the Fourteenth Amendment. The current doctrine as accepted by the high court is that the whole of the Bill of Rights is incorporated in this way — with the exception of the Second, Ninth, and Tenth amendments.

But why should the Second Amendment not be applicable to the states? That question is more topical than ever after *Heller*. Several cases have been filed in federal court asking for a ruling that the Second Amendment is applicable to the states too. Watch this space.

Chapter 16

The Third and Fourth Amendments: Protecting Citizens from Government Forces

. . . .

In This Chapter

▶ Recognizing your home as your castle

▶ Analyzing "unreasonable searches and seizures"

▶ Understanding how the Supreme Court has changed the law

. . . .

T he Third and Fourth amendments (which are part of the *Bill of Rights* — the first ten amendments that were all ratified together in 1791) both safeguard people against intrusion. In brief, the Third Amendment prohibits the quartering of soldiers in your house without your consent. The Fourth Amendment prohibits "unreasonable searches and seizures" of "persons, houses, papers, and effects."

Keeping the Feds Out of Your House

Before the American Revolution, a rumor spread among the colonists that the British government was about to force homeowners to accommodate troops free of charge in their homes. This fear was the product of a mistaken reading of the Quartering Acts of 1765 and 1774, which in fact allowed the British colonial authorities to quarter troops only in "uninhabited houses, outhouses, barns, or other buildings." Despite this restriction, the 1774 Act was soon labeled by the colonists as one of the "Intolerable Acts."

During the course of the Revolutionary War, both sides in fact quartered troops in private homes. The Framers of the Constitution believed that quartering troops in private homes was an evil — but recognized that in times of war it was a necessary evil. So, in drafting the Third Amendment, they drew a clear distinction between war and peace.

The Third Amendment is a bit of a Cinderella. It hasn't had the attention lavished on so many other parts of the Constitution. The U.S. Supreme Court has never had to interpret it, and the amendment has been the direct subject of litigation in a federal court only once since it was ratified in 1791. But I think this is a blessing in disguise, because when the courts get their teeth into any part of the Constitution, they tend to make a meal of it — and sometimes one that is not too appetizing!

The Third Amendment is neither long nor complicated. Here's what it says:

> *No Soldier shall, in time of peace be quartered in any house, without the consent of the Owner, nor in time of war, but in a manner to be prescribed by law.*

This wording looks pretty straightforward, but there's always room for debate about the meaning of any part of the Constitution. The potentially controversial terms here are as follows:

- **Soldier:** This word evokes multiple questions:

  - Does this word include navy seamen, marines, air force personnel, and coastguard personnel as well? Probably. In 2007, a couple hundred supporters of the National Anti-Quartering Association (NAQA) descended on a private residence in Fairfax, Virginia, in the belief that three navy seamen were demanding to be quartered there. The NAQA members sheepishly dispersed when the three sailors turned out to be the sons of the house owner who were home on shore leave!

  - Does this word include National Guardsmen, who are under state control? Yes. This was decided by the Second Circuit Court of Appeals in the 1982 case of *Engblom v. Carey.* The court based this decision on the controversial *incorporation* doctrine — the belief that most of the rights in the Bill of Rights are applicable to the states (as well as to the federal government) as a result of being incorporated into the Due Process Clause of the Fourteenth Amendment. I discuss this thorny problem in the later section "Rewriting the Fourth Amendment," as well as in Chapter 17.

  - Could this word include nonmilitary government agents, like maybe a police SWAT team snooping on a neighboring house? Hard to say. This practice is sometimes employed, but I don't know of any legal complaints about it.

- **quartered:** In Colonial times, courts often ordered felons to be "hanged, drawn and quartered" — meaning that, after being cut down, the felon's body was cut in four. So, does the Third Amendment mean that you mustn't cut a soldier's body in four? Ummm, probably not. Quartering means the same as *billeting,* which means that the homeowner has to provide the soldier with free board and lodging.

✔ **in time of peace . . . in time of war:** Troops were quartered in private homes in the War of 1812 — a formal war declared by Congress — without any legal provision for it. In the Civil War — an undeclared war — the U.S. government quartered troops in both "rebel" and Union states without any legal authority. But what about times when the United States is fighting an undeclared war purely on foreign soil — like the Korean War, the Vietnam War, or the war in Iraq? Do these actions entitle the government to quarter troops in private homes in the United States? Possibly — but then such quartering must be done "in a manner . . . prescribed by law."

✔ **in any house:** *House* must be understood as covering any form of residential accommodation, including an apartment, a condominium, or possibly even a dorm-style room — which was the form of residential accommodation at issue in the *Engblom* case.

✔ **Owner:** The court in *Engblom* rejected a narrow view of this term in favor of a broad interpretation covering anyone "who owns or lawfully possesses or controls property."

✔ **but in a manner to be prescribed by law:** *But* means "except." So, this phrase means that in wartime, no quartering is allowed except in ways laid down by law. What sort of law does this refer to? Although the reference is vague, this presumably refers to legislation passed by Congress.

Putting the Third Amendment in perspective

Your doorbell rings. You open the door to a troop of smartly uniformed GIs. Their sergeant hands you an official-looking document identifying your home as their billet for an indefinite stay.

How do you react to this prospect? With enthusiasm? With resignation? With horror? Most homeowners would probably be less than enthusiastic about this scenario — and this reaction is reflected in the Third Amendment.

But what is the legal basis for the Third Amendment? Its legal foundation goes all the way back to the old English legal maxim "An Englishman's home is his castle," which traditionally gave homeowners extensive rights to protect their property against intruders — even to the point of being allowed to kill such intruders with impunity. In England this protection has now largely been lost — but it still survives in the United States.

The position in U.S. law generally is that if someone tries to break into your house and you have a reasonable fear that there is a present or immediate danger that the assailant intends to commit a felony or to attack yourself or your family, then the law allows you even to kill the intruder to stop him from entering your house.

This legal rule is based on property rights rather than on any right of privacy. But the concept of privacy actually grew largely out of property rights. In the case of *Griswold v. Connecticut* (1965), which first established a constitutional right to privacy, Justice William O. Douglas, writing for the majority, identified the Third Amendment as creating a "zone of privacy."

A restatement of the Third Amendment would read something like this:

> *In peacetime, neither the federal government nor any state is permitted to billet troops in any residence without the consent of the owner, tenant, or lawful occupant. In wartime, the federal government and the states may not billet troops in private residences except in ways permitted by an Act of Congress.*

Keeping the Government Off Your Back

The Fourth Amendment reads as follows:

> *The right of the people to be secure in their persons, houses, papers, and effects, against unreasonable searches and seizures, shall not be violated, and no Warrants shall issue, but upon probable cause, supported by Oath or affirmation, and particularly describing the place to be searched, and the persons or things to be seized.*

A careful reading reveals that the amendment is in two parts:

- ✔ "unreasonable searches and seizures" are prohibited.

- ✔ valid warrants require "probable cause," as well as a precise description of "the place to be searched, and the person or things to be seized."

What is the connection between these two parts? Although the two halves of the amendment are linked by the word "and," there is a logical gap between them. Does the amendment say that a warrant is needed for a search to be lawful? Not really — although it is often taken for granted that the amendment does require a warrant for a search and seizure to be lawful.

Unlike the Third Amendment, the Fourth Amendment is often applied and interpreted. It's most often called into question in criminal cases involving searches of property that result in seizure of evidence that is later intended to be used at trial against a criminal defendant. But, as is so often the case with the U.S. Constitution, the Fourth Amendment raises more questions than it answers. Here are some of those questions.

- ✔ What exactly are "unreasonable searches and seizures"?

- ✔ Does the Fourth Amendment prohibit "unreasonable searches and seizures" only by government agents, or by just anybody?

- ✔ Does the Fourth Amendment apply to "unreasonable searches and seizures" by the feds alone, or does it also cover actions by state governments?

- ✔ What is the meaning of "probable cause"?

✔ Why does a valid warrant have to describe the specific "place to be searched, and the persons or things to be seized"?

✔ Is a warrant always required for a lawful search and seizure?

I answer each of these questions in turn.

Prohibiting "unreasonable searches and seizures"

"The Fourth Amendment protects people, not places," said the Supreme Court in *Katz v. United States* in 1967. In that case, Justice John Marshall Harlan came up with a twofold test that the court has now accepted: "first that a person have exhibited an actual (subjective) expectation of privacy and, second, that the expectation be one that society is prepared to recognize as 'reasonable'." Justice Harlan explained:

> *Thus, a man's home is, for most purposes, a place where he expects privacy, but objects, activities, or statements that he exposes to the "plain view" of outsiders are not "protected," because no intention to keep them to himself has been exhibited. On the other hand, conversations in the open would not be protected against being overheard, for the expectation of privacy under the circumstances would be unreasonable.*

In the *Katz* case, Charles Katz was convicted of illegal gambling on the basis of a recording made by the FBI of a telephone conversation that Katz made from a public phone booth. Was Katz's conversation protected by the Fourth Amendment? The high court said yes, even though the feds' recording device was attached to the *outside* of the phone booth.

In the words of Justice Potter Stewart:

> *No less than an individual in a business office, in a friend's apartment, or in a taxicab, a person in a telephone booth may rely upon the protection of the Fourth Amendment.*

Had Katz committed a federal crime by placing that bet? Sure he had. So, why couldn't the feds nail him? Because they didn't have a warrant. Could they have gotten a warrant? Ummm, it depends . . . I deal with that thorny question a bit later in this chapter.

The feds ought not to have recorded Katz's conversation without a warrant. But the real problem was that they couldn't use the recording in evidence at the trial against Katz. The *exclusionary rule* stops the authorities from using evidence obtained in breach of the Fourth Amendment. But that rule isn't absolute.

Excluding evidence

English common law didn't concern itself with *how* evidence was obtained. Even if evidence was stolen, it was still admissible in court. U.S. law followed suit until 1914, when the Supreme Court ruled that evidence obtained illegally — in particular, contrary to the Fourth Amendment — could not be used.

The Supreme Court first adopted this *exclusionary rule* in the case of *Weeks v. United States.* Missouri police and a federal marshal entered Fremont Weeks's house in his absence and seized a lot of stuff — including some candy! The candy wasn't the problem. The search turned up evidence that Weeks had been sending lottery tickets through the mail — a federal offense. Neither the police nor the federal marshal had a warrant, so the search and seizure was held to be a violation of the Fourth Amendment — and the evidence derived from it was excluded.

The exclusionary rule makes sense because if police know that they can use evidence even if it has been obtained by illegal search and seizure, they can simply ignore the Fourth Amendment. On the other hand, strict enforcement of the exclusionary rule in the 1970s and 1980s wrapped criminal defendants in a protective cocoon and made it harder to get convictions.

An extension of the exclusionary rule may also exclude evidence indirectly obtained with the use of illegally obtained information. The evidence obtained in this situation is called "the fruit of the poisonous tree." The scope of this extension of the exclusionary rule is not always clear.

In the 1980 case of *United States v. Crews,* three women were robbed in a women's restroom by a 16-year-old boy. The robber's description was circulated, and he was picked up by police ostensibly for truancy. He was later charged with armed robbery. His victims identified him in a court-ordered lineup. But his lawyers argued that the identification evidence should be excluded as "fruit of the poisonous tree" because it derived from the initial arrest, for which there was no probable cause. The District of Columbia Court of Appeals bought this argument. But a unanimous U.S. Supreme Court disagreed and allowed the identification evidence to stand. Justice William Brennan, writing for the court, made the point that the identification evidence was independent of the original truancy arrest.

Addressing a police convention in 1981, President Ronald Reagan attacked the exclusionary rule, which he described as based on the "absurd proposition that a law enforcement error, no matter how technical, can be used to justify throwing out an entire case," even when the defendant was plainly guilty of a serious criminal offense.

The U.S. Supreme Court recognizes that the exclusionary rule is "a judicially created remedy designed to safeguard Fourth Amendment rights generally through its deterrent effect, rather than a personal constitutional right of the party aggrieved." On this basis, the court has carved out more and more exceptions to the exclusionary rule. Here are some of these exceptions:

- ✔ **The exclusionary rule doesn't apply to evidence before a grand jury.** This was decided by the Supreme Court in *United States v. Calandra* in 1974.

- ✔ **Evidence obtained illegally is admissible if it would have been found legally anyway.** Here is an example of this exception to the exclusionary rule: On Christmas Eve 1968, Robert Anthony Williams abducted and murdered a 10-year-old girl. He confessed to the police and pointed out to them where he had hidden the body. Because the police had agreed not to question Williams until his attorney was present, the finding of the body was technically a violation of Williams's Fourth Amendment rights. A strict application of the exclusionary rule would have made the body and the autopsy inadmissible at Williams's trial — as a result of which a brutal killer would probably have walked. Fortunately, however, the Supreme Court decided in *Nix v. Williams* in 1984 that this evidence was admissible because the police would inevitably have found the body anyway.

- ✔ **Evidence obtained from an independent legal source is admissible.** This exception to the exclusionary rule is similar to the previous exception. Here is an example: Police followed suspects into an apartment without a warrant. One of the suspects was found to be in possession of cocaine and was immediately arrested. Two officers remained in the apartment until a search warrant was issued — 19 hours later! *After* getting the warrant, the officers found cocaine and records of drug dealing. The case reached the Supreme Court in 1984 under the name of *Segura v. United States*. The court ruled that "whether the initial entry was illegal or not is irrelevant to the admissibility of the evidence, and exclusion of the evidence is not warranted as 'fruit of the poisonous tree'." The court reached this eminently sensible decision only by the narrowest of margins, 5 votes to 4.

- ✔ **Good faith is an exception to an unduly strict interpretation of the rules.** A literal application of the exclusionary rule can easily result in injustice by giving undue protection to criminal defendants. The good faith exception is a welcome commonsense counterblast to the exclusionary rule — which, it must always be remembered, is just a judge-made rule anyway. A good example of this exception is the 1984 case of *United States v. Leon*. After an anonymous tip, the police placed Alberto Leon under surveillance. On this basis, the police got a warrant from a judge to search Leon's house. Large quantities of illegal drugs were found there, and Leon was charged. His lawyers objected that the information on which the search warrant was based was too vague, so the warrant should be set aside and the evidence obtained under the warrant should be excluded. But the Supreme Court ruled that, even if the police should not have been given a search warrant, they acted in good faith, so the evidence obtained under the warrant was admissible in court. In the words of Justice Byron White, writing for the majority, "Indiscriminate application of the exclusionary rule may well generate disrespect for the law and administration of justice."

Avoiding making "a crazy quilt of the Fourth Amendment"

Does the Fourth Amendment prohibit "unreasonable searches and seizures" only by government agents, or by just anybody?

The wording of the first part of the amendment is unhelpful on this score. But the mention of "Warrants" in the second part makes it clear that the amendment as a whole deals only with government actions. If a private person breaks into your house, ties you up, and grabs stuff belonging to you, that person is guilty of several felonies, for which he may go to jail. You can also file a civil suit against such a person. But he hasn't violated the Fourth Amendment.

The distinction between public and private actions is not always quite so clear-cut. For example, in a 1979 high court case, *Smith v. Maryland,* a woman received threatening phone calls from somebody who had robbed her. She identified the man to the police, who got the phone company to install a "pen register" on the man's home phone. This device made a list of all the numbers the man called but didn't record the content of the calls themselves. The man claimed that the pen register violated his Fourth Amendment rights.

Writing for the U.S. Supreme Court, Justice Harry Blackmun ruled:

> *We are not inclined to make a crazy quilt of the Fourth Amendment, especially in circumstances where (as here) the pattern of protection would be dictated by billing practices of a private corporation. We therefore conclude that petitioner in all probability entertained no actual expectation of privacy in the phone numbers he dialed, and that, even if he did, his expectation was not "legitimate." The installation and use of a pen register, consequently, was not a "search," and no warrant was required.*

As a result of this sensible decision, the police were able to nail the assailant — and it allows law enforcement agencies a useful tool.

The relevant points here are as follows:

- ✔ When you make a phone call, the phone company automatically knows what number you dialed.
- ✔ The phone company is a private corporation, so it's not under any duty to you under the Fourth Amendment.
- ✔ You don't have a legitimate expectation of keeping secret the identity of the number you dialed.
- ✔ If the phone company makes a list of all the numbers you dial, that is not a "search" within the meaning of the Fourth Amendment.
- ✔ So, it's okay for the phone company to hand that list to the police.

Rewriting the Fourth Amendment

Okay, so the Fourth Amendment applies only to government searches and seizures. But which government? Does the amendment apply only to the feds, or to the states as well?

The Sixth, Tenth, and Eleventh amendments specifically mention the states — but not the Fourth. Was James Madison, who drafted the whole of the Bills of Rights, such a sloppy thinker as to assume that the Fourth Amendment applied to the states without bothering to say so in so many words? No way!

So how come the Supreme Court now says that the Fourth Amendment — and most of the rest of the Bill of Rights too — binds the states as well as the feds? This ruling is based on the Due Process Clause of the Fourteenth Amendment, which reads as follows:

> *nor shall any State deprive any person of life, liberty, or property, without due process of law.*

This clause sure binds the states. But can the little phrase "without due process of law" really burden the states with the obligations of much of the rest of the Bill of Rights?

This question opens up a huge can of worms labeled the *doctrine of incorporation,* which can be blamed on the vague wording of the Due Process Clause. For a full discussion of this controversial doctrine, see Chapter 14. The draftsmen of the Fourteenth Amendment, which was ratified in 1868, weren't in the same ballpark — or even in the same league — as James Madison. But could even these little league draftsmen have been *that* dumb that they just assumed they'd incorporated the bulk of the Bill of Rights in one vague five-word clause? Most unlikely.

The thinking behind the draftsmen of the Fourteenth can be seen from the so-called *Blaine Amendment.* In 1875 — just seven years after the ratification of the Fourteenth Amendment — James G. Blaine, a leading politician who had been a member of Congress during the passing of the Fourteenth Amendment, proposed a constitutional amendment that passed the House of Representatives but was four votes shy of the necessary two-thirds majority in the Senate.

The Blaine Amendment read:

> *No State shall make any law respecting an establishment of religion . . .*

Familiar? Sure. The wording is lifted straight from the First Amendment but applies specifically to the states. This wording can mean only one thing: that Blaine and the majority of Congress did not think that the First Amendment already applied to the states through the Fourteenth Amendment.

Despite this evidence, in 1949 the Supreme Court decided in *Wolf v. Colorado* that the Fourth Amendment was incorporated into the Due Process Clause of the Fourteenth Amendment and that the Fourth Amendment therefore applied to the states as well as to the federal government — but that the exclusionary rule did not apply to the states. So, the states were bound by the Fourth Amendment, but any evidence found by state police in violation of the Fourth could still be used in court!

In 1961, the high court abandoned this position for a more extreme but more logical position in *Mapp v. Ohio,* which brought the states' obligations under the Fourth Amendment into line with the feds' obligations. The court ruled that "all evidence obtained by searches and seizures in violation of the Constitution is, by [the Fourth Amendment] inadmissible in a state court."

This decision was one of many made by the Supreme Court under Chief Justice Earl Warren that favored criminal defendants. Although the wording of this ruling looks clear enough, it presented the court with the problem of how and when to exclude evidence in individual cases. I discuss the exceptions to the exclusionary rule earlier in this chapter.

Defining "probable cause"

The concept of probable cause holds the key to the second part of the Fourth Amendment, which says that "no Warrants shall issue, but upon probable cause."

The word *but* here means "except." *Warrant* refers to a legal document issued by a judge or magistrate authorizing law enforcement officers to do something that would otherwise be against the law — in particular, to search and seize evidence for use in a criminal prosecution.

So this clause means that a valid warrant needs to be based on probable cause. But what is the meaning of *probable cause*? In 1878, the Supreme Court defined it like this:

> *If the facts and circumstances before the officer are such as to warrant a man of prudence and caution in believing that the offense has been committed, it is sufficient.*

But, "good faith on the part of the arresting officer is not enough" to constitute probable cause:

> *If subjective good faith alone were the test, the protections of the Fourth Amendment would evaporate, and the people would be 'secure in their persons, houses, papers, and effects,' only in the discretion of the police.*

The case of *Illinois v. Gates,* heard by the high court in 1983, is a good example of the commonsense approach now adopted by the court on the question of probable cause. The police received an anonymous tip accusing a husband and wife of interstate drug trafficking. After finding that the couple's movements conformed to the pattern described in the anonymous letter, the police got a search warrant and found drugs and weapons in the couple's car and house. The couple challenged the legality of the search on the ground that the anonymous letter couldn't constitute probable cause. However, the high court ruled that the question of probable cause could not be reduced to a formula but depended on "the totality of the circumstances" — and in this case the anonymous tip-off plus police corroboration of some of its details did amount to probable cause. Justice William Rehnquist put the whole question in context by remarking that "[t]he most basic function of any government [is] to provide for the security of the individual and of his property."

Prohibiting police fishing expeditions

The second half of the Fourth Amendment reads as follows:

> *no Warrants shall issue, but upon probable cause, supported by Oath or affirmation, and particularly describing the place to be searched, and the persons or things to be seized.*

Why are there such detailed requirements for a valid warrant? To answer this question, we have to go back to colonial times.

In 1765, Lord Camden, Chief Justice of the Court of Common Pleas in England, handed down an historic decision against the British Government known as *Entick v. Carrington.* Three government agents had entered the house of John Entick, a radical journalist, armed with a "general warrant" issued by the Secretary of State allowing the agents to search through all of Entick's papers and possessions. The agents spent several hours doing just that.

Lord Camden's judgment was in strong terms. Here is an extract from it:

> *The great end for which men entered into society, was to secure their property . . . By the laws of England, every invasion of private property, be it ever so minute, is a trespass.*

From that time onward, general warrants were banned — and couldn't be issued by the government itself anyway. In order to conduct a lawful search and seizure, the government had to get a warrant from a judge on the basis of a sworn statement specifying the place that was to be searched and the persons or things to be seized.

The Fourth Amendment essentially repeats these requirements, as a safeguard of the liberty of the individual against the government.

But too literal an application of these provisions can hinder law enforcement. So it is fortunate that in recent years the U.S. Supreme Court has relaxed the rigor of its application of these requirements.

For example, in the 1987 case of *Maryland v. Garrison*, police intending to search an apartment occupied by the McWebbs had a warrant specifying "third floor apartment." In fact, there were two apartments on the third floor, although the police didn't realize this fact at the time. The police accidentally entered the wrong apartment — and found drugs and cash. They arrested the occupant, Mr. Garrison, who objected that the warrant wasn't valid.

The Supreme Court rejected this contention and held that the search and seizure were lawful. In the words of Justice John Paul Stevens, writing for the majority:

> *There is no question that the warrant was valid and was supported by probable cause . . . Prior to the officers' discovery of the factual mistake, they perceived McWebb's apartment and the third-floor premises as one and the same; therefore their execution of the warrant reasonably included the entire third floor. Under either interpretation of the warrant, the officers' conduct was consistent with a reasonable effort to ascertain and identify the place intended to be searched within the meaning of the Fourth Amendment.*

Searching without a warrant?

The Fourth Amendment says that a warrant is required for a lawful search and seizure to take place — or does it? The two halves of the amendment are linked by the word *and,* but not by any clear, logical connection.

In certain circumstances, the Supreme Court is prepared to allow evidence in on the basis of probable cause alone — even in the absence of a warrant. *Terry v. Ohio,* heard by the Supreme Court in 1968, is a good example of this approach. A very experienced police officer observed two men walking up and down past a store window and stopping to look into the same window no fewer than 24 times in the space of a few minutes. The officer suspected the men of "casing a job, a stick up." He stopped the men, patted them down, and found a concealed revolver on each of them. The question before the Supreme Court was whether the revolver found on one of the men was admissible in evidence against him — because the police officer who arrested him did not have a warrant. The high court held that the evidence of the revolver was admissible in court because the men's suspicious behavior constituted probable cause, and in the circumstances no warrant was needed.

Can the police ever search premises without a warrant? Yes. In 1999, in *Flippo v. West Virginia,* the high court ruled that "police may make warrantless entries on to premises if they reasonably believe a person is in need of immediate aid and may make prompt warrantless searches of a homicide scene for possible other victims or a killer on the premises." But the court rejected a general "murder scene exception" allowing the police to conduct a warrantless search of premises just because a homicide had been committed there.

Protecting America without a warrant?

What about the lawfulness of a wiretap without a warrant? In *Katz v. United States,* discussed earlier in the chapter, the high court ruled that a recording of a telephone conversation was unlawful — even though the call was made from a public phone booth and the recording device was attached to the outside of the booth.

How does this decision apply to national security? The *Katz* court didn't consider this angle. But the question has become topical since then. Here are a few of the controversial issues that have been raised in this connection:

✔ **FISA:** The Foreign Intelligence Surveillance Act (FISA) of 1978 set up two courts, the Foreign Intelligence Surveillance Court (FISC) and the Foreign Intelligence Surveillance Court of Review (FISCR), both of which meet in secret. FISC hears requests from the FBI and other government agencies for surveillance warrants against suspected foreign spies inside the United States. FISC operates like a grand jury; the government is the only party that appears before it. If FISC denies a government application for a warrant, the case goes to the FISCR. Most applications are granted, though sometimes with modifications.

Is this set-up in accordance with the Fourth Amendment? Despite the secrecy, this arrangement doesn't violate the Fourth Amendment. After all, any ordinary application for a search warrant will normally be made to a judge or magistrate without the other side being present.

✔ **Call database:** In 2006, the press broke the story that the National Security Agency (NSA) had compiled a database of more than 1.9 trillion phone-call-detail records. The Bush administration neither confirmed nor denied this report. Is the database a violation of the Fourth Amendment? Not if it's just a list of numbers called without recording the content of the calls themselves.

✔ **Protect America Act:** This Act was passed by Congress in 2007 and expired because of a "sunset clause" in February 2008. The Act allowed wiretapping by the federal government of any phone calls that begin or end in a foreign country — without a warrant from the FISC. Is this power a violation of the Fourth Amendment? The President said no, on the ground that it was an extension of his powers as Commander in Chief. But this argument would probably fail if challenged in court. I deal with the President in Chapter 10.

Chapter 17

Taking the Fifth — and a Bit of the Fourteenth

. . . .

In This Chapter

▶ Avoiding self-incrimination

▶ Indicting suspects with a grand jury

▶ Banning double jeopardy

▶ Disentangling due process

▶ Trying to understand the incorporation doctrine

▶ Taking private property for public use

. . . .

*T*he Fifth Amendment, ratified in 1791, is one of the meatiest of all the articles of the Constitution, and one of the most controversial. It deals with some heavy-hitting issues:

✔ The so-called "Great Right" against self-incrimination

✔ The role of the grand jury

✔ Double jeopardy

✔ Due process

✔ Eminent domain

Due process is picked up in the Fourteenth Amendment, ratified in 1868. For that reason, I tackle part of the Fourteenth in this chapter as well. (I give the rest of the Fourteenth Amendment its due in Chapter 21.) But first we need to give our rapt attention to the Fifth so you can be the most informed *Law & Order* viewer on the block.

Invoking the "Great Right" Against Self-Incrimination

If you watch movies or TV shows, you've heard of the Fifth Amendment. (If you don't watch movies or TV shows, I'm guessing you're better read and more muscular than the rest of us.) "I'll take da Fift(h)" is the gangster's stock in trade. Why? Because the Fifth Amendment doesn't allow anyone to be "compelled in any criminal case to be a witness against himself."

This is the "Great Right" that gives protection against self-incrimination. If you're asked a question in court (or in some other formal proceeding) and your reply could amount to an admission of a crime on your part, you can refuse to answer.

The Miranda warning

The Fifth Amendment clearly states that you can't be forced to give evidence against yourself. But if you choose to answer an incriminating question, you must accept the consequences. Do you have to be warned about this fact in advance? Not in a court of law. But in 1966, the U.S. Supreme Court decided that you do have to be warned if you are being questioned by police. The case in question was *Miranda v. Arizona,* and the statement a police officer must make to a suspect is the well-known Miranda warning:

> *You have the right to remain silent. Anything you say may be used against you in a court of law. You have the right to an attorney. If you cannot afford an attorney, one will be provided for you.*

The wording varies slightly from state to state, but unless you're cautioned in proper form, any statement you make to the police should be thrown out by the court.

Not everyone has been thrilled by this requirement. In 2000, Chief Justice William Rehnquist stated the problem with the Miranda warning this way: "Statements which may be by no means involuntary, made by a defendant who is aware of his 'rights,' may nonetheless be excluded and a guilty defendant go free as a result."

In 1968, Congress passed a law seeking to reverse the worst excesses of the Miranda rule. If a confession was voluntary, said Congress, it should be allowed as evidence even if no Miranda warning was given. But in 2000, *Dickerson v. U.S.* set the Congressional law aside and put the Miranda rule back in the driving seat. The argument was that the Miranda rule had become part of the Constitution, and the law passed by Congress was therefore unconstitutional.

I would argue (as others, like Justice Antonin Scalia, have done) that the Miranda rule isn't part of the Constitution; it's simply *based* on the Constitution. But for now, the Miranda warning is required prior to any police interrogations.

Normally, you have to answer any question that you are asked in court, and lying under oath can expose you to the serious charge of perjury. The Fifth Amendment gives you a way out under some circumstances. The formal way of invoking the Fifth is by saying "I refuse to answer the question on the ground that it might incriminate me." A witness may claim this privilege in criminal cases as well as civil cases — if the witness is afraid that his answer is likely to expose him to a criminal charge.

However, there is a catch: Taking the Fifth is often interpreted as an admission of guilt. For example, the label *Fifth Amendment Communists* was attached to people who refused to answer questions before the House Un-American Activities Committee just after World War II.

The Fifth Amendment, like the rest of the Bill of Rights, was originally taken to apply only to federal law. To what extent it now applies to state law (if at all) has been the subject of heated debate. I present the basics of this debate in a sidebar later in the chapter called "The scope of the Fourteenth Amendment's Due Process Clause."

Peeking Behind the Closed Doors of the Grand Jury

The opening clause of the Fifth Amendment actually isn't related to self-incrimination. Instead, it deals with the grand jury system. It reads, in part:

> *No person shall be held to answer for a capital, or otherwise infamous crime, unless on a presentment or indictment of a Grand Jury . . .*

The words "infamous crime" have been interpreted to mean that a grand jury is required only for felonies — not for misdemeanors.

The grand jury is a wonderful American institution. Like so many others, it long predates the U.S. Constitution. Its origins lie in the earliest days of the English Common Law, even before the Norman Conquest of 1066. By 1368, grand juries had taken on something very like their modern American form, but they were abolished in England in 1933 and have not survived anywhere else except in the United States.

The grand jury gets its name from its size. A regular trial jury usually has 12 members, but grand juries are generally bigger. Federal grand juries range from 16 to 23 members. However, the real difference between a grand jury and a regular jury is not size but function. Regular juries are *trial* juries. In criminal cases they decide whether the defendant is guilty or not guilty. Grand juries are not trial juries. They come in at a much earlier stage to decide whether a suspect should be indicted with a crime at all.

It's worth noting that although this part of the Fifth Amendment applies only to federal law, grand juries are found in plenty of states too.

Deciding whether to indict

The chief function of a grand jury is to decide whether to bring criminal charges against a suspect. In the federal courts (and in many states), nobody can be charged with a felony unless a grand jury has decided to indict that person. (However, in certain states it's possible for the district attorney to file what's called an *information* or *accusation* as an alternative to a grand jury indictment. This step is followed by a preliminary hearing before a judge at which the defendant can be represented by counsel.)

Grand juries generally do the prosecutor's bidding. Sol Wachtler, former Chief Judge of New York, said in 1985 that a prosecutor could get a grand jury to indict a ham sandwich! A grand jury is very much the prosecutor's show, and its proceedings are secret. No judge is present. The prosecutor presides and can call witnesses, forcing them to come by serving them with a subpoena. Here are some other ways a grand jury hearing differs from a regular trial:

✔ The normal rules of evidence are relaxed. For example, the usually strict "exclusionary rule," which makes any evidence inadmissible if it's obtained on an "unreasonable search and seizure," doesn't apply. (See Chapter 16 for more about this rule.) The practical effect of this is that a prosecutor can use evidence to secure a grand jury indictment that later may not be admissible at the trial on the same charges.

✔ Suspects are not allowed to call witnesses or cross-examine prosecution witnesses, but a suspect can be called to testify.

✔ A suspect or a witness before a grand jury can have a lawyer, but the lawyer can't be inside the jury room! However, generally the suspect or witness is free to leave the proceedings to consult with counsel.

✔ A grand jury witness is normally given a warning against self-incrimination, but if the warning isn't given and the witness lies under oath, the witness can still be prosecuted for perjury. As Justice William Brennan noted in the case that decided this issue, "Our legal system provides methods for challenging the Government's right to ask questions — lying is not one of them."

Victimizing suspects or protecting victims?

The grand jury system has been criticized as unfair to defendants and suspects. After all, they can't be represented by counsel, can't call witnesses, and can't cross-examine prosecution witnesses. Some critics don't like the ease with which prosecutions can be achieved as a result. They particularly don't like the control that prosecutors usually have over grand juries.

There's no doubt that the grand jury process is one-sided. But many people see the grand jury system as acting in the interests of victims of crime, providing a small but essential counterbalance to the elaborate apparatus of protection surrounding criminal suspects and defendants. (For a taste of this apparatus, see the sidebar "The Miranda warning" in this chapter.)

Avoiding Double Jeopardy

I'm not talking about the game show here. *Double jeopardy* means being tried twice for the same crime, and the second clause of the Fifth Amendment forbids it:

> *nor shall any person be subject for the same offence to be twice put in jeopardy of life or limb.*

As with the rest of the Bill of Rights, the ban on double jeopardy originally applied only to federal courts. But in 1969, the U.S. Supreme Court "incorporated" this guarantee into the Due Process Clause of the Fourteenth Amendment, making it applicable to state courts too. (To get a sense of the debate behind this decision, see the upcoming sidebar "The scope of the Fourteenth Amendment's Due Process Clause.")

Applying the principle

Protection against double jeopardy is way older than the U.S. Constitution; it can be traced back to ancient Greece and Rome. There are three practical applications of the principle:

- ✔ If you're *acquitted* (found not guilty) of a crime, you can't be put on trial for it again. This is by far the most important aspect of the principle, which is confined to criminal cases.

- ✔ You can't be tried again for a crime of which you have been convicted.

- ✔ If you've already been punished for committing a certain crime, you can't be given a second punishment for that same offense.

Mistrials are an exception. A *mistrial* occurs when the judge cancels the trial — usually for some procedural reason — before the jury has returned a verdict. If a mistrial occurs, a retrial can be ordered. Another exception is when the original trial is a *nullity* — for example, if a defendant bribes the judge or members of the jury to achieve an acquittal. This offense makes the trial a nullity, or a non-trial. It's as if the original trial never took place.

Allowing for an end to litigation

It seems only fair that after you've faced the music and the music has finally stopped, that should be the end of the matter. Especially if you've been acquitted, it would seem wrong for the same crime to hang over your head for the rest of your life.

However, some arguments against this principle carry weight. Say you've been tried and acquitted of a particular crime and new evidence later comes to light pointing to your guilt. Wouldn't it be fair to your victim for you to be hauled before the court again?

It may not seem fair in every instance, but there is an ancient principle of law going back to Roman times that "it's in the public interest for there to be an end to litigation." In other words, it's not good to keep flogging a dead horse. Doing so would result in an intolerable situation for successful defendants, who would have all their old charges hanging over them indefinitely, or until the statute of limitations ran out. (Or until they were retried and convicted.)

Because of this ancient principle, repackaged in the Fifth Amendment, if someone literally gets away with murder there is nothing to stop that person from crowing about it. Oh, except that the victim's family can take him or her to the cleaners in a civil wrongful death suit. This situation is not considered to be double jeopardy because the parties are not the same as in a criminal prosecution and the standard of proof is different.

Let me explain: A criminal case is brought by the prosecution against a named defendant. In federal cases the prosecutor is the United States, and in state criminal cases the prosecutor is the state (often designated "The People" or sometimes "The Commonwealth"). The burden of proof is on the prosecution, and the standard of proof is "beyond a reasonable doubt," which is a very high standard indeed.

In a civil suit, the case is brought by the victim or the victim's family, which bears the burden of proof but on a much lower standard. The burden of proof is to demonstrate that a "preponderance of the evidence" indicates the defendant did the deed, which just means that it's more likely than not.

O.J. Simpson provides us with probably the best-known example of the difference between the two types of cases. Simpson was found not guilty of murder in a criminal trial but was later found liable for the death of his ex-wife Nicole Brown Simpson and Ron Goldman in a civil wrongful death suit.

Jeopardizing "life or limb"

The Fifth Amendment clause on double jeopardy talks about being "put in jeopardy of life or limb." What's with this "life or limb" business? You may interpret that to mean that double jeopardy applies only to really serious crimes. "Life" refers to the death penalty. But "limb" refers to old-fashioned punishments such as the *stocks* — a wooden frame used to torture and humiliate criminals found guilty of even quite minor offenses. So double jeopardy covers misdemeanors as well as felonies.

In general, what this clause means is that you can't be tried twice for the same offense, no matter whether you were found guilty or acquitted the first time around.

Agonizing over Due Process

If the courts have made a meal of double jeopardy, they have made a gargantuan, indigestible, multi-course banquet of due process. The Fifth Amendment wording goes like this:

> No person shall be . . . deprived of life, liberty, or property, without due process of law.

This wording was picked up in the Fourteenth Amendment, ratified in 1868 during the Reconstruction period just after the Civil War:

> nor shall any State deprive any person of life, liberty, or property, without due process of law.

Why was it necessary for due process to be repeated in the Fourteenth Amendment when it was already included in the Fifth Amendment? The Fifth deals with federal law, and the Fourteenth with the states. Other than that difference, the Due Process clauses in the two amendments are practically identical.

Trying to define the term

What does *due process* mean, anyway? In 1884, the Supreme Court defined due process really broadly. Ready for a mouthful?

> *[A]ny legal proceeding enforced by public authority, whether sanctioned by age and custom, or newly devised in the discretion of the legislative power, in furtherance of the general public good, which regards and preserves these principles of liberty and justice, must be held to be due process of law.*

Let me help you out: *Due process* is really just an old-fashioned way of saying "proper procedure." The Due Process clauses in both amendments originally meant no more and no less than this: You can't be executed, imprisoned, or fined, or have your property confiscated, except after a fair trial conducted according to proper legal procedure. As Supreme Court Justice Felix Frankfurter put it: "The history of American freedom is, in no small measure, the history of procedure."

The next question is, what exactly is proper legal procedure? In 1914, the U.S. Supreme Court gave a short answer to this important question: "The fundamental requisite of due process of law is the opportunity to be heard." This explanation may seem too narrow, but it happens to be one of the two principles of natural justice that have come down to us from antiquity (the other being the rule against bias, which is covered by the Sixth Amendment). *Natural justice* is a philosophy that says that God or nature has laid down certain moral standards that form the basis of civilized society. Thomas Jefferson was strongly influenced by this philosophy. This influence is clear in the Declaration of Independence, of which Jefferson was the main author. (I discuss the Declaration of Independence in Chapter 2.)

Triggering due process

Two important questions emerge:

- ✓ What's needed to trigger a due process claim?
- ✓ How much due process is actually due?

Let's consider an example. A security guard in Cleveland wrote on his job application that he'd never been convicted of a felony. He got the job. But it turned out that he'd been convicted of grand larceny, which sure is a felony. (The guard claimed he thought it was only a misdemeanor!) He was fired without being given an opportunity to explain or defend himself.

In 1985, the U.S. Supreme Court heard the case. It concluded that, because this man's employment could be terminated only "for cause," this meant that it was a property right within the Fourteenth Amendment, which triggered due process. But the extent of due process due to him was only the right to be heard before dismissal — not anything more. What does this example mean? Essentially two things:

- ✔ The word "property" in the Due Process clauses of the Fifth and Fourteenth amendments has a very broad meaning. It can even include possession of a job.

- ✔ There's a whole range of due process rights. The issue is decided on a case-by-case basis, which makes sense but which also makes it difficult to predict what a court will decide in any particular situation.

At the beginning of this section I asked, "What's needed to trigger a due process claim?" Back in 1855, the U.S. Supreme Court said that in order to determine whether a process is due process or not, the court must "examine the Constitution itself, to see whether this process be in conflict with any of its provisions." An unfair trial, for example, is always contrary to due process. In addition, there are some rights that do not appear to be connected with due process but are now regarded by the U.S. Supreme Court as protected by due process:

- ✔ Privacy
- ✔ Contraception
- ✔ Abortion

These all belong to *substantive due process,* which I discuss next.

Wrestling with substantive due process

Due process is about procedure, right? Right. But a significant body of judicial opinion indicates that it can also be about the substance of a law. The doctrine of *substantive due process,* which emerged as early as the mid-19th century, says that due process is not just about *how* something should be done but also *what* should be done.

Substantive due process has undergone some important changes. Justice Hugo Black, who always opposed substantive due process of any kind, particularly criticized the old-style approach to due process. In Black's words, this approach "authorizes courts to hold laws unconstitutional when they believe the legislature has acted unwisely. . . ." In other words, the courts gave themselves the right to second-guess Congress. If the Supreme Court thought Congress had passed a law that the court didn't agree with, the court declared that law unconstitutional. Black opposed this approach because he believed it was unconstitutional for the courts to "substitute their social and economic beliefs for the judgment of legislative bodies, who are elected to pass laws."

Substantive due process greatly expanded the power of the courts — especially the U.S. Supreme Court. The doctrine gave the courts the power to examine not only the procedure used to enforce a law but also the actual content of the law.

Noting some famous early cases

Possibly the earliest use of substantive due process was in the notorious *Dred Scott* case in 1856. Dred Scott was a slave who had moved with his master to various free states and territories. At that time, certain states were designated as slave states and others as free. Dred Scott claimed that after he'd breathed the free air of Illinois, he became a free man and couldn't then be reduced to slavery again on return to a slave state. This claim was rejected by the U.S. Supreme Court, which held that the Fifth Amendment's Due Process Clause protected a slave owner from being deprived of his property — including his slaves — just because he'd brought it into a free state.

The 1905 case *Lochner v. New York* put substantive due process on the map. In those days, journeymen bakers worked very long hours in unhygienic conditions, often in basements. New York State passed the Bakeshop Act of 1895 limiting work to a maximum of 10 hours a day or 60 hours per week. Joseph Lochner owned a small bakery and was fined $50 because one of his employees had worked more than 60 hours in a particular week.

After losing two appeals before the New York courts, Lochner took his case to the U.S. Supreme Court. He argued successfully that the Bakeshop Act was contrary to the Due Process Clause of the Fourteenth Amendment because it infringed on Lochner's "liberty of contract." The Bakeshop Act was struck down as unconstitutional. This is an example of substantive due process because it addresses the fact that certain rights we hold cannot be taken away from us — in this case, Lochner's right to enter into contracts with his employees.

Lochner gave its name to an era because for the next 32 years, a conservative brand of substantive due process dominated the Supreme Court. State laws setting minimum wages; banning child labor; or regulating the banking, insurance, or transportation industries were declared unconstitutional on the basis of substantive due process.

Threatening the New Deal

This trend reached a climax during Franklin Delano Roosevelt's New Deal. In a radio fireside chat, FDR said that the Constitution was "so simple and practical that it can always meet extraordinary needs." But the President hadn't reckoned with the Supreme Court. After initially accepting some New Deal legislation, the court struck down the provisions of Roosevelt's economic recovery program one by one. The cases threatened doom for the New Deal, which had been endorsed by an unprecedented proportion of the popular vote in the 1932 election.

FDR wasn't about to allow a bunch of unelected judges to trample the New Deal. He condemned the court for reverting to "the horse-and-buggy definition of interstate commerce" and came up with a novel plan to counter the judges. Cleverly using the Constitution against the court itself, he proposed to increase the size of the Supreme Court — which was not fixed by the Constitution — by adding one new justice (up to a maximum of six) for every justice over the age of 70, plus up to 44 new lower court judges.

FDR was met with a barrage of criticism for this bold plan. Even the liberal justices on the Supreme Court, who mostly supported the New Deal, were up in arms. But the mere announcement of the proposal was enough to achieve the desired effect. In 1937, in an apparent bow to FDR, the court upheld a Washington state minimum wage law that was practically identical to one declared unconstitutional just a year before. The court similarly upheld the constitutionality of the National Labor Relations Board Act, which created an agency charged with investigating claims of unfair labor practices.

The conservative economic phase of substantive due process was over.

Reemerging in recent decades

In 1965, a new-style substantive due process doctrine appeared thanks to *Griswold v. Connecticut.* The question before the U.S. Supreme Court was the constitutionality of an "uncommonly silly law" (as Justice Potter Stewart called it) banning contraceptives. The court held that it was unconstitutional. Justice William O. Douglas wrote that though the law in question did not exactly breach any express right in the Bill of Rights, it offended against a right of privacy.

But Justice John Marshall Harlan put the matter firmly on the basis of the Due Process Clause of the Fourteenth Amendment. He wrote:

> *In my view, the proper constitutional inquiry in this case is whether this Connecticut statute infringes the Due Process Clause of the Fourteenth Amendment . . . I believe that it does.*

Justice Hugo Black disagreed with Harlan's broad application of the Fourteenth Amendment, arguing that even if the Supreme Court believes that certain laws are "unreasonable, unwise, arbitrary, capricious or irrational," the court shouldn't have such broad authority to strike down those laws. Otherwise, the court would have too much power, which would "jeopardize the separation of governmental powers that the Framers set up and . . . threaten to take away much of the power of States to govern themselves. . . ."

Despite Black's dissent, the new-style substantive due process doctrine continued to gain ground, most notably in *Roe v. Wade* (1973), which struck down two antiabortion state laws. The argument put forward by Justice Harry Blackmun, writing for the majority, was that a woman's right to choose is based on her right of privacy, which in turn is based on the Due Process Clause of the Fourteenth Amendment.

Continuing to stoke controversy

Today, some Supreme Court justices, notably Antonin Scalia and Clarence Thomas, argue against substantive due process, which Scalia has called an oxymoron. In 1994, he wrote that "the Due Process Clause guarantees no substantive rights, but only (as it says) process."

The accepted position is probably still that expressed by Chief Justice William Rehnquist in 1997: acceptance of substantive due process within closely defined limits. But I have no doubt that the court will continue to wrestle with the issue of whether the Constitution permits courts to create or take away rights under the auspices of substantive due process.

Opening Up the Incorporation Debate

Before the ratification of the Fourteenth Amendment, the U.S. Supreme Court understood that the Bill of Rights applied only to federal law and not to the states. But the Fourteenth Amendment changed that understanding for some people, and it opened a can of worms that clogged the legal system for quite some time.

Does the Bill of Rights apply to the states?

Supreme Court Justice Hugo Black, who served the court from 1937 to 1971, argued that the first section of the Fourteenth Amendment — the section that deals with due process — *incorporates* the bulk of the first eight amendments to the Constitution, making all those guarantees of the Bill of Rights binding on the states as well as on the federal government. In other words, because the Fourteenth Amendment mentions due process as a protection under state law, it also provides protection under state law for freedom of speech and the right to bear arms; against unwarranted search and seizure, self-incrimination, and double jeopardy; and for all the other provisions included in the Bill of Rights.

Black prided himself on taking every word of the Constitution at face value. "The Constitution is my legal bible," he would say, referring to the well-thumbed copy that he kept on him at all times. "I cherish every word of it from the first to the last."

But here's the flaw with Black's argument: The Fifth Amendment guarantees due process as one of several separate rights. Nothing in the Fifth Amendment suggests that due process encompasses all the other rights contained in that amendment, let alone in the whole of the Bill of Rights. So why should due process in the Fourteenth Amendment be any different?

If due process in the Fifth Amendment had an all-embracing nature, this fact would surely have been indicated by the wording. Instead, it's listed as one of several guarantees, each on the same level as the others.

If the framers of the Fourteenth Amendment had wanted to incorporate all of the Bill of Rights guarantees, they could easily have listed them or otherwise indicated that those rights were to be applicable to the states as well as to the federal government. Instead, the Due Process Clause of the Fifth Amendment is the only provision in the Bill of Rights repeated in the Fourteenth Amendment.

There is a rule of interpretation that lawyers use, known in Latin as *expressio unius est exclusio alterius,* or "the expression of one thing amounts to the exclusion of another." When a kid asks, "Mommy, can I have some cake?" and the reply comes back "You may have a cookie," this means not only what it says (*expressio unius*) but also that the kid is not allowed any cake (*exclusio alterius*). In the Constitution, the specific mention of due process in the Fourteenth Amendment amounts to an exclusion of all the other guarantees referred to in the Bill of Rights.

Watching selective incorporation in action

The Supreme Court didn't buy Justice Black's *total incorporation* approach to due process. Instead, it adopted the slightly less extreme doctrine of *selective incorporation.* The Supreme Court considered the merits of a variety of cases that dealt with whether the Fourteenth Amendment made the entire Bill of Rights applicable under state law, and it made decisions on a case-by-case basis.

The result is that the court gradually broadened its interpretation of the Fourteenth Amendment until the bulk of the guarantees of the Bill of Rights were accepted as being binding on the states as well as the federal government.

It is commonly said that essentially the whole of the Bill of Rights is now incorporated against the states. However, that is not the case. The true position is much messier. Some amendments in the Bill of Rights are recognized by the high court as completely incorporated; others as partly incorporated; and others again as not incorporated at all. This patchwork is in itself a strong argument against the whole incorporation doctrine. If the drafters of the Fourteenth Amendment really intended their Due Process Clause to have such an uneven effect on the Bill of Rights, how could they have expected that intention to be understood from a reading of the amendment? There is absolutely no indication in the text of the Fourteenth Amendment of any incorporation whatsoever. So why should we not just accept that as being the true position?

Here's a breakdown of the parts of the Bill of Rights that the high court now recognizes as incorporated:

- ✔ **First Amendment:** Completely incorporated; see Chapter 14.

- ✔ **Second Amendment:** Not recognized as incorporated. However, the 2008 Supreme Court ruling in *D.C. v. Heller* has made the question of the incorporation of this amendment a live issue, and several applications have been filed in federal court to get the Second Amendment incorporated. See Chapter 15 for more.

- ✔ **Third Amendment:** Not recognized as incorporated. The possible incorporation of this amendment has never been considered by the high court. But, in the 1982 case of *Engblom v. Carey,* the U.S. Court of Appeals for the Second Circuit accepted that this amendment applied to the states. See Chapter 16.

- ✔ **Fourth Amendment:** Completely incorporated; see Chapter 16.

- ✔ **Fifth Amendment:** Completely incorporated, except for the right to indictment by a grand jury, as decided by the high court in 1884 in *Hurtado v. California.* Justice Stanley Matthews, writing for the majority, pointed out that, as the Fifth Amendment contains both a right to due process and a right to grand jury indictment, the one cannot be included in the other. So the absence of any mention of grand juries in the Fourteenth Amendment must mean that that right does not apply to the states. See Chapter 17.

- ✔ **Sixth Amendment:** Completely incorporated; see Chapter 18.

- ✔ **Seventh Amendment:** Not recognized as incorporated. This amendment guarantees the right to jury trial in civil suits. In the 1974 case of *Curtis v. Loether,* a civil rights case, the high court specifically refused to rule on whether the Seventh Amendment was incorporated, especially in civil rights cases. See Chapter 18.

- ✔ **Eighth Amendment:** The prohibition against "cruel and unusual punishments" is recognized by the high court as incorporated. However, the high court has never ruled on whether the prohibitions of "excessive bail" and "excessive fines" are incorporated. See Chapter 18.

- ✔ **Ninth and Tenth amendments:** Not incorporated. It is commonly assumed that, although these two amendments form part of the Bill of Rights, they do not specifically confer any rights. For a discussion of these amendments, see Chapter 19.

The Blaine Amendment: A compelling argument against incorporation

The framers of the Fourteenth Amendment didn't understand it as incorporating the bulk of the Bill of Rights. How do we know this? James G. Blaine proposed a new amendment to the Constitution mirroring the first clause of the First Amendment but applying it to the states. Instead of starting "Congress shall make no law . . .," the Blaine Amendment began, "No State shall make any law respecting an establishment of religion . . . ."

Blaine proposed his new amendment in 1875 — just seven years after the ratification of the Fourteenth Amendment. If Blaine's proposed amendment was already sitting inside the Fourteenth Amendment, there would have been no need for Blaine to propose it. Was Blaine just plain ignorant of the Fourteenth Amendment? No, sirree. He was one of the most influential members of the House of Representatives, one of the framers of the Fourteenth Amendment, and then Speaker! He wouldn't have gone to all the trouble of putting the Establishment Clause of the First Amendment (the first clause, which refers to "an establishment of religion") into a new amendment applicable to the states if the First Amendment already applied to the states by "incorporation." This is perhaps the strongest argument against the whole incorporation theory.

Note: Those parts of the Bill of Rights that are not regarded as incorporated apply only to federal law. But some of them do apply to the states anyway — by virtue of state law. Prohibition of excessive bail is an example of this, as it's found in every state constitution.

What about *reverse incorporation*? Some commentators have suggested that the Equal Protection Clause of the Fourteenth Amendment, which applies specifically to the states, should be read as applying also to the federal government through incorporation into the Due Process Clause of the Fifth Amendment. Whew! That is not the law at present, and the U.S. Supreme Court has never ruled on it.

Taking Private Property

The last part of the Fifth Amendment hasn't clogged the courts to quite the extent due process has done, but it has generated its share of heated controversy. It reads as follows:

> *nor shall private property be taken for public use, without just compensation.*

Recognizing eminent domain

This clause is intended to offer protection to property owners, but it also recognizes the absolute right of the government to take private property. This had been the case for hundreds of years under English law, and earlier under Roman law. In the words of the famous Dutch jurist Hugo Grotius, written in 1625, "the property of subjects is under the eminent domain of the state." That is why U.S. law uses the term *eminent domain* to refer to the right of the government to take private property.

The taking of private property can only be "for public use," and the definition of this phrase has been highly controversial. At first it was narrowly defined, referring to use by the public, as for example the taking of someone's home to build or widen a roadway. But the U.S. Supreme Court has broadened the definition considerably.

Losing protection

In 1954, the Supreme Court heard a case about a department store that the District of Columbia wanted to take possession of and hand over to a private agency for redevelopment for private use. Because the private agency was redeveloping a larger area surrounding the department store with the intention of removing slum properties, the court refused to interfere with the redevelopment project. The justices argued that the project had to be looked at as a whole. If the success of the larger project depended on clearing a non-slum property such as the department store, that was an acceptable casualty.

In 2005, the U.S. Supreme Court went even further. It ruled that local governments could take private homes and businesses against the wishes of their owners and hand the property over to private developers of shopping malls and hotel complexes. Writing for the liberal majority, Justice John Paul Stevens held that local officials knew better than federal judges what was good for their communities. He also recognized that the states could, if they wished, pass laws granting property owners more rights than under the U.S. Constitution.

The conservative members of the court, and swing-voter Justice Sandra Day O'Connor, registered a strong dissent. "Any property may now be taken for the benefit of another private party," wrote O'Connor, "but the fallout from this decision will not be random. The beneficiaries are likely to be those citizens with disproportionate influence and power in the political process, including large corporations and development firms."

The 2005 decision was greeted with dismay across the nation, and in 2006 no fewer than 34 states adopted some form of eminent domain reform in order to minimize the effects of the judgment.

Chapter 18

Dealing with Justice and Individual Rights: The Sixth through Eighth Amendments

*T*he Sixth through Eighth amendments of the Constitution are part of the *Bill of Rights,* the unofficial name that belongs to the first ten amendments, collectively, which were all ratified together on December 15, 1791.

Amendments six through eight do not have the glamour or pizzazz of the First Amendment, the Fifth, or even the Fourteenth. But amendments six through eight are still pretty important. Here's a brief summary:

✔ The Sixth Amendment guarantees a fair trial to defendants in a criminal prosecution, including the right to a jury trial and the assistance of counsel.

✔ The Seventh Amendment guarantees the right to trial by jury in civil trials.

✔ The Eighth Amendment is best known for banning "cruel and unusual punishments."

I discuss all three amendments in this chapter.

Outlining Defendants' Rights in Criminal Prosecutions: The Sixth Amendment

The Sixth Amendment is quite a mouthful (see the Appendix). It contains no fewer than eight rights applicable to "all criminal prosecutions." Here are the rights that this article guarantees to a defendant in a criminal prosecution:

- The right to a speedy trial
- The right to a public trial
- The right to a trial by an impartial jury from the district where the crime was committed
- The right to be informed of the nature of the accusation
- The right to be informed of the cause of the accusation
- The right to be confronted with the witnesses against him
- The right to compel the attendance of witnesses in his favor
- The right to be represented by counsel

This list of rights looks pretty comprehensive, but it raises quite a few questions, including these:

- Do these eight rights really apply to "all criminal prosecutions," as the Sixth Amendment says? Do they apply to prosecutions for misdemeanors as well as to felonies, and to state and federal prosecutions alike?
- How speedy must a speedy trial be?
- Why is a public trial necessary?
- What exactly is meant by "an impartial jury," and how can it be guaranteed?
- What exactly is meant by the "cause of the accusation"?
- Why is it a right for a defendant to be confronted by the witnesses against him?
- How can witnesses be compelled to attend?
- Is the right to be represented by counsel a general right? What if the defendant can't afford it? And what if a defendant wants to defend himself? Does he have the right to do so?

I tackle each of these questions in turn.

Having the same rights in a state and federal trial

The opening words of the Sixth Amendment state categorically that all the rights guaranteed in that amendment apply "[i]n all criminal prosecutions." But is that really true?

The Bill of Rights originally applied only to federal law, but the U.S. Supreme Court has gradually incorporated more and more of its provisions into the Due Process Clause of the Fourteenth Amendment, which applies to the states. I discuss the whole incorporation debate in Chapter 17.

As of now, the whole of the Sixth Amendment is accepted as incorporated in this way. So the rights listed in the Sixth Amendment do apply to state prosecutions as well as to federal prosecutions (with some exceptions). The crucial case in applying the amendment to state prosecutions was *Duncan v. Louisiana,* decided by the U.S. Supreme Court in 1968.

Gary Duncan, a 19-year-old African American, was charged with slapping a white youth in Louisiana. In law this offense is a misdemeanor called *simple battery.* Under Louisiana state law, jury trial is not available for misdemeanors. Duncan was convicted and sentenced to a fine of $150 and 60 days in jail. He took his case to the U.S. Supreme Court in 1968 on the ground that the state had violated his right to a jury trial under the Sixth and Fourteenth amendments.

Duncan won big-time. The Supreme Court ruled that the right to trial by jury in criminal cases is fundamental and central to the American concept of justice. So the right to a jury trial applies to the states as well as to federal courts — except for "petty crimes" whose maximum possible punishment is a $500 fine and six months jail time.

The Supreme Court held that the whole of the Sixth Amendment was incorporated into the Due Process Clause of the Fourteenth Amendment, and that all the rights enumerated in the Sixth Amendment are therefore available in state courts as well as in federal courts.

How speedy is a speedy trial?

"Justice delayed is justice denied." This old saying puts the importance of a speedy trial in a nutshell. Delaying a trial means that the accusation hangs over the defendant until the case comes to court. In the meantime, witnesses' memories can become increasingly unreliable, and some witnesses may disappear or even die.

If a guilty defendant has posted bail, he can commit more crimes during a long wait for his trial. So the right to a speedy trial is not only in the interest of defendants; it also protects society. And if a defendant can't make bail, he has to sit in jail until his trial; a long wait is unfair to him and adds to the overcrowding of the prisons.

In 1972, the U.S. Supreme Court identified four factors that must be tested to decide whether there has been a violation of the right to a speedy trial:

- ✔ **The length of the delay:** The court held that a delay of a year or more from the date of arrest can usually be presumed to violate the defendant's right to a speedy trial, but the court declined to set any definite limit. The court held instead that this issue has to be decided on a case-by-case basis.

- ✔ **The reason for the delay:** Here, the court proposed a sliding scale. "A deliberate attempt to delay the trial in order to hamper the defense should be weighted heavily against the government," it determined. At the other extreme, "a valid reason, such as a missing witness, should serve to justify appropriate delay."

- ✔ **The defendant's assertion of his right to a speedy trial:** Does a defendant lose his right to a speedy trial if he doesn't assert this right? No, but "failure to assert the right will make it difficult for a defendant to prove that he was denied a speedy trial."

- ✔ **Prejudice to the defendant:** The Supreme Court identified three factors that would likely prejudice (or harm) the interests of the defendant, including "oppressive pretrial incarceration" and "the possibility that the defense will be impaired."

Appreciating the need for a public trial

"Justice must not only be done but must be seen to be done." It would be hard to disagree with this old saying. If you don't know what went on in a trial, how can you be sure that it was fair?

U.S. courtrooms have always been open to the public, and now many trials are even televised, which may not always be a good thing. For example, O.J. Simpson's murder trial in 1995 turned into a media circus. But whether a trial should be televised or not is a different question from whether it should be open to the public.

Is a trial behind closed doors ever justified? If the evidence is so sensitive that it would be dangerous for the evidence to be published, yes. Also, if one of the parties files a motion of *closure* (meaning the trial should be conducted in private), the judge has to decide whether to grant the motion. Closure may be allowed in cases involving organized crime or rape and is routinely ordered in juvenile cases.

It's important to realize that the question of public trials affects rights not only under the Sixth Amendment but may also implicate First Amendment rights of freedom of speech and freedom of the press. I discuss the First Amendment in Chapter 14.

Guaranteeing trial by jury

Trial by jury is an important constitutional right, which can be traced back to Magna Carta in 1215 (see Chapter 2).

Courts have always treated petty offenses as an exception to the right to trial by jury. *Petty offenses* are those that carry a sentence of not more than six months in jail or a fine of not more than $500, or both.

What if a defendant is charged at the same trial with a number of petty offences, so that his total jail time could exceed six months? In 1996, the U.S. Supreme Court said that a trial for multiple petty offenses would not trigger the right to a jury trial.

Selecting an impartial jury

The Sixth Amendment says that criminal defendants have the right to trial by "an impartial jury." But is this really a right that defendants are likely to claim? Aren't they more likely to want juries that are favorably disposed toward them — just as prosecutors prefer juries that are more likely to convict? Of course. Maybe the Framers were a bit naïve in this respect.

But, whether defendants want an impartial jury or not, the system is set up to deliver impartial juries, although it clearly doesn't always succeed in doing so. The states compile lists of people who are eligible for jury service. A jury pool or a jury in waiting is summoned. The actual group of 12 jurors is selected from these potential jurors. The prosecution and the defense can challenge these potential jurors *for cause,* and both sides can also exercise a fixed number of *peremptory challenges*:

✔ **Challenge for cause:** Any potential juror can be challenged "for cause." Examples of "cause" are bias against one party, acquaintance with a party or lawyer, and inability to serve as a juror. The judge and attorneys ask potential jurors a number of questions to find out more about them and whether there is some reason they should not serve on the jury. (*The Simpsons* poked fun at jury selection when Homer Simpson explained how he got out of jury duty: "The trick is to say you're prejudiced against all races.")

✔ **Peremptory challenge:** Both parties also have the right to have a predetermined number of individual jurors excluded from the jury without "cause." This is called a *peremptory challenge* and can generally be freely exercised by a lawyer. However, in 1986, in *Batson v. Kentucky*, the Supreme Court decided that a peremptory challenge could not be used to exclude jurors solely on grounds of race. In other words, a lawyer could not "stack" the jury with members of a certain race. Chief Justice Warren Burger dissented, arguing that the majority decision effectively abolished peremptory challenge, "a procedure which has been part of the common law for many centuries and part of our jury system for nearly 200 years."

So important is jury selection that lawyers increasingly hire jury consultants in high profile or high stakes cases. A jury consultant can charge hundreds of thousands of dollars to pick the right jury for the side that has hired him or her. An apparently innocuous question put to prospective jurors can pay dividends to the perceptive analyst. Prospective jurors may be asked, "Who is your favorite person?" If your answer is Cher, according to jury consultant Howard Varinsky, "It says you're not very bright." Does that mean that such a person should not be selected for the jury? Not at all. Says Varinsky: If the case involves complex information that is unfavorable to your side, a juror who doesn't understand the information could be a plus. This statement echoes the cynical comment made by the humorist Dave Barry: "If you are accused of a crime, you have the right to a trial before a jury of people too stupid to get out of jury duty."

Recognizing the importance of juries

You should never underestimate the importance of jury trials in the whole constitutional framework. The role of the jury is as the *finder of fact*. The judge advises the jury on the law that should be applied to those facts. But the jury's verdict decides whether the defendant is guilty or not guilty.

The power of juries has increased in recent years. For example, in *Ring v. Arizona*, heard in 2002, the U.S. Supreme Court ruled that only a jury was allowed to determine whether there were aggravating factors necessary for imposing the death penalty. This decision struck down the rule in Arizona and some other states that allowed judges to make this determination.

Juries are not usually informed of another power that they have long had: *jury nullification.* The judge is supposed to instruct the jury on the law, and the jury is supposed to accept the judge's instructions. But in practice juries have long reserved the right to ignore the law and to act according to their consciences. This is called jury nullification. During Prohibition, for example, juries often refused to convict defendants charged under the alcohol control laws. This resistance may well have contributed to the repeal of Prohibition by the Twenty-First Amendment.

Most judges are not too happy about jury nullification. In a 1988 case, a judge who was asked by the jury about jury nullification replied, "There is no such thing as valid jury nullification." In 1997, the Second Circuit held that a juror who intended to nullify the law could be dismissed from the jury panel. But perhaps the last word should go to Supreme Court Justice Antonin Scalia, who described juries as "the spinal column of American democracy."

Being "informed of the nature and cause of the accusation"

A fair criminal justice system must let an accused person know exactly what charges he or she is facing. An indictment is normally based on a *statute* — a law passed by Congress or a state legislature. It is essential in the interests of justice that the statute is clear. If it isn't clear, it can be declared void for uncertainty or void for vagueness, and therefore unconstitutional. The tests for vagueness include the following:

- ✔ Is it clear which persons fall within the scope of the statute?
- ✔ Does the statute alert those persons who are subject to it?
- ✔ Are there safeguards against the arbitrary or discriminatory application of this statute?
- ✔ What conduct does the statute prohibit?
- ✔ What punishment does the statute impose?

But clarity in the law itself is not enough. The indictment may have to go beyond the words of the statute and "must descend to particulars," as the U.S. Supreme Court held in *United States v. Cruikshank* in 1875.

Confronting adverse witnesses

Why does the Sixth Amendment guarantee the right of criminal defendants to confront the witnesses giving evidence against them? The alternative would be to allow witnesses' statements to go unchallenged, which is not fair unless the statement is uncontroversial and is accepted by both sides.

The principle that criminal defendants must be allowed to confront their accusers dates back to the revulsion at the way Sir Walter Raleigh was treated in his treason trial in 1603. Raleigh was not allowed to question the witnesses against him, whose signed statements had been extracted under torture.

The right to cross-examine your accusers is important for several reasons:

- ✔ It enables skillful counsel to confront witnesses with inconsistencies in their evidence.
- ✔ It may even result in a witness being caught in a lie.
- ✔ It gives the jury a view of the *demeanor* of the witness — including the witness' body language, which can be revealing.

Child witnesses or other vulnerable witnesses may be allowed to give their evidence in the judge's chambers without being cross-examined. This situation is the main exception to the rule stated in the Sixth Amendment.

Compelling witnesses to attend

If a witness supports your case, that witness will surely be only too happy to come to court to give evidence in your favor, right? Unfortunately not. Too many people are afraid of appearing in court, or just can't be bothered. So it's necessary to be able to compel them to attend. This is done by serving such a witness with a *subpoena* — a formal document issued by the court ordering the witness to appear in court to give evidence at a certain time and place. The reason this procedure is called a *subpoena* — from the Latin, meaning "subject to penalty" — is that a witness who disobeys the order may be found guilty of a contempt of court, for which the penalty can be jail.

Demanding the right to counsel

The Sixth Amendment says that "In all criminal prosecutions, the accused shall . . . have the Assistance of Counsel for his defence." In 1968, the U.S. Supreme Court decided that the whole of the Sixth Amendment was incorporated into the Due Process Clause of the Fourteenth Amendment. In other words, all the rights enumerated in the Sixth Amendment apply to the states as well as to federal courts.

However, the right to counsel has not always been recognized by the courts. In *Betts v. Brady*, the Supreme Court decided in 1942 that criminal defendants in state courts could not claim legal representation unless there were "special circumstances" in their cases — for example, if they were facing the death penalty.

Betts is one of the few Supreme Court cases that have been overruled by a later Supreme Court decision. This overruling happened in the landmark case *Gideon v. Wainwright*, heard by the U.S. Supreme Court in 1963. The court held that the right to counsel in the Sixth Amendment was indeed incorporated into the Due Process Clause of the Fourteenth Amendment and did therefore apply to state trials as well as to trials in federal court.

In an equally famous case, *Miranda v. Arizona*, heard in 1966, the U.S. Supreme Court went further, holding that "The right to have counsel present at the interrogation is indispensable to the protection of the Fifth Amendment privilege" against self-incrimination. As a result of this holding, the right to counsel at public expense is now incorporated into the Miranda warning routinely given to suspects by police officers:

> *You have the right to remain silent. . . You have the right to speak to an attorney, and to have an attorney present during any questioning. If you cannot afford a lawyer, one will be provided for you at government expense.*

But what if a criminal defendant doesn't want legal representation? In 1975 the U.S. Supreme Court held that it is in keeping with the Sixth Amendment for a defendant to represent himself: "A knowing and intelligent waiver" of the right to counsel "must be honored out of that respect for the individual which is the lifeblood of the law."

However, in *Martinez v. Court of Appeals of California*, decided in 2000, the U.S. Supreme Court denied the right of a criminal defendant to conduct his own appeal against a conviction. The court held that the Sixth Amendment right to represent yourself applies to trials but not to appeals.

It's hard to understand the justification for making this distinction. The Sixth Amendment guarantees *rights*, but in *Martinez* the Supreme Court appears to have treated a *right* as if it were an *obligation*. This is a serious logical error. If you're playing *Who Wants to be a Millionaire*, you have the *right* to phone a friend; you don't have an *obligation* to do so.

Guaranteeing Jury Trials in Civil Suits: The Seventh Amendment

The Seventh Amendment preserves an old right of trial by jury in certain civil suits. Here is what the amendment says:

> *In Suits at common law, where the value in controversy shall exceed twenty dollars, the right of trial by jury shall be preserved, and no fact tried by a jury, shall be otherwise re-examined in any Court of the United States, than according to the rules of the common law.*

The right to trial by jury in civil suits long predates the U.S. Constitution. It existed in English law from time immemorial, but it has been largely abolished there. Thanks to the Seventh Amendment, jury trials in civil lawsuits are still alive and well in the United States.

The Seventh Amendment right does not extend to state courts because the U.S. Supreme Court does not regard the Seventh Amendment as incorporated into the Fourteenth Amendment by the Due Process Clause (see Chapter 17). However, most states have provisions for civil jury trials in their individual constitutions, so civil juries are alive and well in state courts too.

What's with the emphasis on the common law in the Seventh Amendment? When this amendment was ratified in 1791, English law drew a distinction between *common law* and *equity*. Not only were the two types of law distinct, but there were separate law courts for each:

- Common law courts tried cases involving contract, tort, and many other types of lawsuits.
- Disputes involving wills, trusts, and real estate went to the courts of equity.

In the common law courts, jury trials were the norm, but in the courts of equity all trials were *bench trials* — heard by a judge sitting alone.

This pattern existed not only in England but also in the 13 American colonies, and it is reflected in the Seventh Amendment. Because jury trials were found only in common law suits, not in equity, the amendment preserves and perpetuates this distinction.

This tradition sometimes results in tedious arguments. For example, in *Chauffeurs, Teamsters & Helpers Local No. 391 v. Terry*, heard in 1990, the U.S. Supreme Court had to decide whether a labor dispute would have been a suit "at common law" back in 1791. Justice William Brennan held that many of the legal rights available today cannot easily be classified in terms of the categories of English law of 200 years ago, and that modern U.S. judges are not qualified to analyze the law in those terms. The right to trial by jury, he added, was too important to depend on such "needless and intractable excursions into increasingly unfamiliar territory."

Prohibiting "Cruel and Unusual Punishments": The Eighth Amendment

The Eighth Amendment is best known for banning "cruel and unusual punishments," but it also contains prohibitions against excessive bail and excessive fines. Here is the entire wording of the Eighth Amendment:

> *Excessive bail shall not be required, nor excessive fines imposed, nor cruel and unusual punishments inflicted.*

Banning excessive bail

After someone has been arrested and booked on suspicion of committing a crime, he or she appears before a judge for *arraignment*. The judge hears the charges and asks the accused person to enter a plea. If the plea is "not guilty," a court date is set for the trial. But that date may be months or even years away. So the court has to decide whether to keep the accused person, or *defendant*, in jail or whether to allow him or her to go free until the trial date.

The bail system is intended to give a defendant an incentive to appear in court as required and not to skip town before the trial date. A defendant facing a murder charge is likely to be given bail of at least $500,000. But in order to *post bail* it's usually necessary to pay only 10 percent of the bail amount up front. If the defendant duly shows up in court, the amount paid is refunded. (However, if a bail bondsman is used to post bail, he retains the 10 percent of the bail amount paid to him as his fee.) If the defendant fails to appear in court, the whole amount of the bail has to be paid to the court.

The words "Excessive bail shall not be required" were lifted directly from the Virginia Constitution, which in turn comes straight from the English Bill of Rights of 1688. This formulation raises some questions:

✔ How much is "[e]xcessive"? You know from the news that celebrities and rich defendants are often required to pay very high amounts of bail, sometimes running into hundreds of thousands of dollars or even more. So, does the appropriate level of bail depend on the seriousness of the charge or on the resources of the accused person? The level of bail set should be just enough to ensure that the defendant in question will not skip town before his trial, but this amount is not easy to assess. If a defendant believes that he has been asked to post too much bail, he can apply to the court for a reduction.

✔ Does the Eighth Amendment mean that criminal defendants must always be given the opportunity to post bail? No. Where a defendant is facing a very serious charge like murder, bail can be denied. At the same time that Congress debated the Eight Amendment, it also considered the Judiciary Act, which defined which offenses were bailable and which were not bailable. As so often is the case, the words of the Constitution have to be read in conjunction with other legislation.

✔ Does the Eight Amendment allow "preventive detention" without bail? The U.S. Supreme Court answered yes to this question in *United States v. Salerno* in 1987. The court was deciding on the constitutionality of the Bail Reform Act of 1984. This law allows a federal court to detain an arrestee pending trial if the government shows that no release conditions "will reasonably assure the safety of any other person and the community." This provision goes way beyond any previous law that allowed denial of bail. Anthony Salerno was alleged to be a mafia boss, but the 1984 law is tailor-made for use against suspected terrorists. In the words of Chief Justice William Rehnquist, here are some factors that have to be considered in deciding whether to deny bail to an arrestee:

  • "The nature and seriousness of the charges,

  • The substantiality of the Government's evidence against the arrestee,

  • The arrestee's background and characteristics, and

  • The nature and seriousness of the danger posed by the suspect's release."

Removing excessive fines

The U.S. Supreme Court has generally taken a narrow view of the meaning of the word *fines*. In 1989, the court adopted the definition of *fines* that was current when the Eighth Amendment was ratified in 1791: "The word 'fine' was understood to mean a payment to a sovereign [government] as punishment for some offense . . . The Excessive Fines Clause was intended to limit only those fines directly imposed by, and payable to, the government."

However, in 1993 the court decided that an order for forfeiture of property could be considered a fine under the Eighth Amendment, though it declined to determine how much forfeiture would amount to an excessive fine.

Barring "cruel and unusual punishments"

The ban on the infliction of "cruel and unusual punishments" is one of the best-known provisions of the Constitution. This prohibition applies to state law as well as to federal law because the U.S. Supreme Court accepts it as incorporated by the Due Process Clause of the Fourteenth Amendment (see Chapter 17). But what exactly is meant by this memorable phrase?

Understanding the importance of "and"

Does the word *and* have any significance? Does "cruel *and* unusual punishments" have a different meaning from "cruel *or* unusual punishments"? The answer is yes. On this basis, the *three strikes laws* have been upheld: laws that allow courts to impose an extra-long jail sentence on anyone convicted of three felonies. This type of punishment sure was unusual, but it was held not to be cruel.

However, some three-strike cases make for worrying reading, like the 2003 California case *Lockyer v. Andrade.* The theft of five videotapes was classified as a felony and, because the offender had a few prior convictions, he was sentenced to jail for 50 years to life. The U.S. Supreme Court ruled that this sentence did not amount to cruel and unusual punishment.

Identifying some completely forbidden punishments

Here are some punishments that are completely forbidden:

- **Torture:** This term presumably includes the use of those old-time favorites, the pillory, the rack, the stocks, and cutting off ears and limbs. The exact meaning of the prohibition on cruel and unusual punishments has been debated since the days of the Framers. In 1789, Representative Samuel Livermore said, "It is sometimes necessary to hang a man, villains often deserve whipping, and perhaps having their ears cut off; but are we in the future to be prevented from inflicting these punishments because they are cruel?" The answer was yes. In 1878, the U.S. Supreme Court in *Wilkerson v. Utah* ruled that all punishments "of unnecessary cruelty" were forbidden by the Eighth Amendment.

✔ **Canceling the citizenship of a U.S. citizen:** Albert Trop, a native-born U.S. citizen, escaped from an army stockade while serving in the U.S. Army in World War II. He was court-martialed, sentenced to three years at hard labor, and received a dishonorable discharge.

Later, Trop applied for a passport and was denied on the grounds that his army desertion had stripped him of U.S. citizenship. In 1958, the U.S. Supreme Court branded this refusal "cruel and unusual punishment." Chief Justice Earl Warren, writing for the majority, held that "denationalization" is "the total destruction of the individual's status in society." Pointing out that desertion from the army can be punishable by death, Justice Felix Frankfurter hit back in his dissent: Can it "be seriously urged that loss of citizenship is a fate worse than death?"

✔ **Punishing someone for suffering from an illness:** Drug addiction, for example, is an illness and should not be criminalized; the Supreme Court said so in *Robinson v. California* in 1962. But this decision put the court on a slippery slope, as the 1968 case of *Powell v. Texas* illustrates. In that case the majority of the U.S. Supreme Court ruled that criminalizing public drunkenness did not amount to cruel and unusual punishment. Where to draw the line? Justice Abe Fortas suggested this test: "criminal penalties may not be inflicted upon a person for being in a condition he is powerless to change." On this basis, Fortas dissented in favor of the drunk in *Powell.* But is an alcoholic really powerless to change his condition? Alcoholics Anonymous might dissent from Abe Fortas!

✔ **Punishments that are cruel and unusual because they're excessive:** Can a punishment be held to be cruel and unusual purely because it is regarded as excessive? Yes. This doctrine was first adopted by the U.S. Supreme Court back in 1910. In *Coker v. Georgia*, heard in 1977, the court held that the death penalty for the rape of an adult female was excessive and amounted to cruel and unusual punishment.

Debating the death penalty

When the Bill of Rights was ratified in 1791, capital punishment was commonplace and taken for granted. Nobody then thought that the death penalty could constitute "cruel and unusual punishments." The Fifth Amendment refers to capital punishment no fewer than three times:

✔ *No person shall be held to answer for a capital, or otherwise infamous crime . . .* A capital crime means one that carries the death penalty.

✔ *nor shall any person be subject to the same offences to be twice put in jeopardy of life or limb.* The word *life* here refers again to the death penalty.

✔ *Nor be deprived of life, liberty or property, without due process of law.* Yep, the good ole Due Process Clause itself takes it for granted that you can be executed by due process.

The Due Process Clause of the Fourteenth Amendment, ratified in 1868, similarly shows that capital punishment was still perfectly acceptable then:

> *nor shall any State deprive any person of life, liberty or property, without due process of law.*

How could a state deprive anyone of his or her life by due process of law if the death penalty was unconstitutional? Obviously, it would be impossible.

In the case of *Wilkerson v. Utah,* heard in 1878, the U.S. Supreme Court made it clear that certain modes of execution did amount to cruel and unusual punishments, but others didn't. Burning people alive at the stake, drawing and quartering, and disemboweling were all unconstitutional as cruel and unusual punishments. But death by firing squad — the form of execution used in Utah — was constitutionally acceptable.

The first real challenge to the death penalty as such occurred in *Furman v. Georgia,* heard by the U.S. Supreme Court in 1972 together with two other death penalty cases. By 5 votes to 4 the court overturned all three capital sentences. Only two justices (William Brennan and Thurgood Marshall) actually went so far as to declare that the death penalty by its very nature constituted cruel and unusual punishment. Three justices concurred in overturning the particular sentences under review but stopped well short of condemning capital punishment as being invariably and inescapably unconstitutional. Instead they focused on the arbitrariness and capriciousness with which the death penalty was imposed, especially as it tended to fall disproportionately on African Americans.

Only four years later the U.S. Supreme Court changed its position on capital punishment. The key case was *Gregg v. Georgia,* which was heard in 1976 together with four other cases. The majority of the court held that

- ✔ The death penalty for murder does not in itself violate the Eighth and Fourteenth amendments.

- ✔ Capital punishment for murder can't be unconstitutional because it was accepted by the Framers of the Constitution and has been accepted by the U.S. Supreme Court for 200 years.

- ✔ Retribution and deterrence are relevant considerations for sentencing.

- ✔ Capital punishment for murder is not disproportionate to the severity of the crime.

In recent years, Congress and 36 states have enacted new statutes providing for the death penalty. This fact seems to show that the death penalty is not contrary to contemporary standards of decency.

In 2008, the high court heard a landmark case on capital punishment called *Baze v. Rees.* The question before the court was whether execution by lethal injection constituted "cruel and unusual punishment." In a 7–2 decision, the court ruled that lethal injection — or, to be more precise, execution by means of the particular cocktail of lethal drugs administered by injection under Kentucky law — is not unconstitutional. Justice Antonin Scalia, in his concurring opinion, concluded with this line:

> *I take no position on the desirability of the death penalty, except to say . . . that it is preeminently not a matter to be resolved here. And especially when it is explicitly permitted by the Constitution.*

Scalia here draws an important logical distinction, which Justices William Brennan and Thurgood Marshall in the 1970s failed to make: namely the distinction between what the Constitution says and what we would like the Constitution to say. Scalia recognizes that there are some strong arguments against the death penalty but that it would be wrong of the court even to get involved in that debate because that would lead to judges amending the Constitution, which is not permitted. The only way that the death penalty could be made unconstitutional would be by means of a proper constitutional amendment proposed and ratified by the procedure laid down in Article V of the Constitution — which I figure ain't gonna happen any time soon!

Chapter 19

The Ninth and Tenth Amendments: Leaving Things Up to the People and States

. . . .

In This Chapter

▶ Recognizing the importance of the Ninth and Tenth amendments

▶ Understanding the meaning of "rights retained by the people"

▶ Getting a load of federalism

▶ Understanding how power is shared between the feds, the states, and the people

▶ Using these two amendments as guides to interpreting the Constitution

. . . .

*T*he Ninth and Tenth amendments are both really important parts of the Bill of Rights. Unlike the first eight amendments, neither the Ninth Amendment nor the Tenth Amendment contains actual concrete rights. Both amendments appear vague, which is why so many people have failed to recognize their importance.

The Ninth Amendment gives guidance on how to interpret the Constitution and makes it clear that rights that are not mentioned in the Constitution belong to the American people. But Judge Robert Bork has described this amendment as "a meaningless inkblot," and other influential commentators have been hardly less flattering.

Thomas Jefferson called the Tenth Amendment "the foundation of the Constitution," but its importance hasn't always been recognized by the U.S. Supreme Court. In 1931, the court commented that this amendment "added nothing to the Constitution as originally ratified." However, in recent years the court has started to give the Tenth Amendment the respect that it deserves.

Reading the Constitution: The Ninth Amendment

The Ninth Amendment is probably the most misunderstood part of the Constitution. It's hard to understand why so many people have made such heavy weather of this fairly straightforward single-sentence provision:

> *The enumeration in the Constitution, of certain rights, shall not be construed to deny or disparage others retained by the people.*

Let me put this amendment in plain English. It may help if I expand it slightly:

- The U.S. Constitution confers or guarantees a number of individual rights.
- But those are not the only rights that individuals possess.
- The rights that are not mentioned in the Constitution belonged to the people before there was a United States of America.
- And those rights still belong to the people.
- The fact that the Constitution doesn't mention those rights doesn't cancel or detract from them.
- The Constitution must not be construed, or interpreted, in a way that deprives the people of those retained rights.

The theoretical underpinnings of the Ninth Amendment

In drafting the Ninth Amendment (and also the Tenth Amendment), James Madison was drawing on a popular theory of his day: the theory of the social contract. This theory says that in the beginning there was no government or law. Everybody did whatever they liked. As a result, there was "a war of every man against every man," and human life was "nasty, brutish, and short." But eventually people got wise to the problem. They decided it was better to trade some of their freedom for order and peace. So they chose a government and entered into a contract with it. The people gave up some rights in return for protection from the new government.

But the people did not give up all their rights, only some. The rest they retained.

Although the idea of a social contract is theoretical, it actually fits in remarkably well with the birth of the United States. The people of the 13 colonies threw off the British yoke. The people then had total independence. But then they got together and chose a government. They devised a constitution, under which they gave up some of their rights to this new government but retained all other rights. Sound familiar? Of course. James Madison was steeped in the fashionable theories of his day.

IN MY OPINION

Is the Ninth Amendment an inkblot?

It's quite alarming to see how many eminent jurists have totally misunderstood the Ninth Amendment:

✔ Judge Robert Bork describes the amendment as "a meaningless inkblot." The meaning of the Ninth Amendment, says Bork, is as indecipherable as it would have been had the text been obscured by an inkblot.

✔ In *Griswold v. Connecticut*, heard by the U.S. Supreme Court in 1965, Justice Arthur Goldberg opined that the Ninth Amendment did not constitute "an independent source of rights protected from infringement by either the States or the Federal Government."

✔ In *Roe v. Wade,* decided in 1972, Justice William O. Douglas wrote, "The Ninth Amendment obviously does not create federally enforceable rights."

✔ Professor Laurence Tribe wrote that "The Ninth Amendment is not a source of rights as such; it is simply a rule about how to read the Constitution."

✔ In *Troxel v. Granville*, Justice Antonin Scalia wrote in 2000: "The Constitution's refusal to 'deny or disparage' other rights is far removed from affirming any one of them, and even farther removed from authorizing judges to identify what they might be, and to enforce the judges' list against laws duly enacted by the people."

Am I right in saying that all these characterizations of the Ninth Amendment are wrong? Of course. Here's why:

✔ The Ninth Amendment is at pains to emphasize that the pre-Constitution rights that the people possessed are still there. So how can that mean that the amendment doesn't "affirm" those rights? It can't.

✔ Can retained rights be claimed in a court of law? Sure. For example, if you're charged with possession of an illegal drug, you can't be convicted if you show that what looked like cocaine was actually a bag of salt. You must assert your right to be in possession of salt. Is there such a right? Of course. It's one of the innumerable retained rights. How do you know you have that right? Because there's no law against being in possession of a bag of salt.

✔ Does the Ninth Amendment tell us how to read the Constitution? Yes, it does. It tells us that we must not construe (interpret) the Constitution to "deny or disparage" — to negate or downplay — the rights retained by the people. So, the Ninth Amendment tells us how to read the Constitution, but it does much more than that. It tells us that the rights stated in the Constitution are not the only rights enjoyed by the people. There are plenty more, and you must not interpret the Constitution in a way that interferes with those rights.

So, what exactly are these rights "retained by the people"? The word *retained* indicates that the people had these rights before. But when? Clearly, before the U.S. Constitution was ratified. In short, these rights derive from English common law, going back at least 600 years before the United States came into existence.

The Constitution confers or guarantees *positive rights,* but the common law works *negatively.* Under the common law, anything that is not prohibited — usually by statute — is allowed.

In drafting the Ninth Amendment, James Madison was anxious to make it clear that the fact that the Constitution contained *some* rights didn't mean that these were the *only* rights people had. He also wanted to make it quite clear that the rights not mentioned in the Constitution didn't somehow fall to the new U.S. government but remained where they had always been — in the hands of the people.

There are hundreds, probably thousands, of these rights "retained by the people." Here are just a few examples:

- **The right to pick your nose in public:** It's not a very nice thing to do, but as long as there is no law against it, you have the right to do it. In a recent poll, the majority of Americans admitted that they did exercise this right!

- **The right to kill bugs:** Certain religions regard the killing of any living thing as a heinous sin, but it's not a crime under U.S. law — not yet anyway!

- **The right to engage in lesbian sex:** Unlike male homosexual activity, which used to be a criminal offense, sex between women was never a crime under U.S. law. Does this mean that you always had a right to engage in lesbian sex? Yes, but it was a bit difficult for about half the population!

Considering the Tenth Amendment

The Tenth Amendment packs some pretty powerful punches. It tackles these topics:

- Federalism
- States' rights
- People power

The Tenth Amendment also provides guidance on how to read the Constitution. This amendment views the Constitution not as the sole source of legal power in the nation, but as only one of three sources, the other two being the states and the people.

Analyzing the wording

Here's what the Tenth Amendment says in its entirety:

> *The powers not delegated to the United States by the Constitution, nor prohibited by it to the States, are reserved for the States respectively, or to the people.*

What does this amendment mean? The key word here is "delegated." To *delegate* a power means to hand it down to somebody else. For example, your boss at work may delegate to you the power to purchase stationery.

The Tenth Amendment looks at the political structure of the nation this way:

✔ In the beginning, all power belonged to the people.

✔ After the Declaration of Independence, the people delegated some of their power to the states.

✔ When the states ratified the U.S. Constitution, they delegated some of their power to the federal government.

✔ The federal government doesn't possess any powers that are not specifically delegated to it by the Constitution.

✔ All powers not delegated to the federal government continue to be "reserved" to the states or to the people.

Balancing power between federal and state governments

Sharing power between the federal government and the states is what federalism is all about, and the United States has a federal form of government (see Chapter 7).

The Tenth Amendment makes it clear that power originates with the states and the people — not with the federal government. In the words of James Madison, the author of the Bill of Rights (including the Tenth Amendment):

> *The powers delegated by the proposed Constitution to the federal government are few and defined. Those which are to remain in the State governments are numerous and indefinite. This division of authority was adopted by the Framers to ensure protection of our fundamental liberties.*

Does this explanation mean that state law is higher than federal law? No. That would be too easy. The U.S. Constitution is supreme, but its scope is limited. The more complicated reality is this:

- ✔ The U.S. Constitution is the highest law in the nation, and any law that conflicts with it is treated as void, or as if it had never existed in the first place. (I discuss the legal status of the Constitution in Chapter 3.)

- ✔ The U.S. Constitution delegates certain powers to the federal government, including the President and the Congress.

- ✔ The federal government has no right to exercise any powers that are not mentioned in the Constitution (known as *unenumerated* powers).

- ✔ In the interests of the liberty of the people, the constitutional powers of the federal government must be strictly interpreted by the courts.

- ✔ All powers other than those delegated by the Constitution to the federal government belong to the states or to the people.

This explanation raises further questions. Here are a few:

- ✔ Exactly which powers have been delegated to the federal government?

- ✔ What is meant by "powers prohibited by [the Constitution] to the States"?

- ✔ What is the split between the powers that are reserved to the states and the powers that are reserved to the people?

I address each of these questions in turn.

Determining the limits of federal power

The Constitution sets out the powers of the federal government, but the precise nature and scope of these powers are open to interpretation. This fact creates a serious problem because neither the courts nor the government stick to the same interpretation all the time. Let me illustrate this problem with a couple of examples.

The Alien and Sedition Acts

The Alien and Sedition Acts of 1798 made the offense of seditious libel a federal crime. *Seditious libel* means writing words intended to subvert the government. This legislation attempted to silence critics of the administration of President John Adams. These laws greatly expanded the power of Congress and came close to claiming that Congress had a power to enforce the *common law* — the case law hammered out by the courts over centuries.

The problem with this view was that the Constitution didn't give Congress any such power. So the Alien and Sedition Acts were clearly in violation of the Tenth Amendment, which restricts the power of the federal government to powers specifically *delegated* to it by the Constitution.

Thomas Jefferson beat the incumbent Adams in the 1800 presidential race. Jefferson then denounced the Alien and Sedition Acts as unconstitutional and void, and he pardoned everyone who had been convicted under them. (The Alien and Sedition Acts in their original form contained four laws. None of these laws has been tested in the courts, and only one of them — the Alien Enemies Act — still survives.)

The Violence Against Women Act

The U.S. Supreme Court under William Rehnquist — who served as Chief Justice from 1986 to 2005 — returned to a more traditional, conservative approach to the Constitution, which some people have named the "Federalism Revolution." (I discuss earlier phases of the Supreme Court in Chapter 12.)

The Rehnquist court enforced the Tenth Amendment by taking a narrow view of federal power and even striking down parts of some federal laws as unconstitutional because they did not conform to the principles of that amendment. One such law was the Violence Against Women Act of 1994.

A freshman at Virginia Tech, Christy Brzonkala, claimed that she'd been raped by two members of the school's football team. A Virginia grand jury was unable to find enough evidence to charge either man with any crime. So Brzonkala filed suit in federal court under the Violence Against Women Act (VAWA), passed by Congress and signed into law by President Bill Clinton in 1994. The act allowed women to file a civil suit in federal court for rape and sexual harassment.

Brzonkala's case reached the U.S. Supreme Court in 2000. The court ruled as unconstitutional the part of VAWA that allowed women to file suit in federal court. Here's how the Supreme Court reached this conclusion:

- Civil suits for sexual assault and harassment fall under the jurisdiction of the state courts.

- Federal courts can hear cases only on issues specifically enumerated in the Constitution or on issues concerned with interstate commerce. (I deal with interstate commerce in Chapter 9.)

- Sexual assault and harassment are not enumerated in the Constitution and have nothing to do with interstate commerce.

- Therefore, the part of VAWA allowing women to file suit in federal court for sexual assaults and harassment is unconstitutional.

President Clinton must have regretted signing VAWA into law, because Paula Jones used that very law against him just a year later! Clinton paid Paula Jones $850,000 to make her VAWA lawsuit go away.

Hanging together: The origins of the Tenth Amendment

The Declaration of Independence of 1776 rejected British rule over the 13 colonies, which became the original 13 states. All 13 states signed the Declaration. But each state claimed independence for itself. The United States of America did not yet exist, and the 13 states did not claim to form a single government.

Benjamin Franklin recognized how important unity was. "We must all hang together," he said, "or assuredly we shall all hang separately." Franklin knew that, unless the 13 states united, the leaders of the American Revolution would all likely be executed for treason against Great Britain.

The delegates from the 13 states took Franklin's advice. Eight days after the adoption of the Declaration of Independence, a constitution for the proposed new country was presented to the delegates. The constitution was called the Articles of Confederation, and the new country was named the United States of America.

The 13 states were in a life-and-death struggle with the British government. The revolutionaries rose up against Britain because the British government denied the colonies autonomy. The revolutionaries regarded British rule as a form of tyranny, and they were not about to substitute one tyranny for another by imposing a new strong central government on themselves.

Thomas Jefferson believed that "The government which governs least, governs best." So the Articles of Confederation created a loose association of the 13 states known as a confederacy. The 13 states retained their individual independence, and the central government of the confederacy was confined to a Congress made up of delegates from all 13 states. George Washington thought that this arrangement was too decentralized. He described the government created by the Articles of Confederation as "little more than the shadow without the substance."

Support grew for a stronger federal government. This consensus led to the drafting and eventual ratification of the U.S. Constitution, which created a much more powerful federal government under a President as head of state, head of the Executive branch, and Commander in Chief.

This arrangement satisfied Washington and the other Federalists, as they were called, but it aroused a lot of hostility among the more radical Anti-Federalists. This opposition was so strong that there was a serious danger that the Constitution might not be ratified by all 13 states. A Bill of Rights was promised in order to ensure ratification.

This is where the Tenth Amendment comes in. As part of the Bill of Rights, it explains that, although the Constitution is the supreme law of the United States of America, the power of the federal government created by the Constitution is strictly limited.

Puzzling over "prohibited" powers

The Tenth Amendment is only one sentence long, but one phrase is slightly puzzling. Let me quote the amendment again and put the phrase in bold:

> *The powers not delegated to the United States by the Constitution, **nor prohibited by it to the States**, are reserved for the States respectively, or to the people.*

Recognizing states' limits

The amendment classifies powers like this:

- Powers delegated by the Constitution to the federal government
- **Powers prohibited by the Constitution to the states**
- Powers reserved to the states
- Powers reserved to the people

The second category refers to Article I, Section 10 of the Constitution. The list of prohibited powers is a long one, including the power

- To make treaties with foreign powers
- To coin money
- To "grant any Title of Nobility"
- To impose import duties
- To "engage in War, unless actually invaded, or in such imminent Danger as will not admit of delay"

These powers all belong to nations, so it's easy to see why they are denied to individual states. Most of these powers are granted to Congress by Article I, Section 8 of the Constitution. (However, the power to grant titles of nobility is specifically denied to the federal government by Article I, Section 9. The Constitution therefore makes it clear that no U.S. institution, either federal or state, has the power to grant titles of nobility. The United States is a republic, and any formal gradations in society just don't belong.)

Probably the most interesting power is the last one I've listed: the power to engage in war. Do the states really have this power? Article I, Section 10 of the Constitution essentially says "yes, but only in exceptional circumstances." It's easy enough to see whether a state has been invaded, but who decides whether a state is threatened by "imminent Danger"? Presumably the state governor and legislature. But the precise interpretation of this provision has never been tested in the courts.

Dragging in the Fourteenth Amendment

Does Article I, Section 10 contain the only restrictions on state power in the Constitution? No. The Fourteenth Amendment also contains major restrictions on the power of the states. When the Tenth Amendment was ratified in 1791, nobody could have anticipated the Fourteenth Amendment, which was a product of the Civil War and became part of the Constitution only in 1868.

But we must read the Tenth Amendment in the light of the Fourteenth Amendment, Section 1, which says:

> No State shall make or enforce any law which shall abridge the privileges or immunities of citizens of the United States; nor shall any State deprive any person of life, liberty, or property, without due process of law; nor deny to any person within its jurisdiction the equal protection of the laws.

These words come from a completely different world than the one that produced the Tenth Amendment. The Tenth Amendment is anxious to emphasize the limitations on federal power, but the Fourteenth Amendment sharply restricts the power of the states. Does the Fourteenth Amendment modify the Tenth Amendment? Yes, undoubtedly.

But, if the Tenth Amendment has to be read in the light of the Fourteenth, doesn't that interpretation nullify the whole purpose of the Tenth Amendment? The answer to this question depends on how broadly or narrowly the Fourteenth Amendment is interpreted. If the Fourteenth Amendment is given a broad interpretation, it seriously diminishes the power of the states, and that sure knocks a dent in the Tenth Amendment. A narrow interpretation of the Fourteenth Amendment is more in keeping with the spirit of the Tenth Amendment. I deal with the Due Process Clause of the Fourteenth Amendment in Chapter 17 and with the rest of that amendment in Chapter 21.

Disentangling states' rights from individual rights

The Tenth Amendment says that any powers not delegated to the federal government are reserved to the states or to the people. But what happens if there is a conflict between the interests of a state and the interests of the people? This situation has arisen quite a few times, and the result is not always easy to predict. Following are a couple of examples.

Protecting freedom of contract?

In 1896, New York State passed a law setting a maximum of 60 hours of work per week in bakeries. Joseph Lochner owned a bakery in Utica, New York. He required his employees to work for more than 60 hours a week. He was charged, convicted, and fined for breaking this state law. Lochner unsuccessfully appealed his conviction to the highest court in New York State.

He then took his case to the U.S. Supreme Court, which heard it in 1905. Lochner's appeal was based on the Fourteenth Amendment, and I discuss this aspect of the case in Chapter 17. But the case is also relevant to an understanding of the Tenth Amendment.

Arguing for individual liberty

Four potentially conflicting forces were involved in this case:

- ✔ The federal government — particularly the U.S. Supreme Court
- ✔ New York State
- ✔ Bakery owners
- ✔ Bakery workers

Lochner said that his employees had freely entered into a contractual agreement to work more than 60 hours a week. Lochner's lawyers argued that the New York State law limiting working hours was contrary to *freedom of contract* and therefore infringed on individual liberty.

New York State claimed that the law about working hours in bakeries was necessary to protect the health of bakery employees.

The high court agreed with Lochner and overturned his conviction under the New York law. The Supreme Court called the New York law an "unreasonable, unnecessary and arbitrary interference with the right and liberty of the individual to contract."

Analyzing the Supreme Court decision

Was the *Lochner* case really a victory for people power, as the Supreme Court claimed? Probably not. Lochner himself wanted his employees to work long hours. His employees agreed to do so. But was their agreement truly free? (Did they really want to put in as many paid hours of work as possible?) Or did they agree to the contract because that was the only way they could keep their jobs? It is impossible to tell.

The majority decision in the *Lochner* case was savaged by Justice Oliver Wendell Holmes, Jr., who in his dissent accused the majority of *judicial activism* — making law rather than interpreting it, as they were supposed to do. Holmes said that the majority decision was based on "an economic theory which a large part of the country does not entertain . . . But a constitution is not intended to embody a particular economic theory."

Let's look at this case from the point of view of the Tenth Amendment. The Tenth Amendment says that the federal government — including the U.S. Supreme Court — is not entitled to exercise any power that is not delegated to it by the Constitution. In my opinion, the Supreme Court had no right to overturn the New York law in the first place. By doing so the court overstepped its constitutional role.

Next, let me look at the New York law. Did the state have the right under its "police powers," as it claimed, to pass a law limiting working hours in bakeries? Note that the term *police powers* is used here in a very broad sense, meaning the power of the state to regulate behavior in the interests of public welfare, security, or morality. So the answer must be yes: The state was right in claiming that the health of the workers was in danger.

Does this conclusion infringe on the rights of the people? No, because freedom of contract is fine in general, but it is not a sacred principle. And in the *Lochner* case it is doubtful that the workers did freely agree to the long working hours that Joseph Lochner required.

In 1937, the Supreme Court rejected the approach that it had taken in *Lochner,* and *Lochner* is no longer an authority followed by the courts. However, *Lochner* is useful in helping to understand the competing interests involved in some legal disputes.

Recognizing gay marriage?

In 2004, the Supreme Judicial Court of Massachusetts legalized same-sex marriage in that state. This is a very controversial topic and one that can be analyzed under the Tenth Amendment.

First, some background: In 2001, seven same-sex couples applied unsuccessfully for marriage licenses in Massachusetts. The seven couples took the matter to court. Chief Justice Margaret Marshall, writing for the majority, held that the state constitution "affirms the dignity and equality of all individuals" and that the state had no "constitutionally adequate reason" for refusing to allow same-sex marriages.

Since May 17, 2004, same-sex marriages have been valid in Massachusetts, and they have also been allowed in Connecticut since October 10, 2008. New Jersey, New Hampshire, and Vermont now also offer same-sex couples the same rights and responsibilities as married couples without using the label "marriage" for same-sex unions. Maine, Hawaii, Oregon, Washington State, and the District of Columbia give same-sex couples varying rights and responsibilities falling short of those of married couples. On the other hand, more than 40 states (including some that allow same-sex couples certain rights) explicitly restrict the use of the term "marriage" to refer to a union between a man and a woman.

Adding the Defense of Marriage Act to the mix

In 1996, Congress had passed the Defense of Marriage Act (DOMA), which was signed into law by President Clinton. This law says that

- ✔ No state is required to recognize same-sex marriages.

- ✔ In federal law the "word 'marriage' means only a legal union between one man and one woman as husband and wife."

Is this law constitutional? It hasn't been tested in the courts as yet, but it has been severely attacked by critics.

Considering the constitutionality of DOMA and gay marriage

The Tenth Amendment provides a simple, logical approach to interpreting the Constitution as a whole, starting with the feds, and then moving to the states, and finally to the people. Using that approach, here I consider the constitutionality of DOMA and same-sex marriages. Let's go step by step:

- ✔ Question: What part of the Constitution gave Congress the power to pass DOMA? Answer: None. For Congress to dictate to the states whether they may or may not recognize a form of marriage is simply unconstitutional.

  DOMA is also unconstitutional because it is an attempt to stop states from obeying Article IV, Section 1 of the Constitution, which says: "Full Faith and Credit shall be given in each State to the public Acts, Records and judicial Proceedings of every other state." If Massachusetts' legalization of same-sex marriage is valid, then all other states must recognize a gay marriage performed in Massachusetts, just as a heterosexual marriage contracted in one state is routinely recognized in every other state.

- ✔ That brings us to the Massachusetts ruling in favor of same-sex marriage. Marriage sure is an area under state control. So the Massachusetts ruling must be kosher, right? Wrong, for at least two reasons:

  - The ruling is an example of *judicial activism* — judges taking the law into their own hands and actually making law instead of just interpreting it, as they are supposed to do.

- The court made a mockery of the English language. Courts are supposed to accept the ordinary and usual meaning of words. Since time immemorial, the English word *marriage* has referred to the union between a man and a woman. What right does the Massachusetts court have to redefine it? None. The court may as well have redefined the word *horse* to include elephants.

Both these reasons make the Massachusetts decision unconstitutional.

✔ Last but not least come the people. The Massachusetts court decision recognizing same-sex marriages polarized opinion. An amendment to the state constitution forbidding same-sex marriage has yet to be put to the people of Massachusetts.

In my opinion, same-sex marriage in Massachusetts is unconstitutional, and the other states therefore don't have to recognize such unions. I am available if anyone wants to take this issue to the U.S. Supreme Court!

The passing in November 2008 of Proposition 8 in California by 52.3 percent of the votes cast is indicative of the highly controversial nature of this issue. Proposition 8 is intended to add a new section to the state Constitution that reads, "Only marriage between a man and a woman is valid or recognized in California." At the time of this writing, the validity of Proposition 8 is being challenged in the California Supreme Court.

Giving the Tenth Amendment its due

The Tenth Amendment was once said by the U.S. Supreme Court to be a mere "truism," just stating the obvious without adding anything new. I don't agree. On the contrary, I think the Tenth Amendment is crucial.

The Tenth Amendment provides a checklist on how to read and interpret the Constitution. Here's how it guides us to determine the constitutionality of a law:

✔ **For federal laws:** What part of the Constitution gives Congress the power to pass this law? If there is no such justification, the law is unconstitutional.

✔ **For state laws:** Does this law belong to one of the areas prohibited to the states by the U.S. Constitution? If it does, it's unconstitutional. If not, the next question is: Have the people delegated to the state — for example, by means of the state constitution — the power to make this law? If so, the law is okay. If not, the law is void.

Part V

Addressing Liberties and Modifying the Government: More Amendments

The 5th Wave   By Rich Tennant

"This is an historic moment, Mr. President. Ratification of the 13th Amendment ending slavery, and Mrs. Lincoln finally selects a pattern for the White House china."

In this part . . .

This part deals with the Eleventh through the Twenty-Seventh amendments — a ragbag of reforms ranging widely in subject matter and date. One of these amendments abolished slavery. Three of them arose out of the Civil War. Six of them directly or indirectly prohibit discrimination. Eight of them are concerned with elections and voting rights. There is also the Prohibition amendment and its repealing amendment, and the curious Twenty-Seventh Amendment, which is both the oldest and the newest amendment of them all.

Chapter 20

States' Rights, Elections, and Slavery: The Eleventh through Thirteenth Amendments

*T*he Eleventh, Twelfth, and Thirteenth amendments are very different from one another, but they all share something in common: Each was introduced to get the Constitution out of some deep doo-doo. Here's a rundown of the amendments with the problem that each was intended to solve:

> ✔ **Eleventh Amendment:** This amendment was introduced to overrule the Supreme Court decision in the case of *Chisholm v. Georgia,* which was viewed by many as an attack on states' rights.

> ✔ **Twelfth Amendment:** This amendment was an emergency measure to prevent the mess of the 1800 presidential election from recurring.

> ✔ **Thirteenth Amendment:** This amendment abolished slavery, which had divided the nation and dragged it into a ruinous civil war.

I discuss each in turn in this chapter.

The Eleventh Amendment: Asserting State Sovereign Immunity?

The Eleventh Amendment, ratified in 1795, contains only 43 words, but it has been interpreted in at least four different ways. Here is what the amendment says:

> *The judicial power of the United States shall not be construed to extend to any suit in law or equity, commenced or prosecuted against one of the United States by Citizens of another State, or by Citizens or Subjects of any Foreign State.*

Overruling the Supreme Court

The Eleventh Amendment was passed to overturn the Supreme Court ruling in the 1793 case of *Chisholm v. Georgia.* Alexander Chisholm of South Carolina filed suit against the State of Georgia for breach of contract, seeking payment for goods supplied to Georgia during the War of Independence.

Georgia refused to play ball, saying that Chisholm couldn't sue a state without its consent because it possessed sovereign immunity from suit. The court didn't like this argument — not surprisingly, because it cut the court's power. The court found in favor of Chisholm and ruled that Article III, Section 2 of the Constitution took away the states' sovereign immunity because in the list of cases that could be heard by the U.S. Supreme Court that section included "Controversies . . . between a State and Citizens of another State."

However, such was the outcry against this decision that two days after the Supreme Court handed down its decision in *Chisholm,* a senator put a proposal before Congress that was to become the Eleventh Amendment. The intention of the amendment was never a secret: It was passed to stop a federal lawsuit from being brought against a state without its consent. But is that really what the Eleventh Amendment says?

Interpreting the Eleventh Amendment

There are four main interpretations of the Eleventh Amendment:

- ✔ The simplest and most straightforward interpretation of the amendment reads it as saying that nobody can sue a state in federal court without the consent of the state concerned.

✔ The second interpretation reads the amendment as permitting a state to be sued by a citizen of another state or of a foreign country, but not by a citizen of the state itself. According to this reading, the State of Utah can't be sued in federal court by a resident of Utah itself, but Utah can be sued by a resident of Nebraska or by a citizen of Outer Mongolia.

✔ The third interpretation is exactly the opposite, excluding only lawsuits against a state by a citizen of a different state.

✔ The fourth interpretation is broader. It says that in general federal courts can't hear cases against states, but Congress can take away a state's sovereign immunity. If Congress does so, that state is no longer protected against suits in federal court.

Cutting across these four different interpretations are four recognized exceptions to the ban on lawsuits against states:

✔ A lawsuit can always be brought in federal court against a state's subdivisions, such as counties, cities, and municipalities.

✔ A state can always consent to a lawsuit being brought against it in federal court.

✔ Congress can *abrogate* — or remove — a state's immunity from suit in federal court, provided Congress's intention to abrogate a state's immunity is "unmistakably clear." However, in the 1996 case of *Seminole Tribe v. Florida,* the Supreme Court ruled that the Commerce Clause in Article I, Section 8 of the Constitution does not give Congress the power to abrogate a state's immunity from suit in federal court. This ruling calls into question the power of federal courts to hear lawsuits against states to enforce congressional legislation under the Commerce Clause relating to environmental law, bankruptcy, or intellectual property, to name but three major areas of commercial law.

✔ If a state violates federal law, the state itself can't be sued in federal court — but a federal court can order state *officials* in their own name to comply with federal law. This was decided by the Supreme Court in the controversial 1908 case *Ex parte Young.* This ruling was based on the fiction that a state official enforcing an unconstitutional state law is a private person — while still remaining a state agent when it comes to remedying the unconstitutional law! For example, in the 1993 ruling in *Martin v. Voinovich,* the high court ordered the governor of Ohio to construct housing for handicapped people to comply with the Americans with Disabilities Act.

The question that lies at the heart of the Eleventh Amendment is whether the individual states can still be regarded as possessing *sovereignty:* complete legal independence. This certainly was the position for the first decade of independence under the Articles of Confederation. But did this position continue under the U.S. Constitution, which was ratified in 1788? In short, are, say, Maine, Ohio, Kentucky, and Texas as independent of one another and of the U.S. federal government as, say, France, India, Brazil, and Australia are of one another? Clearly not, but they obviously have a high degree of autonomy nevertheless. If the states were indeed sovereign states in the fullest sense, immunity from suit would follow. Because they don't have full sovereignty, their immunity from suit is also only partial.

Cleaning Up the Framers' Political Mess: The Twelfth Amendment

The mess that the Twelfth Amendment was intended to clean up reflects the Framers' childish innocence in the dirty world of politics.

The Twelfth Amendment introduced the system of presidential elections that is still in force today — at least in theory. It was intended as an emergency fix for the 1804 presidential election after the two previous elections, held in 1796 and 1800, had gone badly wrong.

Electing the President: The original rules

The original arrangements for presidential elections are to be found in the unamended text of Article II, Section 1 of the Constitution. The arrangements were as follows:

- Each state legislature appointed as many electors for that state as there were senators plus representatives from that state combined. Let's take a hypothetical state with 12 representatives in the House of Representatives. This state would also have had two senators (because every state is entitled to two senators). So, the total number of electors for that state would have been 14.

- The electors of each state met separately.

- Each elector had two votes without differentiating between President and Vice President.

- The candidate with the most votes (provided they amounted to more than 50 percent of the total) became the President, and the runner-up became the Vice President.

✔ If no candidate obtained more than 50 percent of the votes, the presidential election was thrown into the House of Representatives, and the Senate picked the Vice President.

These original rules omitted all mention of political parties. The whole arrangement was undemocratic because the Framers didn't trust the ordinary people to pick the President. Their naïve idea was that the electors would choose the best candidate to be the President and the second-best candidate to be the Vice President.

Not surprisingly, the whole of this arrangement came unstuck as soon as it was put into practice in the first real contested presidential election in 1796.

Understanding politics 1796 style

In the 1796 presidential election, John Adams and Thomas Jefferson, the two main opposing candidates for President, ended up as President and Vice President respectively. It's just as if Jimmy Carter had become Ronald Reagan's Veep!

John Adams, a Federalist, got 71 electoral votes — more than 50 percent of the total — and Thomas Jefferson, a Republican or Democratic-Republican, received 68 electoral votes. Although Jefferson and Adams didn't see eye-to-eye politically, Jefferson was sworn in as Adams's Vice President. What a mess! But worse was to follow.

Tying and vying with your running mate: The 1800 election

The 1800 election was a rematch between Adams and his own Vice President, Jefferson. To avoid a repetition of the same problem as in 1796, the political parties each nominated two candidates, one intended to run for President and the other for Vice President. The Federalist ticket of John Adams and Charles Pinckney was confronted by the Democratic-Republican ticket of Thomas Jefferson and Aaron Burr.

Jefferson and Burr won with 73 electoral votes each. It was well understood that Jefferson was the party's presidential candidate and Burr his running mate, but the Constitution drew no distinction between candidates for the two offices. Each elector just had two equal votes.

Because neither Jefferson nor Burr had a majority, the choice of President was left to the House of Representatives. Here the contest was no longer between Jefferson and Adams but between Jefferson and his own running mate, Aaron Burr!

After 36 ballots and a lot of horse-trading, Jefferson was elected President and Burr Vice President.

This chaotic election made an amendment to the Constitution a pressing necessity, and the Twelfth Amendment was duly ratified on June 15, 1804, less than five months before that year's presidential election.

Preventing future chaos

The Twelfth Amendment has stood the test of time, even though it still doesn't mention political parties. It indirectly recognizes the existence of parties by providing that electors cast a separate vote for President and Vice President.

So, it's no longer a problem if a party's vice-presidential candidate gets the same number of electoral votes as that party's candidate for President — which indeed is what normally happens.

Some people criticize the entire Electoral College system as laid down in the Constitution and the Twelfth Amendment, labeling it undemocratic. I discuss the Electoral College in depth in Chapter 10 and explain why the Framers opted for this method of election instead of relying on the popular vote.

Removing the Blot of Slavery: The Thirteenth Amendment

"All men are created equal," proclaims the Declaration of Independence, written by Thomas Jefferson — a lifelong slave owner. How can slavery be lawful in a nation based on equality? This conundrum took a civil war to sort out.

Although the words *slave* and *slavery* don't appear in the original unamended Constitution, slavery was legally established in a number of states, particularly in the South. And there are indirect allusions to slavery in the text of the Constitution. For example, Article I, Section 9, Clause 1 refers to "the Importation of . . . Persons" — clearly a reference to the slave trade. And Article I, Section 2 allowed slaves to be counted as three-fifths of free persons when calculating state populations for purposes of representation in the House of Representatives — an ironic rule, considering that slaves didn't have the right to vote!

Tracking the debate on slavery

As the United States expanded in the first decades after independence, the question of slavery reared its ugly head at every turn. The main question was whether slavery was to be allowed in the *territories* — the large areas incorporated into the United States but not yet organized into states. As the territories were organized into states, it was crucial to decide whether each new state was to be admitted into the Union as a free state or as a slave state. These decisions had an important effect on the delicate balance of power between the slave states and the free states in Congress, and in particular in the Senate. Here are some of the landmarks in this debate:

- ✔ **The Missouri Compromise:** In 1820, Congress enacted the Missouri Compromise, which prohibited slavery in the unorganized territory of the Great Plains but permitted it in Missouri and the Arkansas Territory.

- ✔ **The Compromise of 1850:** The Mexican-American War of 1846–1848 gave the United States an additional 1.2 million square miles! This huge territory was carved into a number of new states. The question, as always, was whether these states should be free states or slave states. The Compromise of 1850 was made up of five laws passed by Congress that balanced the interests of the southern slave states with those of the free states of the North. The compromise also introduced the concept of "popular sovereignty" into the slavery issue. This doctrine allowed the residents of a new state to decide whether slavery was to be permitted there or not. The Compromise also introduced a stringent new Fugitive Slave Act obliging law-enforcement officers throughout the nation to round up all suspected fugitive slaves and return them to people claiming to be their owners. By making the free states responsible for enforcing slavery, this Act infuriated abolitionists in the North.

- ✔ **The Kansas-Nebraska Act:** This law, passed by Congress in 1854, effectively nullified the Missouri Compromise that had been in place for 34 years. The Missouri Compromise prohibited slavery north of latitude 36°30'. But the Kansas-Nebraska Act allowed "popular sovereignty" in the Kansas Territory and the Nebraska Territory, both of which were north of that line. The act provoked bitter conflict in the two territories — and in the nation as a whole.

- ✔ *Dred Scott v. Sandford:* Dred Scott was a slave whose master was an army doctor who kept moving around, taking Scott with him. Scott was born into slavery in Virginia, a slave state, but lived for a time in Illinois, a free state, and also in the Wisconsin Territory, where slavery was also prohibited. Dred Scott claimed that his residence in a free state and a free territory had emancipated him from slavery.

The U.S. Supreme Court roundly rejected this argument in 1857. Chief Justice Roger Taney, writing for the majority, ruled that the Fifth Amendment prohibited the federal government from depriving anybody of property — including slaves — "without due process of law." The Missouri Compromise of 1820, he held, was therefore unconstitutional. In Taney's words, "An act of Congress which deprives a citizen of the United States of his liberty or property merely because he came himself or brought his property into a particular Territory of the United States, and who had committed no offence against the laws, could hardly be dignified with the name of due process of law." On this basis, the court decided by 6 votes to 2 that Dred Scott was still a slave and, moreover, that no African American, whether slave or free, could ever become a U.S. citizen.

By denying the power of Congress to prohibit slavery in the territories, the Supreme Court incensed antislavery opinion throughout the nation. The widening rift between the free North and the slave-owning South led to increasing talk in the South about secession from the Union.

For the election of 1860, the recently formed Republican Party adopted a platform that opposed the spread of slavery to the territories but did not propose to abolish slavery in those states where it already existed. The Republican presidential candidate, Abraham Lincoln, was a moderate Republican. Lincoln regarded slavery as immoral, but he accepted that it was recognized by the Constitution.

Sliding into secession

The 1860 election revealed just how divided the nation was. Lincoln won handily in the North, while incumbent Vice President John C. Breckinridge swept the South. Lincoln's name didn't even appear on the ballot in nine southern states. Lincoln won less than 40 percent of the popular vote nationwide, but this translated into just under 60 percent of the electoral votes, which put him into the White House.

Although Lincoln was not an abolitionist, the South assumed that he was, and he refused to promise not to abolish slavery altogether. Seven southern states seceded from the Union even before Lincoln was inaugurated on March 4, 1861.

In a last-ditch attempt to placate the South and bring the seceding states back into the Union, lame-duck President James Buchanan asked Congress to propose an "explanatory amendment" to the Constitution based on the *Dred Scott* decision of the Supreme Court.

A special committee of the House of Representatives under Thomas Corwin of Ohio, a Republican, quickly produced a draft. On March 2, 1861 — with just two days of Buchanan's presidency left — Congress passed the proposed amendment with the requisite two-thirds majority in both houses. President Buchanan signed it enthusiastically, although the President's approval is not needed for amendments.

Considering the Corwin amendment

The *Corwin amendment,* as it's usually called, reads as follows:

> *No amendment shall be made to the Constitution which will authorize or give to Congress the power to abolish or interfere, within any state, with the domestic institutions thereof, including that of persons held to labor or service by the laws of said state.*

Despite the absence of the word *slave* or *slavery,* there was no mistaking the meaning of this proposed amendment. It clearly guaranteed the preservation of slavery in all already-existing slave states without, however, dealing with the vexed question of slavery in the territories or new states.

It's significant that this proposed amendment was able to command such widespread support in Congress at a time when many southern members had withdrawn. This means that an amendment guaranteeing the permanent existence of slavery in the established slave states had substantial support among the politicians representing the free states of the North.

Amazingly, two days later, on March 4, 1861, the newly elected President Lincoln also gave the proposed amendment his grudging blessing in his first inaugural address.

The proposed amendment was then sent on its way to obtain the ratification of the states. It was validly ratified by Ohio and Maryland and invalidly by Illinois (by a constitutional convention that just happened to be in session at the time). But Buchanan's and Corwin's frantic efforts to avert a civil war came too late. By the time the proposed amendment passed Congress, not only had seven states seceded; they had already established a breakaway government under the title of the Confederate States of America, or the *Confederacy,* as it's commonly known.

Jefferson Davis, who became the President of the Confederacy, was a U.S. senator from Mississippi from 1857 to 1861. After Mississippi seceded in January 1861 — against Davis's advice — he withdrew from the Senate. In his farewell address, he identified the reason for the secession of the South as the Republican Party's failure "to recognize our domestic institutions [slavery] which preexisted the formation of the Union — our property, which was guarded by the Constitution."

Recognition of slavery where it was already legally established was precisely what the Corwin amendment sought to achieve. The Buchanan-Corwin initiative was not the first time that such a solution had been proposed. But it was the first time that it had reached the stage of being adopted by Congress for ratification as a constitutional amendment.

President Buchanan deplored the secession, saying, "The South has no right to secede, but I have no power to prevent them." Prevention is better than cure, but a cure was at hand — military action. Buchanan regarded that cure as worse than the disease, but it was eagerly embraced by his successor, Lincoln, who was determined to bring the seceding states to heel. With a full-scale civil war raging as of April 1861, the Corwin amendment was quickly forgotten.

Could the ratification of the Corwin amendment have prevented the bloody carnage that followed Lincoln's inauguration? Or was Lincoln's famous earlier remark more accurate? — that "A house divided against itself cannot stand. I believe this government cannot endure, permanently half slave and half free."

Graduating from emancipation to abolition

The Civil War raged from 1861 to 1865. In the early stages, Lincoln didn't allow his generals to free slaves in captured territories, and he even reversed their emancipation proclamations. For example, when General John Frémont freed all slaves in Missouri, Lincoln canceled the general's proclamation and relieved him of his command.

In 1862, in response to a call by a newspaper editor for the total abolition of slavery, Lincoln wrote, "My paramount object in this struggle is to save the Union, and is not either to save or destroy slavery. If I could save the Union without saving any slave I would do it, and if I could save it by freeing all the slaves I would do it."

Lincoln had long been an advocate of sending freed slaves to colonize Liberia, in West Africa. As President he also championed a succession of schemes of black colonization in Panama and off the coast of Haiti.

Lincoln took the view that the Constitution didn't give a peacetime President the power to abolish slavery. However, a mass rally of abolitionists in Chicago held in September 1862 calling for an immediate end to slavery placed the President under pressure.

Later the same month, Lincoln issued his Emancipation Proclamation as a wartime measure. It freed the slaves living in those states of the Confederacy that had not returned to Union control by January 1, 1863. However, it did not have any effect on the slaves in border states that had remained loyal to the Union. Remarkably, the Proclamation also favored the idea of encouraging African Americans to leave the country and establish settlements elsewhere in the Americas or in Africa.

The radical Republicans, hard-line abolitionists, pressed for the immediate and complete abolition of slavery throughout the nation. They thought Lincoln was pussyfooting around the issue of slavery. So in May 1864 they nominated General John Frémont — the radical abolitionist who had had a run-in with Lincoln earlier in the war — to run against Lincoln for President.

Introducing an entirely different thirteenth amendment

In the meantime, the strongly Republican Senate spearheaded the introduction of a very different thirteenth amendment — one abolishing slavery altogether. This was to become the actual Thirteenth Amendment and is still part of the Constitution today. Section 1 reads as follows:

> *Neither slavery nor involuntary servitude, except as a punishment for crime whereof the party shall have been duly convicted, shall exist within the United States, or any place subject to their jurisdiction.*

This amendment was proposed in 1864 while the Civil War was still raging and the slave-owning states of the South still formed part of the breakaway Confederacy. So, an amendment abolishing slavery might have been expected to enjoy widespread support in Congress, from which the Confederate states were excluded.

But in fact abolition was by no means universally popular in the North. For example, Francis Hughes, an influential Pennsylvania Democrat, warned that abolition would flood the state with freed slaves. In the 1862 midterm elections to the House of Representatives, the Republican Party had lost 22 seats, leaving them with only 86 seats out of a total of 185, or just over 46 percent of the seats.

So, although the proposed amendment easily passed the Senate — whose members in those days were not directly elected but appointed by their state legislatures — it was initially rejected by the House of Representatives, which it passed only nine months later, on January 31, 1865.

By this time Lincoln felt much more secure after comfortably winning a second term as President. Congress had taken the initiative over abolition, so Lincoln — always a cautious politician — could now safely come out in its favor. He followed President Buchanan's example (in regard to the Corwin amendment) by writing by hand on the Joint Resolution of Congress passing the proposed new amendment, "Approved February 1, 1865 — Abraham Lincoln."

The proposal was quickly ratified by the free states in the North but was rejected by slave states that had remained loyal to the Union, including New Jersey (which had only a handful of slaves), Delaware, and Kentucky. Nevertheless, by the time the Civil War ended in April, 1865, no fewer than 20 states had ratified the proposed amendment — out of a requisite 27, three-fourths of the 36 states then in existence.

The last seven states to complete the ratification process included some southern states under Union occupation. Ratification was completed with the ratification by the occupied state of Georgia on December 6, 1865. By contrast, Mississippi, another Confederate state, which still had its own elected (Democratic Party) governor at the same time, rejected the amendment on December 5, 1865 — and ratified it only on March 16, 1995!

The importance of the slavery issue in the history of the United States cannot be exaggerated. It has generated — and still generates — strong emotions. To put the whole subject in perspective it may be helpful to read two very different accounts of what slavery was like. First, there is Kenneth M. Stampp's classic negative portrayal of slavery in a 1956 book titled *The Peculiar Institution: Slavery in the Ante-Bellum South.* A very different view of slavery emerges from a 1974 two-volume blockbuster by the Nobel laureate Robert W. Fogel together with Stanley L. Engerman called *Time on the Cross: The Economics of American Negro Slavery.* This radical revisionist work, based on detailed economic data, concluded that the material conditions of slaves compared favorably with those of free industrial workers in the North.

Justifying the draft?

Is conscription, Selective Service, or the draft prohibited by the Thirteenth Amendment as a form of "involuntary servitude"? The Supreme Court in *Arver v. United States,* heard in 1918 during World War I, ruled that performance of a citizen's "supreme and noble duty of contributing to the defense of the rights and honor of the nation, as the result of a war declared by the great representative body of the people" couldn't possibly "be said to be the imposition of involuntary servitude in violation of the prohibitions of the Thirteenth Amendment."

That decision specifically refers to wars declared by Congress. But what about wars not officially declared by Congress? After all, the United States has not issued any formal declaration of war since World War II. Does the 1918 ruling mean that the draft is legal only for wars formally declared by Congress? Probably not, but this question remains open. For more on the President's war powers, see Chapter 10.

Chapter 21

The Fourteenth Amendment: Ensuring Equal Protection

*T*he Fourteenth Amendment, ratified in 1868, is one of the most important — and one of the most controversial — parts of the Constitution. It's a meaty amendment, dealing with some pretty weighty topics. These include:

✔ The definition of citizenship

✔ The obligation of the states to uphold the privileges and immunities of United States citizens

✔ Due process

✔ The obligation of the states not to deny "the equal protection of the laws"

✔ How representation in Congress is calculated

✔ Disqualification from holding office

✔ Denial of any obligation to compensate former slave owners for the emancipation of their slaves

With the exception of due process, which I discuss in Chapter 17, you can sink your teeth into all these topics in this chapter. I hope you're hungry!

Defining Citizenship

The first clause of Section 1 of the Fourteenth Amendment defines citizenship:

> *All persons born or naturalized in the United States, and subject to the jurisdiction thereof, are citizens of the United States and of the State wherein they reside.*

This definition looks pretty straightforward, but it isn't. Here's why:

✔ United States citizenship is based on *birthright* rather than on the "right of blood." Birthright citizenship means that citizenship depends on *where* a person is born rather than *who* his or her parents are. The birthright basis of U.S. citizenship was confirmed by the U.S. Supreme Court in 1898. This ruling was made in the case of Wong Kim Ark, who was born in the United States to Chinese noncitizen parents. The court decided that he was a U.S. citizen even though his parents were not.

Chief Justice Melville Fuller in his dissenting opinion in Wong's case put his finger on a problem with the birthright rule: "It is unreasonable to conclude that 'naturalborn citizen' applied to everybody born within the geographical tract known as the United States, irrespective of circumstances; and that the children of foreigners, happening to be born to them while passing through the country . . . were eligible to the presidency, while children of our citizens, born abroad, were not."

✔ The definition of citizenship in the Fourteenth Amendment is very different from what it would have been at the time when the Bill of Rights was ratified in 1791. Back then, not everybody who was born in the United States "and subject to the jurisdiction thereof" was a citizen, because slaves were not recognized as citizens even though most of them had been born in the United States.

✔ This definition of citizenship contains a twofold test. To be a citizen you have to be "born or naturalized in the United States" *and* "subject to the jurisdiction thereof." Let's see how that pans out in practice:

- The children of U.S. citizens are automatically citizens if they are born in the United States.

- Laws passed by Congress have also given automatic U.S. citizenship to children born outside the United States, provided at least one of their parents is a U.S. citizen — even if they are born out of wedlock. (Precise conditions vary according to the dates of birth of the children concerned.)

- Any child under 18 who has been adopted by a U.S. citizen gets citizenship immediately on arrival in the United States under the Child Citizenship Act of 2000.

- The children of aliens who are lawfully in the United States are automatically U.S. citizens — provided the children are born in the United States.

- What about the children of illegal aliens? The law is clear on this point. All children born in the United States are U.S. citizens, regardless of their parents' legal status. But this law is not universally popular among Americans.

- Where does "subject to the jurisdiction thereof" come in? This provision excludes the children of foreign diplomats from becoming U.S. citizens, even if they are born in the United States. Don't foreign diplomats and their kids have to obey U.S. law while they're in the United States? No. The best evidence of their privileged position is the mountain of parking and speeding tickets that diplomats and their families are allowed to ignore every year.

What about disloyal citizens? Can they be stripped of their citizenship on the ground that they have rejected the jurisdiction of the United States? No. In 2004, the U.S. Supreme Court heard a case involving Yaser Hamdi. Hamdi was allegedly fighting on the side of the Taliban when he was captured in Afghanistan in 2001. Could the U.S. government hold him in Guantanamo Bay and deny him due process as an "illegal enemy combatant"? No, said the Supreme Court, because he was a U.S. citizen. He was born in the United States and raised in Saudi Arabia, of which he was also a citizen. Faced with a judicial brick wall, the U.S. government made a deal with Hamdi. In return for his release, Hamdi gave up his U.S. citizenship and promised to live permanently in Saudi Arabia.

Understanding States' Obligations

The Bill of Rights contains a lot of rights enjoyed by the people against the government. But which government is that: the federal government, state governments, or both? This important question is not directly answered in the Bill of Rights. The U.S. Supreme Court confronted it only in 1833, in the case of *Barron v. Baltimore*.

The court's answer was clear: The Bill of Rights binds only the federal government, not the states. In the words of Chief Justice John Marshall, "The question thus presented is, we think, of great importance, but not of much difficulty." He explained that the U.S. Constitution is concerned only with the federal government and not with the individual states, each of which has its own constitution.

This restrictive reading of the Constitution prevailed right up until the ratification of the Fourteenth Amendment in 1868. The wording of the Fourteenth Amendment makes it quite clear that it applies just as much to the states as to the federal government. Allow me to underline references to the states to demonstrate:

> *All persons born or naturalized in the United States, and subject to the jurisdiction thereof, are citizens of the United States and of <u>the State</u> wherein they reside. <u>No State</u> shall make or enforce any law which shall abridge the privileges or immunities of citizens of the United States; nor shall <u>any State</u> deprive any person of life, liberty, or property, without due process of law; nor deny to any person within its jurisdiction the equal protection of the laws.*

Let's look more closely at the obligations of states contained in this section.

Disentangling state citizenship

> *All persons born or naturalized in the United States, and subject to the jurisdiction thereof, are citizens of the United States and of the State wherein they reside.*

Okay, so all U.S. citizens are also citizens "of the State wherein they reside." Generations ago, that may have seemed simple enough, but these days, few people live their entire lives in the states in which they're born. If you are born in Arizona, go to college in Indiana, and then move to Hawaii, of which state are you a citizen? All of them, at different times. You can get a driver's license in whichever state you move to, vote in that state's elections, and enjoy all the rights of state citizenship as if you were born and raised there.

Analyzing "privileges or immunities"

Look again at the opening of the second clause of Section 1 of the Fourteenth Amendment:

> *No State shall make or enforce any law which shall abridge the privileges or immunities of citizens of the United States . . .*

What exactly does it mean?

- To *abridge* means to shorten, restrict, limit, or reduce.
- A *privilege* is a right that is enjoyed only by some people. The privileges referred to in the Fourteenth Amendment are specifically the privileges enjoyed only by U.S. citizens.
- *Immunities* are really the flip side of privileges. Privileges are positive, immunities negative. Nowadays, the word *immunity* is most often used in reference to disease. But in the Constitution, *immunity* means a special negative right enjoyed by U.S. citizens, such as the right not to be deported to a foreign country.
- The first *shall* means "must" and the second one "will."

Let me rewrite the whole clause in modern English. Here goes:

> *No state is allowed to make or enforce any law that reduces the special positive and negative rights of citizens of the United States.*

But what exactly are these special positive and negative rights?

Dredging the past for "privileges or immunities"

The answer to this question lies in the history of the phrase "privileges or immunities." The "privileges or immunities" clause of the Fourteenth Amendment clearly echoes the first clause of Section 2 of Article IV of the Constitution, which reads:

> *The Citizens of each State shall be entitled to all Privileges and Immunities of Citizens in the several States.*

This wording in turn can be traced back hundreds of years to the English common law.

The phrase crystallized in a wonderful judgment given in 1823 by George Washington's nephew, Justice Bushrod Washington, in *Corfield v. Coryell.* Congress cited this decision when it adopted the "privileges or immunities" clause of the Fourteenth Amendment.

Justice Washington stressed that the phrase "Privileges and Immunities" in Article IV of the Constitution does not refer to *all* the privileges and immunities enjoyed by citizens, but only to "those privileges and immunities which are, in their nature, fundamental." If this is the meaning of "Privileges and Immunities" in Article IV, it must also be the meaning of the phrase in the Fourteenth Amendment, which intentionally echoes it. (The only reason for the switch from "and" to "or" is that the phrase in Article IV is positive, and the phrase in the Fourteenth Amendment is negative. Check it out.)

Listening to George Washington's favorite nephew

Here are some of the privileges and immunities that Bushrod Washington identified:

- "Protection by the government"
- The enjoyment of life, liberty, and property
- "The right of a citizen of one state to pass through, or to reside in any other state"
- The right "to claim the benefit of the writ of habeas corpus"
- The right "to institute and maintain actions of any kind in the courts of the state"
- The right "to take, hold and dispose of property, either real or personal"
- The right to vote

Slaughtering the "privileges or immunities" clause

As Justice Clarence Thomas put it in 1999, the U.S. Supreme Court "all but read the Privileges or Immunities Clause out of the Constitution in the Slaughter-House Cases" in 1873.

The State of Louisiana passed a law that allowed the city of New Orleans to set up a corporation to centralize all slaughterhouse operations. This law threatened the livelihood of a number of independent butchers. The butchers' lawyer figured that the law was unconstitutional because it infringed on the right enjoyed by the butchers "to sustain their lives through labor." The U.S. Supreme Court disagreed with this broad reading of the "privileges or immunities" clause in the recently ratified Fourteenth Amendment. The majority of justices held that the clause was concerned only with the rights of "national citizenship" and not state citizenship — and the right to work for a living was not a privilege attached to national citizenship. So the butchers lost the case, and the state law to which they objected was upheld by the court.

The U.S. Supreme Court has considered the "privileges or immunities" clause of the Fourteenth Amendment on surprisingly few occasions since 1873.

The most recent Supreme Court case on this clause was *Saenz v. Roe*, decided in 1999. The key fact in this case was the higher level of welfare payments available in California by comparison with most other states. In 1992,

California passed a law to discourage people from moving there in order to get the more generous welfare payments. The law said that for their first 12 months' residence in California, welfare recipients would get only the amount to which they were entitled in the state from which they had moved. In 1996, a federal statute was passed that allowed states to operate the sort of system that California had introduced.

The Supreme Court ruled that the California law infringed on the welfare recipients' "right to travel" and settle in any state they liked. The court also struck down the federal law because "Congress may not authorize the States to violate the Fourteenth Amendment."

The "right to travel" certainly is among the "Privileges and Immunities" identified by Justice Bushrod Washington. But does that right include the right to pick up higher welfare checks from day one? Unlikely. We can't ask Bushrod, because, unfortunately, he isn't in the phonebook.

Writing for the majority in *Saenz v. Roe*, Justice John Paul Stevens opined: "The States do not have any right to select their citizens." This is undeniable but irrelevant to the case. California never denied any citizen the right to live in that state. All it did was try to discourage welfare-shoppers from picking California because they regarded it quite literally as the Golden State.

Achieving "Equal Justice Under Law" — Or Not

Equality is one of the big principles of the American Revolution, but more in theory than in practice. The Declaration of Independence proclaims "all men are created equal," but Thomas Jefferson, who drafted the Declaration, was a slave owner.

You may have seen the words "Equal Justice Under Law" emblazoned above the entrance to the U.S. Supreme Court building. (Surprisingly enough, this slogan was coined not by any Supreme Court justice, but by the architects of the building!) The concept encapsulated in this memorable phrase is a close cousin to the Equal Protection Clause of the Fourteenth Amendment:

> nor [shall any State] deny to any person within its jurisdiction the equal protection of the laws.

As is so often the case, this clause raises more questions than it answers. In the following sections, I address some of the topics that are — or could be, if challenged in court — affected by the Equal Protection Clause.

Age discrimination

A 1984 federal law called the National Minimum Drinking Age Act indicates that federal revenue will be withheld from states that allow people under the age of 21 to buy alcohol. Even so, each state technically still has the right to decide the legal drinking age within its borders. Most states set that age at 21 (although some states sidestep the issue somewhat by forbidding the purchase — but not the consumption — of alcohol by people under age 21).

You can vote when you turn 18, so why do you have to wait another three years before you can drink? Is it in accordance with "equal protection of the laws" to allow 21-year-olds to drink but not 18-year-olds? No, but most people would probably regard this kind of discrimination as justified.

South Dakota, which allowed 19-year-olds to buy beer containing up to 3.2 percent alcohol, challenged the 1984 federal law in the U.S. Supreme Court. The challenge was based not on the Fourteenth Amendment but on the Twenty-First Amendment, which gives the states control over liquor (see Chapter 22). South Dakota's challenge failed, and the 1984 federal law was upheld. Would a challenge based on the Fourteenth Amendment have been more likely to succeed? Probably not, mainly because of the problem of drunk driving among young drivers.

Capital punishment

What about executing juveniles or the mentally retarded? Is it right to treat them the same as everybody else? Is that the type of "equal protection" the Fourteenth Amendment refers to?

The U.S. Supreme Court has come out against the execution of anyone who fits in either of these categories. In the case of *Roper v. Simmons,* which was heard in 2005, the court ruled that a 17-year-old murderer could not be executed, even though

✔ He broke into his victim's house, tied her hands, and blindfolded her.

✔ He then drove her to a state park and threw her off a railroad bridge while she was still alive, all for the theft of six dollars!

✔ He had planned his actions carefully.

✔ He videotaped a reenactment of events afterward.

✔ He boasted about his actions.

✔ He confessed to the killing.

Did this killer deserve to be spared the death penalty just because he was a few months shy of his eighteenth birthday? The Missouri jury that sentenced him to death sure didn't think so. This is a case where most people might agree that equal justice was called for. However, the case was not fought on that basis at all, but simply under the Eighth Amendment's prohibition of "cruel and unusual punishments," which I discuss in Chapter 18.

Racial segregation

In the well-known case of *Plessy v. Ferguson*, decided in 1896, the U.S. Supreme Court ruled in favor of a Louisiana law requiring racial segregation on the railroad. The court held that this law did not violate the Equal Protection Clause of the Fourteenth Amendment. The Equal Protection Clause, said the court, was concerned with equality in civil rights, not in social arrangements. The Louisiana law, it held, satisfied the test of reasonableness and was based on "the established usages, customs and traditions of the people."

However, in 1954, in *Brown v. Board of Education,* the U.S. Supreme Court signaled a fundamental change of mind. The court, speaking through Chief Justice Earl Warren, proclaimed that

> *in the field of public education the doctrine of 'separate but equal' has no place. Separate educational facilities are inherently unequal. Therefore, we hold that the plaintiffs and others similarly situated . . . are, by reason of the segregation complained of, deprived of the equal protection of the laws guaranteed by the Fourteenth Amendment.*

I discuss this important case in Chapter 23.

School busing

Does the ban on segregation entitle the courts to enforce mixed schools? In 1971, the U.S. Supreme Court ordered the integration of all 105 schools in Charlotte-Mecklenburg, North Carolina, by busing students to different schools. The intention was to achieve the same whites-to-blacks ratio in the schools as in the population of the area as a whole. The Supreme Court based its unanimous decision specifically on the Equal Protection Clause of the Fourteenth Amendment.

But this important decision backfired. The Supreme Court believed that forced integration would lead to greater equality in the education offered to members of different ethnic groups — and to an improvement in the educational levels attained by minority students. Yet a 1992 Harvard University study found that black and Hispanic students lacked "even modest overall improvement" as a result of busing.

Here are some other bad effects of busing:

✔ Some students were spending as much as three hours a day on the bus! As a result, less time was available for sports and other extracurricular activities.

✔ Busing sometimes transported kids to dangerous neighborhoods.

✔ Kids were often bused from integrated schools to less integrated schools.

✔ "White flight" to the suburbs occurred at least partly in response to forced integration. Another response to busing was for white parents to send their children to private or parochial schools.

✔ The result was that inner city public schools became largely made up of minorities — exactly the opposite of the intention behind busing. Today, Boston public schools are 85 percent African American and Hispanic, even though Boston's black and Hispanic populations together represent less than 40 percent of the city's total population. Similar examples abound. Private schools sprang up in Pasadena, California — 63 at the last count — where white kids now make up only 16 percent of the public school population.

Since 1971, the U.S. Supreme Court has gradually pulled away from the extreme interpretation of the Equal Protection Clause that led to forced busing. In *Milliken v. Bradley,* heard in 1974, the Supreme Court banned forced busing across district lines unless a number of school districts had engaged in deliberate segregation. In *Board of Education of Oklahoma City v. Dowell,* decided in 1991, the Supreme Court recognized that the existence of single-race schools did not necessarily amount to a violation of the Equal Protection Clause.

In two cases decided together in 2007, the U.S. Supreme Court finally almost reversed its harmful 1971 interpretation of the Equal Protection Clause. The Supreme Court now rejects the use of race in assigning students to schools. This turns the 1971 interpretation of the Equal Protection Clause on its head. In the words of Chief Justice John Roberts, "The way to stop discrimination on the basis of race is to stop discriminating on the basis of race" — an important recognition that discrimination in favor of minorities is racial discrimination nevertheless. See Chapter 23, where I discuss these two landmark cases — *Parents Involved in Community Schools v. Seattle School District No. 1* and *Meredith v. Jefferson County Board of Education.*

Affirmative action

A related topic is whether affirmative action is supported by the Equal Protection Clause. In *Grutter v. Bollinger,* heard in 2003, the U.S. Supreme Court upheld the affirmative action admissions policy operated by the University of Michigan Law School. Justice Sandra Day O'Connor, writing for the majority, held that there was "a compelling interest in obtaining the educational benefits that flow from a diverse student body." Justice Clarence Thomas, in a strongly worded dissent, labeled the law school's admissions policy as racial discrimination and "a practice that can only weaken the principle of equality embodied in the Declaration of Independence and the Equal Protection Clause."

The two 2007 decisions mentioned in the previous section are also relevant here — and point to the final emergence of a color-blind Constitution.

TECHNICAL STUFF

The courts' standard of scrutiny

What standard of scrutiny should the courts apply in lawsuits brought under the Equal Protection Clause? The U.S. Supreme Court has identified three levels of scrutiny:

✔ **Strict scrutiny,** applicable to cases involving race, religion, voting rights, and other rights regarded as fundamental. The test here is that a challenged law or decision is unconstitutional unless it is "narrowly tailored" to serve a "compelling government interest."

✔ **Heightened or intermediate scrutiny,** applicable to cases involving sex or gender. The test here is that a challenged law must be "substantially related" to an "important government interest." The U.S. Supreme Court first applied this standard in 1976 in the case of *Craig v. Boren.* This case mounted a challenge of an Oklahoma law that permitted the sale of low-alcohol beer to females over the age of 18 but to males only over the age of 21. The Supreme Court held that the

Oklahoma law didn't pass the requisite test, contravened the Equal Protection Clause, and was therefore unconstitutional.

✔ **Rational basis scrutiny,** applicable to all other cases. The test here is that a challenged law must be "reasonably related" to a "legitimate government interest." The court applied this level of scrutiny to a proposed amendment to the Constitution of Colorado. The proposed amendment banned the passing of any state law that accorded homosexuals or bisexuals "minority status, quota preferences, protected status or a claim of discrimination." The case in question was *Romer v. Evans,* decided in 1996. The U.S. Supreme Court ruled that the proposed amendment was unconstitutional. The majority on the court claimed not to be applying strict scrutiny or even heightened scrutiny, on the ground that the proposed amendment did not even come up to the much lower standard of being "reasonably related" to "a legitimate government interest."

The outcome of a case can easily depend on the level of scrutiny that the court decides to apply to it. The stricter the scrutiny, the harder it is for the law or decision under review to pass muster.

A 1996 case involving the Virginia Military Institute (VMI) provides a good illustration of this important point. VMI, a state military college, had an all-male admissions policy. This policy was challenged in the U.S. Supreme Court under the Equal Protection Clause. The majority on the court held that the school's admissions policy violated the Equal Protection Clause because the school failed to show "exceedingly persuasive justification" for that policy. Justice Antonin Scalia pointed out in his dissent that this test was essentially one of strict scrutiny, which was far too high. The appropriate standard was that of intermediate scrutiny or even just that of a rational-basis review.

Gerrymandering

Gerrymandering refers to redrawing the boundaries of a voting district to favor one political party. The word is the dubious legacy of Massachusetts Governor Elbridge Gerry, whose 1812 redistricting map showed an elongated voting district that resembled a salamander. *Gerry* plus *salamander* produced the new word *gerrymander*.

Obviously, gerrymandering has been practiced for a long time, but is it legal, or does it violate the Equal Protection Clause?

In 2006, the League of United Latin American Citizens challenged the recent redistricting of Texas on the ground that it diluted the Latino vote and amounted to an unconstitutional gerrymander, contrary to the Equal Protection Clause. The U.S. Supreme Court rejected this argument, but the debate is sure to continue.

Apportioning Representatives

Section 2 of the Fourteenth Amendment reads rather strangely to modern eyes. It's a long passage, so I won't quote it here. Take a look at the Appendix to see what I mean, and then allow me to explain.

Recognizing proportionality 80 years too late?

Section 2 says that representatives

shall be apportioned among the several States according to their respective numbers, counting the whole number of persons in each State.

Does the word *numbers* refer to numbers of voters or numbers of inhabitants? The word *persons* shows that it refers to the size of the population, not to the number of voters, though that should not make any real difference. If state X has twice the population of state Y, the number of voters in X is likely to be roughly double that of the voters in Y.

So, a state with a population of 10 million must have twice the number of representatives of a state with only 5 million inhabitants. Fine. Nothing strange about that.

What other basis could there possibly be for apportioning representatives? And how come this basic rule of proportionality first appears in an amendment dating from 1868, 80 years after ratification of the Constitution in its original form?

The answer to this puzzle lies in the Civil War. Under the original Constitution, voting rights were not exactly proportional to population. Slave states were given a special concession. They were allowed an additional three-fifths of a vote for every slave — who of course didn't have the right to vote.

That's why the proportional principle appears for the first time here in the Fourteenth Amendment, after the abolition of slavery by the Thirteenth Amendment, ratified in 1865.

Denying or abridging the right to vote

The whole of the rest of Section 2 is about what happens if a state "denies or abridges" any of its citizens' right to vote. This mammoth clause — all one sentence — clearly envisages a state preventing a sizeable number of its citizens from voting. If a state does that, it loses the relevant proportion of its representation.

Let me take as a hypothetical example a state with 30 seats in the House of Representatives. If that state denies or abridges (reduces in any way) the voting rights of 10 percent of its voters, that state loses 10 percent of its seats. So, that state's representation is reduced from 30 to 27.

This provision has never been put into practice, and the clause doesn't say who has the power to strip a state of part of its representation in this way. Did southern states fall under this provision in the early 20th century by introducing literacy tests and poll taxes in order to reduce the number of black voters? Possibly, but none of those states ever had its representation reduced, although literacy tests and poll taxes were declared unconstitutional.

Let me just explain a couple of dated terms in this section:

✔ **"Indians not taxed":** Native Americans were not automatically U.S. citizens until the passing of the Indian Citizenship Act of 1924. So they were not counted in the population of the states where they lived until then — unless they had acquired U.S. citizenship by marriage, by serving in the U.S. army, or by special treaty.

✔ **Males aged 21:** Why are states to be punished only when they deny or abridge the voting rights of males over 21? Does this mean that it's okay to deny or abridge the rights of women or male voters under 21? Not anymore, because this provision was amended by

  • The Nineteenth Amendment, ratified in 1920, which gave women over 21 the right to vote.

  • The Twenty-Sixth Amendment, ratified in 1971, which lowered the voting age to 18.

✔ **"Rebellion or other crime":** Denying or abridging the voting rights "for participation in rebellion, or other crime" doesn't result in any reduction in representation. Does this mean that it's okay to deny or abridge voting rights for these reasons? Or does it only mean that denying or abridging voting rights for these reasons doesn't reduce a state's representation? There's no agreement on this point. "Participation in rebellion" means siding with the Confederacy in the Civil War. This provision is academic because not too many *graybacks* (Confederate soldiers) are still around. What about felons? Unfortunately, felons are never in short supply. This provision of the Fourteenth Amendment has never been applied to deprive them of the vote, but many states have laws doing so, either only when they are actually doing jail time or, in many cases, even after their release from prison.

Disqualifying Confederates from Office

Section 3 of the Fourteenth Amendment bars from public office anyone in public office before the Civil War who then supported the Confederacy. This section was aimed at the leading figures in the Confederacy, most of whom had held public office in the pre-war United States.

After the war, Jefferson Davis, the first and only President of the Confederacy, was elected to the U.S. Senate again by the state legislature of Mississippi, but this provision in the Fourteenth Amendment prevented him from taking his seat.

The section ends with a clause of remarkable foresight, allowing Congress to lift the service ban on a particular individual by a two-thirds majority vote in both houses. In 1978, Congress applied this provision and lifted the ban posthumously on Jefferson Davis and the Confederate commander, General Robert E. Lee.

Repudiating Confederate Debts

Section 4 of the Fourteenth Amendment is in two parts. The first part proclaims: "The validity of the public debt of the United States . . . shall not be questioned." This provision is hard to understand in isolation, but it becomes clear when you read the second part. This part repudiates all Confederate debts and makes it clear that the United States would not pay compensation to slave owners for the loss of their slaves.

Empowering Congress

The fifth and last section of the Fourteenth Amendment is brief:

> *The Congress shall have power to enforce, by appropriate legislation, the provisions of this article.*

The same wording is also found at the end of the Thirteenth, Fifteenth, Nineteenth, Twenty-Third, Twenty-Fourth, and Twenty-Sixth amendments.

You may wonder why Congress needs to be given this power. Does the amendment not speak for itself? None of the first ten amendments contains any such provision, so why do so many later amendments need it?

The answer is that this provision was first used just after the Civil War, which gave the federal government much more power than before. The Civil War also resulted in great distrust between different sectors of U.S. society.

The Voting Rights Act of 1965 is a good recent example of a law passed by Congress under this provision. Section 4(e) of that Act says that "no person who has completed the sixth grade" in a school in Puerto Rico "shall be disfranchised for inability to read or write English."

This section came before the U.S. Supreme Court in the case of *Katzenbach v. Morgan* in 1966. The question before the high court was whether Congress had the power to enact section 4(e). The objection to this section was that it went well beyond the Fourteenth Amendment itself. Another objection was that it was contrary to the fundamental principle of the separation of powers, because Congress was here usurping the Supreme Court's position as interpreter of the Constitution.

The court in *Katzenbach* ruled that section 4(e) was not unconstitutional and that Congress had been quite entitled to pass it. But the approach of the Supreme Court has changed since then and is now less prepared to allow Congress to interpret the Constitution as it likes.

Chapter 22

Starts, Stops, and Clarifications: Amendments since 1870

. . . .

In This Chapter

▶ Banning race and taxes as voting qualifications

▶ Dotting some i's and crossing some t's in regard to the presidency

▶ Giving the inhabitants of the nation's capital some voting rights

▶ Bringing an amendment back from the dead — after 200 years

. . . .

The U.S. Constitution is more than 200 years old, but it hasn't remained the same over that long period. Here are the stages in its development:

✔ 1788 — The original Constitution is ratified, which is made up of all those heavy articles about what Congress, the President, and the Supreme Court can and cannot do.

✔ 1791 — Ratification of the first ten amendments, or the *Bill of Rights*, takes place.

✔ 1865 — The end of the Civil War ushers in some pretty important amendments prohibiting discrimination on grounds of race and dictating to the states.

✔ 1870 to the present — A grab bag of 13 diverse amendments have been passed, most of which are not very well known.

I deal with the 13 latest amendments in this chapter. I take them one by one.

Removing Race Qualifications for Voting: The Fifteenth Amendment

The Fifteenth Amendment is the last of three amendments introduced in the wake of the Civil War. The Thirteenth Amendment abolished slavery. The Fourteenth Amendment went further and declared that "all persons born or naturalized in the United States . . . are citizens of the United States and of the State wherein they reside."

Didn't this provision automatically take care of voting rights? No, because the states each had their own rules governing voting rights. So citizenship alone didn't guarantee the right to vote. Hence the need for the Fifteenth Amendment, ratified in 1870, the main part of which reads as follows:

> *The right of citizens of the United States to vote shall not be denied or abridged by the United States or by any State on account of race, color, or previous condition of servitude.*

The meaning of this provision is self-explanatory: Racial voting qualifications are no longer allowed. But is this all that the amendment means?

Some people, including some who are regarded as constitutional law experts, have suggested that the Fifteenth Amendment contains a "cluster" of rights that go way beyond the simple right to vote in elections. Where do these people get this idea from? Their argument runs along these lines:

- ✔ The Fifteenth Amendment confers the right to vote.
- ✔ But the right to vote isn't confined to voting in elections.
- ✔ Congressmen and other legislators also have the right to vote — for or against bills.
- ✔ So the Fifteenth Amendment must include the right to run for election to Congress and state legislatures.

Is this argument correct? No. It's one of many examples of trying to change the Constitution by reading stuff into it that isn't actually there. Here's why the argument that I've just summarized is wrong:

- ✔ The original draft of the Fifteenth Amendment presented to Congress contained the right to run for election as well as the right to vote. The right to run for election was dropped from the final version.
- ✔ The reason for this change was that this amendment was difficult enough to pass in its cut-down form. In 1868, 11 of the then 21 northern states denied blacks the right to vote. New York withdrew its ratification of the Fifteenth Amendment and then re-ratified it as power shifted in that state. Delaware ratified it only in 1901, Oregon in 1959, California in 1962, Maryland in 1973, Kentucky in 1976, and Tennessee in 1997.
- ✔ Does the right to vote in elections automatically include the right to run for election? No. Check out the Twenty-Sixth Amendment, whose wording mirrors that of the Fifteenth Amendment in extending the right to vote to all U.S. citizens "who are eighteen years of age or older." Does this amendment give 18-year-olds the right to run for Congress? Not at all. You've got to be at least 25 to run for the House of Representatives, and there are a couple of other requirements too, as laid down by Article I, Section 2 of the Constitution.

The meaning of the Fifteenth Amendment isn't a problem. But the amendment does have two other major problems:

✔ Was the Fifteenth Amendment validly ratified?

- It was proposed in 1869 by a Congress from which the 11 former breakaway Confederate states were excluded.

- Ten of these southern states ratified it only because the First Reconstruction Act of March 2, 1867 — passed over the veto of President Andrew Johnson — gave all adult black males in those states the right to vote as a precondition of readmission of those states into the Union.

✔ Did the Fifteenth Amendment have any effect in practice? In the North, yes. But in the border states, and in the South after 1876, blacks tended to be excluded from the vote by the imposition of literacy tests and poll taxes. Literacy tests were finally outlawed by the Voting Rights Act of 1965, and poll taxes were eventually declared unconstitutional by the U.S. Supreme Court in 1966.

After the end of Reconstruction in 1877, the Republican Party in the South collapsed. The Democratic Party controlled the "solid South," as it came to be known, until the 1960s. So, the really important election in the Southern states was not the general election but the Democratic primary. Here's what a Texas statute said that was still in force in 1924: "in no event shall a negro be eligible to participate in a Democratic party primary election held in the State of Texas." The U.S. Supreme Court declared this particular law unconstitutional, but it was not until 1944 that all-white primaries were completely banned.

Letting Uncle Sam Raid Your Piggy Bank: The Sixteenth Amendment

Can Uncle Sam legally tax you on your income? You may resent this government power, but it is kosher. However, that hasn't always been the case. Income tax is a *direct* tax because it's paid directly to the government. But it was unknown in the early days of the Republic. The earliest form of direct tax was a *capitation tax* — or poll tax — a flat tax of the same amount payable by everybody regardless of wealth or earnings.

Article I, Section 9 contains this little tidbit about direct taxes:

No Capitation, or other direct, Tax shall be laid, unless in Proportion to the Census or Enumeration herein before directed to be taken.

A capitation tax is of course automatically in proportion to population — but income tax normally varies according to income, which prevents it from being proportional to population.

Income tax was first introduced in 1861 to pay for the Civil War. It was abolished in 1872, and when the government tried to reintroduce it in 1894 it was immediately challenged. In 1895 the U.S. Supreme Court declared income tax unconstitutional.

However, most politicians recognized the need for income tax. In the presidential election of 1912, all three main candidates — incumbent President William H. Taft, former President Theodore Roosevelt, and the winner, Woodrow Wilson — supported the legalization of income tax. The Sixteenth Amendment was introduced precisely to achieve that objective. Here's what it says:

> *The Congress shall have power to lay and collect taxes on incomes, from whatever source derived, without apportionment among the several States, and without regard to any census or enumeration.*

Electing the Senate: The Seventeenth Amendment

The Framers of the Constitution didn't trust the people. Under the original, unamended Constitution, the House of Representatives was the only directly elected body. Article I, Section 3 provided that

> *The Senate of the United States shall be composed of two Senators from each State, chosen by the Legislature thereof . . .*

The Senate was intended to balance the House in two ways:

- ✔ By favoring the smaller states — because each state regardless of size is entitled to two senators. California with its population of 36 million has two senators, and Wyoming, with just over half a million, also has two senators.
- ✔ By being *selected* by the state legislatures rather than directly *elected* by the people.

U.S. senators were originally seen as ambassadors of their states. The states kept their senators on a tight rein and actually instructed them how to vote on particular issues — something that never happened with members of the House, who were not chosen by state legislatures.

The system of state-appointed senators worked smoothly at first, but in the run-up to the Civil War, difficulties started appearing. The two houses of a state legislature didn't always agree on who the senators from that state should be. Federal legislation required the winning candidate to have obtained a majority (more than 50 percent) in the state legislature, but some states allowed candidates to be declared elected when they had only a *plurality* of votes in the legislature (meaning more than any other candidate).

In the 1850s, one of the senate seats for Indiana was vacant for two years because of the inability of the Democrats and the fledgling Republican Party to work together. The situation got a lot worse as the 19th century drew to a close. Between 1891 and 1905, there were no fewer than 45 deadlocks in 20 states. For four years Delaware had only one senator. In some states the legislature left the choice of senators to a popular referendum.

Between 1893 and 1902, popular pressure mounted for the Senate to be directly elected, and each year a constitutional amendment to that effect was proposed in Congress only to be defeated — not surprisingly — in the Senate. By 1913, such was the pressure on Congress that only one more state was needed to call a national constitutional convention.

The prospect of a national convention has always terrified Congress, because once a convention was summoned there was no guarantee that it would limit itself to considering the one amendment that had brought it into existence. It could well become a loose cannon destroying the whole carefully crafted fabric of the Constitution. The prospect of a national convention quickly galvanized Congress into action in 1913, and what became the Seventeenth Amendment was soon ratified, simply providing for the direct election of senators by the people of each state.

Outlawing Liquor: The Eighteenth Amendment

The Eighteenth Amendment, ratified in 1919, banned the manufacture, sale, transportation, import, or export of all "intoxicating liquors," which were defined by a companion Act of Congress as any beverage containing over 0.5 percent alcohol.

The evils of alcohol had been preached since early colonial days, and Massachusetts banned the sale of "strong liquor" in 1657. However, the temperance movement really came into its own after the Civil War. The Prohibition Party was founded in 1869, and in 1873 the influential Women's Christian Temperance Union came into existence.

Although only one congressman and one governor were ever elected on the Prohibition Party ticket, the party managed to get liquor banned in many cities and a number of states. During World War I, the pressure on lawmakers by the prohibition lobby was so great that Congress proposed the Eighteenth Amendment in 1917, and it was ratified in 1919. Two states, Connecticut and Rhode Island, rejected the amendment and never ratified it.

The Eighteenth Amendment is an excellent example of just how impossible it is to change human nature by legislation — and how disastrous it is even to try. As a direct result of prohibition, illegal, or *bootleg,* liquor became available in *speakeasies*: illicit, disguised bars. Prohibition was the best thing that ever happened to the mafia, which took full advantage of it.

Giving Women the Vote: The Nineteenth Amendment

Did women first get the right to vote in the United States as a result of the ratification of the Nineteenth Amendment in 1920? Yes and no. The Nineteenth Amendment gave the right to vote to all women in the nation over the age of 21. However, women had the vote in New Jersey between 1776 and 1807. Wyoming Territory gave women the vote in 1869. Colorado followed suit in 1893, and Utah in 1896.

The drive for votes for women across the nation began in earnest with the formation of the National Woman Suffrage Association in 1869. This organization lobbied every Congress between 1869 and 1919. In 1915, a woman's suffrage bill was brought before the House of Representatives but was defeated by 174 to 204 votes.

In 1918, President Woodrow Wilson put his weight behind an amendment extending the vote to women. On January 10, 1918, a bill proposing this amendment passed the House with just one vote more than the two-thirds required. In the Senate, the proposed amendment lost out by two votes in September 1918. When it was presented to the Senate again in February 1919, it was only one vote short of the requisite two-thirds majority.

President Wilson was anxious to get the amendment passed in time for the election of 1920, in which he was planning to run for a third term. He called a special session of Congress to consider the proposed amendment. This time it passed the House with 42 votes to spare, and the Senate also accepted it with a victorious margin of two votes.

The amendment was quickly ratified by the three-fourths of the states required by the Constitution, but a few states held out. The last states to ratify it were eight southern states. Mississippi ratified it only in 1984.

The wording of the Nineteenth Amendment was borrowed from the Fifteenth Amendment. Here's the main part of the amendment:

> *The right of citizens of the United States to vote shall not be denied or abridged by the United States or by any State on account of sex.*

Moving Out of the Horse and Buggy Age: The Twentieth Amendment

In the time of George Washington, travel was slow and roads were bad. So the Founders allowed a period of four months between the presidential election and the inauguration. The original, unamended Constitution fixed March 4 as the date when all presidential and congressional terms started. This arrangement meant that, when there was a change of President, the nation had to endure a four-month period of a lame-duck administration.

The Twentieth Amendment fixed a much earlier date, January 20, for presidential inaugurations, and January 3 for the start of congressional terms.

The amendment also dealt with a couple of other questions, notably: What happens if a president-elect dies before taking office? Answer: The Vice President-elect becomes President. Surprisingly, the Twentieth Amendment did not address the more basic question: If the President dies in office and is succeeded by the Vice President, does the Vice President become President or only Acting President? This issue was left to be dealt with by the Twenty-Fifth Amendment.

The Twentieth Amendment met with very little opposition. It was passed by Congress on March 2, 1932, and was finally ratified on January 23, 1933. The first presidential term it applied to was when Franklin D. Roosevelt succeeded himself as President on January 20, 1937.

Repealing Prohibition: The Twenty-First Amendment

The Eighteenth Amendment introducing Prohibition is the only amendment ever to have been repealed. This was done by the Twenty-First Amendment just under 14 years after Prohibition had been introduced.

What happened in that short time to turn opinion so completely around? In fact, local politicians hadn't really changed their minds because many of them either owed the Prohibition lobby favors or else were afraid of the influence wielded by that lobby in their localities.

But Prohibition had never been that popular among ordinary Americans. After Prohibition ushered in an orgy of crime, Congress was determined to end Prohibition, and it used the nation's deep-seated dislike of Prohibition to achieve this end. So, after handily passing the proposed Twenty-First Amendment, Congress stipulated that ratification was to be effected not by the state legislatures but by the alternative method laid down in Article V of the Constitution — by special conventions in the individual states. The Twenty-First Amendment was the only amendment ever ratified this way.

South Carolina rejected the Twenty-First Amendment, and the voters of North Carolina refused even to call a convention to consider it. But all the other states held conventions that duly accepted the amendment.

It's important to realize, however, that the Twenty-First Amendment doesn't just repeal the Eighteenth Amendment. It does so in Section 1, but it then goes on to provide that

> *The transportation or importation into any State, Territory, or possession of the United States for delivery or use therein of intoxicating liquors, in violation of the laws thereof, is hereby prohibited.*

This section enabled any state that wanted to remain "dry" to do so. Mississippi was the last state to remain dry, which it was until 1966, and Kansas banned public bars until 1987. There are still over 500 dry municipalities in the nation because many states have delegated the power to ban alcohol to local authorities.

Taking George Washington's Lead: The Twenty-Second Amendment

Article II, Section 1 of the original, unamended Constitution set the President's term of office at four years, but it didn't place any limit on the number of times that a president could be reelected.

George Washington was elected President without any opposition in 1788 and again in 1792. He would undoubtedly have been reelected without any problem in 1796 as well, but he decided that he'd had enough. So he delivered his famous Farewell Address — not a live speech, incidentally, but an open letter to the nation carried by many newspapers — and retired to Mount Vernon to dedicate himself to farming and to the construction of a large whiskey distillery.

As two terms were good enough for the Father of the Nation, that should be enough for anybody. That was the conventional wisdom on the subject. Thomas Jefferson recognized the danger of the absence of term limits on the tenure of the presidency. In 1807 he wrote, "If some termination to the services of the chief Magistrate be not fixed by the Constitution, or supplied by practice, his office, nominally four years, will in fact become for life." In other words, according to Jefferson, either the Constitution had to set a limit or else some limit should be set by convention.

Thomas Jefferson, James Madison, and James Monroe — all of whom were two-term Presidents — respected Washington's example and didn't attempt to run for a third term. They effectively established a convention that was followed, sometimes reluctantly, until Franklin Delano Roosevelt decided to run for a third term in 1940.

Roosevelt, ever the wily politician, employed a ruse to get over the two-term tradition. First, he switched the 1940 Democratic Party Convention to Chicago, which was controlled by a tightly organized Democratic Party machine — which of course also controlled the public address system in the convention hall. Then FDR disarmed his opponents by announcing that he would not run unless drafted, and that the delegates were free to vote for whoever they liked. Dead on cue, the loudspeakers in the hall screamed: "We want Roosevelt . . . The world wants Roosevelt!" The delegates joined in the manufactured frenzy and nominated Roosevelt by 946 votes to 147. After that, winning the general election was a walk in the park. And, having shattered the two-term mold, Roosevelt had no trouble getting nominated for a fourth term, which he again easily won, though with a reduced majority. He died less than three months after his fourth inauguration.

When the Republicans swept Congress in the 1946 midterm elections, they were determined to prevent any future president from emulating Roosevelt's successful flouting of the two-term limit. They recognized that to achieve this aim they needed a constitutional amendment. So in March 1947 Congress passed a proposal to enforce the two-term limit. The proposal became the Twenty-Second Amendment, which was finally ratified in February 1951. Only two states rejected it: Oklahoma and Massachusetts.

The main part of the Twenty-Second Amendment reads as follows:

> *No person shall be elected to the office of the President more than twice, and no person who has held the office of President, or acted as President, for more than two years of a term to which some other person was elected President shall be elected to the office of the President more than once.*

Here's what it means:

- ✔ You can't be elected to more than two presidential terms — regardless of whether they are consecutive or not.
- ✔ If you have succeeded to the presidency on the death, removal, or resignation of the President and have served *more than two years* of that President's term, you can't be elected President yourself more than once.

✔ If you have succeeded to the presidency on the death, removal, or resignation of the President and have served *two years or less* of that President's term, you can be elected President yourself a maximum of two times.

✔ If you have been filling in for an indisposed President only as Acting President, you can be elected President yourself for a maximum of two terms, unless you have been Acting President for more than two years, in which case you can't be elected President yourself more than once.

One thing that the Twenty-Second Amendment doesn't do is to place any term limit on the vice presidency. No, sirree! You can be elected Veep as many times as you like — or rather, as many times as the voters like.

Repeal of the Twenty-Second Amendment has been suggested several times, notably in the 1980s in order to "win one more for the Gipper" (Ronald Reagan) and again in the 1990s to elect Bill Clinton to a third term. Those moves came to nothing.

Enfranchising the Nation's Capital: The Twenty-Third Amendment

When the Constitution was ratified in its original form in 1788, New York City was the nation's capital. But the so-called "District Clause" in Article I, Section 8 of the Constitution made provision for a purpose-built new capital, which was to be under the exclusive authority of Congress. Washington, D.C. became the nation's capital and the seat of the federal government on December 1, 1800 — on land ceded by Virginia and Maryland.

William Henry Harrison, the short-lived ninth President who died on April 4, 1841, just one month into his term of office, championed the cause of the inhabitants of the nation's capital in his long inaugural address. He described them as being "deprived of many important political privileges," adding, "The people of the District of Columbia are not the subjects of the people of the States, but free American citizens."

By 1960, when the District of Columbia had a bigger population than 13 of the 50 states, Congress proposed the Twenty-Third Amendment giving the District of Columbia three electoral votes in presidential elections — the same number as the smallest states, whose entitlement is calculated by adding their two senators to their single representative in the House. The amendment was ratified in 1961 and was first applied in the 1964 presidential election.

In regard to presidential elections, therefore, the District is now treated as if it were a state. It is important to realize, however, that the amendment does *not* make the District a state.

The District has no representation in the U.S. Senate, but since 1971 it has sent a *delegate* to the House of Representatives. Until 1993, the delegate from the District, in common with the delegates from the U.S. territories, didn't have voting rights. That changed in 1993, but voting rights (except in committees) were lost again two years later after the Republicans gained control of the House. In 2007, the House gave the D.C. delegate the right to vote in the Committee of the Whole, which considers amendments — subject to the proviso that if the delegate's vote tips the balance, the vote is taken again without the delegate's participation.

Proposed amendments to make the District a state (possibly under the title of "New Columbia," which makes it sound like an encyclopedia), or at least to give it proper representation in Congress, have all failed. Any such amendment would have the effect of repealing the "District Clause" in Article I of the Constitution, which places Washington, D.C. under congressional authority. The real reason for opposition to congressional representation for D.C. is political — because the District is solidly Democratic.

Banning Tax Barriers to Voting: The Twenty-Fourth Amendment

After the end of Reconstruction in the South in 1877, barriers were erected to reduce the number of blacks registering as voters. The two most common ways of discouraging voting were literacy tests and taxation, especially the poll tax. No fewer than 11 southern states introduced a poll tax requirement for voting. This was a simple tax of a fixed sum to be paid by everybody, regardless of race, color, earnings, or wealth.

In what way was the poll tax disadvantageous to blacks? Proof that you had paid your poll tax was often made a condition of voting in an election. But some southern states had a "grandfather clause" that allowed you to vote regardless of whether you'd paid your poll tax or not — provided your grandfather had voted at a named date before the abolition of slavery. This type of clause placed blacks and poor whites at a disadvantage as compared with property-owning white men.

The amount of the poll tax was usually quite low. In Georgia it was limited by law to $1 per person per year. In *Breedlove v. Suttles,* decided by the U.S. Supreme Court in 1937, a 28-year-old white man was denied the right to vote because he hadn't paid his poll tax, which was a condition of voting under Georgia law. He claimed that the tax infringed on his rights under the Fourteenth and Nineteenth amendments. The court dismissed his application. Justice Pierce Butler, writing for the court, pointed out that voting rights are determined not by federal but by state law, and that, within the bounds of the Constitution, "the state may condition suffrage as it deems appropriate." He went on to rule that "The payment of poll taxes as a prerequisite to voting is a familiar and reasonable regulation long enforced in many states and for more than a century in Georgia."

Although Breedlove was white, objections to the poll tax came mainly from blacks. So, in 1962 Congress proposed the Twenty-Fourth Amendment to make it unlawful to make the right to vote conditional on the payment of the poll tax or any other tax. The amendment was finally ratified on January 23, 1964, but several southern states never ratified it.

The main part of the Twenty-Fourth Amendment reads as follows:

> *The right of citizens of the United States to vote in any primary or other election for President or Vice President, for electors for President or Vice President, or for Senator or Representative in Congress, shall not be denied or abridged by the United States or any State by reason of failure to pay any poll tax or other tax.*

The wording of the amendment makes sure it covers all bases — but only in respect to federal elections. It doesn't cover state elections at all.

So it was left to the U.S. Supreme Court to ban the use of poll taxes as a condition for voting in state elections. It did so in the 1966 case *Harper v. Virginia Board of Elections*. Justice William O. Douglas, writing for the majority, ruled as follows:

> *We conclude that a State violates the Equal Protection Clause of the Fourteenth Amendment whenever it makes the affluence of the voter or payment of any fee an electoral standard. Voter qualifications have no relation to wealth nor to paying or not paying this or any other tax.*

Hugo Black, one of the three dissenting justices, stressed that the majority decision "is to no extent based on a finding that the Virginia law as written or as applied is being used as a device or mechanism to deny Negro citizens of Virginia the right to vote on account of their color."

Justice Black then rounded on the majority for departing without good reason from the unanimous decision in *Breedlove* and for amending the Constitution, which the court is not allowed to do under Article V.

Succeeding to the Presidency: The Twenty-Fifth Amendment

The Twenty-Fifth Amendment, ratified in 1967, made some arrangements about the presidency and vice presidency, most of which ought to have been tackled much earlier.

Succeeding as President or Acting President?

When the President dies, resigns, or is removed from office, does the Vice President become President or only Acting President?

By 1967, this question had long been settled in practice. When President William Henry Harrison died on April 4, 1841, just one month after his inauguration, he was succeeded by Vice President John Tyler. But was Tyler then President or only Acting President? Article II, Section 1, Clause 6 of the Constitution was ambiguous. Tyler, a southern Democrat in a Whig administration, was surrounded by enemies who did not want him to be the President but only Acting President — the Vice President acting as President. Tyler himself was equally adamant that he was the President, and he managed to get Congress to agree.

Tyler struck a blow not only for himself but also for all subsequent Vice Presidents succeeding to the presidency, all of whom were recognized as being presidents and not just acting presidents.

The Twenty-Fifth Amendment belatedly endorsed Tyler's position — luckily, otherwise we'd have to renumber all the presidents since 1841 and disqualify a few of them. Section 1 of the amendment provides in clear and simple terms that

> *In case of the removal of the President from office or of his death or resignation, the Vice President shall become President.*

Replacing the Veep

The next question that the Twenty-Fifth Amendment addresses was completely neglected for 180 years: Who takes over as Vice President when the Vice President becomes the President — or when the Veep simply drops dead (which has also happened)?

The answer to this question until the Twenty-Fifth Amendment came along was: nobody. That's right. The Constitution previously just allowed the vice presidency to remain vacant. Was that a problem? Not really, because since 1792 there has been a Presidential Succession Act laying down a long and detailed line of succession to the presidency.

But now Section 2 of the Twenty-Fifth Amendment provides for the appointment of a new Vice President when the vice presidency falls vacant. Here's what it says:

> *Whenever there is a vacancy in the office of the Vice President, the President shall nominate a Vice President who shall take office upon confirmation by a majority vote of both Houses of Congress.*

This provision has been used twice. The first time was when President Richard Nixon picked Congressman Gerald Ford to succeed Spiro Agnew when Agnew resigned as Vice President in 1973. Then, when Ford became President on Nixon's resignation in 1974, Ford appointed former New York Governor Nelson Rockefeller as Vice President.

Acting as President

Sections 3 and 4 of the Twenty-Fifth Amendment deal with another neglected (but this time very real) problem — arrangements for when the President is incapacitated. These sections provide that, when that situation occurs, the Vice President becomes "Acting President."

Amazingly, the presidency lasted for 180 years without any such provision in place — although there was clearly a need for it. For example, in 1881, President James Garfield lingered for 80 days before dying from an assassin's bullet, during which time he was unable to attend to affairs of state. President Woodrow Wilson's incapacity from a stroke was kept even from his Vice President and Cabinet — by his wife, who was the effective President for the last year and a half of his second term.

Section 3 provides for the situation when the President himself recognizes his incapacity, which was done once by President Ronald Reagan and twice by President George W. Bush. On all three occasions, the transfer of power to the Vice President as "Acting President" lasted a very short time.

Section 4, which has never been used, deals with the much trickier situation when the Vice President and Cabinet decide that the President is "unable to discharge the powers and duties of his office." This provision is potentially dangerous, as it could be used as a political weapon against a president who is disliked by his Vice President and a majority of his Cabinet — which is not at all impossible.

Lowering the Voting Age: The Twenty-Sixth Amendment

The voting age was 21 until the ratification of the Twenty-Sixth Amendment in 1971, which lowered it to 18. What was the justification for this change?

The Vietnam War was probably the main reason for lowering the voting age. Young men became liable for the draft at age 18. "Old enough to fight, old enough to vote" was a slogan that became popular during that time.

In 1970, Congress passed a law lowering the minimum voting age to 18 for all elections, state and federal alike. The state of Oregon challenged the law's constitutionality. In *Oregon v. Mitchell,* the U.S. Supreme Court ruled that Congress could set the voting age for federal elections but not for state and local elections.

This ruling was impractical. States wanting to leave the minimum voting age at 21 would have had to establish two voters' rolls, one for federal elections and the other for state and local elections.

Congress therefore decided to short-circuit the court ruling by amending the Constitution. The result was the Twenty-Sixth Amendment, which was ratified on July 1, 1971.

The wording of the amendment is copied from that of the Fifteenth and Nineteenth amendments. The main part of it reads as follows:

> *The right of citizens of the United States, who are eighteen years of age or older, to vote shall not be denied or abridged by the United States or by any State on account of age.*

The amendment was ratified in record time — just over three months from passing Congress to ratification by three-fourths of the states. The reason for this enthusiasm on the part of the states was no doubt because it saved the states from the muddle that would have resulted from an attempt to implement the Supreme Court ruling in *Oregon v. Mitchell.*

Limiting Congressional Pay Raises: The Twenty-Seventh Amendment

A fun amendment at last! The Twenty-Seventh Amendment is of interest less for what it says than for the way it was ratified. It was proposed by Congress in 1789 but was ratified only in 1992, more than 200 years later. I discuss this curious constitutional footnote in Chapter 5. Check it out.

The Twenty-Seventh Amendment reads as follows:

> *No law varying the compensation for the services of the Senators and Representatives shall take effect, until an election of Representatives shall have intervened.*

This seems to be saying that if members of Congress vote themselves a pay raise, the new salaries can't come into effect until after a congressional election. This looks good because voters would be unimpressed by senators and representatives who'd voted themselves more money — so members of Congress would be less likely to do so, in case the voters turned them out in the intervening election.

However, Congress has gotten around this sensible provision by voting themselves annual *cost-of-living adjustments,* or COLAs. The U.S. Court of Appeals for the District of Columbia ruled in 2001 that COLAs are not repugnant to the Twenty-Seventh Amendment. The U.S. Supreme Court has yet to pronounce on this question. Watch this space.

Part VI

The Part of Tens

By Rich Tennant

RICHTENNANT

"Okay, predicting the outcome of this Supreme Court case should be as easy as putting one foot in front of the other."

In this part . . .

These three fun chapters collect together my picks of:

- ✔ Ten landmark Supreme Court cases, including *Brown v. Board of Education* on public school segregation and the *Boumediene* case on the legal rights of foreigners detained at Guantanamo Bay.

- ✔ Ten influential Supreme Court Justices, including John Marshall, who made the Supreme Court the powerful player that it is today, and Thurgood Marshall (no relation), the first African American justice to sit on the court.

- ✔ Two sides of five Constitutional conundrums, including whether the Electoral College system should be abolished and whether the President is too powerful.

Chapter 23

Ten Landmark Constitutional Cases

. . . .

In This Chapter

▶ Understanding that leading cases are not necessarily good decisions

▶ Illustrating how two bunches of judges can disagree totally

▶ Tracing the Supreme Court's attitude toward presidential privilege

. . . .

*T*he best-known Supreme Court decisions have effectively changed the Constitution and expanded the power of the court in the process. But are these decisions necessarily good? No, because the Constitution does not actually give the court the power to encroach on the authority of Congress or the President. Some Supreme Court justices have recognized this problem. In the words of Justice Oliver Wendell Holmes, an advocate of judicial restraint, "I do not think the United States would come to an end if we lost our power to declare an Act of Congress void."

In addition to facts about these cases, in this chapter I sometimes offer commentary, which I've put in italic. To help you see the judicial process in perspective, I don't discuss these cases in chronological order. Instead, after the first one, I've grouped them loosely by subject matter.

Marbury v. Madison (1803)

Marbury v. Madison established the U.S. Supreme Court's right of *judicial review* — the power to strike down a law as unconstitutional. As I explain in Chapter 12, William Marbury was appointed a Justice of the Peace by outgoing President John Adams. But the new Secretary of State, James Madison, refused to deliver Marbury's commission — the formal document of appointment. Marbury asked the U.S. Supreme Court to order Madison to hand him his commission.

Chief Justice John Marshall, writing for the court, held that

▶ Madison's refusal to deliver the commission to Marbury was unlawful. *This is undoubtedly correct.*

✔ But the Supreme Court did not have the power to make such an order. *This is not actually correct.*

✔ Because the law that purportedly gave the Supreme Court this power was itself invalid. *This is also probably wrong.*

✔ And the Supreme Court had the power to strike down invalid laws. *Yeah? The Constitution sure doesn't say so, although Alexander Hamilton in the influential* Federalist Papers, *written in 1788, assumed that the Court had this power.*

This judgment is an excellent example of Marshall's "twistifications" (Thomas Jefferson's term). Note that Marshall should have recused himself from hearing the case anyway because the whole case arose out of the failure of President John Adams's Secretary of State to give Marbury his commission. And who was that Secretary of State? Why, none other than John Marshall himself!

Here's what Jefferson himself said about Marshall's new doctrine of judicial review: "The opinion which gives to the judges the right to decide what laws are constitutional and what not . . . would make the Judiciary a despotic branch."

Brown v. Board of Education (1954)

In *Brown v. Board of Education*, a unanimous Supreme Court outlawed racial segregation in public schools throughout the United States. In so doing, the court declared 17 state laws unconstitutional, including some from northern states. The court also overturned its own 1896 ruling in *Plessy v. Ferguson* that had approved the "separate but equal" formula, which had said that it was okay to provide separate facilities for the different races as long as those facilities were equal.

In *Brown*, Chief Justice Earl Warren crafted a short opinion that commanded unanimous support. Here are the main points he made:

✔ The history of the Fourteenth Amendment with respect to segregated schools was "inconclusive." *Not at all! The Fourteenth Amendment, ratified in 1868, gives Congress the power to enforce it. Congress exercised this power by enacting several laws. But none of these laws says anything about segregation in education — which must mean that Congress did not then regard segregated schools as being a violation of the Fourteenth Amendment.*

✔ "We cannot turn the clock back to 1868 when the Amendment was adopted." *Warren was not interested in finding out the meaning of the amendment in 1868 — nor even the intention of its framers. He adopted the "living Constitution" approach, enabling him to interpret the amendment any way he liked.*

- ✔ "Segregation of white and colored children in public schools has a detrimental effect upon the colored children." *And years of forced integration by busing didn't really help.*

- ✔ "We conclude that in the field of public education the doctrine of 'separate but equal' has no place. Separate educational facilities are inherently unequal." *True. Yet the long-term effect of heavy-handed judicial intervention has been "white flight" to the suburbs, a huge increase in the number of white kids in private education, and a serious decline in the standards of the predominantly black inner city schools.*

Parents Involved in Community Schools v. Seattle School District No. 1 and Meredith v. Jefferson County Board of Education (2007)

These are two separate cases that the high court heard together. Chief Justice John Roberts filed an opinion that marks a major retreat from *Brown v. Board of Education* while cleverly using that case as a precedent.

The main question before the court was this: Is it constitutional for a school district to use race as a factor in assigning students to public schools? Roberts's 5–4 majority said no.

The Chief Justice went on — with the support of only three other justices — to quote the unanimous *Brown II* (a sequel to the original *Brown* decision) holding that school districts should "achieve a system of determining admission on a *nonracial basis*." Doing so enabled him to end his opinion with a flourish: "The way to stop discrimination on the basis of race is to stop discriminating on the basis of race."

West Coast Hotel v. Parrish (1937)

President Franklin Delano Roosevelt had no trouble getting his New Deal legislation passed through Congress, but the Supreme Court struck down one New Deal program after another as unconstitutional (see Chapter 9).

The judicial attack on the New Deal was spearheaded by four conservative justices — nicknamed the "Four Horsemen" (of the Apocalypse) — supported by swing vote Justice Owen Roberts. Their opposition to the New Deal was based on the principle of freedom of contract.

Roosevelt retaliated with a proposal that would have allowed him to pack the court with his own nominees. (The Constitution doesn't establish a specific number of Supreme Court justices, so FDR proposed adding six new justices — one for every member of the Court who was older than 70½ at that time.)

Seeing the writing on the wall, Justice Roberts changed sides in *West Coast Hotel v. Parrish* — the famous "switch in time that saved nine" (justices). The Court's decision upheld a minimum wage law in Washington State, and the outcome signaled a movement away from supporting the freedom of contract (see Chapter 9). In the words of Chief Justice Charles Evans Hughes, "The Constitution does not speak of freedom of contract."

This case is important because it illustrates how two bunches of judges can interpret the Constitution in totally opposite ways. It also shows that a strong president can get in on the act of constitutional interpretation.

United States v. Lopez (1995)

This was the first high court decision since 1937 to limit government regulation of the economy. A 1990 federal law used the Commerce Clause as the basis for prohibiting anyone from knowingly carrying a gun in a school zone. The Supreme Court declared this law unconstitutional, noting that the law in question was a "criminal statute" that had nothing to do with commerce. I discuss this case in much more detail in Chapter 9.

Kelo v. City of New London (2005)

Susette Kelo lost her lovely old house. The City of New London, Connecticut, had condemned her home and 114 other lots in a working-class neighborhood in the interests of "economic development." However, the beneficiaries of this program were not the public at large, but Pfizer, the pharmaceutical giant, and a property development corporation — a private entity.

Does the "takings clause" in the Fifth Amendment of the Constitution entitle a city to take property from private citizens for the benefit of other private citizens and corporations? By a 5–4 majority, the high court said yes, even though the Constitution says that private property can be taken only for "public use."

It's significant that in this case, the four liberal justices on the court (plus swing-vote Justice Anthony Kennedy) supported heavy-handed local government power against the interests of poor property owners. On the other hand, the conservative minority stood up for the rights of the individual. In her dissent, Justice Sandra Day O'Connor cited a 1798 opinion condemning "a law that takes property from A. and gives it to B." as "against all reason and justice."

United States v. Nixon (1974)

Does the President enjoy absolute immunity from judicial process (except impeachment)? A unanimous high court said no.

Claiming "executive privilege," President Richard Nixon refused to hand over audiotapes of conversations that took place in the Oval Office. A unanimous high court (without Justice William Rehnquist, who had recused himself) admitted that the President enjoyed a certain limited executive privilege but that "the legitimate needs of the judicial process may outweigh Presidential privilege." The court ordered Nixon to hand over the tapes. He did so and resigned shortly afterward.

Nixon v. Fitzgerald (1982)

This case decided that the President is "entitled to absolute immunity from damages liability predicated on his official acts" — and he remains immune from suit for his official acts taken while in office, even after he is out of office. Writing for the majority, Justice Lewis Powell based this conclusion on the "President's unique office, rooted in the constitutional tradition of separation of powers and supported by our history."

Does this decision contradict the unanimous ruling in the 1974 case just discussed? Probably not. But it sure seems strange that the President can't be sued for anything he does in his official capacity, yet when it comes to demands for documents produced in his official capacity, the court decides how much executive privilege he's allowed!

Clinton v. Jones (1997)

This case is the flip side of *Nixon v. Fitzgerald.* In that case, the high court ruled that the President is totally immune from civil suits for anything he does in his official capacity. In this later case, a unanimous high court held that the President is *not* immune from suit for anything that he did *before* he became president — and that such private lawsuits can go ahead even while the President is still in office. What about civil lawsuits arising out of private acts that the President commits while in office? Can a sitting president be sued for these too? Yes, apparently so.

The case arose out of a civil suit brought against President Bill Clinton by Paula Jones, who accused Clinton of sexual harassment while he was Governor of Arkansas. The case led indirectly to Clinton's impeachment. (Clinton survived the impeachment process and was acquitted, thereby remaining in office for his entire term.)

Boumediene v. Bush (2008)

Did foreign terrorist suspects detained at Guantanamo Bay, Cuba, have the right to challenge their detention in the U.S. courts? By a 5–4 majority the court ruled that the detainees did have this right, which is known as *habeas corpus.* Here are the points made by the majority on the court:

- ✔ Article I, Section 9 of the Constitution prohibits the suspension of habeas corpus by Congress "unless when in Cases of Rebellion or Invasion the public safety may require it."

- ✔ Habeas corpus had not been formally suspended, so the Military Commissions Act passed by Congress in 2006 amounted to an unconstitutional suspension of habeas corpus.

- ✔ Therefore, the foreign Guantanamo detainees have the right to habeas corpus just like everybody else.

Guantanamo Bay is not part of the United States; it is part of Cuba. But the United States has an indefinite lease and control over it. Justice Antonin Scalia classified Guantanamo as foreign territory. He dissented with what he called the "crazy result" of the majority ruling, holding that

> *Today, for the first time in our Nation's history, the Court confers a constitutional right to habeas corpus on alien enemies detained abroad by our military forces in the course of an ongoing war.*

Chief Justice John Roberts, who also dissented, asked,

> *So who has won? Certainly not the American people, who today lose a bit more control over the conduct of this Nation's foreign policy to unelected, politically unaccountable judges.*

Note this attack by the Chief Justice himself on judicial activism!

As I write these words, President Barack Obama has signed an executive order to close the Guantanamo detention center.

Chapter 24

Ten Influential Supreme Court Justices

*T*he U.S. Supreme Court has experienced an exponential increase in power and influence since it opened for business in 1789. In the early days, the court didn't even have a building to call its own, and it was unsure of the extent of its powers. John Jay, the first Chief Justice, lamented that the court lacked "the energy, weight, and dignity which are essential to its affording due support to the national government."

That all changed with the appointment of John Marshall as Chief Justice in 1801. Marshall started the transformation that has made the court probably the most important branch of government.

But is the expansion of the power of the court necessarily a good thing? The other two branches of government — Congress and the President — are popularly elected. By contrast, the court is made up of unelected justices appointed "during good Behaviour," meaning essentially for life. This arrangement protects the independence of the judiciary. Alexander Hamilton remarked in the *Federalist Papers,* written in 1788 (before the Constitution came into force), that this security of tenure was "the best expedient which can be devised in any government, to secure a steady, upright, and impartial administration of the laws."

But appointment for life also enables the judiciary to butt into areas reserved to the other two branches of government — particularly by *making* law rather than merely *interpreting* it, as judges are supposed to do.

Among the ten most influential Supreme Court justices that I introduce in this chapter, I include some judicial activists and some practitioners of judicial restraint. (Keep in mind that no judge ever labels *himself* a judicial activist. That label yells that the judge in question habitually exceeds the proper powers of a judge or justice.)

John Marshall

John Marshall was the longest serving Chief Justice in U.S. history, holding office from 1801 until his death in 1835. He was also the most influential Supreme Court justice.

As a person, Marshall was easygoing, affable, friendly, and unassuming. Even Marshall's political enemies liked him — except Thomas Jefferson, who was actually a distant cousin of his. Jefferson realized that Marshall's bland exterior concealed a wily nature and a crafty mind. "You must never give him an affirmative answer," said Jefferson, "or you will be forced to grant his conclusion. Why, if he were to ask me if it were daylight or not, I'd reply, 'Sir, I don't know, I can't tell.'"

Some of Marshall's "twistifications of the law" (Jefferson's phrase) occurred in the following leading cases:

- *Marbury v. Madison:* This case established the right of the Supreme Court to declare Acts of Congress unconstitutional and therefore void. I discuss this landmark case in Chapter 23.
- *Fletcher v. Peck*: This was the first case in which the Supreme Court struck down a state law as unconstitutional — while upholding a corrupt contract.
- *McCulloch v. Maryland:* This case established the supremacy of federal law over state law.
- *Cohens v. Virginia:* This case established the power of the Supreme Court to hear all cases involving constitutional issues.
- *Gibbons v. Ogden:* In this case, the Supreme Court held that the Commerce Clause in the U.S. Constitution gave Congress a power overriding state law. I deal with the sticky subject of the Commerce Clause in Chapter 9. Read it at your peril!

John Marshall wrote the opinion of the Supreme Court in all these cases, and in 519 of the 1,106 opinions filed by the court during his tenure.

Marshall had the mind of a lawyer but the heart of a politician. His judicial decisions were heavily influenced by his political views, which

- ✔ Favored a strong federal government over states' rights

- ✔ Promoted the power of the Supreme Court over that of Congress and the Presidency

- ✔ Advanced commercial and industrial interests over rural and agrarian concerns

Oliver Wendell Holmes, Jr.

Oliver Wendell Holmes, Jr., who was an associate justice from 1902 to 1932, is still probably the most oft-quoted Supreme Court justice of all time.

A strong believer in freedom of speech, Holmes nevertheless upheld the conviction of a socialist for exhorting draftees in World War I to oppose the draft. Holmes found that the words used created "a clear and present danger that they will bring about the substantive evils that Congress has a right to prevent." Holmes added that "The most stringent protection of free speech would not protect a man in falsely shouting fire in a theatre and causing panic."

Holmes is less well known for his practice of judicial restraint — his reluctance to interfere with laws passed by elected legislatures. But sometimes he went too far in this direction, as when he upheld Virginia's compulsory sterilization law with the flippant remark, "Three generations are enough."

Louis Brandeis

Louis Brandeis is particularly well known for his championing of the right of privacy. In his dissent in *Olmstead v. United States,* he claimed that the U.S. Constitution protected this right and declared in ringing tones that the right of privacy was "the most comprehensive of rights and the right most valued by civilized men." That was in 1928. But it took nearly 40 years before the majority on the court came around to Brandeis's view, in *Katz v. United States,* decided in 1967 — by which time Brandeis was long dead.

Between 1932 and 1937, Brandeis was known as one of the "Three Musketeers": liberal justices highly supportive of President Franklin Delano Roosevelt's New Deal legislation. Brandeis advocated judicial restraint as part of his respect for two kinds of separation of power that he identified as *vertical* (federal/states/individual) and *horizontal* (legislative/executive/judicial).

Felix Frankfurter

Felix Frankfurter was named to the Supreme Court by FDR in 1939 and served until 1962. Frankfurter was particularly influenced by Oliver Wendell Holmes, Jr., and became the court's firmest adherent of judicial restraint.

Although his politics were liberal, Frankfurter's belief in judicial restraint led him to file some surprising opinions — and earned him the animosity of other liberal justices on the court. In *Minersville School District v. Gobitis,* decided in 1940, two Jehovah's Witnesses were expelled from public school for refusing on religious grounds to salute the flag, which was mandatory under state law. Frankfurter wrote the majority opinion upholding the state law and the expulsions. In a later case on the same subject, he opined, "As judges, we are neither Jew nor Gentile, neither Catholic nor agnostic."

In *Korematsu v. United States,* decided during World War II, the Supreme Court ruled in favor of federal laws that ordered the internment of Japanese Americans. Frankfurter wrote an opinion upholding the constitutionality of the laws, without approving or disapproving of them. "That is their business, not ours," he wrote — an excellent example of his judicial restraint.

When Earl Warren became Chief Justice in 1953, Frankfurter tried desperately to win him over to judicial restraint. Warren's increasing commitment to judicial activism created a rift between them manifested by sharp exchanges in open court. In opposition to Warren's politics-driven approach to law, Frankfurter opined, "The Supreme Court exists to establish rules of law, not to provide justice."

Earl Warren

President Dwight Eisenhower was looking for a conservative Chief Justice when he nominated Earl Warren to fill that seat in 1953. Warren soon turned out to be a liberal activist who hugely expanded the power of the court. Eisenhower regretted his choice, remarking that his nomination of Warren "was the biggest damned-fool mistake I ever made."

A typical example of Warren's views is the opinion that he wrote in 1967 ruling that a member of the Communist Party could not be barred from working in a defense establishment — even though there was a federal law against it. Two justices dissented, noting that "Nothing in the Constitution requires this result."

Warren is best known for his opinion in *Brown v. Board of Education* striking down state laws that established segregated public schools. Referring specifically to this decision, Supreme Court Justice James F. Byrnes said, "The Court did not interpret the Constitution — the Court amended it." (I deal with *Brown* in Chapter 23.)

In *Miranda v. Arizona*, decided in 1966, Warren's opinion commanded only a 5–4 majority. But this was yet another landmark decision that cast a long shadow. The ruling in this case introduced the familiar Miranda warning that you've heard so many times on TV and in the movies: "You have the right to remain silent. . . ." Three dissenting justices maintained that the majority decision "represents poor constitutional law and entails harmful consequences for the country at large."

Thurgood Marshall

Thurgood Marshall was the first African American to sit on the court, serving for 24 years, from 1967 until 1991. A straight line can be drawn from Marshall's appointment in 1967 to the election of another African American lawyer as the first black President in 2008. It's hard to envision the election of President Barack Obama without the long struggle for black civil rights so successfully waged by Thurgood Marshall.

As chief counsel for the National Association for the Advancement of Colored People (NAACP) between 1940 and 1961, Marshall argued 32 cases before the Supreme Court — of which he won no fewer than 29! The best-known of his victories was the earth-shattering 1954 case of *Brown v. Board of Education*, which forever consigned the doctrine of "separate but equal" to the trash can of history.

Marshall's time on the court was marked by his championing of liberal causes, most of which are less fashionable today. Here's a bird's-eye view of two of Marshall's key issues:

✔ **Death penalty:** Marshall and his close ally Justice William Brennan consistently held that the death penalty always amounted to "cruel and unusual punishment" prohibited by the Eight Amendment. Their stance caused the death penalty to be suspended between 1972 and 1976.

Since 1976, the majority on the court has rejected the view that capital punishment is automatically unconstitutional. In the 2008 decision in *Baze v. Rees*, the high court found execution by lethal injection to be constitutional. At the time of this writing, capital punishment is permitted in 36 states.

✔ **Affirmative action:** Allan Bakke, a white man, was twice rejected for admission to medical school by the University of California (UC) Davis. Bakke's qualifications were superior to those of 16 minority students who were admitted under the university's affirmative action program. Bakke claimed that he was the victim of racial discrimination. When Bakke's case reached the Supreme Court in 1978, the majority on the court held that race could be taken into account together with other factors in determining admissions to a university, but that a fixed quota system such as the one operated by UC Davis was unconstitutional.

Marshall robustly dissented from this conclusion. He came out strongly in support of the university's affirmative action program favoring the admission of minorities. Marshall didn't even mention Bakke's claim that he was the victim of racial discrimination himself.

Today, more than 30 years later, the majority on the court opposes discrimination of any kind, and they recognize that affirmative action is by its very nature discriminatory. In the words of Chief Justice John Roberts in a 2007 majority opinion striking down race-based student-assignment systems by public school districts in Louisville, Kentucky and Seattle, Washington, "The way to stop discrimination on the basis of race is to stop discriminating on the basis of race."

William Rehnquist

Only 9 percent of people participating in a 1989 public opinion poll knew that the Chief Justice was William Rehnquist — 54 percent thought that position was held by Judge Joseph Wapner of *The People's Court.*

Despite this rebuff, Rehnquist's name is unlikely to be forgotten — and not only because of his 32-year membership on the court. As Chief Justice, Rehnquist managed to nudge the court in a more conservative direction than before, but he was not completely consistent in his views:

✔ **"The new federalism":** Rehnquist frequently championed the rights of the states against the federal government. This stance is sometimes termed "the new federalism." For example, in *United States v. Lopez,* decided in 1995, Rehnquist was just able to scrape together a majority of justices to strike down a federal law prohibiting the carrying of firearms in a school zone.

✔ *Miranda:* After repeatedly impugning the constitutionality of the *Miranda* warning, in 2000 Rehnquist wrote an opinion that commanded a 7–2 majority in favor of *Miranda.*

> ✓ ***Bush v. Gore:*** Rehnquist headed up a bare majority of the court that handed the presidency to George W. Bush in 2000. Rehnquist's preparedness to get involved in this highly controversial political issue was itself an exercise in judicial activism, which he had so often condemned.

> ✓ **"Illegal enemy combatants":** Rehnquist joined the majority in *Hamdi v. Rumsfeld* in 2004, holding that a U.S. citizen being detained as an "illegal enemy combatant" has the right to apply to a court for judicial review.

Rehnquist said he wanted to be remembered above all as a good administrator. Yet, the Supreme Court over which he presided was very divided. He was able to command a majority only by moderating — and sometimes completely changing — his views. But he held fast to a belief in the right of majority opinion to prevail, which kept him from taking extreme positions.

Sandra Day O'Connor

Sandra Day O'Connor was the first woman ever to sit on the U.S. Supreme Court, which she did from 1981 to 2006. This fact alone earned her a place in history. But she deserves to be remembered for her opinions too — and for her tactics, which gave her added influence as the swing vote in a number of leading cases.

O'Connor adopted a case-by-case approach to her work on the court, which enabled her to switch sides when it suited her. For example, she was on different sides in two cases decided in 2003 about the affirmative action admissions policy of the University of Michigan Law School. The court decided both cases by a 5–4 majority — and O'Connor was in the majority both times!

Among her many skillful tightrope acts was her opinion in *Webster v. Reproductive Health Services,* a case on abortion. She was careful to oppose overturning *Roe v. Wade* while effectively cutting back on it. As so often was the case, she managed to be the swing vote in a 5–4 majority decision.

Antonin Scalia

Antonin Scalia has served as an associate justice of the Supreme Court since 1986. He is an *originalist* — believing that the Constitution means what it meant to the Framers. He is, in general, a conservative in political terms, but his strict view of the Constitution has sometimes given him strange bedfellows.

For example, in *Hamdi v. Rumsfeld,* he was allied with liberal Justice John Paul Stevens in taking an uncompromising stand against the U.S. government.

In general, however, Scalia's conservatism has gotten the better of his originalism when the rights of the President are at stake, as in *Hamdan v. Rumsfeld,* involving the rights of detainees held at Guantanamo Bay.

Scalia's inflexibility and doctrinaire, even pedantic, approach to the law have limited his influence on his fellow justices — except in one respect. Scalia early on started subjecting counsel to the third degree with quick-fire questions. This novel approach soon caught on amongst new appointees to the court (except for Justice Clarence Thomas, who generally maintains a stony silence throughout).

John Roberts

John Roberts has been Chief Justice since the death of William Rehnquist in 2005. Roberts has already put his stamp on the court, although it's still too early to say whether he will emerge as one of the really big hitters of all time.

The first change he introduced was to lose the rather pompous and almost comical gold stripes that Rehnquist had had sewn onto his robe to differentiate himself from mere associate justices. By departing from this non-tradition, Roberts signaled that he was just one of the boys (and girls).

This action chimed in with Roberts's declared aim of achieving more unanimity on the court. But this intention has not stopped him from following his conservative views, even at the expense of bitter recriminations from those who disagree with him. The cases in question have involved police searches, desegregation, and women's rights.

Chapter 25

Two Sides of Five Constitutional Conundrums

Dear Reader, please don't think you've been short-changed. Yes, I know that this is "The Part of Tens" and this chapter contains only five sections. But please don't go back to the bookstore — or worse, the publishers — and ask for your money back! I couldn't do justice to more than these five topics in the limited space available for this chapter. But I have given you both sides of the argument on all these highly controversial issues — and two times five equals ten!

The point of this chapter is to identify some issues that are at the forefront of debate on the Constitution. These are

✔ Whether the Constitution is still relevant today

✔ Whether presidential elections are truly democratic

✔ Whether the Supreme Court has too much power

✔ How to interpret the Constitution

✔ Whether the President has too much power

Is the Constitution Outdated?

The U.S. Constitution is more than 220 years old. If the Constitution were a person, it would be long dead — or, at the very least, extremely frail and completely out of touch with the realities of modern life! Is the Constitution any different?

Here are some arguments in favor of the view that the Constitution is outdated:

- ✔ When the Constitution was drafted, not only were there no cheeseburgers, no cell phones, and no MP3 players — which some people today regard as necessities — but there also were no automobiles, no airplanes, no electricity, no TV, and no computers. It really was a totally different world.

- ✔ Social values were way different then too: Slavery was rife, the death penalty was unquestioned, and women had no legal rights.

- ✔ A constitution emanating from such an alien background can remain relevant only if it's constantly reinterpreted by the Supreme Court to keep abreast of changing values.

But a lot of people reject this approach. Here are some of the arguments against the view that the Constitution is outdated:

- ✔ The core values enshrined in the Constitution are timeless and represent the underpinnings of this country as originally conceived.

- ✔ The Constitution is a force for stability in law, government, and society.

- ✔ Only by sticking closely to the original meaning of the Constitution could the Supreme Court achieve a uniform approach to it.

- ✔ A proliferation of inconsistent interpretations of the Constitution could lead people to lose respect for the Supreme Court — and for the Constitution itself.

- ✔ It's wrong for judges to second-guess the Framers of the Constitution, because that would amount to changing the meaning of the Constitution.

- ✔ The Supreme Court is not allowed to change the Constitution. That can be done only by the elaborate process of amendment as laid down in the Constitution itself.

Should the Electoral College Be Abolished?

The Framers of the Constitution didn't trust the ordinary people. In the original, unamended Constitution, the House of Representatives was the only directly elected body. Senators were originally chosen by the state legislatures, and the President was elected by an Electoral College.

The Electoral College system is still in force for presidential elections. The rise of political parties has made the whole operation much more democratic than the Framers ever intended, but it's still not completely democratic. (See Chapter 10 for an explanation of how the system works.)

Here are some of the undemocratic features of the Electoral College system, which have resulted in calls for its abolition:

✔ Although members of the Electoral College are pledged to support a particular candidate for President, there have been no fewer than 158 "faithless electors" over the years in votes for President or Vice President. Although pledged to vote for a particular candidate, these electors all cast their votes for somebody else.

In 71 of the 158 cases, the voting change made perfect sense because the pledged candidate had died before the election. But the remaining cases have been more complex. The biggest defection occurred in 1836, when all 23 of Virginia's electors who had pledged to vote for Martin Van Buren as President refused to vote for his running mate, Richard M. Johnson, because he had been living with a family slave with whom he had two daughters.

✔ With the exception of Maine and Nebraska, the candidate winning a plurality of the popular vote in a state carries that state and takes *all* its electoral votes. For example, in 2000, the whole election turned on a few votes in Florida. By declaring George W. Bush the winner of the popular vote in Florida, the U.S. Supreme Court gave him all 25 of Florida's electoral votes and thus handed him the presidency.

✔ This winner-takes-all arrangement can result in the candidate with the smaller number of popular votes becoming president. This happened in 1824, 1876, 1888, and 2000, and possibly also in 1960.

✔ In the event of a tie in the Electoral College, the election of the President is thrown into the House of Representatives, with each state having just a single vote — hardly a democratic solution.

On the other hand, the Electoral College also has its supporters, who point out that

✔ The Electoral College system reflects and maintains the federal structure of the nation. No state, however small, has fewer than three electoral votes — because the number of electoral votes allocated to a state is the number of representatives from that state in the House, plus two, for its two senators. This formula compensates the smaller states for their lower levels of population.

✔ Although the election result is calculated by the total number of electoral votes won by each candidate across the nation, the number of *states* carried by each candidate is also important, as is the result in each particular state. Take, for example, the significance of Al Gore's failure to carry his home state, Tennessee, in the 2000 election — which cost him the election. He wouldn't have needed to carry Florida if he'd had Tennessee's 11 electoral votes under his belt.

✔ The Electoral College favors the two-party system by making it harder for a third party to break through. Some people think this is a bad feature of the Electoral College system. But if the President was directly elected by popular vote, the practical result of a serious third-party challenge would likely throw the election into the House of Representatives. In both 1992 and 1996, the Reform Party candidate, Ross Perot, took enough votes to deprive either of the major party candidates of a majority of the popular vote. Without the Electoral College, both of these elections would have been decided by the House.

Does the U.S. Supreme Court Have Too Much Power?

Thomas Jefferson completely rejected Chief Justice John Marshall's claim in *Marbury v. Madison,* decided in 1803, that the Supreme Court had the exclusive right to decide the constitutionality of a law. Jefferson remarked, quite correctly, that "there is not a word in the Constitution which has given that power to them [the Supreme Court justices] more than to the Executive or Legislative branches."

However, Marshall had the last word and scored a lasting victory over Jefferson in that case, which I discuss in Chapter 23. A century later, Chief Justice Charles Evans Hughes could say, "We are under a Constitution, but the Constitution is what the judges say it is." (Hughes's remark was not meant as a criticism.)

Hughes's observation is still correct and, since 1791, the Constitution has changed far more as a result of judicial interpretation than through formal amendments. Here are some major constitutional changes brought about by the court's decisions:

✔ Enforcing "freedom of contract" as a supposed constitutional principle in 1905 — and abandoning it 30 years later. The court then went to the opposite extreme of supporting tight central government control of the economy through a broad interpretation of the Commerce Clause. Since 1995, there have been intermittent signs of a return to more states' rights. I discuss the Commerce Clause in Chapter 9.

- Outlawing segregation in public schools in 1954 — overruling a Supreme Court decision from half a century earlier.

- Approving the use of busing to achieve desegregation of public schools. Busing is now largely abandoned.

- Providing additional protection for criminal defendants, for example by requiring the well-known *Miranda* warning.

- Disapproving of the death penalty in 1972 in *Furman v. Georgia* — even though it's explicitly referred to in the Constitution. Within four years, the Supreme Court pulled back from this position. Capital punishment is now lawful in 36 states and in federal law.

- Establishing the expectation of privacy as a constitutionally-protected right.

- Supporting a woman's right to have an abortion (within certain time constraints).

The question here is not whether you agree or disagree with any of these Supreme Court rulings, but rather whether these are matters that should be decided by judges at all. Most of them have involved striking down state laws, and in some cases they struck down federal laws as well. In my opinion, these decisions should have been left to legislators. Here's why:

- Judges are unelected, so they should not strike down laws passed by democratically elected legislatures. In the words of Chief Justice William Rehnquist, "How can government by the elected representatives of the people coexist with the power of the federal judiciary . . . to declare invalid laws duly enacted by the popular branches of government?"

- Supreme Court decisions have no teeth. (I'm not referring here to the justices' dental health, although they are allowed to continue to sit on the bench until they drop stone dead!) The court has no police force to ensure obedience to its decisions.

- Judge-made law is also contrary to the fundamental constitutional principle of the separation of powers. The Supreme Court is part of the judiciary, but laws are supposed to be created only by a legislature.

- The U.S. Supreme Court is a branch of the federal government. When it strikes down state laws, this amounts to an attack on federalism and democracy alike.

Why do some people believe it's a good idea for the high court to have such sweeping powers? The most common argument in favor of the court's power relates to the concept of the *living Constitution*. The idea is that the Constitution needs to be constantly reinterpreted in order to reflect society's changing values and needs. For example, Professor Michael C. Dorf wrote a 2008 article in support of the living Constitution position, arguing that those who ratified the Constitution in its original form didn't include any women or slaves — but "the Constitution's current authority derives at least in substantial part from the fact that we the living people accept it as authoritative."

Why Is There No Agreed-Upon Interpretation of the Constitution?

"Do you think the Constitution of the United States could have one meaning this week and another meaning next week?" Senator James Eastland hurled this challenge at William Brennan during the Senate hearings to confirm Brennan as a high court justice in 1957. The senator was expressing a widely shared concern about unelected judges taking it upon themselves effectively to amend the Constitution in accordance with their personal beliefs and opinions.

Brennan had a ready retort, explaining, "We look to the history of the time of framing and to the intervening history of interpretation. But the ultimate question must be, what do the words of the text mean in our time?" Brennan maintained that if the words of the text mean something different today from what they meant 220 years ago — or even 20 years ago — the court must simply dump the old meaning in favor of the current meaning.

Brennan belonged to the *living Constitution* school of thought, which I discuss in Chapter 12 (along with the competing schools of thought regarding how to interpret the Constitution).

For example, Brennan, following Chief Justice Earl Warren, held that the phrase "cruel and unusual punishments" in the Eighth Amendment "must draw its meaning from the evolving standards of decency that mark the progress of a maturing society." This approach allowed Brennan to conclude that the death penalty is always automatically a violation of the Eighth Amendment and is therefore unconstitutional.

Brennan's approach has a certain attraction. A point in its favor is that figuring out what a particular word or phrase meant to the Framers two centuries ago can be tough. It's also undeniable that concepts and values change over time.

But, in my opinion, adherents of the living Constitution school fall into a serious logical trap, for these reasons:

✔ Values may have changed since 1788, but current values are far from unanimous. For judges to decide what the applicable values are today gives them a blank check to fill out with their own personal values. The death penalty is a good example. Justice Brennan was totally opposed to capital punishment in any shape or form, but polls show that about three-fourths of the U.S. population consistently supports the death penalty.

✔ Champions of the living Constitution are in danger of confusing what the Constitution says with what they would like it to say. For example, the Constitution clearly recognizes and accepts capital punishment, which is mentioned three times in the Fifth Amendment and again in the Fourteenth Amendment.

So, if the Constitution accepts the death penalty as valid, what does it mean by "cruel and unusual punishments"? A long line of cases shows that this phrase refers only to *extreme* forms of the death penalty and other punishments, such as burning at the stake, boiling in oil, racking, and other forms of torture.

For those people who would *like* the Constitution to say that any kind of capital punishment constitutes "cruel and unusual punishments," Article V of the Constitution tells them how to get their wish — by means of the proper democratic process of amendment.

Does the President Have Too Much Power?

The U.S. president is arguably the most powerful leader in the world. But this has not always been the case. In the 19th century, the only presidents who interpreted their constitutional powers broadly and acted accordingly were Andrew Jackson, James K. Polk, and Abraham Lincoln. The 20th century began with another strong president, Theodore Roosevelt, but it was only Franklin Delano Roosevelt who established the modern *imperial presidency,* where the President is more powerful than he is entitled to be under the Constitution.

Two areas of particular concern about the degree of presidential power are terrorism and war powers. Let me look briefly at these.

✔ **Terrorism:** What powers does the President have to curb terrorism?

- Does the President have the power to detain a U.S. citizen indefinitely as an "enemy combatant"? In *Hamdi v. Rumsfeld,* decided in 2004, a majority on the Supreme Court said no. Justice Clarence Thomas in a powerful lone dissent opined that "This detention falls squarely within the Federal Government's war powers, and we lack the expertise and capacity to second-guess that decision."

- In *Hamdan v. Rumsfeld,* decided in 2006, the President lost again. (Note that despite the similarity in name, this case is entirely separate from *Hamdi v. Rumsfeld.*) The question before the Supreme Court was whether it was legal for "enemy combatants" to be tried by military commissions. The majority on the court said no. Justice Clarence Thomas, dissenting, claimed that the majority opinion "openly flouts our well-established duty to respect the Executive's judgment in matters of military operations and foreign affairs."

✔ **War powers:** The Constitution gives Congress the power "To declare War," but it makes the President the Commander in Chief. Does this mean that the President's role as Commander in Chief takes effect only after Congress has made a declaration of war? If that is the right interpretation, then most presidents since World War II have acted unconstitutionally — because Congress has not made a single formal declaration of war since that time. And even the War Powers Act of 1973 would be unconstitutional because, although the Act limits the President's power to wage war without the consent of Congress, it does not prohibit it. However, the War Powers Act has never been declared unconstitutional.

In October 2002, Congress passed a Joint Resolution authorizing President George W. Bush "to use the Armed Forces of the United States as he determines necessary and appropriate in order to defend the national security of the United States against the continuing threat posed by Iraq." This resolution was certainly not a declaration of war against Iraq but claimed to be based on the War Powers Act. Did this Joint Resolution authorize the President to invade Iraq? It's not clear, but the President certainly applied it in that sense.

So, does the President have too much power in the two areas we have looked at? He certainly has a good deal of power, which, however, is restricted by a Constitution that clearly was not intended to create an imperial presidency. If the Supreme Court or Congress wishes to rein the President in on the basis of a close reading of the Constitution, it would be difficult for the President to break free.

In 1861, without consulting Congress, President Abraham Lincoln suspended *habeas corpus* — the right of a detained person to challenge his detention in court. Chief Justice Roger B. Taney roundly condemned the President's action in the case of John Merryman. Lincoln, said the Chief Justice, "certainly does not faithfully execute the laws if he takes upon himself the legislative power, by suspending the writ of habeas corpus, and the judicial power also, by arresting and imprisoning a person without due process of law." Lincoln simply ignored Taney's ruling. A 21st-century president could hardly do the same!

Appendix

Constitution of the United States of America

· ·

*F*ollowing is the complete text of the U.S. Constitution, which was adopted by the Philadelphia Convention on September 17, 1787. It's followed by the 27 amendments that have been made to the Constitution since its ratification.

Preamble

We the People of the United States, in Order to form a more perfect Union, establish Justice, insure domestic Tranquillity, provide for the common defence, promote the general Welfare, and secure the Blessings of Liberty to ourselves and our Posterity, do ordain and establish this Constitution for the United States of America.

Articles

ARTICLE 1

Section 1. All legislative Powers herein granted shall be vested in a Congress of the United States, which shall consist of a Senate and House of Representatives.

Section 2. The House of Representatives shall be composed of Members chosen every second Year by the People of the several States, and the Electors in each State shall have the Qualifications requisite for Electors of the most numerous Branch of the State Legislature.

No Person shall be a Representative who shall not have attained to the age of twenty five Years, and been seven Years a Citizen of the United States, and who shall not, when elected, be an Inhabitant of that State in which he shall be chosen.

[Representatives and direct Taxes shall be apportioned among the several States which may be included within this Union, according to their respective Numbers, which shall be determined by adding to the whole Number of free Persons, including those bound to Service for a Term of Years, and excluding Indians not taxed, three fifths of all other Persons.] *[The preceding section in square brackets was changed by Section 2 of the Fourteenth Amendment.]* The actual Enumeration shall be made within three Years after the first Meeting of the Congress of the United States, and within every subsequent Term of ten Years, in such Manner as they shall by Law direct. The Number of Representatives shall not exceed one for every thirty Thousand, but each State shall have at Least one Representative; and until such enumeration shall be made, the State of New Hampshire shall be entitled to chuse three, Massachusetts eight, Rhode-Island and Providence Plantations one, Connecticut five, New-York six, New Jersey four, Pennsylvania eight, Delaware one, Maryland six, Virginia ten, North Carolina five, South Carolina five, and Georgia three.

When vacancies happen in the Representation from any State, the Executive Authority thereof shall issue Writs of Election to fill such Vacancies.

The House of Representatives shall chuse their Speaker and other Officers; and shall have the sole Power of Impeachment.

Section 3. The Senate of the United States shall be composed of two Senators from each State, [chosen by the Legislature thereof,] *[the preceding section in square brackets was changed by the first paragraph of the Seventeenth Amendment]* for six Years; and each Senator shall have one Vote.

Immediately after they shall be assembled in Consequence of the first Election, they shall be divided as equally as may be into three Classes. The Seats of the Senators of the first Class shall be vacated at the Expiration of the second Year, of the second Class at the Expiration of the fourth Year, and of the third Class at the Expiration of the sixth Year, so that one third may be chosen every second Year; [and if Vacancies happen by Resignation, or otherwise, during the Recess of the Legislature of any State, the Executive thereof may make temporary Appointments until the next Meeting of the Legislature, which shall then fill such Vacancies.] *[The preceding section in square brackets was changed by the second paragraph of the Seventeenth Amendment.]*

No Person shall be a Senator who shall not have attained to the Age of thirty Years, and been nine Years a Citizen of the United States, and who shall not, when elected, be an Inhabitant of that State for which he shall be chosen.

The Vice President of the United States shall be President of the Senate, but shall have no Vote, unless they be equally divided.

The Senate shall chuse their other Officers, and also a President pro tempore, in the Absence of the Vice President, or when he shall exercise the Office of President of the United States.

The Senate shall have the sole Power to try all Impeachments. When sitting for that Purpose, they shall be on Oath or Affirmation. When the President of the United States is tried, the Chief Justice shall preside: And no Person shall be convicted without the Concurrence of two thirds of the Members present.

Judgment in Cases of Impeachment shall not extend further than to removal from Office, and disqualification to hold and enjoy any Office of honor, Trust or Profit under the United States: but the Party convicted shall nevertheless be liable and subject to Indictment, Trial, Judgment and Punishment, according to Law.

Section 4. The Times, Places and Manner of holding Elections for Senators and Representatives, shall be prescribed in each State by the Legislature thereof; but the Congress may at any time by Law make or alter such Regulations, except as to the Places of chusing Senators.

The Congress shall assemble at least once in every Year, and such Meeting shall [be on the first Monday in December] *[the preceding section in square brackets was changed by Section 2 of the Twentieth Amendment]*, unless they shall by Law appoint a different Day.

Section 5. Each House shall be the judge of the Elections, Returns and Qualifications of its own Members, and a Majority of each shall constitute a Quorum to do Business; but a smaller Number may adjourn from day to day, and may be authorized to compel the Attendance of absent Members, in such Manner, and under such Penalties as each House may provide.

Each House may determine the Rules of its Proceedings, punish its Members for disorderly Behaviour, and, with the Concurrence of two thirds, expel a Member.

Each House shall keep a journal of its Proceedings, and from time to time publish the same, excepting such Parts as may in their judgment require Secrecy; and the Yeas and Nays of the Members of either House on any question shall, at the Desire of one fifth of those Present, be entered on the Journal.

Neither House, during the Session of Congress, shall, without the Consent of the other, adjourn for more than three days, nor to any other Place than that in which the two Houses shall be sitting.

Section 6. The Senators and Representatives shall receive a Compensation for their Services, to be ascertained by Law, and paid out of the Treasury of the United States. They shall in all Cases, except Treason, Felony and Breach of the Peace, be privileged from Arrest during their Attendance at the Session of their respective Houses, and in going to and returning from the same; and for any Speech or Debate in either House, they shall not be questioned in any other Place.

No Senator or Representative shall, during the Time for which he was elected, be appointed to any civil Office under the Authority of the United States, which shall have been created, or the Emoluments whereof shall have been encreased during such time; and no Person holding any Office under the United States, shall be a Member of either House during his Continuance in Office.

Section 7. All Bills for raising Revenue shall originate in the House of Representatives; but the Senate may propose or concur with Amendments as on other Bills. Every Bill which shall have passed the House of Representatives and the Senate, shall, before it become a Law, be presented to the President of the United States; If he approve he shall sign it, but if not he shall return it, with his Objections to that House in which it shall have originated, who shall enter the Objections at large on their Journal, and proceed to reconsider it. If after such Reconsideration two thirds of that House shall agree to pass the Bill, it shall be sent, together with the Objections, to the other House, by which it shall likewise be reconsidered, and if approved by two thirds of that House, it shall become a Law. But in all such Cases the Votes of both Houses shall be determined by yeas and Nays, and the names of the Persons voting for and against the Bill shall be entered on the Journal of each House respectively. If any Bill shall not be returned by the President within ten Days (Sundays excepted) after it shall have been presented to him, the Same shall be a Law, in like Manner as if he had signed it, unless the Congress by their Adjournment prevent its Return, in which Case it shall not be a Law.

Every Order, Resolution, or Vote to which the Concurrence of the Senate and House of Representatives may be necessary (except on a question of Adjournment) shall be presented to the President of the United States; and before the Same shall take Effect, shall be approved by him, or being disapproved by him, shall be repassed by two thirds of the Senate and House of Representatives, according to the Rules and Limitations prescribed in the Case of a Bill.

Section 8. The Congress shall have Power To lay and collect Taxes, Duties, Imposts and Excises, to pay the Debts and provide for the common Defence and general Welfare of the United States; but all Duties, Imposts and Excises shall be uniform throughout the United States;

To borrow Money on the credit of the United States;

To regulate Commerce with foreign Nations, and among the several States, and with the Indian Tribes;

To establish an uniform Rule of Naturalization, and uniform Laws on the subject of Bankruptcies throughout the United States;

To coin Money, regulate the Value thereof, and of foreign Coin, and fix the Standard of Weights and Measures;

To provide for the Punishment of counterfeiting the Securities and current Coin of the United States;

To establish Post Offices and post Roads;

To promote the Progress of Science and useful Arts, by securing for limited Times to Authors and Inventors the exclusive Right to their respective Writings and Discoveries;

To constitute Tribunals inferior to the supreme Court;

To define and punish Piracies and Felonies committed on the high Seas, and Offences against the Law of Nations;

To declare War, grant Letters of Marque and Reprisal, and make Rules concerning Captures on Land and Water;

To raise and support Armies, but no Appropriation of Money to that Use shall be for a longer Term than two Years;

To provide and maintain a Navy;

To make Rules for the Government and Regulation of the land and naval Forces;

To provide for calling forth the Militia to execute the Laws of the Union, suppress Insurrections and repel Invasions;

To provide for organizing, arming, and disciplining, the Militia, and for governing such Part of them as may be employed in the Service of the United States, reserving to the States respectively, the Appointment of the Officers, and the Authority of training the Militia according to the discipline prescribed by Congress;

To exercise exclusive Legislation in all Cases whatsoever, over such District (not exceeding ten Miles square) as may, by Cession of particular States, and the Acceptance of Congress, become the Seat of the Government of the United States, and to exercise like Authority over all Places purchased by the Consent of the Legislature of the State in which the Same shall be, for the Erection of Forts, Magazines, Arsenals, dock-Yards, and other needful Buildings;—And

To make all Laws which shall be necessary and proper for carrying into Execution the foregoing Powers, and all other Powers vested by this Constitution in the Government of the United States, or in any Department or Officer thereof.

Section 9. The Migration or Importation of such Persons as any of the States now existing shall think proper to admit, shall not be prohibited by the Congress prior to the Year one thousand eight hundred and eight, but a Tax or duty may be imposed on such Importation, not exceeding ten dollars for each Person.

The Privilege of the Writ of Habeas Corpus shall not be suspended, unless when in Cases of Rebellion or Invasion the public Safety may require it.

No Bill of Attainder or ex post facto Law shall be passed.

[No Capitation, or other direct, Tax shall be laid, unless in Proportion to the Census or Enumeration herein before directed to be taken.] *[The preceding section in square brackets was changed by the Sixteenth Amendment.]*

No Tax or Duty shall be laid on Articles exported from any State.

No Preference shall be given by any Regulation of Commerce or Revenue to the Ports of one State over those of another; nor shall Vessels bound to, or from, one State, be obliged to enter, clear, or pay Duties in another.

No Money shall be drawn from the Treasury, but in Consequence of Appropriations made by Law; and a regular Statement and Account of the Receipts and Expenditures of all public Money shall be published from time to time.

No Title of Nobility shall be granted by the United States: And no Person holding any Office of Profit or Trust under them, shall, without the Consent of the Congress, accept of any present, Emolument, Office, or Title, of any kind whatever, from any King, Prince, or foreign State.

Section 10. No State shall enter into any Treaty, Alliance, or Confederation; grant Letters of Marque and Reprisal; coin Money; emit Bills of Credit; make any Thing but gold and silver Coin a Tender in Payment of Debts; pass any Bill of Attainder, ex post facto Law, or Law impairing the Obligation of Contracts, or grant any Title of Nobility.

No State shall, without the Consent of the Congress, lay any Imposts or Duties on Imports or Exports, except what may be absolutely necessary for executing its inspection Laws: and the net Produce of all Duties and Imposts, laid by any State on Imports or Exports, shall be for the Use of the Treasury of the United States; and all such Laws shall be subject to the Revision and Controul of the Congress.

No State shall, without the Consent of Congress, lay any Duty of Tonnage, keep Troops, or Ships of War in time of Peace, enter into any Agreement or Compact with another State, or with a foreign Power, or engage in War, unless actually invaded, or in such imminent Danger as will not admit of delay.

ARTICLE II

Section 1. The executive Power shall be vested in a President of the United States of America. He shall hold his Office during the Term of four Years, and, together with the Vice President, chosen for the same Term, be elected, as follows:

Each State shall appoint, in such Manner as the Legislature thereof may direct, a Number of Electors, equal to the whole Number of Senators and Representatives to which the State may be entitled in the Congress: but no Senator or Representative, or Person holding an Office of Trust or Profit under the United States, shall be appointed an Elector.

[The Electors shall meet in their respective States, and vote by Ballot for two Persons, of whom one at least shall not be an Inhabitant of the same State with themselves. And they shall make a List of all the Persons voted for, and of the Number of Votes for each; which List they shall sign and certify, and transmit sealed to the Seat of the Government of the United States, directed to the President of the Senate. The President of the Senate shall, in the Presence of the Senate and House of Representatives, open all the Certificates, the Votes shall then be counted. The Person having the greatest Number of Votes shall be the President, if such Number be a Majority of the whole Number of Electors appointed; and if there be more than one who have such Majority, and have an equal Number of Votes, then the House of Representatives shall immediately chuse by Ballot one of them for President; and if no Person have a Majority, then from the five highest on the list the said House shall in like Manner chuse the President. But in chusing the President, the Votes shall be taken by States, the Representation from each State having one Vote; a quorum for this Purpose shall consist of a Member or Members from two thirds of the States, and a Majority of all the States shall be necessary to a Choice. In every Case, after the Choice of the President, the Person having the greatest Number of Votes of the Electors shall be the Vice President. But if there should remain two or more who have equal Votes, the Senate shall chuse from them by Ballot the Vice President.]

[The preceding section in square brackets has been changed by the Twelfth Amendment.]

The Congress may determine the Time of choosing the Electors, and the Day on which they shall give their Votes; which Day shall be the same throughout the United States.

No Person except a natural born Citizen, or a Citizen of the United States, at the time of the Adoption of this Constitution, shall be eligible to the Office of President; neither shall any Person be eligible to that Office who shall not have attained to the Age of thirty five Years, and been fourteen Years a Resident within the United States.

In Case of the Removal of the President from Office, or of his Death, Resignation, or Inability to discharge the Powers and Duties of the said Office, the Same shall devolve on the Vice President, and the Congress may by Law provide for the Case of Removal, Death, Resignation or Inability, both of the President and Vice President, declaring what Officer shall then act as President, and such Officer shall act accordingly, until the Disability be removed, or a President shall be elected. *[The preceding provision has been affected by the Twenty-Fifth Amendment.]*

The President shall, at stated Times, receive for his Services, a Compensation, which shall neither be encreased nor diminished during the Period for which he shall have been elected, and he shall not receive within that Period any other Emolument from the United States, or any of them.

Before he enter on the Execution of his Office, he shall take the following Oath or Affirmation: "I do solemnly swear (or affirm) that I will faithfully execute the Office of President of the United States, and will to the best of my Ability, preserve, protect and defend the Constitution of the United States."

Section 2. The President shall be Commander in Chief of the Army and Navy of the United States, and of the Militia of the several States, when called into the actual Service of the United States; he may require the Opinion, in writing, of the principal Officer in each of the executive Departments, upon any Subject relating to the Duties of their respective Offices, and he shall have Power to grant Reprieves and Pardons for Offences against the United States, except in Cases of Impeachment.

He shall have Power, by and with the Advice and Consent of the Senate, to make Treaties, provided two thirds of the Senators present concur; and he shall nominate, and by and with the Advice and Consent of the Senate, shall appoint Ambassadors, other public Ministers and Consuls, judges of the supreme Court, and all other Officers of the United States, whose Appointments are not herein otherwise provided for, and which shall be established by Law: but the Congress may by Law vest the Appointment of such inferior Officers, as they think proper, in the President alone, in the Courts of Law, or in the Heads of Departments.

The President shall have Power to fill up all Vacancies that may happen during the Recess of the Senate, by granting Commissions which shall expire at the End of their next Session.

Section 3. He shall from time to time give to the Congress Information of the State of the Union, and recommend to their Consideration such Measures as he shall judge necessary and expedient; he may, on extraordinary Occasions, convene both Houses, or either of them, and in Case of Disagreement between them, with Respect to the Time of Adjournment, he may adjourn them to such Time as he shall think proper; he shall receive Ambassadors and other public Ministers; he shall take Care that the Laws be faithfully executed, and shall Commission all the Officers of the United States.

Section 4. The President, Vice President and all civil Officers of the United States, shall be removed from Office on Impeachment for, and Conviction of, Treason, Bribery, or other high Crimes and Misdemeanors.

ARTICLE III

Section 1. The judicial Power of the United States shall be vested in one supreme Court, and in such inferior Courts as the Congress may from time to time ordain and establish. The Judges, both of the supreme and inferior Courts, shall hold their Offices during good Behaviour, and shall, at stated Times, receive for their Services a Compensation, which shall not be diminished during their Continuance in Office.

Section 2. The judicial Power shall extend to all Cases, in Law and Equity, arising under this Constitution, the Laws of the United States, and Treaties made, or which shall be made, under their Authority;—to all Cases affecting Ambassadors, other public Ministers and Consuls;—to all Cases of admiralty and maritime Jurisdiction;—to Controversies to which the United States shall be a Party;—to Controversies between two or more States;—between a State and Citizens of another State *[The Eleventh Amendment limited federal jurisdiction over civil litigation brought against a state.]*;—between Citizens of different States;—between Citizens of the same State claiming Lands under Grants of different States, and between a State, or the Citizens thereof, and foreign States, Citizens or Subjects.

In all Cases affecting Ambassadors, other public Ministers and Consuls, and those in which a State shall be Party, the supreme Court shall have original jurisdiction. In all the other Cases before mentioned, the supreme Court shall have appellate Jurisdiction, both as to Law and Fact, with such Exceptions, and under such Regulations as the Congress shall make.

The Trial of all Crimes, except in Cases of Impeachment, shall be by Jury; and such Trial shall be held in the State where the said Crimes shall have been committed; but when not committed within any State, the Trial shall be at such Place or Places as the Congress may by Law have directed.

Section 3. Treason against the United States, shall consist only in levying War against them, or in adhering to their Enemies, giving them Aid and. Comfort. No Person shall be convicted of Treason unless on the Testimony of two Witnesses to the same overt Act, or on Confession in open Court.

The Congress shall have Power to declare the Punishment of Treason, but no Attainder of Treason shall work Corruption of Blood, or Forfeiture except during the Life of the Person attained.

ARTICLE IV

Section 1. Full Faith and Credit shall be given in each State to the public Acts, Records, and judicial Proceedings of every other State. And the Congress may by general Laws prescribe the Manner in which such Acts, Records and Proceedings shall be proved, and the Effect thereof.

Section 2. The Citizens of each State shall be entitled to all Privileges and Immunities of Citizens in the several States.

A Person charged in any State with Treason, Felony, or other Crime, who shall flee from Justice, and be found in another State, shall on Demand of the executive Authority of the State from which he fled, be delivered up, to be removed to the State having jurisdiction of the Crime.

[No Person held to Service or Labour in one State, under the Laws thereof, escaping into another, shall, in Consequence of any Law or Regulation therein, be discharged from such Service or Labour, but shall be delivered up on Claim of the Party to whom such Service or Labour may be due.] *[This paragraph refers to slavery and indentured servitude, abolished by the Thirteenth Amendment.]*

Section 3. New States may be admitted by the Congress into this Union; but no new State shall be formed or erected within the Jurisdiction of any other State; nor any State be formed by the Junction of two or more States, or Parts of States, without the Consent of the Legislatures of the States concerned as well as of the Congress.

The Congress shall have Power to dispose of and make all needful Rules and Regulations respecting the Territory or other Property belonging to the United States; and nothing in this Constitution shall be so construed as to Prejudice any Claims of the United States, or of any particular State.

Section 4. The United States shall guarantee to every State in this Union a Republican Form of Government, and shall protect each of them against Invasion; and on Application of the Legislature, or of the Executive (when the Legislature cannot be convened) against domestic Violence.

ARTICLE V

The Congress, whenever two thirds of both Houses shall deem it necessary, shall propose Amendments to this Constitution, or, on the Application of the Legislatures of two thirds of the several States, shall call a Convention for proposing Amendments, which, in either Case, shall be valid to all Intents and Purposes, as Part of this Constitution, when ratified by the Legislatures of three fourths of the several States, or by Conventions in three fourths thereof, as the one or the other Mode of Ratification may be proposed by the Congress; Provided that no Amendment which may be made prior to the Year One thousand eight hundred and eight shall in any Manner affect the first and fourth Clauses in the Ninth Section of the first Article; and that no State, without its Consent, shall be deprived of its equal Suffrage in the Senate.

ARTICLE VI

All Debts contracted and Engagements entered into, before the Adoption of this Constitution, shall be as valid against the United States under this Constitution, as under the Confederation.

This Constitution, and the Laws of the United States which shall be made in Pursuance thereof; and all Treaties made, or which shall be made. under the Authority of the United States, shall be the supreme Law of the Land; and the judges in every State shall be bound thereby, any Thing in the Constitution or Laws of any State to the Contrary notwithstanding.

The Senators and Representatives before mentioned, and the Members of the several State Legislatures, and all executive and judicial Officers, both of the United States and of the several States, shall be bound by Oath or Affirmation, to support this Constitution; but no religious Test shall ever be required as a Qualification to any Office or public Trust under the United States.

ARTICLE VII

The Ratification of the Conventions of nine States, shall be sufficient for the Establishment of this Constitution between the States so ratifying the Same.

Signatures

Done in Convention by the Unanimous Consent of the States present the seventeenth Day of September in the Year of our Lord one thousand seven hundred and Eighty seven and of the Independence of the United States of America the Twelfth. IN WITNESS whereof We have hereunto subscribed our Names,

George Washington,

> President and deputy from Virginia.

New Hampshire:

> John Langdon,
>
> Nicholas Gilman.

Massachusetts:

> Nathaniel Gorham,
>
> Rufus King.

Connecticut:

> William Samuel Johnson,
>
> Roger Sherman.

New York:

> Alexander Hamilton.

New Jersey:

> William Livingston,
>
> David Brearley,
>
> William Paterson,
>
> Jonathan Dayton.

Pennsylvania:

> Benjamin Franklin,
>
> Thomas Mifflin,
>
> Robert Morris,
>
> George Clymer,

Thomas FitzSimons,

Jared Ingersoll,

James Wilson,

Gouverneur Morris.

Delaware:

George Read,

Gunning Bedford Jr.,

John Dickinson,

Richard Bassett,

Jacob Broom.

Maryland:

James McHenry,

Daniel of St. Thomas Jenifer,

Daniel Carroll.

Virginia:

John Blair,

James Madison Jr.

North Carolina:

William Blount,

Richard Dobbs Spaight,

Hugh Williamson.

South Carolina:

John Rutledge,

Charles Cotesworth Pinckney,

Pierce Butler.

Georgia:

William Few,

Abraham Baldwin.

(Ratification of the Constitution was completed on June 21, 1788)

AMENDMENTS

The first ten amendments constitute the Bill of Rights, ratified December 15, 1791.

AMENDMENT 1

Congress shall make no law respecting an establishment of religion, or prohibiting the free exercise thereof; or abridging the freedom of speech, or of the press; or the right of the people peaceably to assemble, and to petition the Government for a redress of grievances.

AMENDMENT 11

A well regulated Militia, being necessary to the security of a free State, the right of the people to keep and bear Arms, shall not be infringed.

AMENDMENT 111

No Soldier shall, in time of peace be quartered in any house, without the consent of the Owner, nor in time of war, but in a manner to be prescribed by law.

AMENDMENT 1V

The right of the people to be secure in their persons, houses, papers, and effects, against unreasonable searches and seizures, shall not be violated, and no Warrants shall issue, but upon probable cause, supported by Oath or affirmation, and particularly describing the place to be searched, and the persons or things to be seized.

AMENDMENT V

No person shall be held to answer for a capital, or otherwise infamous crime, unless on a presentment or indictment of a Grand Jury, except in cases arising in the land or naval forces, or in the Militia, when in actual service in time of War or public danger; nor shall any person be subject for the same offence to be twice put in jeopardy of life or limb; nor shall be compelled in any criminal case to be a witness against himself, nor be deprived of life, liberty, or property, without due process of law; nor shall private property be taken for public use, without just compensation.

AMENDMENT VI

In all criminal prosecutions, the accused shall enjoy the right to a speedy and public trial, by an impartial jury of the State and district wherein the crime shall have been committed, which district shall have been previously ascertained by law, and to be informed of the nature and cause of the accusation; to be confronted with the witnesses against him; to have compulsory process for obtaining witnesses in his favor, and to have the Assistance of Counsel for his defence.

AMENDMENT VII

In Suits at common law, where the value in controversy shall exceed twenty dollars, the right of trial by jury shall be preserved, and no fact tried by a jury, shall be otherwise re-examined in any Court of the United States, than according to the rules of the common law.

AMENDMENT VIII

Excessive bail shall not be required, nor excessive fines imposed, nor cruel and unusual punishments inflicted.

AMENDMENT IX

The enumeration in the Constitution, of certain rights, shall not be construed to deny or disparage others retained by the people.

AMENDMENT X

The powers not delegated to the United States by the Constitution, nor prohibited by it to the States, are reserved to the States respectively, or to the people.

AMENDMENT XI

(Ratified February 7, 1795)

The judicial power of the United States shall not be construed to extend to any suit in law or equity, commenced or prosecuted against one of the United States by Citizens of another State, or by Citizens or Subjects of any Foreign State.

AMENDMENT XII

(Ratified June 15, 1804)

The Electors shall meet in their respective states, and vote by ballot for President and Vice-President, one of whom, at least, shall not be an inhabitant of the same state with themselves; they shall name in their ballots the person voted for as President, and in distinct ballots the person voted for as Vice-President, and they shall make distinct lists of all persons voted for as President, and of all persons voted for as Vice-President, and of the number of votes for each, which lists they shall sign and certify, and transmit sealed to the seat of the government of the United States, directed to the President of the Senate;—The President of the Senate shall, in the presence of the Senate and House of Representatives, open all the certificates and the votes shall then be counted;—The person having the greatest number of votes for President, shall be the President, if such number be a majority of the whole number of Electors appointed; and if no person have such majority, then from the persons having the highest numbers not exceeding three on the list of those voted for as President, the House of Representatives shall choose immediately, by ballot, the President. But in choosing the President, the votes shall be taken by states, the representation from each state having one vote; a quorum for this purpose shall consist of a member or members from two-thirds of the states, and a majority of all the states shall be necessary to a choice. [And if the House of Representatives shall not choose a President whenever the right of choice shall devolve upon them, before the fourth day of March next following, then the Vice-President shall act as President, as in the case of the death or other constitutional disability of the President.] *[The preceding section in square brackets was superceded by Section 3 of the Twentieth Amendment.]* The person having the greatest number of votes as Vice-President, shall be the Vice-President, if such number be a majority of the whole number of Electors appointed, and if no person have a majority, then from the two highest numbers on the list, the Senate shall choose the Vice-President; a quorum for the purpose shall consist of two-thirds of the whole number of Senators, and a majority of the whole number shall be necessary to a choice. But no person constitutionally ineligible to the office of President shall be eligible to that of Vice-President of the United States.

AMENDMENT XIII

(Ratified December 6, 1865)

Section 1. Neither slavery nor involuntary servitude, except as a punishment for crime whereof the party shall have been duly convicted, shall exist within the United States, or any place subject to their jurisdiction.

Section 2. Congress shall have power to enforce this article by appropriate legislation.

AMENDMENT XIV

(Ratified July 9, 1868)

Section 1. All persons born or naturalized in the United States, and subject to the jurisdiction thereof, are citizens of the United States and of the State wherein they reside. No State shall make or enforce any law which shall abridge the privileges or immunities of citizens of the United States; nor shall any State deprive any person of life, liberty, or property, without due process of law; nor deny to any person within its jurisdiction the equal protection of the laws.

Section 2. Representatives shall be apportioned among the several States according to their respective numbers, counting the whole number of persons in each State, excluding Indians not taxed. But when the right to vote at any election for the choice of electors for President and Vice President of the United States, Representatives in Congress, the Executive and Judicial officers of a State, or the members of the Legislature thereof, is denied to any of the male inhabitants of such State, being twenty-one years of age, *[see the Nineteenth and Twenty-Sixth amendments]* and citizens of the United States, or in any way abridged, except for participation in rebellion, or other crime, the basis of representation therein shall be reduced in the proportion which the number of such male citizens shall bear to the whole number of male citizens twenty-one years of age in such State.

Section 3. No person shall be a Senator or Representative in Congress, or elector of President and Vice President, or hold any office, civil or military, under the United States, or under any State, who, having previously taken an oath, as a member of Congress, or as an officer of the United States, or as a member of any State legislature, or as an executive or judicial officer of any State, to support the Constitution of the United States, shall have engaged in insurrection or rebellion against the same, or given aid or comfort to the enemies thereof. But Congress may by a vote of two-thirds of each House, remove such disability.

Section 4. The validity of the public debt of the United States, authorized by law, including debts incurred for payment of pensions and bounties for services in suppressing insurrection or rebellion, shall not be questioned. But neither the United States nor any State shall assume or pay any debt or obligation incurred in aid of insurrection or rebellion against the United States, or any claim for the loss or emancipation of any slave; but all such debts, obligations and claims shall be held illegal and void.

Section 5. The Congress shall have power to enforce, by appropriate legislation, the provisions of this article.

AMENDMENT XV

(Ratified February 3, 1870)

Section 1. The right of citizens of the United States to vote shall not be denied or abridged by the United States or by any State on account of race, color, or previous condition of servitude.

Section 2. The Congress shall have power to enforce this article by appropriate legislation.

AMENDMENT XVI

(Ratified February 3, 1913)

The Congress shall have power to lay and collect taxes on incomes, from whatever source derived, without apportionment among the several States, and without regard to any census or enumeration.

AMENDMENT XVII

(Ratified April 8, 1913)

The Senate of the United States shall be composed of two Senators from each State, elected by the people thereof, for six years; and each Senator shall have one vote. The electors in each State shall have the qualifications requisite for electors of the most numerous branch of the State legislatures.

When vacancies happen in the representation of any State in the Senate, the executive authority of such State shall issue writs of election to fill such vacancies: Provided, That the legislature of any State may empower the executive thereof to make temporary appointments until the people fill the vacancies by election as the legislature may direct.

This amendment shall not be so construed as to affect the election or term of any Senator chosen before it becomes valid as part of the Constitution.

AMENDMENT XVIII

(Ratified January 16, 1919)

After one year from the ratification of this article the manufacture, sale, or transportation of intoxicating liquors within, the importation thereof into, or the exportation thereof from the United States and all territory subject to the jurisdiction thereof for beverage purposes is hereby prohibited.

The Congress and the several States shall have concurrent power to enforce this article by appropriate legislation.

This article shall be inoperative unless it shall have been ratified as an amendment to the Constitution by the legislatures of the several States, as provided in the Constitution, within seven years from the date of the submission hereof to the States by the Congress.

[The Eighteenth Amendment was repealed by Section 1 of the Twenty-First Amendment.]

AMENDMENT XIX

(Ratified August 18, 1920)

The right of citizens of the United States to vote shall not be denied or abridged by the United States or by any State on account of sex.

Congress shall have power to enforce this article by appropriate legislation.

AMENDMENT XX

(Ratified January 23, 1933)

Section 1. The terms of the President and Vice President shall end at noon on the 20th day of January, and the terms of Senators and Representatives at noon on the 3d day of January, of the years in which such terms would have ended if this article had not been ratified; and the terms of their successors shall then begin. Section 2. The Congress shall assemble at least once in every year, and such meeting shall begin at noon on the 3d day of January, unless they shall by law appoint a different day.

Section 2. The Congress shall assemble at least once in every year, and such meeting shall begin at noon on the 3d day of January, unless they shall by law appoint a different day.

Section 3. *[See the Twenty-Fifth Amendment.]* If, at the time fixed for the beginning of the term of the President, the President elect shall have died, the Vice President elect shall become President. If a President shall not have been chosen before the time fixed for the beginning of his term, or if the President elect shall have failed to qualified, then the Vice President elect shall act as President until a President shall have qualified; and the Congress may by law provide for the case wherein neither a President elect nor a Vice President elect shall have qualified, declaring who shall then act as President, or the manner in which one who is to act shall be selected, and such person shall act accordingly until a President or Vice President shall have qualified.

Section 4. The Congress may by law provide for the case of the death of any of the persons from whom the House of Representatives may choose a President whenever the right of choice shall have devolved upon them, and for the case of the death of any of the persons from whom the Senate may choose a Vice President whenever the right of choice shall have devolved upon them.

Section 5. Sections 1 and 2 shall take effect on the 15th day of October following the ratification of this article.

Section 6. This article shall be inoperative unless it shall have been ratified as an amendment to the Constitution by the legislatures of three-fourths of the several States within seven years from the date of its submission.

AMENDMENT XXI

(Ratified December 5, 1933)

Section 1. The eighteenth article of amendment to the Constitution of the United States is hereby repealed.

Section 2. The transportation or importation into any State, Territory, or possession of the United States for delivery or use therein of intoxicating liquors, in violation of the laws thereof, is hereby prohibited.

Section 3. This article shall be inoperative unless it shall have been ratified as an amendment to the Constitution by conventions in the several States, as provided in the Constitution, within seven years from the date of the submission hereof to the States by the Congress.

AMENDMENT XXII

(Ratified February 27, 1951)

Section 1. No person shall be elected to the office of the President more than twice, and no person who has held the office of President, or acted as President, for more than two years of a term to which some other person was elected President shall be elected to the office of the President more than once. But this Article shall not apply to any person holding the office of President when this Article was proposed by the Congress, and shall not prevent any person who may be holding the office of President, or acting as President, during the term within which this Article becomes operative from holding the office of President or acting as President during the remainder of such term.

Section 2. This article shall be inoperative unless it shall have been ratified as an amendment to the Constitution by the legislatures of three-fourths of the several States within seven years from the date of its submission to the States by the Congress.

AMENDMENT XXIII

(Ratified March 29, 1961)

Section 1. The District constituting the seat of Government of the United States shall appoint in such manner as the Congress may direct:

A number of electors of President and Vice President equal to the whole number of Senators and Representatives in Congress to which the District would be entitled if it were a State, but in no event more than the least populous State; they shall be in addition to those appointed by the States, but they shall be considered, for the purposes of the election of President and Vice President, to be electors appointed by a State; and they shall meet in the District and perform such duties as provided by the twelfth article of amendment.

Section 2. The Congress shall have power to enforce this article by appropriate legislation.

AMENDMENT XXIV

(Ratified January 23, 1964)

Section 1. The right of citizens of the United States to vote in any primary or other election for President or Vice President, for electors for President or Vice President, or for Senator or Representative in Congress, shall not be denied or abridged by the United States or any State by reason of failure to pay any poll tax or other tax.

Section 2. The Congress shall have power to enforce this article by appropriate legislation.

AMENDMENT XXV

(Ratified February 10, 1967)

Section 1. In case of the removal of the President from office or of his death or resignation, the Vice President shall become President. Section 2. Whenever there is a vacancy in the office of the Vice President, the President shall nominate a Vice President who shall take office upon confirmation by a majority vote of both Houses of Congress.

Section 2. Whenever there is a vacancy in the office of the Vice President, the President shall nominate a Vice President who shall take office upon confirmation by a majority vote of both Houses of Congress.

Section 3. Whenever the President transmits to the President pro tempore of the Senate and the Speaker of the House of Representatives his written declaration that he is unable to discharge the powers and duties of his office, and until he transmits to them a written declaration to the contrary, such powers and duties shall be discharged by the Vice President as Acting President.

Section 4. Whenever the Vice President and a majority of either the principal officers of the executive departments or of such other body as Congress may by law provide, transmit to the President pro tempore of the Senate and the Speaker of the House of Representatives their written declaration that the President is unable to discharge the powers and duties of his office, the Vice President shall immediately assume the powers and duties of the office as Acting President.

Thereafter, when the President transmits to the President pro tempore of the Senate and the Speaker of the House of Representatives his written declaration that no inability exists, he shall resume the powers and duties of his office unless the Vice President and a majority of either the principal officers of the executive department or of such other body as Congress may by law provide, transmit within four days to the President pro tempore of the Senate and the Speaker of the House of Representatives their written declaration that the President is unable to discharge the powers and duties of his office. Thereupon Congress shall decide the issue, assembling within forty-eight hours for that purpose if not in session. If the Congress, within twenty-one days after receipt of the latter written declaration, or, if Congress is not in session, within twenty-one days after Congress is required to assemble, determines by two-thirds vote of both Houses that the President is unable to discharge the powers and duties of his office, the Vice President shall continue to discharge the same as Acting President; otherwise, the President shall resume the powers and duties of his office.

AMENDMENT XXVI

(Ratified July 1, 1971)

Section 1. The right of citizens of the United States, who are eighteen years of age or older, to vote shall not be denied or abridged by the United States or by any State on account of age.

Section 2. The Congress shall have power to enforce this article by appropriate legislation.

AMENDMENT XXVII

(Ratified May 7, 1992)

No law varying the compensation for the services of the Senators and Representatives shall take effect, until an election of Representatives shall have intervened.

Index

BUSINESS, CAREERS & PERSONAL FINANCE

Accounting For Dummies, 4th Edition*
978-0-470-24600-9

Bookkeeping Workbook For Dummies†
978-0-470-16983-4

Commodities For Dummies
978-0-470-04928-0

Doing Business in China For Dummies
978-0-470-04929-7

E-Mail Marketing For Dummies
978-0-470-19087-6

Job Interviews For Dummies, 3rd Edition*†
978-0-470-17748-8

Personal Finance Workbook For Dummies*†
978-0-470-09933-9

Real Estate License Exams For Dummies
978-0-7645-7623-2

Six Sigma For Dummies
978-0-7645-6798-8

Small Business Kit For Dummies, 2nd Edition*†
978-0-7645-5984-6

Telephone Sales For Dummies
978-0-470-16836-3

BUSINESS PRODUCTIVITY & MICROSOFT OFFICE

Access 2007 For Dummies
978-0-470-03649-5

Excel 2007 For Dummies
978-0-470-03737-9

Office 2007 For Dummies
978-0-470-00923-9

Outlook 2007 For Dummies
978-0-470-03830-7

PowerPoint 2007 For Dummies
978-0-470-04059-1

Project 2007 For Dummies
978-0-470-03651-8

QuickBooks 2008 For Dummies
978-0-470-18470-7

Quicken 2008 For Dummies
978-0-470-17473-9

Salesforce.com For Dummies, 2nd Edition
978-0-470-04893-1

Word 2007 For Dummies
978-0-470-03658-7

EDUCATION, HISTORY, REFERENCE & TEST PREPARATION

African American History For Dummies
978-0-7645-5469-8

Algebra For Dummies
978-0-7645-5325-7

Algebra Workbook For Dummies
978-0-7645-8467-1

Art History For Dummies
978-0-470-09910-0

ASVAB For Dummies, 2nd Edition
978-0-470-10671-6

British Military History For Dummies
978-0-470-03213-8

Calculus For Dummies
978-0-7645-2498-1

Canadian History For Dummies, 2nd Edition
978-0-470-83656-9

Geometry Workbook For Dummies
978-0-471-79940-5

The SAT I For Dummies, 6th Edition
978-0-7645-7193-0

Series 7 Exam For Dummies
978-0-470-09932-2

World History For Dummies
978-0-7645-5242-7

FOOD, GARDEN, HOBBIES & HOME

Bridge For Dummies, 2nd Edition
978-0-471-92426-5

Coin Collecting For Dummies, 2nd Edition
978-0-470-22275-1

Cooking Basics For Dummies, 3rd Edition
978-0-7645-7206-7

Drawing For Dummies
978-0-7645-5476-6

Etiquette For Dummies, 2nd Edition
978-0-470-10672-3

Gardening Basics For Dummies*†
978-0-470-03749-2

Knitting Patterns For Dummies
978-0-470-04556-5

Living Gluten-Free For Dummies†
978-0-471-77383-2

Painting Do-It-Yourself For Dummies
978-0-470-17533-0

HEALTH, SELF HELP, PARENTING & PETS

Anger Management For Dummies
978-0-470-03715-7

Anxiety & Depression Workbook For Dummies
978-0-7645-9793-0

Dieting For Dummies, 2nd Edition
978-0-7645-4149-0

Dog Training For Dummies, 2nd Edition
978-0-7645-8418-3

Horseback Riding For Dummies
978-0-470-09719-9

Infertility For Dummies†
978-0-470-11518-3

Meditation For Dummies with CD-ROM, 2nd Edition
978-0-471-77774-8

Post-Traumatic Stress Disorder For Dummies
978-0-470-04922-8

Puppies For Dummies, 2nd Edition
978-0-470-03717-1

Thyroid For Dummies, 2nd Edition†
978-0-471-78755-6

Type 1 Diabetes For Dummies*†
978-0-470-17811-9

---

* Separate Canadian edition also available
˘ Separate U.K. edition also available

Available wherever books are sold. For more information or to order direct: U.S. customers visit www.dummies.com or call 1-877-762-2974.
U.K. customers visit www.wileyeurope.com or call (0)1243 843291. Canadian customers visit www.wiley.ca or call 1-800-567-4797.

INTERNET & DIGITAL MEDIA

AdWords For Dummies
978-0-470-15252-2

Blogging For Dummies, 2nd Edition
978-0-470-23017-6

Digital Photography All-in-One
Desk Reference For Dummies, 3rd Edition
978-0-470-03743-0

Digital Photography For Dummies, 5th Edition
978-0-7645-9802-9

Digital SLR Cameras & Photography
For Dummies, 2nd Edition
978-0-470-14927-0

eBay Business All-in-One Desk Reference
For Dummies
978-0-7645-8438-1

eBay For Dummies, 5th Edition*
978-0-470-04529-9

eBay Listings That Sell For Dummies
978-0-471-78912-3

Facebook For Dummies
978-0-470-26273-3

The Internet For Dummies, 11th Edition
978-0-470-12174-0

Investing Online For Dummies, 5th Edition
978-0-7645-8456-5

iPod & iTunes For Dummies, 5th Edition
978-0-470-17474-6

MySpace For Dummies
978-0-470-09529-4

Podcasting For Dummies
978-0-471-74898-4

Search Engine Optimization
For Dummies, 2nd Edition
978-0-471-97998-2

Second Life For Dummies
978-0-470-18025-9

Starting an eBay Business For Dummies,
3rd Edition†
978-0-470-14924-9

GRAPHICS, DESIGN & WEB DEVELOPMENT

Adobe Creative Suite 3 Design Premium
All-in-One Desk Reference For Dummies
978-0-470-11724-8

Adobe Web Suite CS3 All-in-One Desk
Reference For Dummies
978-0-470-12099-6

AutoCAD 2008 For Dummies
978-0-470-11650-0

Building a Web Site For Dummies,
3rd Edition
978-0-470-14928-7

Creating Web Pages All-in-One Desk
Reference For Dummies, 3rd Edition
978-0-470-09629-1

Creating Web Pages For Dummies,
8th Edition
978-0-470-08030-6

Dreamweaver CS3 For Dummies
978-0-470-11490-2

Flash CS3 For Dummies
978-0-470-12100-9

Google SketchUp For Dummies
978-0-470-13744-4

InDesign CS3 For Dummies
978-0-470-11865-8

Photoshop CS3 All-in-One
Desk Reference For Dummies
978-0-470-11195-6

Photoshop CS3 For Dummies
978-0-470-11193-2

Photoshop Elements 5 For Dummies
978-0-470-09810-3

SolidWorks For Dummies
978-0-7645-9555-4

Visio 2007 For Dummies
978-0-470-08983-5

Web Design For Dummies, 2nd Edition
978-0-471-78117-2

Web Sites Do-It-Yourself For Dummies
978-0-470-16903-2

Web Stores Do-It-Yourself For Dummies
978-0-470-17443-2

LANGUAGES, RELIGION & SPIRITUALITY

Arabic For Dummies
978-0-471-77270-5

Chinese For Dummies, Audio Set
978-0-470-12766-7

French For Dummies
978-0-7645-5193-2

German For Dummies
978-0-7645-5195-6

Hebrew For Dummies
978-0-7645-5489-6

Ingles Para Dummies
978-0-7645-5427-8

Italian For Dummies, Audio Set
978-0-470-09586-7

Italian Verbs For Dummies
978-0-471-77389-4

Japanese For Dummies
978-0-7645-5429-2

Latin For Dummies
978-0-7645-5431-5

Portuguese For Dummies
978-0-471-78738-9

Russian For Dummies
978-0-471-78001-4

Spanish Phrases For Dummies
978-0-7645-7204-3

Spanish For Dummies
978-0-7645-5194-9

Spanish For Dummies, Audio Set
978-0-470-09585-0

The Bible For Dummies
978-0-7645-5296-0

Catholicism For Dummies
978-0-7645-5391-2

The Historical Jesus For Dummies
978-0-470-16785-4

Islam For Dummies
978-0-7645-5503-9

Spirituality For Dummies,
2nd Edition
978-0-470-19142-2

NETWORKING AND PROGRAMMING

ASP.NET 3.5 For Dummies
978-0-470-19592-5

C# 2008 For Dummies
978-0-470-19109-5

Hacking For Dummies, 2nd Edition
978-0-470-05235-8

Home Networking For Dummies, 4th Edition
978-0-470-11806-1

Java For Dummies, 4th Edition
978-0-470-08716-9

Microsoft® SQL Server™ 2008 All-in-One
Desk Reference For Dummies
978-0-470-17954-3

Networking All-in-One Desk Reference
For Dummies, 2nd Edition
978-0-7645-9939-2

Networking For Dummies,
8th Edition
978-0-470-05620-2

SharePoint 2007 For Dummies
978-0-470-09941-4

Wireless Home Networking
For Dummies, 2nd Edition
978-0-471-74940-0